Methodology for the Human Sciences

SUNY Series in Transpersonal and Humanistic Psychology
Richard D. Mann and Jean B. Mann, Editors

Methodology for the Human Sciences

SYSTEMS OF INQUIRY

Donald Polkinghorne
SAYBROOK INSTITUTE

State University of New York Press
ALBANY

To Judy, Deborah, Kyle, and Shanti

Published by State University of New York Press, Albany
©1983 State University of New York
Printed in the United States of America

For information, address State University of New York Press, State University Plaza, Albany, N.Y., 12246

Library of Congress Cataloging in Publication Data
Polkinghorne, Donald, 1936-
  Methodology for the human sciences.

  (SUNY series in transpersonal and humanistic psychology)
  Includes bibliographical references.
   1. Psychology—Methodology. 2. Psychological research. I. Title. II. Series.
BF38.5.P64 1983   300'.72   82-5895
ISBN 0-87395-663-X   AACR2
ISBN 0-87395-664-8 (pbk.)

6·17·92

Contents

Illustrations

Preface

I teach at the Saybrook Institute of San Francisco, a research center and graduate school. The institute was formed to provide encouragement and support to students and faculty members interested in seeking solutions to the significant personal and social problems confronting our society. The members of the institute experiment with a variety of research strategies, letting each question posed determine which strategies are most useful for answering that question. The general framework within which projects are conducted stands in the tradition of the human sciences, a tradition which extends back to Wilhelm Dilthey.

Our students, as well as students from neighboring schools, have asked for a book that would provide an overview of the human science approach in its present condition. This book is written primarily to serve those students. Its purpose is to provide a statement of the conceptual issues which inform research designs directed toward understanding human action and social structure. Methods accepted in the past decades are now seen to rest on assumptions about research that have come under increasing attack, and questions once thought to have been answered are being asked again. Consequently, researchers now need to reconsider the tenets upon which they base their designs. Moreover, they are free to construct new designs based on alternative tenets and epistemological commitments. In the present climate of renewal of methodology, researchers are called upon to understand the "why" of their designs as well as the "how" for carrying them out.

The scientific study of human and social phenomena began after the scientific study of the natural world had been successful. In order for the human sciences to be successful, too, it was proposed that they should emulate the methods used in the natural sciences. Before the beginning of this century, Dilthey and the neo-Kantians of the Southwest German school argued that such a strategy was inappropriate and that the sciences that explored human phenomena required different methods. The idea that two approaches to knowledge are needed—one for the natural world and one for human phenomena—has continued to resurface from time to time during the hundred years since Dilthey wrote, but the argument that there is only one approach to science, first developed for the study of nature, has gained a clear victory over Dilthey's proposal. Thus psychology, sociology, economics, and anthropology have adopted the methods of the natural sciences for themselves. The disciplinary journals, textbooks, and dissertation standards reflect the victory of the single-science point of view.

The orthodox approach to research design calls for experiments using measurable variables, and it is based on the idea of hypothesis testing and the covering-law model of explanation and prediction. Research proposals calling for qualitative and nonexperimental designs that are based on teleological, reasonable, or descriptive explanatory models clearly do not meet the standard criteria for acceptable research in most institutions.

During the past two decades, however, this standard conception of research criteria has been criticized from many angles, and the question of methodology for the human sciences has once more reappeared. In its new form, the debate is not merely a repetition of the arguments used by Dilthey, for the context of the debate has changed. On the one hand, the logical-empirical philosophy of science, which was the form in which the single-science approach triumphed, has failed to hold up under continued self-examination. It had been assumed that the logical-empirical system provided a secure foundation for certain and indubitable knowledge. This system, however, has proved vulnerable in several areas: its inability to verify hypotheses through inductive methods, its lack of attention to the role of hypothesis creation or context of discovery, its inability to demonstrate that the analytic-synthetic distinction between theoretical and observation statements could hold up, and its failure to answer the criticism offered by Stephen Toulmin, Thomas Kuhn, Paul Feyeraband, Imre Lakatos, and other historians of science. On the other hand, developments outside the logical-empirical system have offered an expanded understanding of science and alternative systems of inquiry. Action theory, systems and structural research, Peter Winch's application of Ludwig Wittgenstein's later theories to social science, Hans-Georg Gadamer's development of interpretation theory, and the existential phenomenology of Maurice Merleau-Ponty have all added to the complexity of the environment in which the debate about methodology and human science is taking place. Paul Ricoeur's integration of structural and interpretative approaches, Jürgen Habermas's discussions of science and human interests, and Anthony Giddens's combination of reflective action and social structures are examples of contemporary scholarship involved in the new debate.

I refer to the object or subject matter of the human sciences with different phrases in the book. "Human action and social structure," "the life and history of human beings," "the sphere of *Geist* and its contents," "human action in general," "the human realms," "human phenomena" and others are used. The choice of these terms reflects my position that methods and research design for the human sciences must be able to yield information about being human as we experience it as embodied, historical, and integral. This position holds that human science requires a syncretic approach which integrates the results obtained through multischematic and multiparadigmatic systems of inquiry.

The renewed discussion of methodology for the human sciences is still in process. This book is meant to serve as a guide to present discussions, rather than as a report of the outcome. Its purpose is to encourage others to join in the debate. What is needed most is for practitioners to experiment with the new designs and to submit their attempts and results to examination by other participants in the debate. The new historians of science have made it clear that methodological questions are decided in the practice of research by those committed to developing the best possible answers to their questions, not by the armchair philosophers of research.

This book presents the historical background of the development of methodology for the human sciences, in order to provide readers with a context for understanding the present concerns and issues in research methodology. An examination of the origins of notions which have become taken for granted as postulates of research design provides the reader an occasion to reconstruct the insights originally gained by these constructions and to reintegrate them into expanded approaches to research. Because the purpose of the book has seemed best served by moving rapidly through the century of exploration on which we stand, an author's complete thought, with all of its nuances and complexity, has sometimes had to be simplified, and significant portions of it have had to be neglected. The more I became acquainted with an author's work, the more appreciative I became of his or her commitment to confronting the problems of human knowledge honestly. I hope that my simplifications do not prevent the reader from acknowledging the sophistication and thoroughness of these writers. It is serious work with high stakes, and the positions taken by many of these writers have cost them friendships and professional standing. Perhaps the book will incite its readers to delve more deeply into the thoughts of those who have struggled to understand how we can achieve a deepened and reliable knowledge of the human realm.

I thank the students and the faculty of the Saybrook Institute. This book was prompted by their concern for addressing questions about human existence and by their willingness to engage themselves with the problems and uncertainties of untested research designs. Their commitment to integrity and rigor in research, along with our discussions about how we could venture into untried approaches, provided guidance for my preparation of the text. I also extend my thanks to the institute's trustees, who offered generous support and provided release time from my normal teaching and administrative duties so that the book could be completed.

D. P.

March 1982

Berkeley, California

Introduction

Developments in Anglo-American and Continental thought over the last several decades have brought about a shift in the understanding of the nature of science. The shift is from a "positivist" conception of science to a "postpositivist" conception. Although the consequences of this shift are significant for all areas of scientific work, this book is concerned with its effect on the understanding of scientific study of the human realm.

The positivist conception of science has its roots in a definition of knowledge which holds that only those things of which we are absolutely certain can be counted as knowledge. If a knowledge claim fails the test of certain truth, then it cannot be included within the body of scientifically approved statements. Western thought has remained within this tradition that requires certainty of science since its beginnings in Greece. Various foundations have been proposed upon which the claims of certainty could be grounded—Plato's realm of ideas, Descartes's clear and distinct ideas in consciousness, the empiricists' realm of sense data, and the rationalists' realm of logical and mathematical truths, When scientific procedures were directed to the study of the human realm, beginning in the nineteenth century, the debate about appropriate methods was carried out within a context which assumed this traditional understanding of science. The question around which the debate centered concerned which methods could provide certain knowledge while also addressing the unique characteristics of the human realm. The standard by which such methods were judged was whether they produced certain or "objective" truth. Some argued that only those methods which had been used to study natural objects could produce "objectivity," while others proposed that methods that recognized the unique features of the human realm—such as meaning—and also provided certain knowledge could be developed. Over time, the search for methods

1

that would both address the human realm and produce "objective" or certain truths reduced the range of acceptable methods to those that incorporated the principles of deductive logic and intersubjectively verifiable data.

Many of those who studied the human realm thought that the standards of positivist science required that too much of what was central to human experience had to be neglected if study was limited to those areas that submitted to research tools designed to produce certainty. Biologists, too, were concerned that the concept of "life" could not be captured by the tools of certainty. An unresolved tension between the requirements of producing indubitable truths and the requirements of addressing the most significant questions about the human realm has accompanied human science since its origins.

The shift to a postpositivist understanding of science calls for a reassessment of human science methodology and the adjustments it has made in order to conform to the demands of positivist science. The purpose of this book is to contribute to such a reassessment. Unlike positivism, postpositivist science does not propose a unified view of science. Its point is not that the positivist conception of what constitutes proper methods for obtaining certain knowledge should be replaced by another conception of how apodictic knowledge should be produced. Instead, postpositivism challenges the tradition that knowledge actually is apodictic truth. Postpositivism holds that we do not have access to indubitable truths. The knowledge claims that a community accepts are those that withstand the test of practical argument and use. Knowledge is understood to be the best understanding that we have been able to produce thus far, not a statement of what is ultimately real. Postpositivism is not a school of thought with an agreed-upon set of propositions. It is an attitude about knowledge.

This attitude was brought to expression by four different, though somewhat overlapping, movements in the last several decades. (1) The "linguistic turn" in the philosophy of science as expressed in Wittgenstein's later writings. The implications of this turn are spelled out by Quine, Kuhn, Toulmin, Hesse, and others, who call into question the truth status of the statements of science and the kind of link such statements have to an extralinguistic reality. (2) The continued development and increased sophistication of systems theory and its application to the study of the workings of complexly organized wholes such as human beings. (3) The concerted effort to develop a theory of human action that includes the notions of purpose and deliberative activity. (4) The challenge of Heidegger and Gadamer in philosophical hermeneutics to the idea of a foundational epistemology that yields apodictic truths. These movements have brought about a concept of science as a human activity which answers our historically given problems with the conceptual tools that are available or can be created at the time. Knowledge claims are accepted by a community when they have the power to convince the community that they are an improvement over previous understanding. This convincing takes place through arguments that use an enlarged sense of reasoning—the kind of multifaceted reasoning used in making practical decisions.

The purpose of this book is not to replace positivist methodology with a new postpositivist methodology. For in the postpositivist understanding of science there is no correct method to follow. Science is not seen as an activity of following methodological recipes that yield acceptable results. Science becomes the creative search to understand better, and it uses whatever approaches are responsive to the particular questions and subject matters addressed. Those methods are acceptable which produce results that convince the community that the new understanding is deeper, fuller, and more useful than the previous understanding. Such an understanding of methodology means that it is not enough to know the recipe for carrying out a research design. It also means that methods that were discarded because they did not produce certain knowledge need to be reexamined for their usefulness in improving our present understanding of the human realm.

The book is organized according to the following ground plan. Chapter 1 explores the original debate over the type of methods that were to be allowed into the then-emerging human sciences. Chapter 2 describes the clarification of positivism that resulted from the combination of the new logic of Russell and the previously developed sense-data theory to provide a foundation for science. Chapter 3 presents the recent developments and challenges to the logical-positivist clarification. Chapter 4 presents the development of systems theory and structuralism and describes their challenge to the positivist conception of science. Chapter 5 explores the attempts at developing a theory of human action that recognizes the intentional character of action. Chapter 6 describes the Continental schools of phenomenology and hermeneutics.

The final chapter lists and describes some of the conceptual tools needed by a human science researcher working within the context of the postpositivist conception of science. The first conceptual tool needed is a clear understanding of the nature of knowledge. It is such an understanding that is the base from which the researcher works, since postpositivism has cleared methodology of prescibed rules and boundaries. The acceptance of a knowledge claim finally stands within the community to whom the researcher will present his or her results for acceptance. The goal of research is to answer a question in such a way that it is convincing and can be defended with cogent arguments. Methods are to be developed as responses to specific questions. The positivist notion that research should be limited to questions which yield up information to prescribed methods is replaced by the idea that questions have priority and that it is the researcher's responsibility to devise strategies and methods that will provide the best possible answers to the posed questions. The second conceptual tool needed by the human science researcher is the understanding that methods need to be responsive to the special characteristics of the realm under investigation. The special characteristics of the human realm are outlined, with particular emphasis placed on the use and importance of the linguistic data type for research in the human realm.

Underlying the selection of materials discussed in the book and the positions I take toward them, there exist, of course, my own presuppositions and assumptions. In order to make these presuppositions and assumptions clear to readers before they move through the main chapters of the book, I present here a brief outline of my own position. Clarifications and definitions of some of the basic terms used in the discussions are also given.

Methods and Methodology

This is a book about methodology. It is a consideration of the procedures and the methods that are to be used in the human sciences. Most discussions of methodology take one of two forms—prescriptive or descriptive. Prescriptive methodology sets down standards which researchers are advised to follow. Descriptive methodology lays out the procedures adopted by successful researchers. This book, however, takes neither of these two forms; instead, it is more of an exploratory study of methodology. It is concerned with what kinds of methods can be constructed in order to provide the best possible answers to questions about human actions and creations.

At present, the notion that there is a foundation on which prescription could rest is under challenge, and there is no one approach used by successful researchers of human phenomena that can serve as the source of description. Human science research is in constructive turmoil as a result of successful challenges by philosophers of science during the past several decades. Previously agreed-upon boundaries have come under attack, and new postpositivist approaches to research, such as ethnomethodology and interpretive sociology, are currently being tried out. Researchers in the human sciences find themselves in the middle of a renewed methodological controversy, and the stance that researchers take regarding methodology will substantively affect the conduct of their research and the results they achieve.

Methods are the particular activities that are used to achieve research results. Methods include various experimental designs, sampling procedures, measuring instruments, and the statistical treatment of data. The word *method* retains the meaning of its etymological roots. It is made up of the root words *meta* and *hodos*: *meta* means "from or after," and *hodos* "journey." The word *method* is thus "a going-after" or "a pursuit." In the case of science, it is a pursuit of knowledge. The term usually refers to the procedures or the detailed and logically ordered plan used to "go after" knowledge. *Methodology* adds the root word *logos*, which has a rich history beginning with Greek philosophy where it was used to refer to the principle of reason, the source of world order and intelligibility. The contemporary suffix "-ology" retains some of this meaning, and when combined with "method" gives a term which denotes a study of the plans which are used to obtain knowledge. Methodology is thus the examination of the possible plans to be carried out—the journeys to be undertaken—so that an understanding of phenomena can be obtained. In the human sciences, the phenomena are, of course, human phenomena. The study of methods, however, is concerned with particular procedures for research.

In this book, the emphasis will be placed squarely on methodology. Little attention will be given to how to use particular methods—for instance, how to conduct interviews, how to administer questionnaires, or how to develop measuring instruments—and major attention will be given to why such methods do or do not produce valid, reliable, or genuine understanding.

The general thesis presented in this book is that in postpositivist science various systems of inquiry, each providing internal coherence and meaning to a research project, can be useful in developing knowledge. Methods, then, take their validity and reliability from their participation in a particular system of inquiry. Within one system of inquiry—for example, reason-explanation—interview methods are understood to provide a particular type of data susceptible to a kind of interpretation which has validity only within that system; within another system of inquiry, however—for example, structural explanation—interview methods are understood to provide a different kind of data with different meaning. Particular methods do not operate independently of a system of inquiry; the use of a method changes only as a researcher uses it in different systems of inquiry. The use of a method is not an isolated activity, for the method is shaped by its implicit or explicit reference to a particular system of inquiry. The meaning of a particular research conduct is determined by the context of its system of "going after" knowledge.

This book draws on many of the insights offered by Abraham Kaplan in his classic study of methodology, *The Conduct of Inquiry* (1964).[1] While retaining his emphasis on an eclectic and programmatic approach to research, this study attends to the greater diversity within methodological thought which has developed since Kaplan's book was written. The impact of a postpositivist philosophy of science has enlarged the context in which the discourse on inquiry takes place. The present interest in human science methodology is reflected in more recent work, such as Amedeo Giorgi's *Psychology as a Human Science* (1970) and Anthony Giddens's *New Rules of Sociological Method* (1976).[2]

Methodology as Problem Solving

Researchers are problem-solvers. The questions they are concerned with are questions of how to gain understanding and knowledge of a situation or a process. Thomas Kuhn[3] describes scientists as "puzzle-solvers" and believes that the challenge of puzzles is an important element in the motivation of scientists. Larry Laudan[4] proposes that if the philosophy of science would approach science as an activity fundamentally aiming at the solution of problems—instead of focusing on such issues as degrees of confirmation, corroboration, explanatory content, and the like—it would overcome much of its present confusion.

Typically, a researcher approaches his or her problems with a toolbox that contains conceptual instruments which, when used properly, produce answers to the questions of knowledge that have been posed.[5] The conceptual instruments are usually given to researchers during their graduate training, and many researchers add no new tools throughout the rest of their careers. Some researchers possess only one tool, which they carry with them and attempt to use for solving all of the problems they come across. A well-known proverb tells us that when a man possesses only a hammer he will view all problems as problems requiring the pounding of nails. Psychologists, at times, have been given only one tool—the true experiment—and have been told that all problems can be solved with that tool.

Many graduate schools are now giving a variety of instruments to their students. Quasi-experimental designs, Q-sorts, field studies, interviews, and case studies are being included in the repertoire. Yet even these tools are not always adequate for solving the complex problems which need answers in our society. Merely pulling tools from the box will not always work. Researchers frequently need to construct new sets of tools that are designed especially for the specific problems before them. This does not mean, however, that the tools in the box are totally useless. Experience with approaches that have worked for other problems is essential if new and suitable instruments are to be built for the various problems the researchers have chosen to study.

This book is concerned with the issues involved in constructing research strategies. Its purpose is not merely to hand down previously developed tools but to explore the issues involved in the construction of new research designs—designs that are essential for solving the problems that require increasing understanding and knowledge of human beings as acting agents.

Methodology and the Human Realm

Human beings present the most complex kinds of problems. We have histories, we are animate organisms, and we act through and in a matrix of social and linguistic meanings. We deliberate and make rational plans, we are driven by physical needs and desires, and we are pulled by socially instilled values. We are caught in a web of internal and external structures, and yet at times we seem to transcend these structures and produce novel and creative ideas. As a consequence, those problems of understanding that focus on us and our communities present the greatest challenge to our methods and our tools of comprehension. Our solutions to problems of the physical universe have provided an understanding that has allowed us to transform energy from one form to another and have enabled us to replace "natural engines" (human beings and animals) with constructed engines as the sources of mechanical work. Yet the problems of living and working together in our families, our businesses, and our nations remain puzzles.

Our knowledge about the physical universe does not change it as it is in itself, although this knowledge suggests, of course, how we can manipulate it to produce steel and engines, to grow more food, to heal our bodies, and to create more powerful weapons. Our knowledge about ourselves, however, does change something: our self-understanding and our relationships with others. Mario Bunge[6] notes the often-expressed belief that we fear knowledge of ourselves because we are afraid that it can be used to manipulate and manage us in the same way that knowledge of the physical world has been used to manipulate and manage it. The examples usually given are advertising and political and ideological manipulation. But there is, of course, an answer to this fear: we can use knowledge of ourselves that does indeed account for our complexity and for our essential qualities to overcome manipulation. This knowledge can also be used to enable us to make decisions that will improve our ability to live together harmoniously on our small planet.

Developing sets of conceptual tools that will provide the understanding necessary to approach more successful solutions to our human problems requires a knowledge of the principles of tool-making, a familiarity with previous attempts (both successful and unsuccessful) at developing such tools, and an awareness of the job to be performed with the tools. It is a characteristic of tools that they are not worthy in themselves—their value is dependent upon the particular job to be done. Although a screwdriver may be a valuable instrument in itself, especially when it is constructed of hard steel and has a comfortable handle, it is worthless when the carpenter's task is cutting a piece of wood. And although a jeweler's screwdriver is perfectly suited to the task of putting a watch together, it is inappropriate for loosening a large bolt that holds a chair upright.

The human sciences have developed some finely honed tools. The statistical operations created by Karl Pearson and R. A. Fisher, along with the added sophistication in multivariate designs, possess their own aesthetic qualities as well as power for analyzing data. Many measuring devices for translating concepts into quantified data are ingenious, including the pigeon bar as an instrument for measuring learning capacity. Donald Campbell and Julian Stanley's clarification of the logical limits of various types of experimental designs[7] and the more recent Cook and Campbell quasi-experimental design for field settings[8] are important tools for all researchers. In addition to these tools, which are usually included in the training of researchers in the human sciences, mention must be made of tools developed in linguistics, action theory, and depth hermeneutics, which are not usually presented to human science students at conventional institutions.

The researcher as tool-builder—and as tool-user—will need an understanding of the conceptual bases out of which the previously developed tools have been derived. These completed tools belong to periods of "normal science," and "normal science" is unlikely to provide useful answers to the most important questions surrounding the object of inquiry in the human sciences, the life and history of human beings. For the researcher in the human sciences, design problems will be more like those of a skilled and creative architect, who fashions a unique design to fit the multiple requirements of the client, the environment, the costs, the existing materials, and the land. The creative architect cannot profit from following a set of plans that have been drawn up for tract houses, and the researcher in the human sciences cannot profit from following a set of plans that have been designed for an entirely different set of purposes.

Fruitful research in the human sciences needs to remain in a "state of crisis" as Kuhn defines it—that is, it must question methodological assumptions, and it must experiment with various epistemological frameworks. The pull toward a single methodological perspective with its clearly defined tools needs to be resisted because this single perspective, designed for research in "normal science," overlooks the anomalous quality of human experience. The difficulty for human science arises, not from a need to change from one paradigm to another, but from a need to resist settling down to any single paradigm.[9]

Researchers who work within the context of the methodological pluralism of postpositivist science cannot assume the validity of their particular tools for inquiry. They need to begin their work at a deeper level where the assumptions and relationships of the systems of inquiry themselves are examined. This deeper level provides a much broader range of choice in the use of particular methods and designs, but it also places a responsibility on researchers to understand and explain the assumptions they have incorporated into their approaches.

Methodology and Certainty

The methodological debate between positivist and postpositivist scientists is taking place within the framework of the distinction between *doxa* (opinion or belief) and *epistēmē* (certainty and knowledge). This distinction has its origins in the early Greek attempt to clarify the differences between experience and reality. In the dialogue *Theatetus*, Plato points out that there is a difference between what we believe to be true (*doxa*) and what we know to be true (*epistēmē*). What we believe to be true sometimes turns out to be false. Believing is not enough to assure certainty, and acting on what we believe can lead to calamitous results when what we have thought to be so turns out to be wrong. Thus Plato held that there is a need to develop a method of inquiry that provides an absolutely certain ground so that beliefs can be changed into trustworthy knowledge.

Epistemology (the *logos* or study of *epistēmē*) has become the search for methods and foundations which enable us to be assured of the truth of our beliefs. *Epistēmē* is the thing upon which we can stand (*epi* means "upon," and *[hi]stanai* means "to stand"), and epistemology is the search for such a foundation. While the word *epistemology* is etymologically related to Greek, our other word for knowledge has Latin roots: *science* is derived from *scīre*, which means "to know." Connoted in these terms is the distinction we make between our beliefs and opinions (our ordinary understanding of the world and each other) and our knowledge (the true and certain understanding of reality). As a term, *science* retains this distinction, but in practice it has lost the broad implication of the search for knowledge and has come, instead, to stand for a particular method by means of which certain knowledge is believed to be established.

We human beings have an ordinary awareness of the world which serves as the basis for our responses and actions. This ordinary awareness is built up through interpretive schemes that are passed on to us from our culture and from our interaction with the environment. By means of experiences of success and failure in these interactions—through what Freud called the reality principle and what Skinner calls reinforcement—our stock of knowledge is altered. In our ordinary or natural attitudes, we hold beliefs and opinions about the objects of the world, about ourselves, and about other persons.[10] This is our common sense of what is. It is our *doxa*.

This common stock of knowledge is usually held tacitly or implicitly; ordinarily, a question of its accuracy is not raised. If doubt is raised about it, however, a new level of awareness arises. When we are asked "Are you sure? Do you really know it to be so?," we can no longer take the stock of knowledge for granted. Doubt calls for a defense, and the skeptic asks for a justification of knowledge. Knowledge can no longer be held innocently, and then a search is begun for the reasons that lie behind the common belief.

Historically, one of the most significant groups of "doubt-raisers" in the development of Western thought was the Sophists. Men such

as Protagoras, Hippias of Ellis, Prodicus of Ceos, and Thrasyma-
chus—who lived in Athens in the fifth and early fourth centuries
B.C.—lifted the Greek philosophers from their satisfaction with a
commonsense knowledge. They provided the irritation of doubt by
asking whether one could really know anything. It was in response
to the Sophists that epistemology, the examination of the foundations
and methods of knowledge, arose. Plato and Aristotle could not take
the possibility of knowledge for granted, once the Sophists had raised
a doubt, and thus began a dialogue between the doubters and the
defenders of knowledge which has continued as a central theme in
Western thought since that time. The contemporary scholarly community is still operating on the principle of this doubt-defender
dialogue. A thesis is proposed in a dissertation or an article, the
community assumes the role of skeptic and questions the truth of
the thesis, and the proposer responds by calling forth evidence which
argues for this truth. Because of the nature of the dialogue, proposals
for the adequacy of any kind of knowledge depend upon the nature
of the doubts to which they are a response. The most characteristic
form of skepticism about knowledge is presented in the assumption
that we ought not to claim knowledge about anything unless we are
absolutely sure about it, unless there is absolutely no possibility that
we might be wrong.

We normally claim knowledge about something when we are sure
about it, but this claim to know something is very different from a
strict claim that we have absolute certainty. To defend the claim
that what one proposes is true usually requires only that there be
the best of grounds for what is claimed and that one can argue
cogently before one's community, defending against critiques and
providing appropriate evidence for the thesis offered. Thus, the
requirement demanded by skeptics—that only that which passes
muster before the standard of absolute certainty can be accepted as
knowledge—is too stringent.

Nevertheless, the standard of apodictic knowledge—absolute, indubitable certainty—has been accepted by Western epistemologists,
and almost all of what we ordinarily claim we know—our common
sense of the world—has come under the shadow of doubt. What
we have claimed as knowledge is transformed by the standard of
certainty into mere opinion. No longer can we claim to hold true
knowledge—*epistēmē*—and we must accept our understandings as
doxa.

So the search begins for any aspect of our stock of knowledge
that can pass the test of apodictic certainty. If the apodictic standard
is to be applied, it is possible that most of the things we ordinarily

claim to know are wrong. Everyday knowledge of objects of perception, knowledge derived from memory, knowledge of other minds, and inductive knowledge cannot stand up to the test of absolute certainty. Is there any ground that withstands the test and can thereby provide a base upon which to build true knowledge?

Western epistemologists have proposed two primary things that measure up to the standard of certainty: rationalists have proposed that ideas such as mathematical axioms meet the apodictic standard, and empiricists have claimed that internal sense experience (not to be confused with projected external objects) provides a certain ground which cannot be doubted. Each group, using its base of absolute truth, then rebuilds the world of ordinary knowledge. The rationalists attempt to demonstrate that the certain truths of reason are related to ordinary truths in the same way that the axioms of geometry are related to theorems. The truths of ordinary knowledge can be saved, because they follow deductively from the primary truths of reason. The empiricists rebuild ordinary knowledge from a foundation of the truth of facts—the facts of sense data. Beginning with the primary truth of sense experience, they say, one can inductively demonstrate the reality of what we normally accept as knowledge.

The debate, as formulated by the skeptics, provides only two categories of propositions—apodictic and problematic. Either a proposition is infallible and beyond doubt or it is dubious and therefore not *epistēmē*. It is possible, however, to reformulate the debate so as to include a third term between the apodictic and problematic alternatives. Chapman[11] calls this third type of knowledge "assertoric." Assertoric propositions can be denied without contradiction and do not qualify as apodictic, but they are supported by evidence. They remain open to future confirmation and correction as more experience is gained.

Postpositivist philosophy of science has raised questions about whether the certainty required by the concept of *epistēmē* is possible. Logical positivism has sought to reconstruct science on the base of sense experiences plus statements connected by logical necessity, and its epistemological framework has provided the grounding for hypothetical-deductive research. But its attempt to find a strictly apodictic base for knowledge has not been successful. At best, the attempt provides a system for developing assertoric knowledge. Statements asserting knowledge cannot be verified and certified; they can only be confirmed with degrees of probability or pronounced false. The acceptance of assertoric knowledge as a legitimate goal for science has reopened a possibility for alternative epistemological frameworks to be proposed, so long as the frameworks meet the criteria for this kind of limited understanding.

Wittgenstein's later work (and Winch's interpretation of it for social science), Whorf's hypothesis, and Gadamer's hermeneutics[12] all propose that apodictic knowledge is impossible, because human beings cannot stand outside their language systems and cultures and obtain an absolute viewpoint. All of our knowledge is conditional knowledge, constructed within our conceptual systems, and thus knowledge is a communal achievement and is relative to time and place. One need not retreat to a complete relativism, however, just because a perspectival or context-bound aspect of knowledge is recognized. Between the extremes of absolute certainty (with no relativity) and absolute uncertainty, statements of knowledge can be judged against each other, and some of them can be accepted and used as the base for action while others can be rejected.

Another consequence of the postpositivist challenge is that the line of demarcation between "science" and other scholarly attempts at gaining knowledge loses its edge. The methods developed in history, literary criticism, and the other humanities are not clearly separated from the methods of psychology, sociology, anthropology, and the other sciences of the person. Part of the notion underlying the distinction between the sciences and the humanities is the assumption that science provides certain knowledge (*epistēmē*) while the humanities provide only opinion (*doxa*). If this dichotomy no longer informs our understanding of science—if, instead, we are all seeking to create the best possible assertoric knowledge of human beings— then the divisive wall which has been built between types of scholarship needs to be removed so as to allow interaction for mutual benefit. Commenting on a "possible psychology for a possible postpositivist world," Sigmund Koch has suggested that important sectors of psychological study should "require modes of inquiry more like those of the humanities than the sciences."[13] This advice can be expanded to include all of the human sciences.

The point of view from which this book approaches science holds that the effort of science should be directed toward refining its assertions according to their fruitfulness. Admitting only apodictic attempts as "real" science, thus excluding most of the serious accomplishments of scholarship, and relativizing all scholarship because nothing is certain can only be harmful to our efforts as we seek to increase our understanding.

1

The Original Debate

The sciences concerned with the study of the human realm have continuously struggled with the question of appropriate methods for dealing with their subject matter. The question has invariably been framed in some kind of relationship to the methods developed by the physical sciences, mainly because the methodical study of the natural order preceded the methodical study of the human order. Rarely has the relationship been reversed; rarely has anyone asked whether the physical sciences might use the special methods developed by the human sciences.

The traditional debate remains essentially this: Should the human sciences emulate the methods of the natural sciences or should they develop their own methods? The advocates of special methods base their argument on the premise that human beings are different in kind from the objects of study in the physical world and that they therefore require different methods. On the opposite side of the debate are those who hold that the methods of the natural sciences will work for all of the sciences. It is in this conceptual framework that the debate was formed nearly a century ago, and it is in this same framework that it continues.

I believe that the structure of this old debate has ceased to produce useful discourse. In recent decades, investigations in the philosophy of science, along with the development of alternative systems of inquiry, have brought about vast changes in our understanding of the nature of the scientific enterprise. The context in which the debate is carried on has changed since it began. The debate, I believe, should be refocused, so that emphasis is placed on these recent developments. By this means, methodology can move beyond the sterility of the debate itself; it can stimulate us and bring about new conceptions of how we know and understand the human realm.

15

It is important, nevertheless, to understand the original debate and to trace its development, for it continues to influence all discussions of methodology in the human sciences, and often its form, as well as its substance, emerges in what are said to be "revised" formats.

Positivism

The movement toward empirical investigation, begun by the crafts guilds during the Middle Ages, gradually accelerated, and it eventually burst forth as a "great awakening" during the late Renaissance period and the Baroque era. Francis Bacon's *Novum Organum* of 1620 championed the inductive-experimental method as a replacement for Aristotle's methods, which, Bacon said, had not overcome the "idols" which obscure our understanding.[1] In 1632, Galileo published *The Dialogue Concerning Two Chief World Systems*, in which he held, as had the Greeks before him, that nature is consistent in its operations and is not random. Because of this consistency, Galileo said, it can be seen that nature varies in a systematic way, and it is possible to discover and describe nature's patterns by using mathematical formulas. But he excluded the teleological explanations that has been part of Aristotle's scheme; according to Galileo, we need not suppose that variation in nature takes place so that some purpose is accomplished.[2] Newton's *Mathematical Principles of Natural Philosophy* (1687) stressed the need for experimental confirmation of theses about the order of nature. According to Newton, such an approach not only proved fruitful for advances in medicine and for solving problems of technological production, but also for a general understanding of the natural world.[3]

This "great awakening" in the natural sciences was paralleled some two centuries later by the burgeoning of a systematic study of human phenomena, particularly history, languages, and social institutions. Before the nineteenth century, answers to questions about human beings were sought from the Bible, from the church, and from philosophers. The scholarly examination of evidence as a method for answering questions about the human realm is thus a recent development in human history.[4]

Thomas Hobbes was the first to comprehend and express the view that humans could be studied with the new methods of science. Hobbes visited Galileo in 1637, and using Galileo's notion that the cause of everything was merely a variation of matter in motion, he wrote in the *Little Treatise* that human sensation could also be explained as variations of motion. According to Hobbes, thinking, in all its forms, is an activity, and thinking is therefore a kind of motion. Mind is simply the name for the sum of a person's thinking activities; it is thus nothing but a series of motions in an animal organism. Consciousness, or mind, can be studied in the same way that any object in motion is studied. Hobbes composed a series of objections to Descartes's *Meditations* which were included in its publication in 1641. Hobbes objected to Descartes's separation of mind and matter; instead he proposed that mind is part of nature and need not be seen as a second basic substance. Hobbes ended up with one universe made up of matter in regular motions—motions that could be described by mathematical formulas. In Hobbes's view, there was no need for a separate study of human phenomena because they are, in principle, no different from any other phenomena.[5]

Closer to the contemporary period, Auguste Comte, writing between 1830 and 1850, proposed that the study of human phenomena be brought into conformity with the methods used in the natural sciences. All fictitious or "negative" philosophical speculation about the human realm, he said, should be given up, and instead, the "positive" or scientific study of human beings should be undertaken. Through such scientific approaches, a new order of society could be developed that would alleviate the suffering and chaos caused by social systems built upon the speculative ideas of philosophers. In Comte's description of the evolution of the human mind, it passed through three stages. The first was a theological stage: humans were held under the spell of supernatural beings, and the world was explained in terms of the will of anthropomorphic gods and spirits. The second was a metaphysical stage: conceptual abstractions were substituted for animistic beings, but these abstract concepts were merely fictional inventions and wishful projections. The third, which, according to Comte, was about to emerge, was a stage of positive knowledge: the inventions of the earlier stages would be rejected, and it would be recognized that the only truth is knowledge of the necessary regularities of phenomena. Within the third stage—the stage of knowledge—there would exist a hierarchy of sciences that would recognize the "positive" conception of truth. The highest of the sciences would be "sociology," which would discover the laws— the regularities—of social behavior. Human beings would then be able to establish a perfect society based on these laws of behavior.[6]

John Stuart Mill's *System of Logic* (1843) provided a firm philosophical and logical foundation for empiricism as the ground of knowledge. Mill did not propose a society or "sociocracy" based on an absolute and final knowledge (as Comte did), but he did call for the use of natural science methods in the study of human phenomena, stating that "the backward state of the moral sciences can only be remedied by applying to them the methods of physical science, duly extended and generalized."[7]

A more restricted version of positivism was developed in the late nineteenth century by Richard Avenarius and Ernst Mach. Avenarius's ideas were developed in the 1870s, although his most influential work was published from 1888 to 1890. This was the two-volume *Critique of Pure Experience*, in which he presented his system of "empiriocriticism," an epistemological theory according to which the task of philosophy is to develop a "natural concept of the world" based on "pure experience." Avenarius believed that "pure experience" must be recognized as the sole admissible source of knowledge. He proposed that we eliminate all the metaphysical ingredients that we import into experience through introjection. This could be done, he said, by attending only to that which is directly given by pure perception, "the sensa."

Mach also proposed that knowledge be limited to sensations. In *The Analysis of Sensations* (1886), he held that the world we encounter in casual observation as a complex and unorganized flux contains, on close inspection, objects with common qualities. However much the objects may differ from one another, they are made up of the same colors, textures, shapes, sounds, and so forth. Similarly, when we analyze experience, we find in it elements that are accessible to one or another of the five senses. Mach argued that the most accurate and economical description of the natural world can be stated in terms of these basic elements. By limiting science to a description of these elements, he said, possible error can be avoided. For example, two people are asked to describe what they experience when they look at a particular object and one person calls the object "chair," while the other calls it "stool." According to Mach, the distinction between "chair" and "stool" does not exist in the basic experiences of the perceiving persons; it exists in what persons infer about the object based on the elements of sensation. If the two people were to be asked to describe the sensations they have, they would give the same report—that is, they would describe the object as "a white, round plane with four rectangular legs attached." For Mach, "the world consists only of our sensations." It is only sensation that is certain and indubitable, and thus a science built on sensation has a foundation of certainty.

The positivist tradition might also be called a single-method tradition. Its primary themes can be summed up in three statements: (1) All metaphysics should be rejected and knowledge confined to what has been experienced or can be experienced. Thus science should restrict itself to discovering reliable correlations within experience. (2) The adequacy of knowledge increases as it approximates the forms of explanation which have been achieved by the most advanced sciences. (3) Scientific explanation is limited to only functional and directional laws (Comte) or to only mathematically functional laws (Mach).

There is a strong reformist flavor to the positivist movement; its members preached a gospel of good news in which all human problems would finally be solved by applying the one correct method. Traditional beliefs and practices were to be cast aside and replaced by prescriptions developed by applying to human problems the methods that had succeeded in uncovering the secrets of the natural world. All metaphysical ideas should be exorcised since they were not merely wrong—they stood in the way of progress. Positivist methodology was ultimately supposed to guarantee progress through technical means applied to the social realm.

Mill and Comte were only exemplars of a general movement. Other elements entered into and influenced the use of the natural science approach for the study of the human realm. Beginning in the 1860s, a loose combination of naturalism, empiricism, and positivism was adopted by most researchers concerned with human phenomena as well as by those investigating the natural world.[8] Naturalism held that all phenomena can be explained in terms of natural causes and laws without attributing moral, spiritual, or supernatural significance to them. Empiricism held that experience of the senses is the only source of knowledge. This combination of naturalism, empiricism, and positivism has continued to dominate the methodological framework for the behavioral and social sciences until the present time.

Chapter 2 will trace the continued development of the empirical approach, carrying it through its logical-empirical period and bringing it to the beginnings of its breakdown with the discovery of quantum physics at the beginning of the twentieth century and with changes in the philosophy of science during the 1960s. Meanwhile, however, recent texts in research methods continue to promote the naturalism-empiricism-positivism tradition. For instance, as recently as 1979 Kerlinger has written:

> The general approach to knowledge and understanding of physics and psychology is the same, but the details of theory and investigation are quite different. . . . To measure aspects of human behavior . . . is usually more difficult than to measure properties of physical bodies.[9]

The next section of this chapter will describe the early anti-positivist formulations of methodology for human science.

The Anti-Positivist Response

In the last decades of the 1800s it had not yet been decided which methodological principles would be used for the newly developing studies of the human realm. The previous section outlined the position that these new studies should use the principles which had proved so successful in studies of the physical realm. This section will present an outline of six thinkers who represent the alternative position. In common they held a position that the methodology of the natural sciences was inadequate for studying human phenomena. They had considerable differences among themselves as to the nature of the human realm and how it ought to be studied; yet they believed that these studies should address the fullness of human experience, including values and meaning in addition to perception. The struggle to understand and define the human realm shows through in their writings. They attempted in various ways to define the human realm as a prelude to establishing ongoing research programs. However, their anti-positivist position did not carry the day, and the sciences of the human realm ended up with a methodology grounded in the procedures and logic of the physical sciences.

The early anti-positivist attempts to define the human realm and to answer how access to it could be gained and what kind of procedures and logics were appropriate, are a fertile field for a renewed debate about human science methodology. Giambattista Vico was an early eighteenth-century forerunner of the debate. The focus of the anti-positivist exposition was carried on in Germany from 1880 to 1920. The leaders in the endeavor were Wilhelm Dilthey, Wilhelm Wundt, Franz Brentano, Edmund Husserl, Max Weber, and, in the United States, William James. Each approached various problems inherent in constructing a human science and focused on particular issues.

As early as 1725, however, Vico anticipated the growth of the empirical approach to human phenomena. In *The New Science*, Vico resisted the trend by asserting that we can gain a true knowledge of human phenomena through the study of our history. We can understand history, he said, because we have made it ourselves:

The whole world of culture has, for certain, been produced by the physical and mental activity of man, and for this reason one can, and, in fact, has to, find its principles and regularities within the modes of existence of the spirit of the self-same people.[10]

According to Vico, the laws of historical development are laws of the structure of meaning. His call for a science of human society preceded that of the positivists, and it was a call for a study of the forms of social life developed by and created through human meaning. Although his ideas went practically unnoticed at the time, they are significant because they asked for a study of human phenomena freed from theology and metaphysics and because they suggested an alternative approach to the study of human nature (an approach anticipating the structuralism developed much later by Lévi-Strauss). In recent years, Vico's work has become the subject of increasing study and has served, in fact, as a source for ideas about methodological issues in the human sciences.

The main context of the late nineteenth-century anti-positivist response was the idealistic and Romantic legacy of the movements of Herder, Fichte, and Schelling in Germany from earlier in the century. These movements recognized the life experience of humans, the emotional and vital feeling of life, and the engagement that humans have with others and with the world. The new science of humans proposed by the positivists overlooked the very experience of life in favor of the physical and mental regularities that could be caught up in a network of laws. Novel and creative acts, the personal pain of suffering, and the joy of happiness were not the focus of the perspective they advocated.

The anti-positivist response was not unified and did not develop a coherent and systematic alternative to the positivist-inspired approach to the study of human phenomena. There was, however, general agreement in the anti-positivist response that what was wrong with positivism was that it neglected the unique sphere of meaningful experience that was the defining characteristic of human phenomena. What the anti-positivist response—in its broadest interpretation— was calling attention to was the sphere of reality that exists because of human beings. If human beings did not inhabit the planet, there would be no such constructions as roads and homes, there would be no social institutions, there would be no cultural-belief systems, and there would be no developed systems of conceptual communication through spoken and written words. It appeared that positivism did not appreciate or intend to investigate this "human-added" realm. Although there was agreement among the anti-positivists that the human realm needed to be included in the sciences, no single program of methods for studying this realm gained preeminence.

Neo-Kantian Response

The first person to introduce a dichotomy of method between the physical and human sciences appears to have been the German historian Johann Gustav Droysen. In 1858 he used the terms *erklären* (explanation) to describe physical science methods and *verstehen* (understanding) to describe human science methods. According to Droysen's plan, the physical sciences were to explain phenomena by uncovering necessary and predictive laws, while the human sciences were to provide an understanding of human experience. The difference between the two approaches is a difference between kinds of knowledge. For example, through the physical sciences we can come to know that a rock falls because of the law of gravity, while through the human sciences we can come to know the meaning that someone is trying to communicate to us.[11]

The anti-positivist response drew on the distinction that Kant had made between theoretical and practical reason. For Kant, theoretical reason was concerned with the knowledge of appearances—with the realm of nature—and practical reason was concerned with moral decisions. Kant asserted that human history was a part of nature, and he did not accept a distinction between the human sciences and the natural sciences. The neo-Kantians of the late nineteenth century, however, thought that cultural phenomena, as expressions of meaning, needed to be comprehended apart from events in nature. Moreover, the realm created by human action—the cultural realm—needed to be comprehended with a kind of reason akin to Kant's practical reason. Cultural phenomena required *verstehen*, a mode of understanding which the neo-Kantians considered a legitimate source of knowledge. The positivists were opposed to the use of the *verstehen* mode on the ground that different interpreters could come to different understandings of the same phenomena. Understanding was said by the positivists to be merely speculative and therefore open to challenge; they attacked it for lacking certainty and refused to include it in science (*epistēmē*).

A leading center of the neo-Kantian opposition to Mill's "logic of the moral sciences" was the so-called Southwest German (or Baden) school, which placed extreme stress on the activity of the mind in knowledge and on the priority of value. Wilhelm Windelband and Heinrich Rickert, the leaders of this school, held that there was a fundamental difference between the natural sciences and the studies of history, jurisprudence, and economics. However, they proposed that there were not two realms, a human and a physical, but one realm that could be approached from two perspectives.

Windelband, in an address called "History and Natural Science" given in 1894, coined the labels "nomothetic" (*nomos* means "law") and "idiographic" (*idio* means "personal," "particular," or "distinct") to distinguish between the natural science and historical science approaches to phenomena. Windelband argued that the natural science approach aims at the construction of physical causality and "explanation" (Droysen's *erklären*) of events by identifying them as instances of a general law. The historical science approach, by contrast, is individualizing; it concentrates on the uniqueness of the event and attempts to identify its meaning and specific characteristics. Windelband believed that any given event could be studied by either kind of science. A mental event viewed from the perspective of physical causality—as an instance of the working of some general law—could be explained as a natural event. But that same mental event, described in its individuality and valued for its deviation from the class or form to which it belonged, became an object approached from the idiographic perspective. The human sciences were not, then, distinguished by attending to a different realm, but by using the idiographic method. The use of this method allowed certain unique and human characteristics to be understood.[12]

Rickert was the most influential member of the Southwest school. He, too, believed that the difference between the human and natural sciences was the perspective each took, rather than that they studied different realms. In *Culture Science and Natural Science* (1889), he stated that "reality becomes nature if we consider it in regard to what is general; it becomes history if we consider it in regard to the particular or individual."[13] Rickert rejected Dilthey's term *human science* and substituted for it the term *culture science (Kulturwissenschaft)*. Dilthey proposed that the object of study was the "lifeworld," or experience. Rickert believed that this proposal emphasized the study of individual experience to the detriment of the study of cultural products and institutions. It is these and their meanings that the sciences of human phenomena should seek to understand, not inner experience. When the originally "immeasurable manifold" is viewed from the perspective of understanding concrete individual cases that are suffused with meaning, rather than abstract generalized laws, the cultural sciences result.

It was Rickert's position that meaning cannot be understood except in terms of values. Values are what provide the meaning of individual events. Culture science should attend to understanding values, and this is done by looking at their historical manifestations. Values are not psychic or mental phenomena; instead, they are universal and ahistorical standards. Although they are never actualized in history, they can be studied by looking at how they are approached by various cultures. Rickert approached the position that culture science should focus on the transcendent realm of values and how they are manifested in human actions. Such an approach was opposed by Dilthey, who believed that values were contingent and subject to change and historical development.

Georg Simmel, although included among the neo-Kantians, was not part of the Southwest school. He lived most of his life in Berlin, where his major works were written between 1892 and 1908. Simmel proposed a theory of the origin of human society. He believed that concrete social phenomena could be traced back to the modes of individual behavior and that the particular form of such modes should be understood through detailed description. Simmel represented the position that social forms were dependent upon individual needs, in opposition to the idea that these forms had a reality of their own. His key concept was that of reciprocal effect. This notion holds that the drives of individuals—such as hunger or love—make up the *content* of social life. On the other hand, reciprocal effects between individuals such as competition, domination, cooperation, and solidarity are the *actualizing forms* of social life. His distinction between content and actualizing forms provided a way to understand how experience is constructed. In experiences, the objects of the world are constituted in different forms; for example, a painting can be experienced as beautiful and simultaneously can be revered as an object of worship. Simmel focused on the structuring activity of the agent in producing what is experienced.[14]

These three are representatives of the ideological context in which an anti-positivistic human science was undertaken in Germany. We shall turn now to six advocates of a methodology for human science that could rigorously study the fullness of the human realm.

Wilhelm Dilthey (1833–1911)

Wilhelm Dilthey was the principal architect of the anti-positivist movement in human science. He agreed with the positivist position that the only real knowledge is rigorous scientific knowledge, and he believed that the claims for speculative knowledge, intuitive knowledge, poetic knowledge, and knowledge of faith were riddled with contradictions. He also appreciated Mill's emphasis on the need for an empirical base for true knowledge. His argument with the positivists was not over their concern to build a knowledge freed from the traditional sources of revelation and pure reason, but over the question of what is the appropriate empirical science for the study of human phenomena. It was Dilthey's particular appreciation for the wealth and variety of human life that informed his understanding of the limitations of a merely explanatory model of science for the study of human beings.

Dilthey's explication of a methodology for the human sciences must be viewed within the context of his "philosophy of life." Life, he said, cannot be understood as a machine, as Hobbes had suggested. Neither can it be explained merely as an organic system shared with other life forms, because human life is something far more than organic metabolism and mechanical movement. For Dilthey, life is what we experience in our activities and reflections as we live out our personal histories. He did not believe that human life could be understood by using the explanatory model that classifies events according to the laws of nature:

> The expression "life" denotes what is to everyone the most familiar and intimate, but at the same time the darkest and even most imponderable. . . . One can describe it. One can elucidate its peculiar and characteristic traits. One can, as it were, inquire after its tone, rhythm, and melody. But one cannot analyze it totally into all its factors, for it is not totally resolvable in this manner. What it is cannot be expressed in a simple formula or explanation. Thought cannot fully go behind life, for it is the expression of life.[15]

The accumulation of the innumerable lives of individuals makes up the historical and social reality of humankind. For Dilthey, it was an empirical fact that the individual stands in a complex texture of relationships with others. "The individual life is part of life as a whole."[16] The individual life is not an isolated monad; it is merged and integrated into levels of intensity with various group lives, including the group life of humankind. And because individuals do not exist in isolation, Dilthey said, they cannot be studied as isolated units; they need to be understood in the context of their connections to cultural and social life.

The object of inquiry for the human sciences, then, includes not only the hopes and fears and thoughts and acts of individuals, but also the institutions that have emerged out of life activity, which, in turn, provide part of the context in which individual experience is formed. Other expressions of human life must also be included— for instance, the laws that guide conduct, the religions that are believed in, the creations that organize and give meaning to experience, such as art, literature, and philosophy. The activity of science—even science that studies inanimate nature—is an expression of life, and as such it must be included in the subject matter of human science. Human science takes as its field of study all of human life and all of life's expressions. Its goal is to understand the order that underlies the process of human existence, an order that provides the form for experience.

Dilthey's "philosophy of life" proposes that the only proper focus for human science is the concrete life—the experience—of historical agents and their actions. Dilthey dismissed two alternative focal points as inadequate. The first of these was transcendentalism in any form. He did not believe that there is any ultimate reality "behind" life, such as, for example, Kant's thing-in-itself or Rickert's universal values. There is no point outside of life on which a knower can stand to observe, he said, and thus knowledge of life is an activity of life itself focused on itself. There are no transcendent, absolute standards of truth that can be utilized as grounds of certainty, and thus the study of life is an activity of particular individuals living at a particular time in a particular place. Human scientists are influenced by their circumstances, by their cultural traditions and cognitive structures, by their social environment, and by the horizons of their historical setting. Therefore all knowledge developed by life reflecting on itself is tinged with relativity.

The second focal point dismissed by Dilthey was the empirical view that we "experience" only sensations and impressions, such as, say, green patches of color. Such descriptions of experience, he said, are abstractions from the fullness of the experience that makes up our life-world. Ordinarily, experience consists of concrete things— for example, people we recognize and feel something toward, a painting we see as beautiful, objects which appear as useful. And it is this experience, which is part of our everyday lives, that must be the source of material for the human sciences. Knowledge begins with this experience, Dilthey asserted, and in his view empiricists and positivists were mistaken in their belief that knowledge begins with such things as blobs of color and twinges of pain. He accused the positivists of metaphysical dogmatism for insisting that knowledge must be sought in "pure sensation," itself an abstraction resulting from a particular analytic attitude taken toward the life-world in its richness.

Categories of life. The task of the human sciences, as Dilthey saw it, was to examine the life experience both in its individual manifestations and in its social expressions. Life experience, he maintained, is not a mass of random and disconnected experience; we do not experience a buzz of impressions. Experience is already organized as it appears; it makes sense, and it is understandable. And it is already full of meaning. What human scientists must seek to make explicit, then, are the principles of organization. Dilthey called these principles "categories of life." They are the processes by means of which experience appears as related and meaningful. The goal of human science is to explicate these processes, not to seek causal connections. This explication would result from the use of a kind of reason different from the reason used to establish the laws of nature. Dilthey called this reason "historical reason" to distinguish it from "pure reason," which Kant used for the study of nature.

Dilthey believed that his own task was to develop a critique of historical reason that would stand in contrast to Kant's critique of pure reason. Kant sought to understand how it is that we experience physical reality. He attempted to describe the mental processes that organize our sensations into our experiences of an ordered, connected world of objects in space and time, and he named the principles of this mental ordering process "categories." Dilthey extended Kant's approach: whereas Kant undertook to order the experience of the physical world, Dilthey undertook to order the whole of the life experience.

Dilthey wanted to produce a list of categories of life, those principles by means of which we organize experience, but his approach to recognizing the categories differed from Kant's approach. According to Kant, the categories exist a priori—that is, they exist before any experience is acquired, and thus they are not learned— and no experience is available that has not already been organized through the activity of the categories. Using a somewhat mechanistic metaphor, we might say that a person's brain is prewired, so that it operates on any data that come into the system according to the patterns already wired into the brain. Kant's concept was just the opposite of Hume's empirical concept. Hume held that all organization of experience is the result of previous experience and that there are no pregiven organizational patterns; instead, these patterns are built up through the association of various experiences. The position that Dilthey took in regard to his categories of life is closer to Hume's position than to Kant's. Dilthey did not believe that the categories are a priori; in his view, they can vary, depending upon the historical setting and the individual experiences.

Dilthey's method for uncovering the patterns uses empirical generalization. Examining the life experience itself, the researcher notices forms and relationships shaping the way in which the experience is meaningful. Some of the patterns Dilthey discussed are the relationships of self and world; power; part and whole; means and ends; and development. The pattern of self and world is at the base of symbolism, and it organizes the relationship between objects and meaning—for example, between frown and anger or between a combination of alphabet letters and concepts. The pattern of power organizes experience so that we are aware of our impact on things and their effect on us; it is at the base of our planning activities, and it corresponds to causality in the physical world.

The categories of life operate primarily at a level underlying conscious awareness and deliberation. For example, usually we do not notice a person's turned-down lips and consciously infer from them that the person is angry; instead, we experience an angry person. These patterns can be used consciously, however, when an appearance is confusing and may at first seem meaningless. In such an instance, we can try to understand an experience and make sense of it. Dilthey believed that religions, myths, proverbs, and works of art are all constructions of meaning that provide order in experience and that social understanding, legal codes, and written constitutions are all manifestations of the ordering process, providing contexts in which present actions and future plans are made meaningful.

Moreover, the categories of life are part of a researcher's own experience. The human scientist is a human being who is affected, like everyone else, by the circumstances of his setting. Dilthey saw this as an advantage, not as a disadvantage to be overcome, because a researcher gives meaning to his own experience through the organizing processes. These processes, then, are not abstract, as are relationships in the physical realm; they are experienced by the researcher and are part of his own interpretation of life. The processes themselves are used in the researcher's activity to gain knowledge.

In Dilthey's scheme, there are levels of organizing processes. At the most comprehensive level, there are those processes that provide an overall integrative interpretation or world view. The world view of a culture can be defined as that which provides the basic assumptions and the total attitude of life. It is the meaning environment that envelopes individuals; it presents the conceptual and interpretive organizing patterns that individuals integrate into their own meaning-creating process. Dilthey discerned three basic types of world views: naturalism (positivism), subjective idealism (the idealism of freedom as exemplified by Kant), and objective idealism (as exemplified by Hegel). For Dilthey a world view is coherent and stabilizing, but it is not self-enclosed or static, for it is attended by an "inner dialectic" that forces the revision of premises and brings about changes in the meaning network.

When Dilthey emphasized that the task of human science is to make explicit the organizing themes that render experience meaningful, he was seeking to describe the structural coherence that gives meaning to experience. As a goal for human science, description of structure differs broadly from the goals of Mill's science. Mill sought to trace the causal genesis and to state the laws of explanation, while Dilthey looked to human science to uncover the structures of meaning. These structures are not independent of life; they are handed down to individuals through the cultures into which the individuals are born. The structures do adapt and change over periods of time, however. The sources for the human scientist who is uncovering these organizing processes are literature, religious practices, everyday assumptions about nature and people, artistic works, and any other expressions of life. Because researchers express their own life-worlds and local organizing themes in their attempts to understand, they are unable to achieve a purity of knowledge that is freed from situatedness in various life contexts. But if researchers were to base their findings merely on the life within and around them, they would become parochial. Such a limited data base would make it possible for researchers to mistake their own organizing principles or categories for the whole.

For Dilthey, the understanding and recognition of categories required the broadest possible context and the deepest possible investigation of life's manifestations. Limiting the search for categories to a particular disciplinary perspective or historical period would, he felt, miss the interactive aspect of the categories. Human science research needs to address life in all of its manifestations. It needs to examine human actions and expressions; it needs to examine the developing and historically changing life patterns; it needs to examine the patterns of social organization. In short, it needs to address the intersection of life patterns and the individual's interpretive efforts toward meaning-giving. Synchronically, life appears multi-tiered; diachronically, it appears slow-changing.

Verstehen. The positivists had declared that knowledge should be derived from perception. This position implied that what we perceive is the manifestation of physical objects, transmitted by the sensory apparatus into consciousness. Knowledge, in the positivist view, should be limited to what can be implied from this one type of experience. Dilthey emphasized his belief that there is another type of "perceptual" experience and that human science must use it. In addition to recognizing physical objects, Dilthey said, we also recognize meaning. When people communicate to us through books, we experience more than the visual sensation created by black marks on white paper; we also perceive the meanings of the words and the message of the author. When we perceive physical objects, we see more than those objects; we "perceive" or understand (*verstehen*) meaning in the world. Dilthey held that this second type of experience needs to be included as part of the repertoire of human science and that it ought to be recognized as a legitimate means for acquiring knowledge.

Because of his belief in its importance, Dilthey tried to analyze this type of experience, much in the same way that the positivists had tried to analyze the perceptual experience of physical objects. According to Dilthey, the cognitive process of understanding (*verstehen*) is focused on expressions of life, rather than on physical objects. One does not "understand" a garbage can. The choice of the *verstehen* mode of cognition is appropriate only for studying the objects investigated by the human sciences. The objects studied by the physical sciences are not expressions of life—that is, they do not order and give meaning to their experience.

Dilthey described three conditions which make it possible to understand (*verstehen*) another's meaning: (1) One needs to be familiar with the mental processes through which meaning is experienced and conveyed. Since each person is involved in trying to communicate meaning to others, everyone is familiar with these processes to some extent, but researchers can enlarge this familiarity through the study of biographies and descriptive psychology. (2) One needs a knowledge of the particular concrete context in which an expression is made. A word is understood in the context of its sentence; an action is understood in the context of its situation. (3) One needs a knowledge of the social and cultural systems that provide the meaning for most expressions. To understand a sentence, we need to know the language; to understand a chess move, we need to know the rules of chess.

The human science researcher uses *verstehen* in addition to other modes of cognition. Starting with experience as it is given and including its meaningfulness, the researcher uses all of the tools of knowledge available as he or she seeks to describe, as accurately as possible, the organizing patterns by means of which the experience appears with the particular sense that it has. These tools—all of which are necessary—include observation, logical reasoning, comparison, classification, abstraction, hypothesis framing and testing, and analysis by means of statistical techniques. But along with information obtained with these methods, the human scientist must also take into consideration the information that is developed by the use of *verstehen*. Dilthey emphasized the interdependence of the kinds of knowledge required to understand the full, concrete experience of life.

Human science studies the manifestations of life in order to identify the patterns of organization that are operative in giving form to the manifestations. Manifestations of life appear in an individual's experience and in the productions of that experience. Access to one's own experience requires introspection—that is, examination of one's own consciousness. Dilthey came to have reservations, however, about the use of introspection as a useful means for gaining access to the organizing principles of life experience. In the process of introspection, he said, we interfere with the very life experience we seek to understand. Because of this fact, he rejected this method as an acceptable base upon which to build a human science:

> The concrete content of these structural relations [the life categories or organizing patterns] is not provided in the observation of the self, but rather in the understanding of expression, that is, mental creation.[17]

Because of what he saw as the limits of introspection, Dilthey turned to the expressions of life for a source in which to study the life categories. The expressions of life are, for example, the words or gestures produced by a person or the texts in which the words are written. As he worked with written expressions of life, Dilthey made use of the techniques that had been developed in hermeneutic studies. Biblical, legal, and classical scholars had developed methods for interpreting and understanding the meanings of the texts they were studying, and Schleiermacher had recently enlarged the scope of hermeneutics by claiming that traditional interpretive techniques could be used to understand the meaning of any kind of text. Dilthey expanded this possibility. If the techniques of hermeneutics could be used for the systematic interpretation of written texts, he asked, why could they not be used to interpret spoken words? Speeches, conversations, and interview responses might thus be systematically interpreted. Moreover, if spoken expressions could be interpreted, then why not nonverbal expressions, such as facial expressions, gestures, and actions? (This subject will be taken up again in chapter 7, where the specific techniques of the contemporary hermeneutic approach will be described in detail.)

Dilthey continued to influence the "search for a method" in the behavioral and social sciences. He functioned more as a stimulator of the debate, however, than as a creator of a consistent and complete system for the human sciences. He reminded the debaters that an integrative position, instead of an extreme position, would be the most appropriate for a fruitful human science.

H. P. Rickman has listed nine of Dilthey's ideas about psychology, and these ideas hold for all of the various disciplines within human science; I enumerate them by way of summary of Dilthey's contribution to the debate. (1) Humans are embodied and social beings, and therefore a balance should be maintained between studies of the physiological bases of behavior and experience and studies of the structures of the life experience. (2) The life experience is a structural whole that affects and modifies its various parts. (3) The life experience expresses itself in various ways, including facial expressions, gestures, postures, actions, spoken and written languages, and artistic expressions. (4) The most substantial sources of knowledge about the life experience are the expressions of life—for example, the pictures painted, the letters written, the poems and stories composed, and the institutions created. (5) The life categories that give coherence to a person's expression of life are not necessarily explicitly present to this person's awareness at the time the expression is produced. (6) Since humans are psychosocial beings, they cannot understand life in isolation; they understand it only in the context of the social relations and cultural influences that intersect at particular times and places. (7) Life is historical, and as individuals manifest life, it changes. Consequently, an unchanging human nature cannot be assumed. The structures of meaning evolve in a one-way process, so that they are different in various historical periods. (8) Life is found at the level of meaningful experience. If human science concentrates on a lower level, with less complex and more easily isolated phenomena (such as sensations, instincts, and reflexes), then the very subject matter of the human sciences—life itself—will be missed. (9) In addition to explanations in which individual events are subsumed under laws usually causal in nature, human science needs "detailed, searching description of complex, mental phenomena and human behavior."[18]

Dilthey's student, Eduard Spranger (1882–1963), carried forward the anti-positivist understanding of the human sciences by extending Dilthey's argument and method (with Hegelian overtones) into psychology and personality theory. Spranger's chief work is *Die Lebensformen* (*Life Forms*) (1914), translated into English as *Types of Man* in 1928 by W. Pigors.

Wilhelm Wundt (1832–1920)

Wilhelm Wundt has been recognized as the father of psychology. The founding of his Psychological Institute in Leipzig in 1879 is held to mark the beginning of psychology as a science distinct from philosophy. His own distinction between physiological psychology and folk psychology (*Völkerpsychologie*) illustrates the struggle within the human sciences to establish the kind of discipline that psychology was to become. The first was Wundt's model of a psychology that would be entirely a physical science, while the second model would have only one foot in the physical sciences. Edwin G. Boring's *History of Experimental Psychology*, the classic text of the history of psychology, is written from the perspective of the first model and does not give full treatment to the nonpositivistic parts of Wundt's approach.[19]

Boring identifies the most prominent proponents of the "new" psychology as Oswald Kulpe, Herman Ebbinghaus, and E. B. Titchener. What these men had in common was a commitment to the new positivism associated with Avenarius and Mach. Those who advocated that the new discipline of psychology should follow the Machian outline of science understood that the fundamental tasks of psychology would be observation and description for the purpose of providing the most economical summary of the relationships among the elements of sensation. The earlier positivism of Comte allowed no place for psychology in science, but the revised and restrained positivism of Avenarius and Mach had considerable respect for it. Danziger describes Avenarius and Mach's perspective on psychology:

> [They] rejected the metaphysical dualism of the mental and the physical. As positivists they refused to go beyond what is given in experience; but we do not have two kinds of experience, physical and mental— experience is simply experience. The elements of our experience, however, can be studied from two points of view: We can study relationships among experiences that are independent of the particular biological system to which they belong—in that case we have the basis for physical science—or we can study relationships among experiences that depend on the particular biological system to which they belong—in which case we practice psychology. The difference between psychology and physical science is therefore not an essential difference; there is no reason why psychology should not aspire to a scientific status comparable to that of the physical sciences.[20]

Psychology, however, should give up all mentalistic explanatory concepts. Sensa do not show up a "self" or personal agency, and thus the investigation of individual experience is of the biological individual, not of the psychic individual.

On the other hand, Wundt himself held that psychology should be the scientific study of immediate experience. This experience, however, is not to be understood as the interaction of biological senses with the world; instead, it is a psychological entity interacting with the environment. Psychology studies all of experience—including subjective elements, such as feelings—directly, as it is given in consciousness and as it develops from the psychological state of the observer. Wundt's German students spoke of his approach as *Ganzheit* or "wholeness" (though not in the sense of "gestalt" or other contemporary uses of the term).

In opposition to the approach of the positivists, Wundt emphasized the role of apperception. For him, apperception refers to the activity of attending to something and integrating and creating the perceptive experience; it stands in opposition to the notion of perception as a passive, receptive occurrence or a reproductive play of associations. Wundt believed that we have control over our minds, that we practice a voluntarism in which we analyze and synthesize and direct our attention where we will, although in accordance with lawful principles. He also took a "centralist" position, claiming that voluntary movement provides the basis for involuntary movement, and not the other way around; according to Wundt, it is a central generative process that causes attention to be given to various phenomena. This, too, was a response to the positivists, who held that such a psychological force, insofar as it is not directly available to sensation, must be rejected.

The positivists called for a study of experience stripped of all subjective elements, including even the projection on the sensa of reference to objects in the world. In direct contrast, Wundt was interested specifically in the subjective elements of experience. He believed that conscious experience and physiological events (independent, biologically related sensa) are so different that they cannot be causally related. For Wundt, experience is a complex mental event resulting from a mental synthesis of elements into a higher unity. By breaking up experience into simple elements, he maintained, the unity created by feeling and will is missed. Wundt designated three areas for psychological investigation: (1) immediate experience, to be studied through experimentation and the use of internal perception; (2) the processes of thought themselves, to be studied through a nonexperimental psycholinguistics which he developed in extensive detail; and (3) the area made up of feelings, affects, and processes of volition, to be studied through examining the historical development of the human species.

For the study of immediate experience, Wundt distinguished between "self-observation" and "internal perception." (English translations frequently do not retain this distinction; usually both terms are translated as "introspection.") He wanted to avoid the difficulties that would arise from reporting memories of experience—that is, the concept of "retrospection" as developed by Mill in reply to Comte's attack on "introspection"—and so he tried to develop a procedure in which the observation and report of one's experience would follow immediately on the original perception without time for reflection and self-consciousness. Wundt trained observers for the purpose of increasing quick and attentive observation. He also replicated experiences in a laboratory setting, gathering multiple reports of internal perception of the same event, so as to provide a reliable source of data for dependable descriptions of experience. In these experiments, "observers" (Wundt's term) would sit in a darkened room facing a projection screen. For just an instant, a four-by-four matrix of four-letter groups would be flashed on the screen, and the "observers" would immediately report their experiences. Wundt's question was: How many ideas can be presented in consciousness at a given moment? By varying the letters from nonsense combinations to word forms to words whose meanings were connected, he hoped to determine the way experience is apperceived or synthesized into wholes.

Wundt believed that his experimental approach was limited to those mental phenomena that are directly responsive to physical influences. His term for this kind of psychology was "physiological psychology," which was appropriate in this instance because he had borrowed his approach from his original field, physiology. The higher mental processes could not be revealed by this method of experimental "internal perception." Something else was needed in addition to the experimental methods, and this was the study of the products of mental life, Wundt's "folk psychology." The study of language, myths, and customs, he believed, would provide clues to the higher operations of the mind. For example, he held that sentence production begins with a unified idea that one wants to communicate and that it is from this "whole mental configuration" that the sentence is produced. He was also concerned with gesture language, meaning change, and the origins of language in involuntary, expressive sounds. David Leary has summarized Wundt's two approaches:

According to Wundt experimental psychology and folk psychology differed both in terms of subject matter and in terms of method. They were fundamentally different disciplines, and yet both were valid and necessary to give a rounded understanding of human experience and the psychological processes underlying that experience. There was simply no way . . . that social phenomena such as language, myths, and customs could receive a definitive treatment, or be understood, in terms of the more primitive psychological processes. . . . The best that can be done is to provide careful genetic and comparative descriptions as well as critical analyses of social phenomena.[21]

In 1894 Wundt published his monograph on *Psychic Causality*. This was the same year that Avenarius wrote his first paper on psychology and Dilthey published his *Ideas on Descriptive and Analytical Psychology*. Wundt's assistant, Kulpe, wrote his *Groundplan of Psychology* in 1893, which marked the beginning of his break with Wundt over the nature of psychology. Kulpe came to favor a positivist approach for psychology while Wundt continued to develop a model of psychology that borrowed certain experimental methods from the physical sciences and yet still allowed for other methods for studying the higher mental processes. Wundt did not accept Avenarius and Mach's position that science must limit its data to sensa and avoid all subjective additions to and projections from these supposedly apodictic givens. Thus his role in the anti-positivist side of the debate must be recognized, even though he is often presented as a champion of the physical science model.

Franz Brentano (1838–1917)

Franz Brentano shared with Dilthey and Wundt the belief that the object of inquiry for psychology should be human experience in its fullness. Unlike Mach and Avenarius, who believed that sense data were primary, Brentano sought to understand experience as it is lived—which means the inclusion of judgments and valuing as well as perceptions of objects. He wanted to emancipate knowledge of human phenomena from the speculative efforts of scholastic philosophers, and in the spirit of the time he looked for an empirical base for such knowledge. He engaged in considerable correspondence with Mill, and he shared the ambitions of the positivists to adopt the methods of the natural sciences for studying human phenomena. Unlike the positivists, however, Brentano wanted to use these methods to approach such final metaphysical questions as the relationship between the mind and the body and the possibility of immortality.

In 1869, Brentano published an article on Comte, exploring in a sympathetic way the possibility of a positivistic renewal. He could not accept Comte's repudiation of psychology, however, and finding support in Mill, he held that psychology—that is, the study of experience itself—was the proper vehicle for the positivist reform. He contended that the problem with the study of experience thus far was a lack of groundwork that would clarify the fundamental categories and basic divisions in experience. In his view, this preparatory work needed to be done before the metaphysical questions he had in mind could be addressed from an empirical standpoint.

Brentano's most important book is *Psychology from an Empirical Standpoint* (1874; 1911). The book opens with a direct statement of his position:

> The title I give to my book characterizes its subject matter and its method. My standpoint in psychology is empirical: Experience alone is my teacher. But I share with others the conviction that a certain ideal intuition [*ideale Anschauung*] can be combined with such a standpoint.

His acknowledgment of the empirical source of knowledge is straightforward, but the additional source of knowledge he cites—the "ideal intuition"—is not fully explained and considered in the book. Herbert Spiegelberg[22] believes that Brentano was referring to the type of knowledge that one has of the goodness or badness of something, a type of knowledge acquired at one stroke without induction from experience. Brentano wanted to recognize a special kind of experience that is not allowed for in traditional empiricism and that is wide enough to include such phenomena as love and hate. In addition to experiencing objects in the world, one experiences love of an object or love of a person. Brentano wanted an empiricism that would recognize these aspects of experience.

It became clear to Brentano that his approach went beyond the psychology of Mill and opened up the realm of experience in such a manner that what was to be found had not yet been categorized and clarified. Consequently, he proposed that the new psychology should be made up of two major divisions: genetic psychology and descriptive psychology. Genetic psychology would study the causal relationships among the various aspects of the widened empirical realm—but before causal relationships could be established, a full descriptive psychology needed to be developed. The empirical realm needed to be mapped out before it could be causally explained. He drew on the subdivision between descriptive and explanatory (genetic) efforts that had been made in other sciences—such as, for instance, the subdivision between anatomy and physiology—and he took his name for a descriptive psychology from a descriptive subdivision of geology, called "geognosy." He coined the term *psychognosie* (*psycho* means "soul"; *gnosie* means "knowledge") for the study of the organization and structure of everyday experience. The problem for *psychognosie* was how to delimit and articulate the sprawling, elusive, and amorphous flow that makes up experience. The first step was to isolate and to identify the basic divisions of experience, and to this end Brentano devoted most of his time.

His concern was to give a basic articulation of the chief categories that can be used in describing the experiential field. For instance, are sensations, feelings, and judgments separate phenomena, or are they overlapping? Are they on the same level of experiential strata, or are they on different levels? The work of a descriptive psychologist differs from the work of, for example, a bird watcher: the bird watcher works within an already developed classificatory system, and he has only to identify the category to which a bird belongs; but the descriptive psychologist does not have an already developed system, and so must identify the basic categories themselves and describe their structural features. After this basic work is done, then it is possible to determine in which category a particular experience belongs. Lacking the categorical structure, it is not possible to develop genetic psychology, for until the categories are clarified one does not know what events produce what causes.

Thus Brentano qualified his initial enthusiasm for methods drawn from the physical sciences. The inquiry into the categories of experience, he decided, must precede the formation of knowledge about the relationships among events, and it needs to use methods that cannot be obtained from the physical sciences.

Ever since Comte's attack on introspection, access to the data of experience had been viewed as problematic. As mentioned in the discussion of Wundt, the notion of introspection (*Selbstbeobachtung*) naively assumed that the data of consciousness or experience are available through self-observation. But as one observes one's own experience, something interferes with the experience; it is no longer what it would be if one were merely experiencing and not trying to observe oneself at the same time. Self-observation transforms the very experience it tries to observe. Mill, in answer to Comte (who was joined by Lange), held that this difficulty of interference could be overcome if self-observation could be conceived of as a kind of "retrospection" in which what is observed is not the experience itself as it is happening, but a memory of the original experience. This observation of a memory, however, along with the distortions of the memory act itself, would obviously not measure up to the standards of empirical observation, for empirical observation addresses itself to the experience of events as they occur and not to their memory images.

Like Wundt, Brentano maintained that the criticism of self-observation did not hold for "inner perception" (*innere Wahrnehmung*). Inner perception is the immediate awareness of one's own psychological phenomena, of one's joys, sadness, desires, and rage. As Brentano saw it, inner perception is possible only "in the margin" of experience while one's main attention is focused on external objects. He believed that it is possible to observe the immediate trace of an inner perception while it is still within the range of immediate memory. Thus the "empirical" data which Brentano sought to describe and classify could be developed only through the act of inner perception—that is, by conscious awareness of one's own experience as it occurs.

As he approached the task of describing mental phenomena, Brentano's first problem was to separate them out from the other data of consciousness. "All data of our consciousness," he wrote, "are divided into two great classes—the class of physical and the class of mental phenomena."[23] The examples he gave of physical phenomena in consciousness included "a color, a figure, a landscape . . . , a chord . . . , warmth, cold, odor which I sense; as well as similar images which appear in imagination."[24] Mental phenomena in consciousness were mental activities: "Every judgement, every recollection, every expectation, every inference, every conviction or opinion, every doubt, is a mental phenomenon."[25] The basic characteristic of mental phenomena was "intentionality" (a technical term Brentano borrowed from scholastic philosophy). The property of mental activity was that it referred to an object. The mental phenomenon in consciousness referred to something, and the thing referred to was the physical phenomenon. In the new positivism of Mach and Avenarius, the only phenomena to be attended to were what Brentano called the physical phenomena—that is, the objects of direct sense perception. Brentano identified psychology as the study of the rest of experience, the intentional acts themselves; *acts* referring to objects were the proper study of psychology.

Having delineated the subject matter of psychology, Brentano turned to an investigation of the basic types of these acts. He found three basic categories of mental phenomena: representations, judgments, and acts of love and hatred. Representations (*Vorstellungen*) are ideas, thoughts, and presentations; they provide the foundation for the second and third categories. The second category, judgment, is nonpropositional for Brentano; the object of one's judgment is simply the object itself (for example, a horse), and judgment is the act of accepting, affirming, or acknowledging that it is there. The object of the judgment is not a proposition (such as "the being of horses") that is accepted; the mental act accepts or denies the object itself.[26] The third category could be described as emotive acts; they include desires and feelings ("love and hate," in Brentano's terms), with the physical phenomena (things and persons loved and hated) as the referents.

Brentano was also interested in the question of how time is given in experience. He was particularly concerned with the difference between the way we experience present time and the way we experience past and future time. The difference lies, he believed, in the way we refer to a phenomenon when we "represent" it—that is, how we treat it in the first of the three basic categories of mental phenomena. Time is thus not part of the second category, judgment. Moreover, present time is given directly while past time and future time appear only indirectly by way of present time. Consequently, past time and future time are not real in consciousness by themselves; they are dependent upon present events. Husserl was later to use Brentano's ideas about the experience of time as the starting point for his significant work on inner time-consciousness.

Brentano's explorations in descriptive psychology differed from the inductive generalizations recommended by Mill. Writing about his own method, Brentano had this to say:

> Just as deduction is opposed to induction when we speak of kinds of proof, in this case explanation by means of subsumption under a general term is opposed to explanation by means of particulars, through examples. And the latter kind of explanation is appropriate whenever the particular terms are clearer than the general ones. Thus it is probably a more effective procedure to explain the term "color" by saying that it designates the class which contains red, blue, green and yellow, than to do the opposite and attempt to explain "red" by saying it is a particular kind of color. Moreover, explanation through particular definitions will be of even greater use when we are dealing, as in our case, with terms which are not common in ordinary life, while those for the individual phenomena included under them are frequently used. So let us first of all try to clarify the concepts by means of examples.[27]

Brentano represents part of the original effort to define the nature of human science. He contributed to our recognition that the human realm is not merely a reflection of the physical realm but is a realm in its own right. He also contributed to our awareness that experience contains more than sensa, that it demonstrates the subject's contribution to and active engagement in the world.

Edmund Husserl (1859–1938)

Edmund Husserl is the father of the phenomenological movement. He published a series of books on phenomenology, beginning with the first volume of the three-volume *Logical Investigations* in 1900 and concluding with *Cartesian Meditations* in 1931 and *The Crisis of European Sciences and Transcendental Phenomenology* in 1936. (After his death, the Husserl archives were founded to preserve his considerable legacy of unpublished manuscripts; more than twenty volumes of his collected works have appeared so far.) Unlike the other participants in this debate, Husserl looked to the rationalistic rather than to the empiricist tradition for suggestions for investigating the organizing structures of consciousness. He held that the organizing structures cannot be explained in terms of generalizations "learned" from experience but are rather presumed by experience. What creates our lived experience, he said, are the essential structures or ideas that order and give form to experience. He did not believe that these forms are built up from "more primary" elements of experience, such as "sense data," but that experience is already and always shaped by the essential structures. Like the other participants in this debate, then, he was concerned to understand the nature of these forms rather than of the sensa of experience.

Although Husserl followed many of the traditions of rationalism, he did not advocate a mere replication of earlier rationalistic methods. He was aware that his work came after the full development of empiricism and its success in producing the technological sciences at the end of the nineteenth century. He could not only build on what had already been accomplished by empiricism, but he could also add to it certain neglected insights drawn from the nonempirical tradition. In a letter to Lévy-Bruehl, Husserl described phenomenology as "a method by which I want to establish, against mysticism and irrationalism, a kind of super-rationalism (*Überrationalismus*) which transcends the old rationalism as inadequate and yet vindicates its inmost objectives."[28]

Husserl attempted to update the tradition of rational science as an addition to—not a replacement for—empirical science. What follows is a description of phenomenological research as it has been developed from Husserl's methodological ideas.

Phenomenology is the science of the essential structures of consciousness. It is a study based on the intuitive grasping of the essences of phenomena; it is not a study based on empirical generalization. Phenomenology holds that what is experienced by people is the result of a constitutive process within consciousness. Thus the sense data already appears within meaningful configurations. The meaning "borrows" the facts; the empirically present factual material that may be disengaged by subsequent analysis is more originally within the framework of the essential, nonempirical *eidos* (essence, essential structure) that is the object of consciousness. Objectivity becomes a region that is constituted or built by consciousness and is not a statement about a quality of empirical realities. The essence is thus what is necessary for recognizing a certain kind of thing.

Essences are present in everyone's stream of consciousness, giving form to experience; usually, however, they are "anonymous" or "latent" in our "performances." By reflecting in a methodical way on experiences themselves, one can bring to light the previously hidden eidetic (having to do with eidos) activity. In everyday awareness, one does not attend to the constitutive process of the essences; instead, one focuses on the final result of the constitutive process, the contents of our lived world. Because we usually do not attend to the structuring process and because the lived experience itself involves all of our motor and affective functions as well as our sensory functions, then in order to uncover the essences, we must go through a process similar to the process an archaeologist goes through when he or she excavates a prehistoric site. For the structure of essence of experience has undergone a process of sedimentation, and, like the archaeologist, we must carefully describe the various strata in order to reveal the meaning-giving structures that are taken for granted in everyday experience.

Phenomenological reflection does not produce factual statements or generalizations derived from particular experiences. Instead, it produces descriptions of what is essential or invariant to such-and-such a kind of experience. These essences are grasped by "intuiting" or "seeing," after applying a method that enables them to come to light. The method involves looking reflectively at an instance (or several instances) of the kind of experience under consideration. The instance (or instances) is then altered in imagination. This process of imaginative variation of altering allows for the sifting through of those aspects of the experience that are contingent and variable, thus leaving to be gleaned the necessary and sufficient ingredients—that is, the essence of the object of consciousness. For example, in determining the invariant structures of this essence "ball," the researcher imagines variations of balls. A football, beach ball, croquet ball, and so on are examined to explicate the structures which are present in each instance. The grasping of essences is not the result of passive waiting; it is the result of a strenuous, active search that makes possible the intuiting or seeing of the essence.

Phenomenological research is not concerned to frame theories; it focuses on examining and then describing the phenomena or essences as they present themselves to view. The commitment is to examine all phenomena carefully and to take none of them as familiar or understood until each has been carefully explicated and described. Phenomenology is held to be not only descriptive but presuppositionless. This obviously does not exclude the possibility that at any given time an individual phenomenologist may still be operating with certain unexamined assumptions—such a thing can always happen. The claim of presuppositionlessness expresses, instead, a resolution to eschew all unexamined assumptions. Phenomenology attempts to examine all premises, including its own, so as to permit the phenomena to show themselves in their essential structures.

It must be emphasized that essences, in the phenomenological sense, are not entities or existents of any sort. They are not objectlike; they cannot be perceived, inspected, or studied in the manner of objects. They have to do with the "how," rather than with the "that," of objects. That is, How is it that the experience of "ball" is possible?; not, Is that object a ball? The essence is that which is constant as the "given" of consciousness in the constitutive process; furthermore, the essence is what remains identical in all possible variations of what is being investigated. Moreover, essences are not restricted to experiences based on sense but include such nonsensuous experiences as relations, abstract entities, values, and the like. Essences vary in exactitude from the precision of mathematical and logical concepts to the more open structure of various feelings.

Use of examples. As conceived by Husserl, phenomenological method takes its beginning from carefully selected examples. Typically, only the most promising examples are seized upon, those that exhibit essential structures with a maximum of evidential clarity. For this reason, considerable care needs to be taken in the preliminary choice of examples, since it is by examining the examples that the essential structures can be intuited. It is the example itself that serves as the basic mediating factor which will show the essence. Examples may come from the researcher's own experience or from the experience of others. This approach to examples is of a different sort than the inductive requirement for a random sample of examples.

Once selected, the *epochē* or "reduction" is performed on the example. Claims about the reality or existence of the example are set "out of play" and attention is turned to the example as a phenomenon, i.e., as an object of consciousness rather than as a representation of an existing fact. The example is treated neither as a brute fact nor as an illustration of a conceptual truth; it is treated precisely as an example—as an instance of an essential structure whose necessary and invariant features are to be sought.

Free imaginative variation. After the researcher has identified his own "original phenomenon" or other examples of the phenomenon, these examples are submitted to a series of "free imaginative variations." This process is comparable to what contemporary Anglo-American philosophers call the method of "counterexamples." In this process, the example is described, and then the description is transformed—possibly, by adding a predicate or deleting one of the predicates contained in the description. Using the example of the *eidos* "ball," the predicate "round" would be deleted as an invariant structure, since nonround balls such as footballs exist. With each addition or deletion, the researcher questions whether the amended description still describes an example of the same kind of object or phenomenon as that which the original example was said to exemplify. Sometimes when a predicate is added or deleted from the description, what remains is a description of a different kind of phenomenon from the original. At other times, the additions and deletions do not affect the essential features of the kind of phenomenon exemplified by the different examples. Through this process of mental experimentation, the necessary and invariant features, the identical core of meaning or essence of the original phenomenon, become apparent and can be distinguished from features that are accidental and hence irrelevant to the eidetic description.

In the process of variation, the possibilities are infinite. But it is not necessary to go through the infinite variety of aspects of the phenomenon. Somewhere along the line, it will be seen or intuited that there is an identical element underlying all of the variations. It is this identical element that is the "sense" or essence of the phenomenon under investigation. Thus, grasping the essence of something does not require collecting some minimal or optimal number of instances of the phenomenon; it involves, instead, seeing that no additional variations can be significant for the investigation. It is this operation, however, that makes it possible for personal limitations of imagination to truncate a researcher's fullness of variation and completeness of investigation.

Intuiting. After the researcher has selected the examples of the phenomenon to be investigated and after he or she has performed the free imaginative variation, the necessary and sufficient aspects of the phenomenon begin to become obvious. Although the grasping of the essential structure is prepared for by the previous operations, it reaches completion through the "seeing" of the essential ingredients. Husserl used the term *Anschauung* to describe the awareness through which the researcher arrives at insight regarding the essence. It is not easy to translate this German term or even to find approximate equivalents for it in English. *Anschauung* (looking at) differs from *Erfahrung* (experience); "experience" always refers to cases which are assumed real, whereas *Anschauung* may also occur in imagination or recollection. *Anschauung* also differs from "intuition," especially in the sense of an inspirational idea of instinctive anticipation. Unless one uses a literal English parallel like the made-up word *intemplation*, one can do little else but speak of "direct intuition" or use the gerund *intuiting*. The term has also been translated as "seeing" as in "Oh, now I see."

Objects that are seen (in the ordinary sense of the term) are empirical objects. Essences are not empirical objects, and so they are not seen in this ordinary way. The point stressed by the concept of *Anschauung*, however, is that essences are not inferred from the individual examples but are given directly. They are not given through abstraction or generalization; neither are they induced from an enumeration of examples. Instead, they come to light and can be seen as the researcher reflects on examples and variations of the phenomena.

Husserl's point was that logical insight, in its most adequate and self-evident form, cannot be described in terms of mere sensibility. Just as one "sees" that the syllogism is true, so one intuits or sees that the description of the essence is true. The intuiting of essences (*Wesensschau*) is not a mystical or lyrical leap; it is a rational insight or cognition of a nonempirical structure of consciousness. It is not "ineffable"; it is undertaken in a fully articulate way.

Validity. After a researcher has identified the phenomenon to be investigated, carefully gathered rich examples either from his/her own experiences or from the experiences of others, and has creatively submitted the examples to free imaginative variation in which he or she comes to see (*Anschauung*) those aspects of the phenomenon that are necessary and sufficient, the research is complete. The final criterion for the validity of the research is the clarity of insight of the phenomenon's essence, for the insight is self-validating. The results of the research are then written up to be shared with the community of scholars. If the insight is communicated well, then others will also recognize the description as a statement of the essence of the phenomenon for themselves. Ernest Keen[29] has suggested four criteria for the descriptive statement: vividness, accuracy, richness, and elegance. Vividness is the quality that draws readers in, creating a feeling of genuineness. Accuracy is the dimension that makes the writing believable, creating a focus that enables readers to see the phenomenon as their own. Richness is the quality that deepens the description through colorful use of language, graphic depiction or shades of meaning, and detail, relaying something of the sensual-aesthetic tones of the phenomenon. Elegance is found in an economical use of words, disclosing the essence of the phenomenon through simple expressions that unify the description and give it grace and poignancy.

Ideally, the validity of phenomenological research is guaranteed through the self-validation of an insight that is communicated in a rich, full, clearly written description. In practice, however, different phenomenological researchers have investigated "the same" phenomenon and have arrived at different results, although each claims to have obtained the results through valid insight. In these instances, the process of submitting examples to variation can provide a basis for "internal" criticism by showing that the "essence" arrived at was or was not justified by the process itself. These differences in descriptions of essences can also be interpreted as part of a process of uncovering deeper and fuller understanding of the essences. Just as the insights into mathematical truths have developed through the work of various mathematicians, so the insights into other essences can develop as researchers build on each other's work. In his later writings, Husserl himself, giving his attention to the historical and the cultural, suggested that this process is at work. Validity of an essential description need not be an all-or-nothing judgment. Insights deepen as various researchers return to explore a phenomenon, and phenomena initially taken to be examples of "the same" essential structure may turn out to belong to essentially different types.

There are at least two trends within the Husserlian tradition with regard to validity. Both agree that the results of phenomenological research are not claims to be "proved" in the ordinary meaning of that term. According to one school of thought, however, when one has properly "seen" the essence of a phenomenon, one must also see that no one else can justifiably see it in any other way. Consequently, members of this school are rarely concerned with the opinions of other phenomenological researchers, except perhaps to reject those opinions with which they disagree or to accept those with which they do agree.

The other school of thought is exemplified by Gabriel Marcel,[30] who believes that dialogue, as well as the intuition of essences, is indispensable to phenomenological research. For Marcel, an individual intuition has little significance by itself. Like other phenomenologists, he appeals to essential insight, but he does so on the assumption that other people have had and do have similar experiences. On this basis it is possible, through discussion, to seek to persuade others to see in these experiences the same intuitions one has gained oneself. At the same time, it is very possible that one will be brought to modify one's own "intuition" by contact with the "intuition" of others. The result may very well be a sort of "social intuition" which has more validity precisely because humans are more truly human when they are acting in accord with others. The contributions of others, both in the past and in the present, are extremely important, since humans think authentically only when they are thinking in a framework that is both historical and social. This is not to bring truth down to the level of "mere opinion"; it is to recognize that intersubjectivity is essential to human experience.

Husserl, too, recognized that the constitution of phenomena within consciousness is both concretely historical and concretely multiple. In theory, he recognized that consciousness is not confined to some process within the individual but can be considered transindividual. The process of gaining clarity can therefore be the work of a group of researchers over time, for the particular essence being examined becomes clearer through subsequent work.

Max Weber (1864–1920)

Max Weber was a German sociologist who was influenced by neo-Kantianism and especially by the Southwest German branch led by Wilhelm Windelband and Heinrich Rickert. Weber, however, attempted to draw this tradition into a closer relationship with the positivistic emphasis on causes, empirical verification, and the search for laws.

Weber considered the social and cultural sciences to be the sciences of "human action." "In 'action,'" he said, "is included all human behavior when and in so far as the acting individual attaches a subjective meaning to it."[31] His distinction between "action" and "behavior" (the biological, instinctive level) holds that action is more than an event in nature; it is behavior guided by meaning, values, and other human attributes. His general notion is of a human subject making decisions, interpreting situations, and acting in terms of meanings and intentions and in relation to other actors. The purpose of social science is to inquire about this dimension that makes human action more than a behavioral response. At times, however, the line between action and behavior is difficult to determine.

Weber organized actions into four basic types: (1) a purposeful action (*Zweckrational*)—one that is oriented toward achieving a discrete end and has been rationally selected to achieve that end; (2) a value (*Wertrational*)—an action undertaken because it is believed to be valuable in and of itself and not because it leads to any other end; (3) a traditional action—one undertaken because of tradition, which is thus closer to undirected behavior than either of the two kinds of reasoned action; and (4) an affectual action—one that is an expression of emotion and is thus undeliberated, close to a pure event of nature—that is, behavior. These four types of action inform his understanding of development. According to Weber:

> [Biological analogies] may throw light on the question of the relative role in the early stages of human social differentiation of mechanical and instinctive factors, as compared with that of the factors which are accessible to subjective interpretation generally, and more particularly to the role of consciously rational action. It is necessary for the sociologist to be thoroughly aware of the fact that in the early stages even of human development, the first set of factors is completely predominant. Even in the later states he must take account of their continual interaction with the others in a role which is often of decisive importance.[32]

Weber understood that there are two strata in human beings: the animal level, which is mechanical and biological, and the rational level of subjective meanings. In the investigation of human action, it is the second level that is the object of inquiry. It is in this stratum that choices based on achieving purposes and ends are made. The first stratum, however, is mixed in with the second, and actions are not purely determined by reason. As a consequence, irrational behavioral elements lead to deviations from the pure type of rational action. For the purpose of attempting to understand the operation of these irrational factors, Weber constructed an "ideal type" which represents what action would be like if no irrational elements were present. By comparing the actual action with the ideal action, one can observe the effect of irrational elements:

> It is possible to understand the ways in which actual action is influenced by irrational factors of all sorts . . . in that they account for the deviations from the line of conduct which would be expected on the hypothesis that actions were purely rational.[33]

In Weber's view, people choose to act in certain ways to achieve goals they have chosen; their actions are the means for attaining what they set out to bring about. At the same time, these goals are bound to overall life goals or values. Human actions therefore take place in the context of ultimate goals—which is to say, in terms of the meaning of life. Values intervene in the natural world through the medium of action directed toward achieving them. These values, however, are not part of the natural world and are not derived from it, and consequently empirical investigation cannot demonstrate which values are correct but can merely demonstrate the effect a commitment to a value position has on human action. As the science of human action, sociology studies the expressions of value commitments as they relate to the choices people make in attempting to attain them.

The object of inquiry for social science, according to Weber, is the meaning (*Sinn*) an action has for the actor—that is, the purpose an actor has for carrying out the action. "Meaning" is not a phenomenon that can be subjected to empirical observation. The behavioral aspect of an action appears—and thus can be viewed—in the realm of empirical phenomena, but the "meaning" of the action does not. Access to this nonobservable realm of meaning is attained by interpretive understanding (*verstehen*). Weber distinguishes two kinds: "direct observational understanding," where the purpose or the meaning of the action is immediately apparent to the observer, and "explanatory understanding," which seeks to grasp the motivation or final cause toward which the action is a means "by placing the act in an intelligible and more inclusive context of meaning."

In direct observational understanding, we know immediately why or to what purpose an act is performed. We understand "the meaning of the proposition $2 \times 2 = 4$ when we hear or read it"; we understand "an outbreak of anger as manifested by facial expression, exclamation, or irrational movements"; and we understand "the action of a woodcutter or of somebody who [has] reached for the knob to shut a door." In explanatory understanding, we comprehend why a person has done something because we know his or her motive and why he or she attaches importance to the action. We can explain what impels a person to write down the equation $2 \times 2 = 4$, why she balances a ledger, what moves him to give vent to his anger. In explanatory understanding, the action is placed in a broader context.

With these two types of interpretive understanding, Weber transformed the division between understanding (*verstehen*) and explanation (*erklären*) into two sequential parts within the method of social science. Understanding becomes the premise of explanation. As Weber saw it, researchers must understand the meaning of an action before they can explain why it occurs. In addition, the process of interpreting the meaning of social action should be undertaken by social science researchers with the aim of meeting the same standards of precision and verifiability as are met by researchers in the natural sciences.

Weber spoke of the "causal adequacy" of an interpretive explanation: "According to established generalizations from experience, there is a probability that [the action] will always actually occur in the same way."[34] A correct causal explanation of why someone did something is both causally adequate and adequate at the level of meaning. By developing a structure of instrumental action as the framework for causal explanation, Weber was able to subsume individual actions under lawlike statements that concerned what the action taken by someone would be if he or she were freed from irrational elements in order to attain this goal. The person's action is not dependent on subjective choice; the rationally adequate decision has an objective standing. An explanation is adequate at the level of meaning "according to our habitual modes of thought and feeling," and the component parts of the activity, taken "in their mutual relations," are "recognized to constitute a 'typical' complex of meaning."[35]

Weber recognized that the study of human action means sacrificing other values—such as precision and conclusiveness of findings—that are possible to attain in the study of purely natural phenomena. He struggled with the problem of objectivity in interpretation and realized that knowledge gained through *verstehen* is particularly susceptible to an investigator's subjective bias. He admitted that "this additional achievement of explanation by interpretive understanding, as distinguished from external observation, is of course attained only at a price—the more hypothetical and fragmentary character of its results."[36] Still, Weber was pleased that the human sciences could venture into the realm of human phenomena. "We can accomplish something which is never attainable in natural science," he said.[37]

William James (1842–1910)

Mach had presented his idea of sensationalism in *The Science of Mechanics* in 1883. In 1912, William James, the American philosopher and psychologist, published his *Essays in Radical Empiricism*. Along with Mach, James held that science should admit nothing unless it is given in direct experience. Mach, however, admitted only isolated sensa from experience—that is, the elements of sense data (sounds, colors, thermal data, extension, durations, feelings of pain or pleasure, volitions, images, or memory). It was the goal of science, he believed, to describe these elements.

James called for a radical empiricism that would extend what is to be admitted from direct experience by declaring that nothing should be excluded which is directly experienced. He held that there are connections and conjunctions in direct experience which are as real as the elements of sense data. Both these elements and their relationships, he said, are "integral members of the sensational flux."[38] Whenever an element of sensation appears, it is always related to, grouped with, and joined to other elements. What is given in direct experience is not isolated bits of sensation which are then coordinated by some agency into an appearance of a physical object; what appears in experience is already ordered. Moreover, consciousness appears as a continuity or flow, not as a single cross-section in time. And experience does not appear as a mass of heterogeneous data; one of its components is at the center of focus, and the rest of the components lie in the margin.

Such organizational patterns, he maintained, are given in direct experience, and thus they qualify for inclusion in science. James took Mach's dictum that only what appears directly in experience should be admitted for scientific study and used it to support an investigation into the structural patterns that form part of the organized nature of experience.

The Recurring Debate

In spite of the ferment stirred by the anti-positivist response during the formative stage of the sciences of the human realm, the positivist position clearly won the debate. The study of human phenomena has come to be conducted under standards and procedures adopted from the physical sciences. Experimental procedures with operationally defined variables are used to determine correlations and lawlike relationships among various aspects of the human realm. The triumph of the positivist position occurred when the center of work in the behavioral and social sciences shifted to the United States in the early decades of this century. Kurt Danziger proposes that social forces in the United States during the period in which these sciences developed supported a positivism-grounded psychology and sociology:

In the United States . . . psychologists had to justify themselves before a very different tribunal [than psychologists in Europe]. Control of university appointments, research funds, and professional opportunities was vested in the hands of either businessmen or their appointees, or politicians who represented their interests. If psychology was to emerge as a viable independent discipline, it would have to be in a form acceptable to these social forces.[39]

What the sponsors of a research program wanted was the kind of information that might be useful in situations "where a group of people had the power to control the conditions under which others would have to act." The social environment in the United States was conducive to the development of research programs based on a methodology on which a promise could be given to answer the questions of the educational, industrial, marketing, and political enterprises.

Seymour Sarason, in his recent *Psychology Misdirected*, says that psychology optimistically promised to provide these answers. "Social science believed that scientifically attained, so-called hard knowledge had an inexorable quality that society could neither resist nor avoid. The assumption was that society needed *and* wanted that knowledge, which, when forthcoming, would help transform the social order."[40] Sarason holds that psychology has failed to deliver on this promise, and as a discipline does not have enough assets to meet the obligations it took on. Thus he calls for a new birth in psychology which will "come to value understanding and deemphasize the role of measurement."

While the social sciences in the United States almost completely adopted a positivist stance, the victory was not as thorough on the Continent. The anti-positivist response which had been formulated there retained its influence. Since the initial triumph of positivism in the early decades of the century, and before the reforms in science begun in the 1960s, several challenges to positivism have had an impact in the United States. Two of these, Gestalt psychology and humanistic psychology, had their roots in Europe; the other, symbolic interaction, seems indigenous to the United States and grounded in American pragmaticism. Thus even during the period of positivist dominance, the anti-positivist opposition continued to have advocates.

Gestalt Theory

In the closing paragraphs of *Principles of Gestalt Psychology* (1935), Kurt Koffka wrote that "if there is any polemical spirit in this book, it is directed not against persons but against a strong cultural force in our present civilization for which I have chosen the name positivism."[41] For the Gestaltists, positivism represented an approach to science that was distinguished by an overriding concern with the accumulation of facts.

Max Wertheimer, a leader of the Gestalt movement, held that "traditional" science is characterized not only by certain methods, but also by an approach to explanation that is oriented about an assumption deriving from the Newtonian and empirical world views—namely, that phenomena consist of discrete elements and that these elements are bound together by some extrinsic, linear force. For the phenomena that appear in consciousness, Wertheimer said, this extrinsic force can only be association. In opposition to this traditional understanding, Wertheimer wrote in 1924 that Gestalt theory is "neither more nor less" than the belief that "there are wholes, the behavior of which is not determined by their individual elements, but where the part processes are themselves determined by the intrinsic nature of the whole. It is the hope of Gestalt theory to determine the nature of such wholes."[42]

To illustrate: A tune (the whole) is made up of sensory elements (the various sounds). The sensory elements can be changed—for instance, the tune can be transposed into another key or played on a different instrument—and yet the tune is recognized as the same tune. That is because a tune is not merely a collection of elements (individual sounds), but a form (gestalt); the tune is an organizing pattern that gives meaning to the elements. An individual note from the tune is not experienced as the same element when it is heard in isolation and is not part of the organized pattern of sounds which make up the tune. Another example: A triangle (the whole) is made up of three elements (the three sides). But a triangle is not experienced as three lines; it is experienced as a form that possesses a quality that might be called "triangleness."

The Gestalt theorists rejected the notion of atomistic elementalism. Both Brentano, with his act psychology, and Christian Ehrenfels, who discussed "gestalt qualities" as early as 1890, held that the source of form—the organizational quality—is the mind. Sensory elements, they said, are derived from the interactions with "the world," but it is the mind, in a mental act, which adds the structuring form-quality. However, the Gestalt psychologists rejected the idea that form-qualities are produced by mental acts that organize intrinsically atomistic sensa. In 1912, they carried out their famous phi phenomenon research. In this experiment, two spots of light were flashed on and off alternately. When the flashing interval was less than 0.2 seconds, the observer no longer saw two lights flashing—he saw one light in continuous motion. The experiment showed that sensational "atoms" do not "hit" the retina and are then experienced.

Perception is a qualitatively different kind of experience. What appears in consciousness as perception may emerge as the result of simple sensations, but perception is of a different order and cannot be reduced to sensations.

For the Gestaltists, experience is produced by the dynamic interaction of various parts of the field of sensation. In the phi phenomenon, the "parts" of the field—the two flashing lights—interact to give the perception of motion. The form produced by the interaction, however, is not understood as the addition of an active mind, as claimed by the act psychologists. The Gestaltists explained these perceptions in physical-field terms. It is, they said, a dynamic field-process in the brain that produces the perceptual effects of organization.

George Herbert Mead (1880–1949)

In 1934, George Herbert Mead published his *Mind, Self, and Society*, which, along with his other publications, described the symbolic interaction approach to understanding human beings. Symbolic interactionism was a call for a methodology for human science that would recognize the special importance of symbols and the meaning they carry in understanding human behavior.

In Mead's view, human beings do not typically respond directly to stimuli; instead, they assign meanings to the stimuli and then proceed to act on the basis of these meanings. Moreover, the meanings are not individually determined but are derived through social interaction. There are shared group meanings that make up the world of individual actors, and these shared meanings provide the framework in which action is carried out, although they do not cause or fully determine behavior.

According to Mead, human action is the result of some degree of choice within the context of the social network. People can modify the social influences, and they can create and change their behavior. Action is the result of an internal dialogue between the "I," which is a spontaneous and impulsive aspect, and the "Me," which is a set of internalized social definitions. Out of the interplay between these two components of the self, action is generated.[43] The study of human behavior, Mead said, must include the actor's own view of his social world and the meaning his behavior has for him.

Humanistic Psychology

Another call for a human science whose methodology would be more than the application of physical science principles to the human realm came from the humanistic psychology movement, which began in the United States around 1958. Like the other anti-positivist movements, humanistic psychology was unified more by its opposition to what the behavioral and social sciences had become than by an organized alternative methodology grounded in a human science approach. The lines of the old debate were redrawn at a 1963 symposium held at Rice University which was titled "Behaviorism and Phenomenology: Contrasting Bases for Modern Psychology."[44] Under the influence of John Watson, the father of behaviorism, American psychology had defined its object of inquiry rather narrowly in the years following 1927. Consciousness and direct human experience were dropped as psychology's subject matter, and only behavior was studied, in order to ensure that data could be made observable to the researcher and intersubjectively verified. Several books—particularly *Existence* (a book edited by Rollo May, which contained several chapters by him along with translations of essays by European writers on phenomenological psychology) and books by Carl Rogers on "person-centered" psychotherapy—reemphasized the importance of people in creating their actions and self-understanding. Humanistic psychology was concerned with the individual, the exceptional, and the unpredicted rather than with general laws that describe only what is regular and repeatable. To borrow Windelband's terms, it might best be called idiographic rather than nomothetic; thus it is understandable that its greatest successes seem to have been in psychotherapies oriented toward the unique human being, rather than in human science research *per se*.

In *Humanistic Psychology* (1978), John Shaffer stated the five central emphases in humanistic psychology: (1) While humanistic psychology recognizes that the primary data for the human sciences come from conscious experience, it places a greater emphasis on the differences to be found in experience than did Brentano and Weber, and it enthusiastically accepts the variety of perspectives that makes up the lived world of different individuals. (2) Humanistic psychology emphasizes the wholeness and integrative aspects of experience and rejects the atomistic elements of Machian postivism. (3) While humanistic psychology recognizes the constraining biological and social structures inherent in human existence, it insists upon the essential autonomy and freedom of choice in human action. (4) Humanistic psychology maintains that human existence is an emergent quality and cannot be understood by examining aspects of lower strata— for example, animal behavior, libido energies, and basic physiological drives. (5) Humanistic psychology maintains that humanness is not defined by biological givens but is refined by its historical developments of conceptual and meaning processes and by the effects of human actions on each other and on future generations; the property of humanness is thus always undergoing historical change and development and can never be finally defined.[45]

Summary

The debate was framed at a time when the physical sciences were committed to a theory of explanation in which events were understood as instances of universal laws and when the entire universe was thought to be made up of a small number of entities arranged in various patterns. The metaphor commonly in use was based on the system of chemical elements. Only three entities—protons, neutrons, and electrons—in ninety-two different arrangements in space produced the diversity of the elements. Differences in the powers and qualities of materials were attributed to differences in the structure of their arrangements—that is, qualitative differences were reduced to, and explained by, differences in the quantitative relationships among the parts. When one came to apply this metaphor to human behavior, one attempted to relate the behavior of a crowd of people to the behavior of its individual members. The characteristics of a crowd were said to be merely the sum of individual actions. Similarly, the behavior of an individual could be explained in terms of less complex elements.

Since the time the debate began, a greater understanding of emergent qualities has developed in science. It is now understood that many groups of elements form more complex structures or conditions and have properties that are not the same as those of the individuals that make them up. Individual molecules, for example, do not have pressure or temperature; only groups of molecules do. Individual cells cannot think or talk; the structural integrity that is a human being can. This conception provides an explanation of the parts in terms of the characteristics of the whole. The process is called *emergence*.

The explanation of emergence is that the holistic properties derive from the structure, not from the entities that are structured. The explanation has to do with the unique ensemble of simple properties. A living thing contains nothing but chemical reactions, but its aliveness derives from its particular, mutually supporting ensemble of interactions—and the explanation for this unique interaction cannot be reduced to laws of chemistry.

During the hundred years since Dilthey engaged Mill in dialogue, the physical science approach that Mill proposed for the human (moral) sciences has itself undergone considerable change. The debate no longer centers around whether or not human science should adopt Mill's science. The first transformation in Mill's science was brought about by a combination of Mach's empiricism of sensa and a new logic of relations described by Bertrand Russell. This revision held sway for thirty years, and its influence has not yet completely disappeared. During the next thirty years, Mill's science underwent even more changes. It became a science of structure; a science of living organisms and human actions; and a science that undertook the understanding of human communication. The debate over methodology for human science now needs to address itself, not to Mill's science, but to the new science.

2

The Received View of Science

The original question concerning the nature of a methodology for the human sciences was put forth in clear form by Mill: Should human science adopt the methodology of the physical sciences? Mill took the affirmative side of the question, while Dilthey took the negative side. Those who have stood with Mill have won the debate, and their position has been adopted as the standard methodology for the human sciences by university departments, textbooks, and journals. There are still a few supporters for Dilthey's side of the debate, but they argue from a minority position and can hope only that the victorious side will pay them some attention and respond to their critiques.

Those who have triumphed, however, have paid less attention to the supporters of the alternative view than to the efforts within their own camp to develop and refine their position. The most significant refinement within this camp emerged during the 1920s when Russell's new logic was added to the empirical tradition. This refinement has come to be called "the received view," and it is the subject of this chapter. The received view supplies the methodological underpinnings for most of the contemporary behavioral and social sciences committed to Mill's thesis.

The discussion of the development in the philosophy of science may be organized into the five phases proposed by Frederick Suppe.[1] The first phase includes the integration of Russell's logic and Mach's positivism by the Vienna circle in the 1920s. During this phase it was proposed that science should limit its statements to descriptions of the regularities that held in observations. In the second phase, which began in the 1940s, philosophy of science expanded to include theoretical statements that referred to nonobservable entities and the construction of an axiom-based network of universal statements. The third phase, in the 1960s, consisted of the critique of the assumptions of logical positivism and was paralleled by the fourth phase, which proposed alternative systems for science based on an analysis of the history of science. The contemporary or fifth phase is a reconstruction of science based on pragmatic reason and an acceptance of the influence of historical conditions on scientific inquiry. This chapter is concerned with the first two phases of this development; the next chapter with the last three.

The First Phase: The Vienna Circle

Positivism, as developed by Mill and Comte, had its heyday in the middle of the nineteenth century. This period was followed by the anti-positivist reaction during the late nineteenth and early twentieth centuries. But in the period between the two world wars—that is, the 1920s and 1930s—a renewal of positivist thought occurred. This renewal movement was called neo-positivism or logical positivism, or, later, logical empiricism. Although the philosophy of science developed during this renewal period has come under increasing criticism since the 1960s, it continues to inform the contemporary approach to research in both the physical and the social sciences. Because of its pervasive influence, it is recognized as the dominant approach in contemporary science.

This dominant system provides the epistemological support for experimental designs based on empirical data. It constitutes the approved approach to science, and it is communicated within the social and behavioral sciences through the primary agencies of disciplinary orthodoxy. The standard textbooks on research, the editorial policies of disciplinary journals, and the guidelines for acceptable doctoral dissertations call for the use of a methodology based on this approach.[2]

What is variously called the dominant, standard, or mainstream approach for contemporary science was first articulated by members of the Vienna circle during the 1920s. Although it has undergone continuous revision since the first formulations were made, the basic epistemological commitments have remained. Moritz Schlick, a professor of philosophy at the University of Vienna, was the leader of the Vienna circle, and its members included Rudolf Carnap, Otto Neurath, Herbert Feigl, and Kurt Gödel. The group met on a regular basis to discuss, among other issues, how knowledge could be placed on a firm foundation that would assure the elimination of all metaphysical and speculative errors. The foundation they adopted was an empiricism that was based on Mach's sensationism. Mach had been a professor at the University of Vienna from 1895 onward, and his influence was felt strongly in the group—in fact, the group's original name was the Ernst Mach Society.

The group was also heavily influenced by another former Viennese professor, Ludwig Wittgenstein. Wittgenstein's *Tractatus Logico-Philosophicus*, written in England in 1921, reflected the new approach to language that he had helped develop, which was contained, as well, in Bertrand Russell and Alfred North Whitehead's *Principia Mathematica*. Wittgenstein's work was read aloud and discussed, sentence by sentence, at the group's regular meetings from 1924 to 1926.[3]

One of the first publications by members of the group was Carnap's *Logical Structure of the World*. Also allied to the group were the Berliners Carl Hempel and Hans Reichenbach and the Englishman Sir Alfred Ayer. Ayer's book *Language, Truth and Logic* (1936) was written after he had attended the group's meetings in Vienna; it made the group's approach available to the English-speaking world, and it remains the classic introduction to the group's thought.

The viewpoint developed by the Vienna circle was adopted by the general community of scientific philosophers as the appropriate viewpoint for use by researchers who were attempting to describe scientific knowledge. Various problems in the position were clarified and refined, and it continued to expand its influence.[4] Over time, certain basic commitments were changed—for instance, there was a move from phenomenalism to physicalism (see the next section). In the late 1950s and the early 1960s, self-scrutiny began to uncover some basic difficulties in one of the position's fundamental claims, namely, its claim to have described a method which gives "certainty" to scientific statements. Contemporary critics—for example, Polanyi, Hanson, Toulmin, Kuhn, Feyerabend, Scriven, and Hesse—refer to the position as it stood before these more recent emendations were made as "the received view."[5]

The Vienna circle focused its attention on the products of science that are statements about the world. Members of the group believed that by prescribing what kind of statements would work for describing the world, they could assist scientific work. Statements in forms that were ambiguous or nonreferential could not provide real descriptions, they said, and so such statements should be identified and removed from scientific work. The Vienna circle, it should be noted, concerned itself with the form of statements, not with actual research procedures or the practice of developing evidence. The Vienna circle's members were concerned with the finished products of science—that is, with completed articles and the way those articles presented their theses and justified and defended them to the scientific community. The distinction to be made here is this: the body of science is made up of the statements about the world that have been produced by the scientific community; the received view initiated by the Vienna circle is concerned about the form of these statements.

The philosophers of the Vienna circle brought together two perspectives for their analysis of scientific statements. The first was the positivism described by Mach, which was closer to the skeptical position of Hume than to the positivist position taken by Mill and Comte, and the second was the "new logic" developed by Russell and Whitehead. These two perspectives provided the base for an analysis of statements to determine whether the statements were tied to sensations and connected through necessary logical relationships. The process was defined in a somewhat simplified manner by Carnap: "The senses provide the material of cognition, reason synthesizes the material so as to produce an organized system of knowledge."[6] For the logical positivist, knowledge (*epistēmē*), i.e., what is known with certainty and not just a matter of belief or opinion, is limited to what can be stated in forms that pass the tests of sensationism and relational logic.

The next two sections will examine in more detail logical positivism's two forms of "certainty," positivism and logic.

Positivism: Phenomenalism and Physicalism

Since for the Vienna circle knowledge is in the form of words and statements, the problem to be addressed has to do with the relationship of words to the world. How is it possible for language to express what is not language—that is, the extralinguistic world? Logical positivism identifies some words as being linked to the world through their function; these words refer to specific sensations or to worldly objects. They are words that "stand for" or "mean" particular objects. For instance, in the behavioral interpretation of language acquisition, one simply points to a table and utters the word *table*, and in this way the word comes to refer to the object. This theory of meaning is called the referential theory, and it is basic to the link between sense data and statements in logical positivism. If a word does not refer to a sense datum, then it has no reference, and there is no way to know what it is referring to. In short, it has no meaning in this sense. The word *electron*, for example, does not have a referent that can be pointed to. Neither does the word *good*. In the original attempt at purifying scientific language, such terms were to be excluded because they are not referential.[7]

The move to exclude from scientific discourse words that did not have direct referents in the sensa was more stringent than anything required by the earlier positivism of Mill and Comte. Mill and Comte allowed the use of words that referred to generalizations or described concepts; for instance, they would allow the word *tables* to describe the general category of "table." During the development of logical positivism, the phenomenalists[8] preferred only words and statements that described immediate sense experience or could be verified by direct sense experience. A table would thus need to be described in a specific way—for example, as a white rectangular plane with four extensions downward to another plane which, in turn, extends to walls. The positivists wanted to limit inquiry and belief to what can be firmly established.

Since the connecting link between language and the world was said to be words that refer directly to sense data, certain theories had to be questioned. Newton's theories, for instance, contain the word *force*, which was considered suspect because it does not point to a direct sensation. But the phenomenalists believed that limiting scientific discourse to accurate and economical descriptions and predictions of sensory experience would assure it of a base of certainty free from error and dubious interpretation. Only words connected to direct and immediate awareness of sense impressions, they said, could provide an infallible source of knowledge.

Descriptions of sense data were to be the focus of scientific work. The term *data* is the Latin word for "given." "Sense data" are what are directly given in sensation, and it is this special, direct "givenness" which makes data the ground for certainty. Any words that attempt to describe realities beyond those things that are directly given can only be speculative and should thus be eliminated from scientific statements. Science should concern itself only with certain knowledge (*epistēmē*). Any statement that can be doubted should not be included in scientific discourse, and only statements of direct sensation cannot be doubted. References to ultimate designs or "organizing principles" do not stand up to this test of verifiability. Statements made up of words that refer directly to sense data are called "basic statements" or "protocol statements." Protocol statements provide the foundation upon which all statements of knowledge stand.[9]

The early version of logical positivism emphasized this kind of phenomenalism—that is, it was a claim that what can be known is limited to what appears in consciousness by way of sense data. Kant had earlier distinguished between phenomena, which appear in consciousness ("a chair appears"), and noumena, which are the entities of the world. According to logical positivism, we have access only to what appears in consciousness, the phenomena; we cannot know how things are but only how they appear. In the early version of logical positivism, what appears are patches of color, outlines and shadings, sounds, and the like. There was, furthermore, no need to postulate unknowable objects in the world that cause these sense data to appear.

By the mid-1930s, the logical positivists had abandoned their effort to establish a thoroughly phenomenalistic language and had developed an alternative doctrine called physicalism. They no longer insisted that only words referring to classes of sense data were acceptable; they now proposed admitting words referring to recognizable physical objects and qualities within our ordinary environment. Limiting description to words referring to sense data was not necessary, they believed. Phenomenalism was too stringent, too restrictive to be imposed on scientific statements. Phenomenalism had also opened itself to the criticism of solipsism, since the protocol statements referred only to the private experience of individuals.

The move to physicialism was a recognition that scientific statements were supposed to refer to objects and relationships in the world, not merely to private experience. If two people make statements about their private sense experiences and the two statements are different, then there is no way to know which statement should be accepted, for there are no standards of preference. By moving to a language that accepted simply physical terms referring to objects in the world, the logical positivists opened up the possibility of intersubjective verification. Physicalism was closer to the actual language used in the descriptions of working scientists, and it allowed for the basic mode of scientific verification, the intersubjective agreement that such objects were "there in the room."

With the move to physicalism, logical positivism gave up the classical empiricist insistence that knowledge must be *epistēmē*, that is to say that it must be justified or proved with certainty. The move was from a position that based knowledge on a thing-language where one speaks of material things and ascribes observable properties to them. Such a move marked a significant change in empiricism. From the seventeenth century until well into the twentieth century, the base of knowledge had to be shown to be apodictic in the most stringent sense, i.e., beyond correction and amendment. If something like "sense data" was the only unimpeachable source of base knowledge, the problem was how to move to other levels of knowledge— for instance, to generalizations or statements about physical objects.

In early empiricism of the 17th and 18th centuries, the movement from base knowledge to derived knowledge had to be adequately justified if the derived statements were to be admitted as truly standing for things or *epistēmē*. The justification for the movement from the base knowledge of sensation to the derived knowledge about physical objects was attempted by causal and phenomenalistic theories holding that the sense data were caused by the transmission of information about physical objects through light and sound, and so on, impacting on the senses and producing the indubitable sense data. The attempt to justify generalizations presented a different kind of problem because they dealt with scientific laws and theories. Theories of induction were developed that tried to demonstrate how general statements could be derived from base knowledge in an indubitable and unimpeachable way. Writing in the latter half of the 18th century, Hume made a number of skeptical attacks on such attempts to justify derivable knowledge. He demonstrated that if base knowledge was limited to sensation and a priori knowledge, then neither knowledge of physical objects nor inductively obtained general knowledge was possible. Although there were various attempts to answer Hume's attacks and save derived knowledge,[10] none of them could defeat his arguments, and it was his skepticism that prevailed in empiricism until logical positivism made the move to physicalism.

After giving up sense data and a priori knowledge as base knowledge, the logical positivists moved to a position in which potential intersubjective agreement provided sufficient justification for knowledge. They took this position, we should notice, in spite of the possibilities for collective delusion. In this new position, observational evidence that conferred a high probability on generalizations was accepted as sufficient for obtaining general knowledge. Thus the physicalist move weakened the "adequate evidence" requirement of indubitable connection to sense data. By the mid-1930s logical positivists like Carnap came to hold that evidence making the derived statement highly probable or likely was acceptable.[11]

The move from phenomenalism to physicalism was accompanied by a change in the name of the school of thought from *logical positivism* to *logical empiricism*. (The two terms, however, continue to be used interchangeably.) Scientific statements were those that referred to physical objects or space–time points—that is, objects that appear through the senses—and such statements needed to be verifiable publicly, not just by one person. For instance, the statement, "I see a person in this room but you cannot see him because he lets only me see him," was not verifiable, since it did not allow others to recognize the object, and was therefore not allowable in science. After the move to physicalism, the verifiability criteria allowed any statement into science that could, in principle, be observed publicly, even though such a thing might be difficult to do. A favorite pre-1960s example was, "The far side of the moon has mountains." Although no one had or could at that time test the statement, it was still allowable because it was testable in principle.[12]

The verifiability criteria were further complicated by the development of sense-aiding instrumentation. Previously, such a statement as "There is a germ in the blood" was not acceptable because the germ did not appear to sense experience. The development of more powerful microscopes, however, made such a statement acceptable. And with the arrival of the electron microscope, matters became even more complex. Did the observer actually see something through the microscope, or was what appeared an artifact of the instrument itself?

The positivist or empirical root of the logical positivist synthesis proposed that discourse purporting to be scientific—therefore constituting statements of knowledge—needed to be grounded in terms that referred to observable objects and events in space and time. Statements that consisted of such observational terms were called "synthetic" statements, and they were the only acceptable descriptions of the world of facts. All other statements in science were pronounced tautological, and they were said to be logically derived from synthetic statements. These statements were called "analytic," a term taken from the second root of logical positivism, Russell's relational logic.

The New Logic

The second part of logical positivism, the part added to positivism, was the new logic of Russell. The central topic of logic is valid reasoning. It is concerned with determining the conditions under which propositions are valid in relationship to other propositions and the conditions under which one proposition may be inferred or deduced from other propositions. Logic does not establish the verifiability of a statement. Whether or not a statement accurately describes the world is determined by the criteria of experienced sensation or intersubjective observations. But if a statement is true, then the other statements that can be validly deduced from it are also true. For example, if it can be established by observation that a plastic ball is lighter than water and that all things lighter than water will float in water, then it can be established by logic that a plastic ball will float in water. One need not establish this conclusion by observation because it follows from the nature of the words used in the first two observation sentences.

Until the nineteenth century, it had been assumed that logic was a finished and completed subject. Kant had proclaimed that Aristotle's logic left no room for any further advances. Just as it had been thought that Euclid had completed the necessary work in geometry and that it was the scholar's task to learn and use this completed tool, so it was thought that no further development was possible in logic. Beginning with Gottlob Frege's work at the end of the nineteenth century, however, and culminating with Russell and Whitehead's *Principia Mathematica*, which was published in three volumes in 1910 and 1913, a new and much more inclusive system of logic was developed.

Aristotle and other logicians had distinguished between the "truth" of component statements and the "validity" of an argument. But until the development of mathematical logic, the full significance of this distinction had not been grasped. This is a technical use of the term *valid*. In common speech, a valid argument is often simply a persuasive argument. Validity in logic, however, has to do with deductive consequences—that is, the form of one proposition implies or is implied by the form of another proposition. According to Russell, logic is concerned exclusively with validity, and what determines validity is not the truth of the content of propositions (i.e., not what is judged about) but their *form*.[13] In 1929, Russell had this to say about the new logic:

> In every proposition and in every inference there is, besides the particular subject matter concerned, a certain "form," a new way in which the constituents of the proposition or inference are put together. . . . Take the series of propositions, "Socrates drank the hemlock," "Coleridge drank opium," "Coleridge ate opium." The form remains unchanged throughout this series, but all the constituents are altered. Thus form is not another constituent, but is the way the constituents are put together. It is the forms, in this sense, that are the proper object of philosophical logic.[14]

It is possible for the statements to be false while the argument is valid. For example, the statement "John left the house" may, in fact, be false. Nevertheless, the statement itself implies a second statement, "John was in the house." When the statements in the premises imply the conclusion, the argument is valid. If, in addition, the premises are true, the argument is said to be sound.

Validity and Form

An argument is contained in the conjunction among its statements, and what determines its validity is the relationship that holds between its parts. If the relationship is one of *implication*, the argument is valid; if not, the argument is invalid. In order to tell if the relationship among the parts of a deductive argument is one of implication, one might simply try to imagine a counterexample to the conclusion which could be implied by the premises. For example, take the statement, "If the ability to learn a language is largely innate, then children will all learn to speak at about the same age; but the ability to learn a language is not largely innate, and therefore children will not all learn to speak at about the same age." In this statement, the conclusion is not implied by the premises, for all children might learn to speak at the same age because of cultural training. The argument is not valid and contains the fallacy of denying the antecedent. The use of imagination to supply counterexamples, of course, is very limited as the means for validating deductive arguments, because even though one might not think of a counterexample there might still be some counterexamples that are conceivable.

There is a link between relationships among statements that are implicative and specific patterns or forms of langauge usage. For example, if we let the letters P, Q, and R stand for statements, any network of statements that conform to the pattern "All P's are Q's and all Q's are R's" will imply that all P's are R's. By identifying the linguistic pattern underlying a network of statements, it is possible to identify the network as one that contains an implication and is thus a valid argument. These patterns of inference make up the subject of formal logic. Most of the patterns studied in logic are those of artificial languages, but there are several elementary patterns that are applicable to networks of statements in ordinary language. Russell's logic resulted in a great expansion of the kind of patterns of relationship studied in logic. The syllogistic pattern was now no longer regarded as the whole of logic, but as only one relatively minor subdivision of logic.

Aristotle's logic could establish valid relationships only between statements that described inclusion in or exclusion from a class. It dealt with attributive predicates—that is, statements in which a quality is attributed to a subject. The classic example is: "The entity Socrates has the quality of humanness. All things with the quality of humanness have the attribute of mortality. Therefore, Socrates is mortal."

The new logic expanded the kinds of statements that could be connected by implication, and it could work with relational predicates. The statement "This thing is bigger than that thing" does not merely assign a quality to "this thing"; it relates "this thing" to another thing. Said Russell:

> But the forms of propositions giving rise to inferences are not the simplest forms: they are always hypothetical, stating that if one proposition is true, then so is another. Before considering inference, therefore, logic must consider those simpler forms which inference presupposes. Here the traditional logic failed completely: it believed that there was only one form of simple proposition [i.e., a proposition not stating a relation between two or more propositions], namely the form which ascribes a predicate to a subject. . . . If we say "This thing is bigger than that," we are not assigning a mere quality of "this," but a relation of "this" and "that." Thus propositions stating that two things have a certain relation have a different form from subject-predicate propositions.[15]

The new logic uncovered implications between statements whose forms were relational. Terms and constructions like "and," "or," and "if . . . then" form relationships. For example, if statement A, "John is wearing a brown coat," and statement B, "Mary is wearing a red coat," are related by the use of "and," and if they are individually true, then the compound statement "John is wearing a brown coat and Mary is wearing a red coat" is true. If either statement A or statement B is false, then the compound statement will be false. The rules for determining the validity of the deductions from relational statements are called rules of inference, and all the consequences of relating statements can be set out in a table of truth conditions.

Of special significance for relating statements in scientific discourse is the form of hypothetical relationships "if . . . then." Two types of inference that can be drawn from a hypothetical proposition are important for the discourse used in systems of explanation that subsume events and laws under more general laws: The "modus ponens" (method of affirming) and the "modus tollens" (method of denying). The modus ponens is the simplest form of conditional argument. Its pattern is: "If P, then Q. P is. Therefore Q." If a conditional statement and its antecedent are true, so is its consequent. The modus tollens form is an argument that goes: if a conditional statement is true but its consequent is false, then its antecedent is false. Its pattern is: "If and only if this, then that. But not that. Therefore not this." Examples of these arguments are given by Bell and Stains:

Modus Ponens:

> If P ("The ability to learn a language is largely innate"), then Q ("Children will all learn to speak at about the same age").
>
> P ("The ability to learn a language is largely innate").
>
> Therefore Q ("Children will all learn to speak at about the same age").

Modus Tollens:

> If P ("The ability to learn a language is largely innate"), then Q ("Children will all learn to speak at about the same age").
>
> Not Q ("It is not the case that children all learn to speak at about the same age").
>
> Therefore not P ("The ability to learn a language is not largely innate").[16]

The point of these examples is to demonstrate that it is the form of the argument to which one looks to determine its validity. If the argument passes the test of validity then it implies or guarantees the conclusion, and it is thus a valid explanation. A statement that is implied by the premises of an argument is said to be explained.

In addition to his contribution of relational logic, Russell helped the logical positivists solve the problem of mathematical entities. Russell's work in logic was, to begin with, driven by a desire to understand the foundations of mathematics. Drawing on the work of Gottlob Frege, Russell was able to show that mathematics is a branch of logic, and to uncover the nature of mathematical axioms. The first step toward the merging of mathematics and logic was taken as a result of the discovery of non-Euclidean geometry. This discovery made it clear that geometry was not a description of some eternal pattern in the universe; it was, instead, a particular logical system relating statements to each other irrespective of what the world was "really" like. Consequently, mathematics in general could be understood as a system of relationships between statements derived from postulated axioms.[17]

Russell was able to demonstrate that the entire theory of natural numbers could be derived from the three primitive ideas—class, belonging to a class, and similarity—all of which were purely logical notions. Thus mathematical statements did not refer to some mysterious realm in the world; they merely constituted a powerful logical system with only internal references, all held together by tautological deductions. The deomonstration that mathematics was reducible to logic—and therefore was made up of analytic statements that were not linked to the world as such—solved a problem for logical positivism by eliminating a "worldly" realm of numbers inaccessible to direct observation. As a result, the limitation of synthetic statements to references of sense data could be maintained. There was no other realm except the realm made up of sense data and logical relationships.

The Second Phase: Theoretical Networks

The early positivists, especially Mach, had argued against the introduction of hypothetical terms into science. The logical positivists were willing to admit only those terms that were ultimately linked to some observable manifestation. Mach held that the business of science was only the description of facts and of the observable relationships between them. However, in the second phase of its development the received view was expanded to include statements that included purely theoretical terms. The expansion allowed for a form of explanation which answers the question of why an event has happened by describing the law under which the event has occurred. These laws in turn were explained by being subsumed under more general laws, and finally all events were explained from a network of deductive relationships stemming from a few basic axioms. Thus the logical positivists came to accept the idea that the aim of scientific research was not only to describe events; more importantly, its aim was to explain and understand why events occur as they do. Scientific inquiry, they now said, seeks to render facts intelligible—that is, to rationalize reality. The world is more than a random appearance of disconnected events, and independent statements about specific observations fail to describe the ways in which events are related. Scientific discourse, then, needs to include a set of systematically related statements. As Richard Rudner said in *Philosophy of Social Science*:

> It is not the business of science merely to collect unrelated, haphazard, disconnected bits of information; it is an ideal of science to give an "organized" account of the universe—to connect, to fit together in relations of subsumption, the statements embodying the knowledge that has been acquired. Such organization is a necessary condition for the accomplishment of two of science's chief functions, explanation and prediction. But the sort of systematic relatedness exemplified among the statements of scientific theories is *deductive* relatedness. Accordingly, to the extent that a theory has been fully articulated in some formulation,

it will achieve an *explicit* deductive development and interrelationship of the statements it encompasses.[18]

The change from descriptive statements about observable events to general statements related to other general statements raised scientific discourse above the mundane realm of "hard" description to the realm of theory. The connection between the "hard or brute data" of observation statements and the general statements of law or theory continues to be problematic for a scientific discourse based on a clear distinction between synthetic statements of observation and analytic statements of logical relationships. The ideal model implied in this system is a model in which statements of greater and greater specificity are derived from a few axioms until a statement of "fact" is implied; one can then test to see whether the fact implied in the deductive system appears to observation. This scheme describes the ideal of a fully formalized system of scientific statements that are all linked deductively to one another. Such a completely unified system of scientific discourse has not been achieved, however. In fact, most of the discourse fails to relate one discipline to another, and even within a single discipline the discourse is not all deductively related. Among the scientific discipline, physics has come closest, within its own field, to attaining the model, but the social and behavioral sciences still fall far short of the ideal.[19]

The type of network of statements proposed in the second phase of the received view relied on the kind of relations Russell had discovered, especially relations between statements of the hypothetical "if . . . then" kind. The type of logical network in which these statements are linked is called "deductive." The other primary type of logic—the "inductive" type—is also important for scientific discourse directed at verifying the premises that make up the deductive network. The inductive inferences will be discussed in the next chapter; here the concern is with the more fundamental model of statement connections underlying the hypothetical-deductive model of research and experimental testing.

In deductive networks, the logical relationship between the premises and the conclusion is such that if the premises are true, then the conclusion *must* be true. The conclusion follows necessarily from the premises. This is so because the deductive system is based on tautological or purely logical reasoning. The conclusion merely makes explicit what is already implicit in the premises. No new factual or observational information is needed for one to know that the conclusion is true if the premises are true. Thus a deductive network produces statements that are certain and indubitable if the premises are true.

The models of deductive linkages in explanation are the modus ponens and the modus tollens. A statement of the sort "If it is raining, then the streets are wet" describes a type of relationship between the protasis "if it is raining" and the apodosis "then the streets are wet."[20] When "it is raining" is true, then necessarily "the streets are wet" is also true. Russell called this type of relationship "implication."

Given the basic network, it is possible to test a premise by seeing if the conclusion of the premise holds when the protasis is true. For example, the premise "If an object is heavier than water, then it will sink if placed in water" can be tested by placing an object that is heavier than water in water and observing the consequences. Such a test is a scientific experiment. If the object that is heavier than water does not sink when placed in what is undoubtedly water, then the premise cannot be true (the modus tollens inference). Because of the nature of deductive networks, a premise can be used to predict a conclusion logically. In scientific discourse, premises are referred to as "laws." A law necessarily implies a conclusion if the law is true. If the conclusion is observed not to be true, the premise or law must be false (as stated).

When it is seen that laws can be treated as premises in hypothetical statements, explanations take on the form of deductive arguments in which events are subsumed under laws. In a series of papers written from the late 1940s to the 1960s, Carl G. Hempel[21] sought to translate or to reconstruct the network of scientific laws through the use of the deductive network framework. The notion that proper explanation for science requires that the event to be explained must be identified as an implication of a law was not new with Hempel, but his explicit description of scientific explanation as a logical form of deductive argumentation renewed the discussion about the nature of scientific theory.

The renewed discussion and defense of the position that the deductive-nomological explanation is the basic model of scientific explanation was set in motion in 1948 with a paper by Hempel and Paul Oppenheim. The authors viewed functional or teleological explanations, genetic explanations, and historical or reason-explanations as incomplete in their present form and in need of translation into the deductive-nomological (*nomos* = law) form if they were to be useful for prediction and were to meet the scientific goal. It is the predictive force, as well as its explanative power, they said, that gives the deductive-nomological model its importance for science.

Subsumption of events (or less general laws) under general laws provides an explanation for past events and a prediction of future events.[22] The proposals in the 1948 paper were refined in the 1950s and 1960s in a series of papers and books by Hempel, Richard Braithwaite, Ernest Nagel, and Karl Popper.[23] Although the deductive-nomological model has come under increasing criticism (see chapter 4), it continues to exert a strong influence on the assumptions of science expressed in textbooks.

As we have already seen, the deductive-nomological model of explanation has the form of a deductive argument. In the deductive argument, the conclusion is implied or guaranteed by the premises. It is this certainty that is the aim and the reason for the law-deductive type of explanation. The deductive form of argument or explanation also provides an account that is applicable both to events that have happened and to events that have not yet happened. When the event to be explained has already occurred, the argument *is* an explanation; when the event has not yet occurred, the argument is a prediction. It is the power of the deductive argument to connect statements relating to future events with statements of premises that makes it the preferred logical model for experimentation and testing for the truth of the statements in the premises.

Within the context of the received view, the terms of the deductive argument are given special names. The event that is to be explained—the conclusion of the deductive argument—is called the *explanandum phenomenon.* The premises in which the explanandum is implied are called the *explanans sentences.*[24] The explanans sentences—the premise-set—consist of general law statements that are the conditional statements (for example, in the modus ponens deduction, "If P, then Q") and statements describing the initial conditions ("P is true"). The form of the logical explanation is given in Figure 1 along with the parallel terms.

The template for the deductive model of explanation is as follows:

A. The event to be explained, the explanandum or conclusion of the deductive argument (for example, "Why did the walls of a room painted in white blacken?")

B. The laws and statements describing the relevant initial conditions, the explanans or premise set of the argument.

   (1) Laws or conditional statements in the premise (for example, "If an object is lead carbonate and combines with sulfur to form lead sulfide, then it will turn black").

Deductive Argument   **Deductive Explanation**

Premise-set $\left\{ \begin{array}{l} \text{L (If P, then Q)} \\ \\ \text{P} \end{array} \right\}$ law statements   Explanans sentences
(pl. explanantia)

Conclusion   Q   Explanandum sentence
(pl. explanda)

Figure 1. Deductive Model of Argument and Explanation

(2) Antecedent conditions (for example, "The paint contained lead carbonate, and sulfur was contained in the gas used for lighting the room").[25]

The deductive form consists of the relations among the statements in the argument. If one focuses on the conclusion or explanandum, the argument provides an explanation of this event in terms of the premise set. If one focuses on the premise set, the argument provides a prediction in the form of a conclusion. In the example above, changing the focus to the premise set gives an answer to the question: "What will happen if the walls are covered with a paint containing lead carbonate, and gas containing sulfur is used for lighting the room?" The answer is: "The walls will blacken." This characteristic of the deductive argument provides a symmetry of explanation and prediction.

To summarize: Hempel called the kind of explanation described above a *deductive-nomological explanation*. It is deductive because it follows the format of the deductive argument, and it is nomological because the premise set contains general laws. The event to be explained is implied or subsumed within the law statement. Laws invoked in this kind of explanation are called *covering laws* when used in the explanans. (Laws as well as individual events can be explained within the deductive-nomological model. In these instances, the covering laws are more general than those to be explained, and they imply or subsume the explanandum laws under them.)

The deductive-nomological explanation is valid if the explanandum sentences are implied in the explanans sentences. The problem of relating the implications between the statements of the argument to descriptions of the "real" world will be addressed later in this chapter.

In this type of explanation, the emphasis is placed on the logical relationship between the forms of statements within the argument.

In Hempel's representation, science is a series of statements that argue for or give reasons for certain conclusions. Science is not merely the accumulation of conclusions—such as, for instance, "Water freezes at 0 degrees centigrade" or "Behaviors that have been reinforced are likely to be repeated." Understanding the nature of science includes understanding the statements used in supporting and arguing for those conclusions. Hempel and others in the later developments of the logical empiricist tradition sought to examine the structures of the arguments used in science to support its conclusions—that is, they sought to reconstruct the reasoning processes that scientists use when they justify their conclusions. When these processes are made explicit, they in turn can be used as norms to determine whether a scientist is reasoning appropriately.

In a completely stated argument, all of the premises and the conclusion they support are given. In many instances in the scientific literature, however, authors are content to leave parts of their arguments unstated. If an author's argument is elliptic—if it omits a premise—it is called an *enthymeme*. In order to reconstruct the reasoning process to support the conclusion, it is necessary to insert the omission and make explicit what was implicit in the enthymeme.

When the reconstruction of the scientific process is undertaken, what is revealed, according to Hempel, is that science is primarily an argumentation process. It does not consist merely of statements that describe observations; it consists primarily of a network of inferences between statements, only some of which are observation statements. The form of the network is argument. An argument is a logical structure in which some statements are given as reasons for other statements. The classic form of argument, the Barbara-type syllogism, is a network of statements in which the conclusion "Socrates is mortal" is supported by the statements "All men are mortal" and "Socrates is a man."

An argument is not a single statement; it is a conjunction of statements in relation to each other. An argument is understood as a whole, and its meaning is located in the relationships between and among its statements. The function of the whole is to provide reasons in support of one or more of its statements. The form of the unitary argument—that is, an argument that does not have intermediate conclusions as do extended arguments—is one element consisting of a statement that puts forth a particular view and another element consisting of statements that specify the reasons for that view. The element that puts forth the point of view ("Socrates is mortal") is the conclusion, and the element which offers reasons in support of the conclusion ("All men are mortal," "Socrates is a man") is made up of the premises. The connection between the elements is usually indicated by such words as "therefore," "thus," "so," "it follows that," and "it can be seen that."

For Hempel, a statement is explained when it is a supported conclusion in an argument. To explain why it is that children all learn to speak at about the same age, one needs to demonstrate that the statement itself can be supported by premises that enable one to accept it as true. The argument, "If the ability to learn a language is largely innate, then children will all learn to speak at about the same age; the ability to learn a language is largely innate, therefore, children all learn to speak at the same age"[27] is the explanation for why "all children learn to speak at the same age."

Laws

The base of the deductive system of science is provided by the premises that form the nodes of the network. These premises are the laws of science. Laws can be deductive, related in the same logical manner that events are related to laws—that is, a lesser law can be deduced from a more general law. A system of deductively related laws constitutes a *theory*. In the deductive system of science, the aim is to generate unified networks of laws—to wit, theories. In his widely used book on research design, Kerlinger explicitly states: "The basic aim of science is theory."[28]

Laws play an essential role in deductive-nomological explanations. They provide the general premises by means of which particular circumstances can serve to explain the occurrence of a given event (the explanandum). Hempel has said that "the laws required for deductive-nomological explanations share a basic characteristic: they are . . . statements of universal form."[29] In other words, whenever and wherever conditions of a specified kind occur, then, without exception, so will certain conditions of another kind occur. If I hold a piece of ice in my uncovered hand (event A), I will experience a cold sensation in my hand (event B). If a particular regularity between two events is postulated to occur at all times and in all places, without exception, then this regularity is expressed in the form of a "universal law." It is the postulation of certain repetitions or regularities between events in the world that is the core of the deductive-nomological model of science. As Carnap has put it:

Day always follows night; the seasons repeat themselves in the same order; fire always feels hot; objects fall when we drop them; and so on. The laws of science are nothing more than statements expressing these regularities as precisely as possible.[30]

Carnap suggests that the word *law* can be confusing. The word is used to describe both laws of the political realm and laws of nature. In the context of science, *law* simply refers to a description of an observed regularity, and thus it may be true or false—which is to say, it may be either an accurate or an inaccurate description of nature. Since there is no other generally accepted word for the kind of universal statement that appears in the deductive framework for making explanations and predictions, it continues to be used.

The use of the word *law* to designate relationships between natural events seems to have originated with the Greeks. They thought that a certain necessity lay behind the natural regularities, something analogous to the moral requirements that operated in relationships between persons. Since the word *law* carries a suggestion that it can be either obeyed or disobeyed, it was assumed that nature could from time to time violate its own laws but did not, for the same reason that a good citizen did not. Something of this feeling about the laws of nature lingers: like civil and moral laws, they are commands to be obeyed. But the laws of nature are not imperatives; they are descriptions drawn by observers of the regularities that have been noted. If there is a discrepancy between a description and a natural occurrence, a question is never raised about whether nature has disobeyed; the question that is raised concerns the adequacy of the description.

The deductive-nomological system of science differentiates between "singular" statements of fact and "law" statements. An example of a singular statement of fact is "Today, during my walk, I saw a monarch butterfly." The singular statement speaks about a specified, single time-and-space. The positivist approach holds that all of our knowledge has its origins in singular statements—that is, that all of our knowledge is based on the particular observations of particular individuals. Of primary concern within the law-explanatory system, however, is the question of how one is able to go from such singular statements to the assertion of universal laws. A universal law states that events of type A and events of type B are always related, although the regularity of the relationships is not directly observable. To return to our example: even if I see a monarch butterfly on each of my daily walks for a full year, the sum of my singular statements cannot lead to the conclusion of such a universal law as "If I take a walk, then I will see a monarch butterfly."

We are never absolutely certain in respect to laws. A law about the world states that in a particular case, at any time and in any place, if one thing is true, then another thing is true. The universal law describes an infinity of possible instances, and thus no finite number of observations, however large, can make the "universal" law certain. Hence it is not apodictic in a stringent sense, but rather is assertoric (see chapter 1).

Universal Laws and Accidental Generalizations

Adherents of the received view have been confronted with the problem of how statements that are laws are to be differentiated from other statements. As already noted, a lawlike statement has a conditional form as well as a universal form. It makes "an assertion to the effect that universally, if a certain set of conditions, C, is realized, then another specified set of conditions, E, is realized as well."[31] The standard form of a lawlike statement is therefore the universal conditional, "If P, then Q." However, not all universal conditionals are lawlike. For example, the statement "*All* of the coins in my pocket on January 4, 1982, were nickels" may be true, but it refers to an accidental occurrence and does not necessarily establish a law (e.g., "If I have coins in my pocket, they will be nickels"). Consequently, laws must be distinguished from other statements by other requirements besides the universal conditional form.

One of the proposed requirements is that laws (nomic generalizations) entail counterfactuals. A counterfactual conditional is an assertion that, even though a certain event has *not* taken place, if it had taken place, then a certain other event would have followed. For example, the statement "If I drop a stone, it will fall toward the earth" entails the counterfactual statement "If I had dropped the stone yesterday (although I did not), it would have fallen toward the earth." Similarly, a law—in contrast to an accidentally true generalization—can support subjunctive conditionals—that is, sentences of the type, "Should P come to pass, then so would B." To take the same example again: "If I were to drop the stone tomorrow (although I might not), then it would fall to the earth."

An accidental universal statement does not hold up to the counterfactual or subjunctive conditional entailments. "If I were to have coins in my pocket tomorrow, they would all be nickels" is not necessarily true. Nelson Goodman has proposed four characteristics of lawlike statements that differentiate them from accidental generalizations:[32]

(1) Lawlike statements must be unrestricted as to space and time. A nomic statement must formulate what is always and everywhere the case, provided only that the appropriate initial conditions are met. Carnap asserts that this condition holds only for basic laws, and he proposes that there are many technical and practical laws that are not accidental generalizations but that are not entirely general with respect to time and space.[33] For example, Kohlberg's "laws" of moral development and Piaget's cognitive development "laws" may not be universal laws because they are limited to particular places (cultures) or particular periods of history (the 1900s). But they are also more than mere accidental generalizations. These "laws" are dependent on a variety of basic laws that determine the intellectual and moral teachings and cultural values of the particular cultures and the particular period of history those researchers have examined.

(2) Nomic generalizations must not be vacuously true—that is, true only because there are no cases that satisfy the conditions—unless the particular generalizations in question are derivable from other laws. (See the fourth characteristic below.) Using the criterion that there are no contrary instances, the statement "If an animal is a unicorn, it will have black fur" is true. Such a statement, however, is not considered lawlike, because nothing satisfies its conditions.

(3) Lawlike generalizations are "open," not "closed." A closed generalization is limited to the cases from which it generalizes. "All the coins in my pocket at this time are nickels" is not a lawlike generalization since it merely restates the evidence. As an open generalization, a lawlike statement goes beyond a description of the specific evidence and makes a universal statement that all examples of something, at all times and places, are something.

(4) A nomic generalization is derivable from other laws. It is part of a scientific theory. A theory is a network of laws in that some laws are derivable from other more general laws that are grounded finally in axioms postulated as the givens in the deductive network. A generalization which summarizes empirical findings but does not relate them to a theoretical network is called an "empirical generalization," not a law. (The notion of empirical generalizations will be discussed in detail in chapter 3).

If a statement meets these criteria, it can be called a lawlike statement. For a lawlike statement to be considered a law, it must be a true statement. Laws are statements that have nomic form and are also true. The difficulties in establishing lawlike statements as true—that is, as actual laws rather than merely as statements in the form of laws—will be discussed in the section on "Confirmation."

Cause

One of the difficulties with the deductive system of inquiry is that the deductive logic dispenses with "the time concept and treats the actual processes of thought as laid down in an eternal present—just in order to avoid contradictions between successives."[34] In the deductive system, the explanation of a fact consists of showing that it is an instance of a general law. From a formal point of view, deductive explanation produces nothing that is new, nothing that is not in some way "contained" in the premise statement. It is this tautological network that gives the deductive system its internal consistency and power of clarity.[35]

The positivists sought to replace inexplicit links in the process of knowing with completely explicit observations (protocol sentences or observation statements) and with completely explicit deductions from these observations. When knowledge is limited to these two sources, causation does not show up. Hume pointed out in 1748 that if all but sense impressions were excluded as a source of knowledge then cause should not be included as *epistēmē*. When one billiard ball strikes another, and the second one then moves, cause is not seen— that is, cause itself does not appear in the sense data. Hume held that cause is a psychological condition, derived from habit, that people add to the sense data. But if one is to be truly faithful to the sense data, it is apparent that cause is not part of the sensa. Thus the most that can be accepted is knowledge that the two events have constantly been conjoined in our sense experience. If one assumes that what was true in the past will remain true in the future (an assumption that cannot be supported within the deductive system), then one can speculate that whenever A (the first ball striking the second ball) occurs, B will also occur (the second ball will move). One could inductively assume the lawlike statement "If a ball strikes a second ball, then the second ball moves." But such a statement does not describe what has traditionally been thought of as causality. The term *causality* usually refers to an event that *produces* something, and that which is produced is explained with reference to the cause.

However, cause, as something which produces an effect, does not show up within the deductive system, for causes are not directly observed. Philosophers of science committed to the deductive system approached the matter of cause in such a way that it could fit into their system. In order to do this they had to replace the notion that a result was produced with the notion that a kind of relationship held between events. The issue of causal production was dealt with as an issue of necessary and/or sufficient relationships between events. If a necessary relationship exists between events, they said, then the presence of one event is necessary for the presence of a second event. For example, oxygen is necessary for fire, but oxygen may be present without fire being present. If oxygen is withdrawn, fire will go out. A necessary relationship answers the question of how it is possible for an event to happen.

In a sufficient relationship, the situation is somewhat different. "If A, then B" is a sufficient relationship when B will be present if A is introduced. B might be present when A is not present, but B must be present if A is present. For example, "If people are shot in the heart, then they will die" is a sufficient relationship. People may die for many reasons, but if they are shot in the heart, then they will surely die. Usually, in the deductive system, when a relationship exists between events of a sufficient condition, it is spoken of as a causal relationship or as a causal law. "If oxygen is removed for a prolonged period of time, then people will die" is a causal law. However, not all sufficient conditions seem to describe what is meant by the term *cause*. The quality of being an equilateral triangle is related to the quality of being an equiangular triangle (in the Euclidean system) in a sufficient way (and also in a necessary way), but this relationship does not appear as a cause of the equal angles. Or, the statement "If there are living people, there must be oxygen" shows a sufficient connection between events, and therefore they are causally connected, but the presence of people is not the cause of oxygen.

The idea of causality is particularly important for the behavioral and social sciences. In the system of inquiry concerned with human reasons for action (discussed in chapter 6), the cause of human action is of central concern. With the systems of inquiry that limit data to observables—such as the logical positivists' deductive system—the idea of causality is problematic.

Carnap describes the logical positivists' reasons for rejecting the common meaning of causality and replacing it with the specialized meaning that has to do with the relationships of invariable sequences. According to Carnap, the concept of causality in nature arose, apparently, "as a kind of projection of human experience into the world of nature." When we move objects—such as tables, for instance—we feel tension in our muscles. By analogy, we imagine that when one ball strikes another it is having an experience similar to ours when we move a table: the striking ball is the agent, and it does something to the other ball to make it move. Carnap holds that this analogy, an anthropomorphic approach to nature, is the basis for our inappropriate idea that in nature one event makes the other occur. Nevertheless, he says, this animistic thinking persists:

> A stone shatters a window. Did the stone intend to do this? Of course not, the scientist will say. A stone is a stone. It possesses no soul capable of intention. On the other hand, most people, even the scientist himself, will not hesitate to say that event B, the breaking of the window, was caused by event A, the collision of the stone with the glass. What does the scientist mean when he says that event B was caused by event A? He might say that event A "brought about" event B or "produced" event B. . . . When he tries to explain the meaning of "cause," he falls back on . . . metaphorical phrases, taken from human activity.[36]

In the deductive system, laws are statements of invariable association between events. One type of invariable association is invariable sequence.[37] Invariable sequences can be described as necessary or sufficient or both. As we have already seen, however, when *cause* is limited to mean invariable sequence, most of the everyday meaning of the term is drained away, and the notion of an event producing or bringing about another event is left out of the system of inquiry. In the deductive system, a reference to causal laws is a reference to an invariable sequence between events, not a reference to a relationship of a cause to its effect, as would be said in everyday usage.

Confirmation

How does one arrive at statements of law? The old understanding, which was summarized by Mill in his *System of Logic* (1843), was that the researcher begins with free and unprejudiced observation of facts and then proceeds, by inductive inference, to the formulation of general statements—laws—about these facts. In the old model, then, laws are formed by generalizing from a set of observations. A series of "evidence reports" or protocol statements is inspected, and a general statement is inductively inferred from it. For example, from the series, "Mary has red hair, and she has a fiery personality," "John has red hair, and he has a fiery personality," "Jim has red hair, and he has a fiery personality," the general statement "People who have red hair have fiery personalities" emerges by inductive inference. Once a law or premise has been proposed, it can be tested according to the deductive system.

For the deductive system of science, the lack of certainty in inductive inference made the latter unacceptable as a central method in the construction of the network of universal statements or laws. Mill's acceptance of inductive inferences was challenged by William Whewell in *Philosophy of the Inductive Sciences* (1840) and by William Jevons in *The Principles of Science* (1877). Jevons proposed that before a hypothesis (a proposed universal statement) is accepted into the network of well-confirmed laws, it should be implied within the network and its consequences should agree with what is observed. Karl Popper, writing after the first efforts of logical positivism had been made, also proposed that scientific discourse should be limited to deductively connected law statements. In his *Logic of Scientific Discovery* (1934), he held that proposed laws could not be "verified" through accumulating evidence. He suggested, instead, that deductive inferences be used to propose evidence statements; these statements could be tested, and if a case was found that did not hold, the proposed law would be falsified. For example, the hypothesis "All swans are white" would be falsified if one swan was found that was not white. The problem, however, was that there was no way in which such a hypothesis could be verified, for no matter how many white swans were observed, it was still possible that there might somewhere exist a swan that was not white. (In fact, there were— and are—black swans in Australia.)

The hypothetical-deductive method replaced the old inductive system of "law making" in the deductive system of science. In the hypothetical-deductive method, possible observations are deduced from the hypothetical or proposed law, and these observations are then tested in an attempt to falsify the statement. This method, however, had little to say in regard to the reasons for suggesting a hypothesis in the first place. It was talked about as if it were an uncertain groping matter, as if it were guesswork, as if it were some sort of psychological or creative work of the researcher. In any event, how hypotheses were developed was not the concern of philosophers of science. Their concern was only how the suggested law was tested. Hans Reichenbach[38] distinguished between the manner in which the scientist actually arrives at a hypothesis, which he called the "context of discovery," and the presentation of the proof that a hypothesis is probably true, which he called the "context of justification."[39] The scientist, he said, is concerned only with the context of justification, not with the context of discovery, which belongs to the province of psychology.

The problem that remained was to connect to the real world the network of deductively joined statements and to ground them in a set of axiom statements. In *Fundamentals of Concept Formation in Empirical Science* (1952), Hempel (see Figure 2) likened the complex of laws that make up a theory to a spatial network:

> [The terms of a scientific theory] are represented by the knots, while the threads connecting the latter correspond, in part to the definitions and, in part, to the fundamental and derivative hypotheses included in the theory. The whole system floats, as it were, above the plane of observation and is anchored to it by rules of interpretation.[40]

The whole system of statements, although logically connected, may merely float above reality, not accurately describing the relationships that exist between the real individual objects in the world. Writing in 1919, N. R. Campbell made a distinction between the axiom system, with its deductively derived statements, and its application to experience (the empiricism side of logical empiricism). He proposed compiling a "dictionary" that would connect parts of the deductive system to empirical observations, so that the floating statements could be fixed to reality. In this way, the boundary between the axiom system and the realm of sense experience could be bridged; the "dictionary" entries would link certain terms of the axiom system with experimentally measurable properties.[41]

The final difficulty for the deductive system came at the point of this connection to empirical observations. The certainty for which the logical empiricists searched could be found only within the system of statements floating above the world. As Popper pointed out, it was possible to draw a conclusion with certainty when a statement was falsified by an observation, but it was not possible to provide a

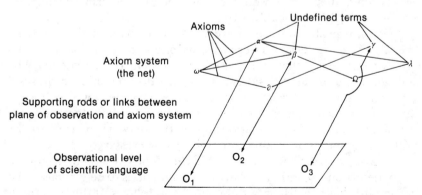

Figure 2. Hempel's Network Model of Theories

link of certainty by means of which the whole deductive system could be established in a positive way. The best that could be done was to try to establish a probability that the system of statements was supported by empirical observation.

Hypothesis Testing

In the deductive system of inquiry, experimentation and the gathering of empirical data take place within the context of the testing of a proposed law or hypothesis. If the hypothesis is true, then certain empirical observations should hold. The experiment is set to determine whether these observations do in fact hold. If they do not, the proposed law is to be rejected. However, if the observations do turn out to be what has been projected from the law proposal, it still does not mean that the law statement is true; it merely means that evidence supports it.

For example: "It is proposed that if students receive training in relaxation techniques then they will learn faster." (Within a full deductive system, this proposed statement would be linked deductively to other statements in the system. At present, however, most research in the social and behavioral sciences does not deal with deductively related proposals but is limited to isolated hypotheses. Moreover, even in the deductive system of inquiry, the goal of linking these isolated law statements into a total system has still not been achieved.) To test this proposed law (hypothesis), one could form two groups of students, the first to receive training in relaxation techniques and the second not. Data on the learning rate would then be collected from both groups. If the statistical analysis of the data showed that the group receiving the training had a faster rate of learning, then there would be evidence to confirm the hypothesis—that is, it is probably true.

It is only probably true, however, and the reason derives from the nature of inductive inferences, as opposed to the kind of deductive inferences that hold within the system of statements. The linkage of the deductive system to empirical observation requires a different kind of inference system than is provided by the linkage between the statements. Because inductive inference does not give certain conclusions, the relationship of the network of laws to the realm of observation is only probable, not necessary.

The goal of experimentation within the deductive system of inquiry is to determine whether a lawlike statement is true or false. To accomplish this goal, the reasoning used is as follows: If the hypothesis is true, then the statements regarding direct observations, which have been deductively arrived at from the general statements of the hypothesis, are true. If the evidence reports—that is, observation sentences or protocol sentences—are in accord with the deductively arrived-at statements about what should be observed, then it can be inductively inferred that the hypothesis is confirmed as probable (see Figure 3).

Because the test of the hypothesis involved translation from general statements to particular cases and back again, not all of the particular members of the general statement—except in limited cases—can be tested. If we return to the example "It is proposed that if students received training in relaxation techniques then they will learn faster," we note that it is impossible to test all students. And since the law is a general statement, it is not supposed to be time-bound; it must refer not only to all present students but also to all past and future students. Thus only a limited sample of deductive implications can be tested. In order to give more power to those tests that are made, it is reasonable to propose that a representative sample of observations be made. Sampling theory provides a basis for selecting— from the many possible observations derived from the hypothesis— those which should be made.

The Human Sciences and the Deductive System of Inquiry

The deductive system of inquiry was developed, first of all, to rationalize the physical sciences. One of the purposes of the deductive

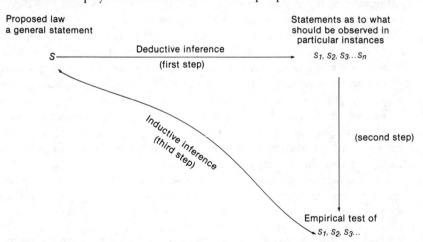

Figure 3. Hypothetico-Deductive Testing of Theories

network, however, was to connect all knowledge to basic axioms. To accept another realm of knowledge derived from a separate set of axioms would defeat the aim of unifying all knowledge into one system. Therefore the deductive system itself implies that all knowledge ought to be justified by the same methodological principles, regardless of the subject matter studied.

Since the time of Mill's call for the sciences of the human realm to adopt the methods of knowledge that had proved successful for the sciences of the physical realm, many philosophers of science, including the logical positivists, encouraged the human sciences to use the refinements of method as they were worked out in the physical sciences. As early as 1942, Hempel had proposed that law explanations and the deductive system were applicable to the study of history. Hempel asserted that historians were already using a deductive system, although they often left out parts of the deductive argument (using elliptical arguments) or merely outlined deductive explanations in an incomplete way (using explanation sketches). As an example of the use of deductive explanation by historians, Hempel cited "Dust bowl farmers migrate to California because continual drought and sandstorms render their existence increasingly precarious, and because California seems to offer so much better living conditions." The law proposed, Hempel said, was "Populations will tend to migrate to regions which offer better living conditions."[42]

For those who held the deductivist position, it was a matter of showing that the models of scientific explanation that had been developed on the basis of an analysis of the natural sciences were applicable to history and that it was therefore unnecessary to devise alternative accounts of the way explanation proceeds in history. There was a disposition on the part of some historians to look with favor on the application of the nomological thesis to their discipline, because they believed that it formulated the basic epistemic demands of the social sciences. These historians were willing to accept the logical conditions laid down by the logical positivists as the legitimate definition of science; they worked for a degree of generality comparable to that of deductive-nomological theory and ruled out in advance any possibility of there being an alternative model of explanation that might prove more appropriate for their use.

The deductive system was attractive to sociologists and psychologists as well as historians. As Peter Berger and Hansfried Kellner have pointed out in *Sociology Reinterpreted* (1981):

Sociology from its beginnings has been haunted by the positivist ideal. This calls for the establishment of universal laws, in the fashion of the natural sciences, allowing for a system of causally connected relationships under which specific phenomena can be subsumed. If these laws are empirically valid, then the specific phenomena can be deduced from them as cases and predictions can be made as to the future course. . . . Laws are supposed to have universal validity.[43]

And Anthony Giddens, who has written several articles on the impact of logical empiricism on sociology, has said:

Many sociologists embraced such positivistic philosophies [i.e., the philosophies of Carnap, Hempel, and Nagel], which were essentially liberalized forms of logical empiricism, with a fervor that blinded them to the fact that the logical empiricist view of science represents only one possible philosophy of science among other available philosophies. The logical empiricist philosophy of science came to be seen as what natural science "is," and as showing what sociology should become.[44]

In psychology, Clark Hull tried to develop a theory of learning that was based on a logical positivist approach. Thomas Leahey, in *A History of Psychology* (1980), has called Hull "the most mathematical, hypothetical-deductive of the formal behaviorists" and has described how he set out to develop an axiomatic system that deductively linked his empirical laws.[45] Another historian of psychology, Duane Schultz, has written:

Hull argued for strict adherence to the "hypothetico-deductive method," which utilizes rigorous deduction from a set of formulations that are determined in "a priori" fashion. The method involves establishing postulates from which experimentally testable conclusions can be deduced. These conclusions are then submitted to experimental test: Failure results in revision; verification allows for their incorporation into the body of science. Hull believed that if psychology was to be an objective science on the order of other natural sciences . . . then the only appropriate method was the hypothetico-deductive one.[46]

In *Naturalism and Social Science* (1979), David Thomas reexamined the usefulness of the deductive system of inquiry for social science. He worked from the perspective of a "postempiricist philosophy of science" and considered the critique of the law-system of explanation, but he advocated, without denying the fruitfulness of other approaches, the "naturalistic" approach to social science:

An advocate of a naturalistic social science would emphasize features such as the unification of knowledge (by means of generalizations, explanations, predictions, etc.) which would be yielded by a powerful naturalistic theory, as against the fragmented insights of non-naturalistic approaches.[47]

The nonnaturalistic approaches include the hermeneutic or interpretive approaches, which will be described in later chapters.

It can be seen, even without the presentation of more detail, that the deductive system has had a powerful effect on the methodological goals of the various human sciences. The human sciences do not have a closely linked system of theory, and it is suggested by positivists such as Hempel that such a system, with its regulative devices, is a goal toward which to strive. The argument goes that the sciences of the human realm are young relatives of the sciences of the physical realm but have not yet grown into fully developed sciences themselves. This is so, the argument continues, because they have not yet developed deductively derived theories from an axiomatic base. It is assumed that the Newton of the human sciences is yet to come along to systematize the diverse, scattered information that at present results from human science investigations.

According to another line of thought, human science researchers should not strive to develop a unified theoretical system, but should concentrate instead on empirical experimentation in which various correlations between variables are collected. The next chapter will discuss this alternate system of inquiry and will offer some critiques of sensation-based empiricism in general and the logical positivist system in particular.

The terms *logical positivism*, *logical empiricism*, *deductive-nomological*, and *"causal" law system* all refer to the system of inquiry that is called the received view or the deductive system in this book. The basic canons of this system are as follows:

1. Knowledge (*epistēmē*), as opposed to opinion, is contained only in statements that are descriptions of direct observation or in statements that are deductively linked to those descriptions of direct observation. (Inductively generated statements of probability are recognized as approximations that have not attained the certainty of deductively valid statements; they are acceptable as the best obtainable knowledge thus far.)

2. The goal of science is a network of knowledge statements linked together by the necessity of deductive logic generated from a few axiom statements and grounded ultimately in observation statements.

3. The only kinds of statements free from methaphysical overtones and personal bias—that is, the only kinds of statements assuring certainty—are those grounded in observation and belonging to the axiomatic system. All sciences are to limit their assertions to these kinds of statements, including the sciences of human phenomena.

Unless statements about "values," "reasons," "meaning," and so on can be reduced to the kinds of statements just mentioned, they are beyond the possibility of inclusion in true knowledge—that is, in *science* or (*epistēmē*).

3

Pragmatic Science

The goal of science, according to the reconstruction based on logic made by the logical positivists, is the development of comprehensive theory. The phenomenon to be explained is shown to be an instance of a deductively connected set of empirical generalizations. For example, when Durkheim set out to explain the connection between religious affiliation and suicide, he did so by showing it to be a deductive consequence of hypotheses about the effects of group cohesiveness on group members.[1] The premises of a theory, called its axioms or postulates, are confirmed by establishing the truth of the theorems that are derived from it.

By the 1950s, however, logical positivism had failed in its attempt to reconstruct science into a logically united system of theoretical statements grounded in the certainty of sense experience. There were two reasons for the failure: the "problem of induction" and an excessively narrow line of demarcation. The "problem of induction" arose because the accumulation of empirical data could not provide proof that the laws being tested were true. Inductive inference from the data was limited to only a degree of probability that the proposed law or hypothesis was correct. Laws could not be verified, and thus the network of necessity was torn, and a comprehensive and unified system of certain knowledge based on empirical observation was transformed into a collection of overlaid threads with various probable relationships.

The excessively small circle, drawn to separate true science according to the prescriptions of logical positivism, excluded much of what had been included in the tradition of science—for example, Darwin's theory of evolution—because it was not predictive. Logical positivism failed to concern itself with the way scientists actually work, the way they place emphasis on inquiry and limited problems and build up their research efforts into generalization. In actual

93

practice, scientists are not always logical. Negative results do not always refute a theory, and a research program often rests on a series of unprovable concepts unrelated to a theoretical or conceptual system.

A return to the study of the historical practice of science provided another base for criticism of the logical positivist program for science. Stephen Toulmin's *The Philosophy of Science* (1953) and Michael Polanyi's *Personal Knowledge* (1958) opened a period in which a number of writers called for a philosophy of science that recognizes a pragmatic, less formalized, problem-centered science.[2] This chapter will examine the efforts made during the 1960s and 1970s to reformulate the philosophy of science in such a manner that it could overcome the problem of induction and would give more consideration to the way that science is actually practiced. This reformulation ultimately had to give up the standard of certainty for scientific knowledge, and it then had to take measures to overcome the immediate relativistic response to the abandonment of certainty. The development of this new formulation is still in progress. It is referred to here as "pragmatic science."

Recall that during the past sixty years, the philosophy of science has moved through a five-phase development: (1) the original development of the received view by the Vienna circle during the 1920s and 1930s; (2) a period of refinements and improvements by the proponents of the received view; (3) a period of criticism of the received view which proposed to show that the received view was untenable and should be abandoned in favor of an alternative approach; (4) a time (overlapping the third phase) in which proposals for alternative analysis of science were offered, proposals whose acceptance presupposed—indeed, required—the rejection of the received view; and (5) a response (during the 1970s) to the skeptical challenges of the fourth phase which included a proposal that scientific practice be understood as a rational enterprise capable of yielding progressively more truthlike knowledge. The first two phases have already been discussed in chapter 2; the remaining phases will be discussed here.

The Third Phase: Criticism of the Received View

All during the 1960s, the received view was strongly criticized. Frederick Suppe reported in 1974 that "the vast majority of working philosophers of science seem to fall on that portion of the spectrum which holds The Received View fundamentally inadequate and untenable."[3] There was a strong feeling that something was wrong with the orthodox view, and yet there was considerable disagreement about just what was wrong with it. Suppe listed nine characteristics of the criticism:

1. The analytic-synthetic categories of statements do not provide a complete separation.
2. The absolute distinction between direct observation and theoretical terms does not hold.
3. Theoretical terms already have culturally embedded meanings before they are incorporated into scientific theories, even though their incorporation into theories may alter their meanings somewhat.
4. The meanings of theoretical terms may derive from references to analogies and iconic models.
5. The linking of theory to the world through observations includes the use of auxiliary hypotheses and theories as part of the definitions of the observations.
6. The linking of theory to the world must allow for time sequences (causal analysis) and experimental correlations.
7. Theories cannot be viewed as entirely axiomatizable or formalizable.
8. The formalization that is involved in systematizing theories must be semantic, not syntactical.
9. The analysis of scientific theories must not limit itself to providing formulations of theories at fixed stages of development and then offer them as finished products; it must include an account of the evolutionary or developmental aspect of scientific theorizing.[4]

This section will discuss in some detail various aspects of the criticism of the received view: first, the criticism of the claim of theory-independence of observation reports; second, opposition to the view that theory is contained in written statements; third, the recognition that there is a need for partial formulations; and fourth, the rejection of the idea of verification by inductive inference.

Theory-Dependence of Observation Reports

A basic tenet of the logical empiricist philosophy of science was the claim of theory-independence of observation reports. According to the logical empiricist view, the truth or falsity of observation reports (protocol statements) can be decided directly without appeal to the sentences of the theoretical level because theories acquire their empirical connection and meaning from the sentences of the observation level. Peter Achinstein and Willard Quine[5] took issue with this separation of observations from theoretical perspective.

Achinstein examined the distinction between observational terms and theoretical terms. In logical positivism, observational terms refer to directly observable entities or to attributes of entities while theoretical terms do not. Achinstein took as his example "observing" a slice of muscle tissue. At various times, muscle tissue can be examined in various ways: with the naked eye, under a microscope, under a microscope after staining and fixing, and under an electron microscope. He asked whether the tissue is observed in each of these instances or whether at some point in the sequence the tissue ceases to be observed. Achinstein's point was that the observable-nonobservable distinction cannot be absolute; it is dependent on the context. The same observation—for example, a stained virus under a microscope—may be classified either as nonobservable, when compared to observation of a table in a room, or as observable, when compared to viewing through an electron microscope.

Quine reaffirmed and developed a thesis suggested by Pierre Duhem[6] which held that our observations are not connected by correspondence rules to one theoretical statement but are connected to the whole system of our theories and assumptions. There is no theoretical statement or lawlike relation whose truth or falsity can be determined in isolation from the rest of the network of statements. Moreover, many conflicting networks may fit, more or less, the same facts. A particular measurement uses theoretical assumptions from other theories. For example, heat is measured by a thermometer, but implied in the measurement, in addition to the level of heat, are theories about the expansion of mercury, the activity of a liquid in a vacuum, and so on. If an observation does not fit the deduced hypothesis, it does not necessarily disprove the hypothesis; adjustments can be made in the network of lawlike statements, including those that refer to measuring instruments, so that the hypothesis can be retained in spite of the falsifying observation.

Quine also held that the sharp distinction between analytic and synthetic statements was incorrect. Since observation reports use language that contains terms of classification, and since these terms also have theoretical implications, it is questionable whether observation statements can be said to be free of theory. Mary Hesse, writing in support of Quine's attack on the idea of theory-free observation, says that it "is quite clear that the netlike interrelations between more directly observable predicates and their laws are in principle just as subject to modifications from the rest of the network as are those that are relatively theoretical."[7] Hesse points out that observation language and theory language are not completely separate; together they form an interacting system, a "network" model of language.

Nonstatement View of Theories

A number of critics opposed the orthodox view that theory is a collection of statements. Frederick Suppe, for instance, proposed a "nonstatement view" of theories.[8] Suppe and others distinguished between a statement and a proposition: a statement is made up of the actual words used in a sentence, while a proposition is made up of the meaning expressed by those words. Several sentences or statements can express the meaning or proposition. For example, the two statements "John loves Mary" and "Mary is loved by John" express the same proposition.

Suppe held that a theory is actually a nonlinguistic entity or meaning (proposition) which is related to linguistic formulations. The orthodox view, he said, was incorrect in maintaining that science is a collection of actual statements; instead, science is a collection of propositions which are described by various statements. Thus, whatever formalization is involved in theory development must be semantic, not syntactical.[9]

Partial Formulations

In its axiomatization of scientific theories, the received view proposed that scientific knowledge can be systematically related by deductive implications. Most theories in the human sciences, however, are insufficiently developed to fit into the kind of logically integrated system required for full axiomatization. Richard Rudner,[10] in *Philosophy of Social Science*, argues for partial formulations of theories in much of social science.

In the received view, it was held that the advancement of knowledge would lead to a progressive unification of science. This would come about as separate laws and theories were linked through inclusion in broader and more general theories, and the progression would continue until all knowledge would be derived from a few basic axioms. In actual practice, however, it appears that more generalizations are accumulated than will fit easily together in large systems. The accumulation of separate generalizations is especially characteristic of the human sciences. Writing about psychology and laws, Rom Harré has said:

But a theory would still be a theory and would still explain the facts it did explain if its laws did not fit easily or at all into a logical system. The laws might only hang together because they were the laws of the same subject matter, that is, the laws describing the behavior of the same kind of things or materials. We have a great deal of knowledge about human behavior, for instance. But this knowledge cannot be formulated in such a way as to fit into a deductive, logical structure. Our theory of human behavior is a rag-bag of principles united by virtue of the fact that they all concern the same subject matter, namely, the behavior of people. We may never find a systematic formulation of these laws. We may never achieve the pragmatic advantages of system.[11]

Although research in the human sciences sometimes arrives at generalizations through inductive inference and then applies them to populations that extend beyond the specific observations made, much of the research is limited to summary statements about actual measurements. Statements of the type "26 people were tested, and the mean score was 45, which correlated at a positive 0.65" abound in the literature. This kind of research is called "evidence reports," and because the observations are not adequate to serve as the sample base for a larger population, the results are not generalized beyond the actual observations.

In psychology, the move toward a less formalistic research program, with a return to the simpler positivism of Mach, was led by B. F. Skinner. Theories are unnecessary, Skinner said, and science should concern itself only with observables. Intervening unobservable variables which make up the language of theory should be eliminated, and explanation should be merely an accurate and precise description of the relationships between observable variables. As Mach had sought to remove any metaphysical references to unobserved causal links in physics, so Skinner sought to exorcise any metaphysical references to unobserved causal links in psychology. Skinner called this kind of science "descriptive behaviorism." He rejected all theory that refers to unobserved hypothetical entities, and in its place he put summary statements of the ways in which observable variables correlate.[12]

In sociology, David Walsh and Anthony Giddens[13] reported on the way that research had taken on the character of observational reports. Emile Durkheim, in *The Rules of Sociological Method* (1895), attempted to establish a scientifically grounded sociology by declaring that social facts should be treated as things and that the role of sociology is to examine the relationships between and among social facts in terms of their observable properties. Durkheim argued that scientific observation and analysis are possible only with regard to overt behavior. Terms, he said, should be defined by the operations used to measure overt characteristics. Scales referring to observables should be devised for terms, with scores on the scales correlated with other observable behavior.

Research prevalent in the behavioral and social sciences is often not intended as a test of hypotheses derived from a theoretical network. Instead, the investigators study a circumscribed set of variables and produce summaries of the observed correlations. The findings are partial formulations or "empirical generalizations" in contrast to "scientific laws" which are the intended result of studies which seek to confirm theoretically derived hypotheses. Such findings do not produce open, universal statements (laws) and may only be closed, accidental generalizations (see chapter 2, "Laws"). Robert Merton believed that by relating isolated facts to each other, a level of empirical generalization could be obtained, and the generalizations would retain a degree of independence from any theoretical framework.[14] Ernest Nagel employed the term *experimental law* to refer to what is called an empirical generalization here:

> Even when an experimental law is explained by a given theory and thus is incorporated into the framework of the latter's ideas, . . . two characteristics continue to hold for the law. It retains a meaning that can be formulated independently of the theory; and it is based on observational evidence that may enable the law to survive the eventual demise of the theory. . . . Such facts indicate that an experimental law has, so to speak, a life of its own, not contingent on the continued life of any particular theory that might explain the law.[15]

Empirical generalizations are statements of regularity in a set of observations—they are not theoretical deductions—and thus they stand on their own, independent of theoretical interpretations.

These researchers do not attempt, primarily, to unify knowledge through a deductive system. Instead, they work on limited problems, seeking to solve them by locating correlations and other regularities among the variables defined through observable events.

The "Problem of Induction"

Logical positivism is based on a deductive model of scientific reasoning. As described in chapter 3, deductive reasoning provides relationships of necessity: if the premises are true, then the properly drawn conclusions must be true. Deductive reasoning has been held out as the superior mode of logic because it supposedly produces a demonstrative reasoning of certainty. It is used to relate statements to one another and to order them into a logically certain network of theory. At the same time, the question of the truth of a law statement (in distinction to its logical validity) is to be established by predicting what instances will occur if the law should prove true and then testing to see if they will occur.

The "problem of induction" is that no sample of possible instances can provide absolutely certain grounds for an inference that the law is true. The inference from instances to a general statement cannot be deductive (except in cases of falsification); it can only be inductive, and this kind of inductive inference (the result of probability or ampliative induction) yields only probability statements about the law.[16] Consequently, laws cannot be verified through testing deduced inferences; all that can be obtained are degrees of confirmation. The "problem of induction" leaves the deductively tied network hovering about the instances of reality without offering any surety that the network actually describes genuine relationships.

Everyday meanings of the terms *deductive* and *inductive* do not agree with the meanings used here and in discussions to be found in the logical empirical literature. Colloquially, *deduction* is used indiscriminately to refer to both types of argument, often referring to any act of drawing conclusions by reasoning. For example, detectives are said to "make deductions" about what happened at the scene of the crime by examining the evidence. *Induction* is usually not used at all in relation to arguments—or if it is used, it carries a narrower meaning than it has in supportive-type arguments. In the present context, the term *induction* is used only to describe supportive arguments that reason to a conclusion about all of the members of a class from an examination of only a few members of the class. For the remainder of this section, these terms will be used in their technical sense.

In induction, the relationship between the evidence and the generalization that is drawn from that evidence is a matter of probability—that is, the evidence confirms the generalization only within a limited range of probability. It is not necessarily certain from the sample that the inference is valid.

The distinction between these two types of argument—deduction and induction—is basic in the literature of law explanation. If one holds to certainty as the standard for acceptable knowledge, then one is required to use arguments of the deductive type, because arguments of the inductive type lend only probable support and cannot guarantee that a conclusion statement is true. The criteria for judging the worth of the two types of argument differ, and thus almost all inductive arguments will be found lacking if they are judged by the criterion used for deductive arguments—that is, that the truth of their conclusions is guaranteed.

The issue in inductive analysis is the confrontation of the generalization with the evidence and the determination of the degree of probability which the evidence offers for the generalization. In induction, rules of "degree of confirmation" are needed. These rules take into account further factual knowledge; the degree of confirmation may change radically in the light of further information. Induction differs from deduction in just this way: additional information impacts on the previous inductive inferences. In deduction, no further information is needed; only the rules of the deductive system within which the deduction is being made are needed. And no additional factual information can change the validity of the deductive inference.

In probability induction, several distinctions are made. The first distinction is that attribute and variable induction are differentiated. An attribute is a quality or property which does not vary in degree. (An example is a nominal-type measurement, such as being an Irishman.) A variable is a quality which varies in degree. (Examples are ordinal scales for measuring by rank order, interval scales for measuring differences according to equal quantities on a scale, and ratio scales which measure on scales with an absolute zero and thus allow for ratio comparisons—for instance, "He is twice as heavy as his brother.") Other distinctions in inductive reasoning include one, two, or more place attributes ("All men are mortal," "War is immoral and expensive") and universal ("All humans can reason") or proportional ("Some people have red hair") attributes.[17]

Inductive reasoning does not lead to validation of a generalization from premises; it provides only a degree of confirmation. For example: five people in a group of twenty, who were asked whom they would vote for in the coming election all reported the same preference, but this does not mean that one can infer that all people in the group prefer the same candidate. There are three rules of induction for increasing the probability of a generalization induced from a limited number of observations: the rule of variety, the rule of randomness, and the rule of numerousness.

Under the rule of variety, the sample considered in making the generalization needs to be varied along the lines of significance for the major generalization. For example, in considering the relationship between smoking and cancer, it is necessary to sample subgroups of both urban dwellers, with their higher rates of air pollution, and rural dwellers, with their lower rates of air pollution, if a sound inductive conclusion is to be drawn. Errors due to the lack of proper stratification in the sample are called "errors of bias." The first Kinsey report did not provide adequate control sampling and failed to include farm dwellers and Catholics, and thus the sample was biased toward urban dwellers and Protestants; as a result, there was an error of bias when the generalization to the whole population was made.

The rule of randomness calls for selection of the sample to be made in such a way that weighting due to peculiarity is avoided. All members of the population need to have an equal chance to be selected for the sample. If a questionnaire is distributed only to college students and an attempt is made to generalize to the whole population, the conclusion is less likely to be a description of the population.

The rule of numerousness is rather simple: the larger the numbers, the better the sample (assuming that the sample also has variety and randomness). However, the rule of numerousness alone will not provide a better induction. If the IQ scores of boys and girls are compared and the girls are taken from the slum area of a city and the boys are taken from a middle-class suburb of that city, increasing the numbers of each group will not lead to increased reliability of the generalization.

In addition to these three rules, generalization from a given set of evidence to competing generalizations can provide a test of comparison to tell which of two possible generalizations is more probable. Experiments are often set up in which two competing generalizations are compared. The statistical "*t*-test" is a comparison of generalizations. When experimenters conclude that the difference in performance between two groups is statistically significant, they are asserting that the hypothesis "There is a difference between the parent populations from which the two groups are drawn" is a better generalization than the hypothesis "There is no difference between the parent populations."

Scientific practice since the time of Bacon has proceeded with the use of an inductive mode of reasoning. Mill developed four principles whereby an empirical generalization can be inferred from instances.[18] As statistical methods have gained increasing sophistication, the movement from enumerations of sample instances to inferences about the population has become more precise. In spite of the logical positivists' attempt to transform science by insisting upon the certainty of deductive relationships, inductive inference has continued to serve science.

This section has described the third phase in the recent philosophy of sciences. This phase consisted of a critique of the received view's notions of theory-independent observational statements, a scientific knowledge consisting in deductively related statements, an axiomatically based unified theoretical network from which all knowledge could be derived, and laws verified by observations. During the same period, the 1960s and 1970s, alternative descriptions of the nature of science were offered which were incompatible with the received view.

The Fourth Phase: Sciences as Expressions of Various World Outlooks

The goal of philosophers of science has been to develop the procedures by means of which *epistēmē* could be achieved. They have believed that by carefully examining how science justifies its conclusions they could clarify observational and logical operations which would grant the certain, universal, and timeless truths that have been the object of human aspiration at least since the time history was first written down. But each attempt at formulating a method which would achieve this perfect knowledge, from Plato's dialogues to the arguments of logical positivism, has been challenged by a skeptical response.

The skeptical response to logical positivism has taken the form called the *Weltanschauungen* (world outlooks) analysis. A précis of this skeptical response might go as follows: All knowledge is relative to one's perspective; there is no absolute point of view outside of one's historical and cultural situation. Neither pure sense data nor formal logic can provide an absolute foundation for knowledge. The character of one's knowledge, the categories according to which experience is formed, what is considered as reasonable, and so on— all of these are functions of one's *Weltanschauung*. One never has access to reality: one can only look through the opaque spectacles of the cognitive apparatus of one's historically given *Weltanschauung*. The problem has been that we have taken our particular constructed and filtered experience as a true expression of reality. We have not recognized it as a distorted vision.

Wittgenstein's later work on language games played a catalytic role in the origin of the *Weltanschauungen* analysis, especially for Toulmin, Hanson, and Winch. An early receptiveness for his ideas was also provided by Benjamin Whorf's theory that people's language systems mold their perceptions of reality and that the world we inhabit is primarily a linguistic construct.[19]

Wittgenstein's Language Games

The motive behind Russell's *Principia* and early Wittgenstein's *Tractatus* was the hope that the development of a formal language would produce a better key to understanding the world without mind—that is, material reality—than any other language (including everyday language) could provide. The question posed was: What would a science look like that conformed to a logically complete language? For Wittgenstein, this project was a "thought experiment," because such a language of pure logical interrelationships was a utopian idea.

If a science based on a formal language were to be developed, it would have to fulfill certain presuppositions. First, it would have to reduce all relevant nonextensional contexts to extensional contexts. Second, the semantics (rules for relating the language to the world) of such a science would have to possess correspondence rules which were theory-independent so that basic "facts" could be related to other basic "facts" as mathematical functions. Third, there would have to be a class of propositions about "facts" which would be unproblematic and which would provide a secure base; obviously, the scientist would need to be in a position to discover these propositions. If such a science could be developed, then research would consist, essentially, of continually expanding the stock of basic propositions and relating them to each other through truth-functional combinations of logical operations.

Although Wittgenstein had little or no sympathy for what later emerged as logical positivism, the logical positivists used his concept as the base for their movement. They, in fact, tried to construct a science according to the world which Wittgenstein's thought experiment described. But Wittgenstein had left open the question of whether reality actually conformed to the model of a formal language, and in attempting to bring the thought experiment into existence, the logical positivists came up against extreme difficulties as they tried to fit reality into the formal system. The problems they encountered, particularly the problems of verification and demarcation, were never solved.

Wittgenstein's proposed thought experiment was set forth in his book *Tractatus Logico-Philosophicus* in 1922. His concern with the relationship of language to reality continued to be a basic theme of his work, and he later began to explore the construction of ordinary language. In 1936, he began to write *Philosophical Investigations*, which presents the development of his thought on the varieties and structures of language games which, he said, give meaning to speech.

He chose not to publish *Philosophical Investigations* during his lifetime, and so it was not published until 1953, two years after his death. In the meantime, however, from 1937 to 1951, he prepared short manuscripts and gave some lectures which dealt with the ideas developed in the book.

In *Tractatus Logico-Philosophicus*, Wittgenstein maintained that there are some words that directly name parts of reality. These words are simple signs or the names of simple objects in experience. (The protocol sentences of logical positivism were supposed to be constructed of these words, thereby linking statements to experience.) In *Philosophical Investigations*, Wittgenstein questioned the possibility that there is such a direct relationship between a word and an object. Words do not have direct referents, he said; the meanings of words are determined by the various contexts in which they are used. Meanings have no rigid boundaries; they are formed by the surroundings or circumstances in which they are used. Consequently, one name cannot stand for one thing and another name stand for another thing. A particular referent for a name is determined by the way in which the term is used. Before one can find out what a name stands for, one must already have mastered the language game to which the name belongs. In order to learn the name of a color, a direction, or other presentation in experience, one must have some understanding of how colors are placed in an order, how a map is read, how words, gestures, and behavior are expressions of aspects of experience. Merely pointing at something and saying a word achieves nothing. The kind of use a word will have, the special circumstances in which it will be said, must be understood before it can even be a name.[20]

The meaning of a word, Wittgenstein continued, is analogous to the meaning assigned to a piece of wood that is used to represent a pawn in a chess game or a marker in checkers. In each use, the meaning of the piece is defined by the rules of the particular game, and the following of the rules involves not only the person using the rules, but also any other persons who understand and follow them. If you are standing next to me, and I point (an ostensive definition) at the mountain we are looking at and say "That is Mount Diablo," then you will know, when I see you again a month later and say "I climbed Mount Diablo last week," just which mountain I am speaking of. And if I then say "Let's meet at the base of Mount Diablo next week for a picnic," you will still know which mountain I am speaking of. Because I know that you understand the rule that I consistently refer to the same mountain with the term "Mount Diablo," I can be assured that you will understand the term whenever I use it.

It is only in a situation in which it makes sense to suppose that somebody else could, in principle, discover the rule which one is following that one can be said to be following a rule at all. If I write down the series of numbers "1, 3, 5, 7," an observer who understands the rule I am following can then continue the series by writing "9, 11, 13, 15." Commenting on this subject, Winch has said that a person's behavior belongs to the category of rule-following "only if it is possible for someone else to grasp what he is doing, by being brought to the pitch of himself going on in that way as a matter of course."[21]

In the category of rule-following, it is possible to make a mistake. A mistake is a contravention of what is established as correct by the rules. If I make a mistake in the use of a word, other people must be able to point it out to me; they must also be able to recognize that I have not made a mistake when I have used a word correctly. If I call the mountain "Mount Angel" when the rule says that it is to be called "Mount Diablo," then other people are able to point out the mistake to me. If there is no rule, then the change in the name for the mountain is not recognized as a mistake. We can see, then, that making a rule or standard which establishes meaning is an activity of a community; it is not the activity of an isolated individual, and to ascribe it to an individual would not make sense.

Words, Wittgenstein said, are not references to preformed meanings or concepts, and words and utterances do not "contain" absolute essences. The meanings of words are bound up intrinsically with the practices that constitute forms of life—which is to say, social activity. To know a language is to be able to participate in the social activity within which it is expressed. To understand the language of chess, for example, one must literally be a chess player. Because words have meanings only within diverse language games that are forms of life, one must enter into the various networks of conventions which are the foundation of intersubjectivity and interaction, meaningful communication and practice.[22]

Wittgenstein's change from his *Tractatus Logico-Philosophicus* position—which allowed for an absolute link between words and observations—to his *Philosophical Investigations* position—in which there is no such link, and meaning varies according to the rules of the language games in which it is used—has had an impact on the methodology of science. As mentioned above, many of the philosophers of science who proposed alternatives to the received view took Wittgenstein's later philosophy as their source—for instance, Norwood Hanson, Stephen Toulmin, Paul Feyerabend, Thomas Kuhn, and (indirectly through Kuhn) Imre Lakatos. Since all language meanings are relative to the "grammars"[23] of the language games in which they take part, all observation statements are theory-dependent—that is, they are dependent on the rules of the games and are not statements of "reality"—and the terms used in theories do not have fixed meanings across theories but vary according to the contexts in which they are placed.

Wittgenstein's On Certainty. In 1949, Wittgenstein visited the United States, and under the urging of Norman Malcolm he began work on a draft of a book about G. E. Moore's "A Defence of Common Sense," particularly Moore's claim to know a number of propositions—such as "Here is one hand, and here is another" and "The earth existed for a long time before my birth"—for certain.[24] The last entry in Wittgenstein's draft was made only two days before his death, and the book was left unfinished. G. E. M. Anscombe and G. H. von Wright edited Wittgenstein's notes and prepared the draft of *On Certainty* for publication; it appeared in 1969.

Wittgenstein had long maintained a radical pluralism based on the possibility of different world views and world pictures. In *On Certainty*, he argued that we continue to believe in our picture of the world not so much because it is useful but simply because it is given; it is ours, and it is there. This view differs from the view of pragmatism. The pragmatists hold that we maintain our world views because they are useful, but Wittgenstein asked: What possible use is derived from a world picture which claims that the king can make rain or that time and the existence of the world began with the coronation of the king? The world view or language game is there when we come into the world, Wittgenstein said. It is what we use to make sense of ourselves and the world. But it is not chosen; it is merely what we are used to.

"Truth" is a function of the world picture which we share, and for Wittgenstein there is a plurality of truths. For example, there are statements that are true in a Euclidean system that are false in another system. What we see as true depends upon our world picture. Truth is not based on a notion of absolute certainty or "super" certainty, as Wittgenstein called it. He was referring to the certainty of Descartes and the tradition which followed him. In this tradition, only those statements were accepted as certain which could stand up to the criterion that they could not be doubted. The notion of "super" certainty is not tenable, Wittgenstein said, because there are "hard" and "soft" certainties. There are some propositions that we never question because "nothing in our world-picture speaks in favor of the opposite."[25] Examples of such propositions, given in *On Certainty*, are: "The external world exists," "I have two hands," "My name is Donald," and "That is a tree." In Wittgenstein's plurality of linguistic worlds, these propositions, while necessary within a particular world picture, are not necessarily universal. It is possible, for instance, to conceive of a society in which the members have no names. Yet these are the "hard" facts which are indubitable and solid within a particular system. Other facts are "soft" and are open to doubt without disrupting the basic system of beliefs—for example, "There is a tenth planet" and "John loves Mary."

Wittgenstein believed that the laws of logic are like the laws of society. Stealing from a store and contradicting oneself are different kinds of violations, but in both instances the conflict which arises exists only between oneself and one's society, not between oneself and some ethereal realm of divine law or logic. Logic does not lie outside one's world picture. Aristotelian logic is a word game, and it is just one of many ways of looking at the world (of making sense of the world); it is conceivable that other "more primitive logics" can serve just as well, so that one is not obliged to follow Aristotle's laws of inference.

Wittgenstein maintained that logic and grammar are historical products and that there might well be as many logics as there are languages with different structures. He differentiated between "broad" reason and "strict" reason. Broad reason has to do with the ability of humans to "put the world together" in a certain way that makes "sense" to them. All humans have broad reason, and they express it by holding a world picture—not an individual picture, but a picture held in common with a community. Strict reason is a derivative form of reason; it is a sub–language game which prescribes certain rules for "correct" thinking.

What are the consequences of Wittgenstein's later philosophy for scientific policy? Because philosophy cannot do more than describe the various language games, all systems or theories should be regarded as "equidistant from God and criticizable from within"—that is, in terms of their own logic. This capacity for criticism from within would appear to hold true for social systems as well—for instance, for liberal democracy, for the National-Socialist movement, for the Stalinist brand of Communism, or for various forms of dictatorships—for there is no point outside their own systems where one can stand to judge.

The task of the social sciences becomes a task of discovering which propositions, values, and so on are held to be true within a given communication community. Since there is no objective knowledge, the sociologist can provide secure knowledge only about what is believed to be true within a particular language game. Thus, a "sociology of knowledge" would be more fittingly labeled a "sociology of belief."[26] The problems of theory preference across systems were dismissed by Wittgenstein, and so some methodologists have concluded that methodology itself is impossible.[27] Moreover, since there are no evaluative positions which span traditions, disciplinary independence reigns. The implications of the language-game approach are that even within disciplines each style of thought, each paradigm, or each research tradition should be considered to have its own language game, its own grammar, or its own logic. Cooperation and interaction between disciplines, including attempts to develop implications for one discipline by another, are deadened by this approach. As mentioned elsewhere in this chapter, an attempt has recently been made to overcome the separation and the relativistic connotations implicit in language-game theory.

The section on hermeneutics in chapter 6 shares many common themes with Wittgenstein's later writings. Although Wittgenstein's ideas have had their strongest effect in the Anglo-American community, he came originally from Vienna, and he wrote in German. He was influenced by the German neo-Kantian tradition, and his idea of language games preserves the richness and diversity of that social and historical tradition.[28] His philosophy, however, does not satisfy the positivists' desire for a knowledge that is "truly descriptive" of an extralinguistic reality. And one does not feel very confident that one's picture of reality is the most accurate of the available alternatives.

Peter Winch

Although Wittgenstein did not focus on the problem of sociological understanding, the consequences of his ideas for social inquiry were drawn out by Peter Winch in 1958 in *The Idea of a Social Science and Its Relation to Philosophy*.[29] Winch described his purpose thus:

> Wittgenstein's account of what it is to follow a rule is, for obvious reasons, given principally with an eye to elucidating the nature of language. I have now to show how this treatment may shed light on other forms of human interaction besides speech. The forms of activity in question are, naturally, those to which analogous categories are applicable; those, that is, of which we can sensibly say that they have a "meaning," a "symbolic" character. In the words of Max Weber, we

are concerned with human behavior "if and insofar as the agent or agents associate a subjective 'sense' (*Sinn*) with it."[30]

Winch maintained that understanding social action amounts to understanding the meaning imbedded in that action. Social scientists' access to their data comes through the actors' way of viewing their world, he said, and so the social scientists must understand the language games that are being played. This kind of understanding is more akin to "tracing the internal relations" of a system of ideas than to "the application of generalizations and theories to particular instances."[31] The "social relations between men and the ideas which men's action embody are really the same thing considered from different points of view."[32]

For Winch, the actions themselves have a meaning; behavior is not merely a series of bodily movements to which a person attaches subjective meaning. The characterization of a sequence of movements, as an action of a certain sort, involves interpreting the behavior as having a purpose or a reason and as situated within a system of rules, norms, standards, and so on. Thus, the action is meaningful within the language game; it is not meaningful in and of itself. For example, if I raise and wave my arm, that is meaningful action because, within the language game of my society, it is interpreted as a type of polite signal that I am going away. Within another language game, even within a subset of my society, the act can have a different meaning—as it does, for instance, when it is used as a signal by basketball referees. Participants in various games use these rules unreflectively to act in meaningful ways.

In his approach to understanding social action, Winch noted a problem involving the relation of categories of explanation of the action, categories which are developed by the scientist independently from those of the language in which the action takes place. What standing do the rules and categories of the social scientist's own language game have when he is investigating another language game? For example, within the language game of a particular culture, a certain food may be considered sacred and thus will not be eaten. The reason given for not eating the food is that to eat it would offend the gods. But within *our* language game, this action is interpreted as a learned behavior because the food does not preserve well and can possibly make those who eat it sick. Within another language game, the reason given for the fact that it rains every spring is that the members of the tribe have offered the proper sacrifices and prayers. But within *our* language game, spring rain comes as the result of seasonal changes which have to do with the tilt of the earth toward the sun and consequent movements in the weather patterns. Whose interpretation is correct? Winch declared that social action must be understood from within the language game of the actors, not from within another language game. One's own system must not be viewed as the only correct system so that another system is labeled "merely primitive."

The standards for what is intelligible and rational vary among language games:

> Rationality is not "just" a concept "in" a language like any other; it is this too, for, like any other concept it must be circumscribed by an established use: a use, that is, established in the language. But I think it is not a concept which a language may, as a matter of fact, have and equally well may not have, as is, for instance, the concept of politeness. It is a concept necessary to the existence of any language; to say of a society that it has a language is also to say that it has a concept of rationality.[33]

By the very nature of the fact that a society has rules, certain connections and relationships make sense while others do not. However, what makes sense—that is, what is rational—is relative to the system of the language game. And what the social scientist does, then, is translate from one language to another.[34]

Winch was reacting to certain anthropologists (Frazer and Tylor, for instance) who appraise societies in terms of the opposition between rationality and irrationality, claiming that their own views are scientific while the views of other societies are "primitive." What Wittgenstein's analysis of language posits is that our "scientific rationality" is merely one of many possible language games and thus is rational only within the context of our own system. The anthropologist fails to understand the context—the language game in which another society is engaged—and to notice how actions are rational within that system. Investigation involves a dialectical process in which the rationality of one game is brought into relationship with the rationality of another game—"their" game with "our" game—so that a new unity for the concept of rationality can be created. As Winch put it: "Seriously to study another way of life is necessarily to seek to extend our own—not simply to bring the other way of life within the existing boundaries of our own."[35]

Winch's book and other writings have brought significant response. I. C. Jarvie, who is unsympathetic to Winch's approach, describes the view as a form of relativism.[36] The issue is whether one can talk in terms of objective reality conceived as outside of language and culture, or whether one is limited to giving descriptions of various cultural views of reality. Can one say that the beliefs of primitives do not accord with objective reality? Jarvie says that Wittgenstein's view of language does not provide any access to an external or objective reality or any discourse about it; consequently, there is no way to distinguish which language game is closer to accurate description of reality. Jarvie, in opposition to Winch and Wittgenstein, believed that "there is something like a community of rationality shared by all men, but recognized or fostered by different societies in varying degrees (none being perfect)."[37] This universal rationality, he said, consists, at a minimum, of learning from experience, especially from mistakes. It is the resistance of reality to our attempt to mold it and make it serve us, or at least to keep it from hurting us, that provides a ground point outside of all language games and the base for determining which cultural views are more accurate in describing reality.

The History of Science and the Philosophy of Science

Hans Reichenbach introduced the terms *context of discovery* and *context of justification* in 1938[38] to mark a distinction between the process by means of which a scientific result is achieved (discovery) and the process by means of which the result is presented, justified, and defended before the scientific community (justification). The received view held that the philosophy of science could be most productive by confining its attention to the finished products of science. Its adherents were not interested in examining the activity of science; they were interested in looking at the results—including the reasons why the hypotheses presented should be accepted and should become part of the system of knowledge laws. In effect, the focus of this orthodox approach was journal articles and formal presentations.

Even as the criticism of the orthodox approach was beginning, a small number of writers expressed the opinion that to understand the nature of science, and thus how one comes to *epistēmē*, the focus had to be changed to the history of the ongoing social enterprise which is the actual practice of science. Science was still to be viewed as the exemplary human activity for obtaining knowledge, but now the search for deepening our comprehension of this basic human achievement was to be directed at the process of science, not at its products. The logical positivist's focus on the products—which comprised a system of theoretical statements tied to each other by deductive implications and to the world by correspondence statements—had not revealed why science gives knowledge. By turning to the practice of science it was hoped that the questions of how and why science produces knowledge would be answered. What is seen when attention is given to the practice of science is that it is an activity undertaken by people who exist within history and culture. The factors governing the discovery, development, and acceptance of scientific theories are related to the conceptual framework within which a scientific activity is carried out. The conceptual perspective determines in large part which questions are seen as worth investigating and what sorts of answers are acceptable. The *Weltanschauung* or world view of scientists conceptually shapes the way in which the world is experienced, and it is closely tied to the language system which one uses when one speaks of understanding the world. Science is thus seen as one of the games played when scientists interact with the world and with other people. It is a special kind of ordering experience, one of Dilthey's "categories of life."

The concerns of the philosophers of science who produced these alternatives to the received view overlapped with those of the historians and sociologists of science. The first influential *Weltanschauungen* analysis was offered by Stephen Toulmin in *The Philosophy of Science: An Introduction* in 1953. Toulmin maintained that the function of science is to build up systems of ideas about nature which have some legitimate claim to "reality." These ideas provide an intellectual framework of thought—or *Weltanschauung*—which determines the questions scientists ask and the assumptions underlying their theorizing. Their theories are neither true nor false; they are ways of looking at phenomena which work or do not work, which are fruitful or are not fruitful. Theories are merely instruments; they are not correct descriptions of reality.[39]

The most influential book in *Weltanschauungen* analysis was Thomas Kuhn's *The Structure of Scientific Revolutions* (1962). According to Kuhn, science takes place within paradigms or conceptual systems. Each paradigm has its own internal logic, but it is not related to other paradigms. At times, when a particular paradigm in use is unable to account for anomalies which appear, a revolutionary switch to a new paradigm occurs. The switch to a different paradigm, Kuhn said, is an arational, discontinuous jump, not an evolutionary or developmental change.[40] Other important contributions to the *Weltanschauungen* approach were Michael Polanyi's *Personal Knowledge* (1958), Norwood Hanson's *Patterns of Discovery* (1968), and Paul Feyerabend's articles in the 1960s culminating in his 1975 *Against Method*.[41] All of these writers employed, to some extent, three theses in their analyses: (1) observation is theory-laden; (2) meanings are theory-dependent; and (3) facts are theory-laden.

(1) *Observation is theory-laden.* Whereas positivism had held that the connections between statements and reality take place through the accurate linguistic description of uncategorized sense data, those who held the alternative view emphasized the role that concepts play in the construction of original experience. They believed that primary experience consists of organized and meaningful appearances. Pure, uncategorized sense data are not actually given in experience, they said; the "sensa" themselves are abstract, constructed from what is given. Experience is built from interaction with one's conceptual framework and with the environment. Moreover, there is a continuity of conceptualization and observation, and thus all observation is relative to the category system one accepts. This does not mean, however, that experience is pure subjectivity and that one merely projects a world. The category system does not prejudge, does not determine beforehand which category an object is to be put into. For example, two people with varying category systems may look at the same figure and see it differently; in Figure 4 one may see an antelope while the other sees a pelican.[42]

In postulating that observation is theory-laden, these writers appeal to Gestalt psychology and its use of "unstable" figures, such as the Necker cube (see Figure 4).[43] The conceptual apparatus which infects or builds an observational field varies culturally as well as individually. The Irish of a few hundred years ago observed Druids in the forests. It is only if one holds that there is an absolute-category-free data base of pure sensation that one can make the judgment that what one observes has been cleansed from projections and believe that others have "really" experienced the same sensations and have merely misinterpreted them. Those who held the alternative view argued that one cannot go beyond an interpreted experience to

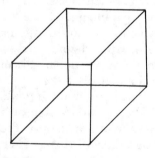

Figure 4. Gestalt Figures

sensation, for our most primary experience is already organized and interpreted.

(2) *Meanings are theory-dependent.* The received view, in order to link various laws deductively, required that if a term was used within the axiomatic system its meaning would be consistent throughout that system. If the meaning of the term changed, depending on context, then the logical linkage of statements using the term would be suspect. Adherents of the alternative view held that theory terms do vary from theory to theory. In addition to the kind of shift in meaning that occurs when technical terms are used in different contexts, there is also a shift when terms from ordinary language, with their pregiven meaning histories, are incorporated into theories. For example, the word *force* changes meaning when it becomes a term in the law of gravitation and the word *significant* takes on a particular connotation when used in the language game of statistics.

Not only are the meanings of terms dependent on the theories into which they are incorporated, but they may also vary from theory to theory.[44] The words *drive* and *learning*, for example, change their meanings, depending upon the theoretical contexts in which they are placed. Consequently, scientific activity cannot assume clear ostensive referents which remain the same in all observation statements that contain these terms. And the same is true for references to such unobservables as *electron* and *force*; neither of these terms retains a single, unambiguous meaning across the theoretical contexts in which it appears.

(3) *Facts are theory-laden.* Adherents of the alternative view questioned the supposition that there is an objective set of facts independent of theoretical assumptions that can be used to test various theories which seek to explain the same events. The argument ran as follows: Facts are not a peculiar sort of activity; facts are what statements state. They are the end products of observation. One observes something and then states that what one has observed is true, that it is a fact. It follows, however, that to the extent that languages differ in what they are able to express they will also differ in the facts that they can assert. Moreover, one's prior knowledge and beliefs, including one's conceptual apparatus, will determine what one experiences as facts. It is impossible to express facts in a language that is neutral. Thus, those things one takes as facts are related to the world view in which one organizes one's experience. And a world view contains theoretical assumptions about reality. We cannot get to purely objective facts which exist independently of human experience, and since human experience is already theory-laden, we do not have access to objective facts.

The alternative view served as a corrective to the received view, and it pointed out cultural effects on scientific activity. Various contexts describe reality differently, and thus all attempts to acquire pure *epistēmē*—knowledge of things as they really are—are futile, because such knowledge is beyond the reach of the scientific enterprise. However, the fourth phase went beyond the recognition of these limits and has been labeled as a "relativism" by writers such as Shapere.[45] It contended that all perspectives were equal in their attempts to approach knowledge. Statements do not progress—that is, they do not become more adequate descriptions of reality—through historical development, and there are no criteria by means of which to judge various contemporary statements. History is not progress, it is merely change; and one opinion or language game is as good as another. Even if a particular language game was more accurate, there would be no way to know this, since in order to make such a judgment, one would have to find "truth" and make a comparison.

The Fifth Phase: Historical Realism

Suppe calls the fifth (and latest) phase "historical realism" because it accepts the insight of the *Weltanschauung* position that science is a human activity which takes place in various *historical* contexts and is not a process of formal logic attaining timeless truths. Yet this new phase does not agree that being historical necessarily implies that various scientific statements are "true" only for their contexts. It holds, instead, that science makes cognitive progress toward more accurate descriptions of *reality*.

During the late 1960s and the early 1970s, it was thought that a viable replacement for the received view would be some sort of world-view analysis like that described as the fourth phase. But the key tenets of those proposals have themselves gradually come under attack by a number of authors, including Dudley Shapere, Gerard Radnitzky, Larry Laudan, and Stephen Toulmin (in his later work).[46] Suppe contends that contemporary philosophy of science, although it has been strongly influenced by *Weltanschauungen* views, has gone beyond them and is heading in new directions.[47]

The fifth phase, which has roots in the 1960s, is still in its beginning stages, although there has been an intensification of effort since 1975. It is characterized by a renewed belief that science does work, that it provides reliable information about the world, and that it is consequently one of the paradigms of human effort to gain knowledge or truths about the physical, psychological, and social realms. Science does far more than make knowledge claims that are coherent within a system; it seeks to say something that corresponds to "how things really are."

The hope of the philosophers of the fifth phase is that a reexamination of science will reveal those essential features which allow it to produce knowledge. There is a reaffirmation of the view that science is a model that yields absolute truth. Consequently, the philosophers of the fifth phase believe that science should be reexamined so that its real knowledge-producing procedures can be retained—those procedures which were missed by logical positivism with its commitments to absolute certainty and deductive logic.

What is showing through in this new examination is that the central and most characteristic activity of science is the use of various patterns of reason rather than simply logic. It is through the processes of reasoning that hypotheses are suggested and developed, and it is through the processes of reasoning that knowledge claims are evaluated. Among contemporary philosophers of science it is believed that the core of scientific activity is to be found in these patterns of reasoning that come into play in postulating and evaluating hypotheses. The patterns of reasoning yield conclusions that go beyond the logical entailments of deductive logic. These patterns are "different systems of rules of the scientific game,"[48] and deductive logic is merely one pattern of rationality.

Imre Lakatos and Stephen Toulmin (in his more recent work) attempt to steer a middle course between the *Weltanschauungen* and the patterns-of-reasoning approaches. Lakatos has described an enlarged reasoning pattern to account for the way in which some scientific research programs may have developed. He has limited himself to just one pattern in his descriptions of the growth of scientific knowledge, however, and often science employs other patterns of reasoning as well, patterns which are incompatible with the one he describes. His pattern applies a corrective to what he says is Popper's "simple falsification,"[49] and he labels his own pattern a "sophisticated falsificationism." As a reasoning pattern, falsificationism is an alternative to "verificationism" and "inductive inference." It retains a skepticism toward scientific statements of law because they can never be proved; they can only be falsified by negation. This reasoning pattern from Popper lies within the deductive-logic mode, but Lakatos expands the notion and uses it to describe a kind of rational pattern which leads scientists to make problem-shifts to more progressive research programs. A program is more progressive if it is more comprehensive, if it predicts and explains "new facts" and resolves inconsistencies or "blank spots" in the old program which it replaces. The reasoning pattern used to create change works, then, at the level of a research program rather than at the level of an individual hypothesis.[50]

Toulmin's *Human Understanding* (1972), the first volume in a projected three-volume series, approaches science as an enterprise in which concepts evolve and change in competition with other concepts. Those concepts which are more fruitful and provide increased understanding survive while others fall away. Toulmin also employs an expanded idea of rationality in his attempt to understand scientific activity:

> The rationality of natural science and other collective disciplines has nothing intrinsically to do with formal entailments and contradiction, inductive logic, or the probability calculus.

> We are free to abandon . . . the philosophers' traditional assumption that rationality is a sub-species of logicality.

> It is arguable that the rationality of intellectual performances should be judged . . . by considering, not the internal consistency of a man's habitual concepts and beliefs, but rather the manner in which he modifies this intellectual position in the face of new and unforeseen experiences.[51]

Toulmin expands rationality to include problem-solving activity and the decision to replace a concept with a more useful alternative. Rationality, he says, is considered with the generation of conceptual novelties and strategies of change as well as with the analysis of static relationships.

Dudley Shapere's work is in progress and will probably undergo further revision and refinement. He approaches science as a historically developing human activity that has achieved some increased understanding of reality. He holds that what science has to offer those who seek knowledge is a variety of reasoning patterns that can be used to solve conceptual and knowledge problems. If we look at the evolution of the "extremely weird beliefs about the world" which we presently hold, we can discover how and why they have rationally developed and changed. Science has used various reasoning patterns and methodologies during its history. In fact, the development of improved patterns of reasoning—those not previously used in the context of science—has been integral to the development of science itself. "We learn how to learn as we learn," Shapere says.[52] Thus, science is not a fixed and finished method; its basic problem is its own development and improvement. As it develops knowledge and runs up against its limits, it seeks to expand those limits, to gain greater understanding and a greater degree of surety. It does this by varying its patterns of reason and by incorporating this new rationality into its own system.

Charles S. Peirce

With the disintegration of the deductive system, with its emphasis on the analysis of how theories are justified rather than on how they are constructed (discovered), many philosophers of science have returned to ideas about science which were developed before the victory of logical positivism during the 1920s. One of the richest sources of ideas for a postpositivist standpoint has been American pragmatism and especially the work of Charles S. Peirce. References to Peirce's ideas appear in the writings of Paul Ricoeur, Jürgen Habermas, Karl-Otto Apel, Gerard Radnitzky, and others.[53] Peirce gave lectures on the logic of science at Harvard as early as 1864, and he continued writing until his death in 1914. His thought has a contemporary ring to it, and it has been taken up again and made part of the current debate about the nature of science in general and the nature of human science in particular.

Like the present-day developers of the alternatives to the received view, Peirce held that science is not "systematized knowledge" but the pursuit itself in which scientists are engaged. His focus of inquiry was not centered on completed articles or on the logic of justification used to defend theories. Instead, he investigated the process of scientific activity. He did not reduce the role of methodology to the logical analysis of scientific theories; instead he identified methodology with the explication of the procedures used to obtain theories. Science, he said, must not be thought of as a mere collection of established truths; it must be conceived of "as a living historic entity" and regarded "as the occupation of that peculiar class of men, the scientific men."[54]

For Peirce, the understanding of what science is requires an examination of the motives of scientists themselves. He held that the scientist is motivated by the pure love of truth and pursues knowledge for the sake of knowledge alone. Peirce distinguished between scientists and practical men. The practical man, he said, is concerned with action and results, and for the practical man to act, he must believe "with all the force of his manhood" that the goal of his action is good and that his plan of action is right. But scientists are so interested in truth that they are willing to reject their present beliefs if experience demands it. "This is the reason that a good practical man cannot do the best scientific work. The temperaments requisite for the two kinds of business are altogether contrary to one another."[55] Because of the quest for truth, the scientist is bound to come upon the right method of proceeding. And because of the commitment to truth, the scientist is attentive to the self-corrective character of the inquiry. "No matter how erroneous your ideas of the method may be at first, you will be forced at length to correct them so long as your activity is moved by that sincere desire."[56] What constitutes science, then, is not so much correct conclusions as a correct method. "But the method of science is itself a scientific result. It did not spring from the brain of a beginner: it was a historic attainment and scientific achievement."[57]

In Peirce's view, a scientist begins an inquiry because of a genuine doubt about something. Peirce rejected the Cartesian notion that one can pretend to doubt everything as an intellectual exercise. The doubt must be real and living, the result of a puzzling event, Peirce said. Doubt originating in the events of one's life leaves one perplexed and unable to act, and so it incites one to inquire into it and seek its explanation.

Eagerness to "find out," generated by a genuine doubt, must be directed according to a method that will best meet the scientist's desire for the truth. Historically, Peirce noted, people have responded in four ways to their need to know. The first way, the poorest way, is the method of tenacity in which one clings steadfastly to the beliefs one already holds. This way represents a refusal to venture into ideas that might disturb one's opinion. The second way is the method of authority in which one assumes that one should believe what one is told by institutions. This way discourages thinking and forbids private investigation. The third way is the a priori method in which one figures out the answer to the doubt through the use of reason alone, independently of observed facts. The fourth way, the most satisfactory way, is the scientific method. This way, Peirce maintained, appeals to nature, both real and public, and will lead every inquirer to the same conclusion. "Experience," he said, "will be the occasion for wonder about nature, and nature herself will ultimately supply the answer to this wonder."[58]

According to Peirce, the answers to all of one's questions will come from the observation of nature. Experience is the necessary beginning for all of our knowledge, since there is no human knowledge that is not based on observed facts. "All knowledge whatever comes from observation," he said.[60] In a brief reference to Mach, however, he complained that Mach "allows thought no other value than that of economizing experiences," and he insisted that the greatest emphasis should be placed on thought, noting that sensation is valueless except as a vehicle for thought. In Peirce's concept, then, observation refers to more than pure perception; observation is perception buttressed by thought and analysis.

Research, to Peirce, was "conversation with nature," and conversation requires intelligence on the part of the investigator. Science joins experience with reasoning, even in the initial observation stage. The starting point of a reasonable inquiry is not the sense impression but the percept. In this conception, we observe the external world directly. We are not like the old-fashioned telephone operator who was isolated from the world but received reports which came through the switchboard as sensa.

Abduction

Like Hanson and Polanyi in their more recent work, Peirce believed that science should be as concerned with the process of discovery as with the process of justification. He saw science as a dialectical interaction between these two processes. The process of discovery begins with the shock of an experience which does not fit into one's system of thought and sets off doubt. A problem arises when the uniformity of nature which one thinks one has understood is disrupted by an experience that causes one to question and change previous understanding. One then begins a scientific inquiry with a conjecture (a hypothesis) which attempts to explain the disrupting phenomenon. Peirce used the term *abduction* to designate the mental activity by means of which the hypothesis is formed. He also called this activity *retroduction, presumption,* and *hypothesis* (i.e., hypothesizing). This is a living process that occurs in the minds of scientists.

The two main functions of science are the framing and testing of conjectures. "Science itself, the living process," Peirce said, "is busied mainly with conjectures, which are either getting framed or getting tested."[60] Science is therefore distinct from thoroughly established truths. In opposition to Hume, Peirce emphasized that our knowledge is not derived from experience alone: "Every item of science came originally from conjecture, which has only been pruned down by experience. . . . The entire matter of our works of solid science consists of conjectures checked by experience. . . . Abduction . . . furnishes the reasoner with the problematic theory which induction verifies."[61] Abduction is one of three types of inference, the other two being deduction and induction. Abduction is the process of suggesting a hypothesis which can serve as an explanation of what has appeared as puzzling.[62]

A conjecture must be connected with the observed facts so that if it is correct it will explain the observations or "save the appearances." Peirce disagreed with the Comtean positivists who maintained that a legitimate hypothesis must be susceptible to direct verification. His position was closer to that of the later logical positivists, who held that theory is an inference transferred from the directly observed to the unobserved. The progress of science, he believed, must be attributed to the human intellect which, fed with the facts of experience, introduces new ideas. Science moves beyond the given of sense data by originating ideas—through imagination—which provide explanations for puzzling events. "It remains true," Peirce said, "that there is, after all, nothing but imagination that can ever supply [the inquirer] with an inkling of the truth. He can stare stupidly at phenomena; but in the absence of imagination they will not connect themselves together in any rational way."[63] Abduction only suggests what may be the case, but what it suggests allows the events to be seen in a different way so that new connections will be noticed. The ideas of understanding originate in the mind.

In the operation of abduction—the "seeing" of possible connections through the use of imagination—there are some requirements that the suggested explanations must meet. Most importantly, the hypothesis must be susceptible to testing. Peirce offered some practical considerations for this principle of testability. Some hypotheses can be eliminated as unsuitable right at the start without testing them, he said, and some will be impossible to test because time and money will not be available. "The best hypothesis, in the sense of the one most recommending itself to the inquirer, is the one which can be the most readily refuted if it is false."[64] But there are other considerations as well: the choice of hypothesis should be determined by its effect on other projects, and a balance between inclusiveness and manageability needs to be maintained. The hypothesis should also be a reasoned or likely explanation of the facts; it should not be an ill-formed guess. It should be something that can be played out in the imagination before it is submitted to experimental testing.

Peirce proposed that an investigator instinctively imagines the correct hypothesis, and he related the investigator's instinct to the instincts of animals. Animals, he said, must "comprehend" their environments in order to guide their activities of feeding and breeding. Correct ideas are needed for survival. Peirce, however, only noted the power of instinct in this regard; he did not exaggerate it. He believed that instinctive guesses are less important than reasoned guesses that are informed by the investigator's "progress in science." All the same, he recognized an element of spontaneity in the "intuitive" leaps that are part of the abductive process.

Peirce held that abductive and perceptual judgments are closely connected and that there is no sharp line of demarcation between them. In his view, there are four important similarities between the processes of perception and abduction. First, they are both seeking to gain a knowledge of the general elements of the world. Perception identifies an object as a member of a class ("That object is a ball"), and abduction makes a conjecture which places an individual in a class (or sometimes in a less extensive class within a more extensive class). Second, perception and abduction are both beyond the control of reflection. Both occur by means of "flash of insight, by the use of imagination, somewhat outside the influence of reason." But while the perceptual judgment is not subject to criticism—for it is the ultimate premise for reason—the abductive judgment is required to be submissible to reasoned testing. Third, there are elements of originality in both perception and abduction. Perception (unlike remembrance) presents the world anew with each look, and abduction is the only form of reason that presents new ideas to science. Abduction leads to a hypothesis not given before (or in the same way before) which will explain observed facts. Fourth, perception and abduction are acts of interpretation. Two examples used by Peirce were the drawing which is seen at first as a serpentine line, then as a stone wall, and the optical illusion which may be seen as steps either ascending or descending. Perceptual judgment abstracts certain features from the object to give it an appearance, but this appearance does not exhaust the meaning of the object. The knowledge grasped in the perceptual judgment is only one of several possible pieces of knowledge. Nevertheless, the perceptual judgment is true in the sense that "it is impossible to correct it, and in the fact that it only professes to consider one aspect of the percept."[65] Abduction is also an interpretation in the sense that it offers a possible explanation of certain events by limiting them to members of a class.

Both perception and abduction classify according to the observer's point of view. Thus, an experienced observer will hit upon the right hypothesis sooner than the inexperienced observer—other things being equal—and the scientist with keener insight and more agile imagination will be more successful than his or her fellows in developing the right guess. The inquirer's ability and experience make important contributions to the way the observations are interpreted. The personal background of the inquirer and the history of the science concerned are important in providing themes for interpreting the phenomena. The interpretation in perception is basically certain and undeniable, but the interpretation in abduction is tentative and often in error. In abduction—but not in perception—interpretation or classification of the objects is not wholly given in the phenomena, and the inquirer can imagine various explanations for what is observed.

Deduction and Induction. In the scientific process, once a conjecture is generated which can possibly explain the puzzle, it needs to be submitted to verifiability testing. After an explanatory hypothesis capable of being tested has been chosen, the investigator deduces experiential predictions from it and then watches for the predictions to be fulfilled. The deductive phase generates observable predictions from the hypothesis.

The next phase of scientific work is induction. Induction is a process that evaluates the proximity of the hypothesis to the facts produced in the experimental test. If the hypothesis is correct, it will explain "an infinite number" of possible observations. Since not all of the observations can be made, a "haphazard specimen of all the predictions which might be based on the hypothesis" is made. Induction treats the limited number of observations, and from them it projects back upon the hypothesis a probability that it is true. Most likely, the hypothesis will not be accurate and will have to be modified somewhat to meet the recommendations of induction. The modification results from the testing and from a new abduction. The modified hypothesis will then have to be submitted to the same sort of testing again.

For the process of induction to be valid, two conditions must be met. First, the investigator must specify, before the observations are made, what they will be if the hypothesis is correct. The actual observations are then compared to the projected observations. For example, if the conjecture states that 75 percent of athletes will retire from competition before they reach the age of 25, and if 100 observations are to be made, the investigator "predesignates" that 75 of the athletes will be observed as retired. Second, the investigator must observe instances that constitute a "fair sample" of the class. The principle used is statistical inference, which states that a representative sample of a class is one that probably exhibits a given characteristic in about the same ratio as the whole class from which the sample is drawn.

Peirce identified three main phases in the inductive process: the classification phase, the probation phase, and the sentential phase. In the classification phase, the observations have to be recognized as the sorts of things that have been predicted by the hypothesis.

In the probation phase, the investigator must observe how many times what the hypothesis has predicted actually occurs within the total number of observations. In some cases, this is merely a matter of counting instances—for example, it is easy to note that in 100 trials the predicted observation has occured 56 times—and Peirce referred to this counting as "quantitative induction." In other cases, which Peirce called "qualitative induction," an estimate is required of the importance of the various characteristics of the class which is being observed. As an example of qualitative induction, Peirce chose a case where the hypothesis that a certain man is a priest is being tested. In this instance, the inquirer must put more value on the man's role in ceremonial functions than on the style of clothing he wears. In the sentential phase, the investigator must make a judgment of the value of the proposed hypothesis based on the probations. An inductive conclusion that the predictions of a hypothesis are probably about 90 percent correct becomes the basis for affirming that the hypothesis itself is about 90 percent correct.

Peirce's consensus theory of truth. In Peirce's definition, as we have seen, science is one of the methods for responding to puzzlement by attempting to discover the truth. Knowledge gained through the scientific method, while it is of greater value than knowledge achieved through the methods of tenacity, authority, and preconceived ideas, is still subject to error and still always open to further attempts at perfection. Peirce repeatedly and firmly asserted that scientific knowledge is not a completely certain and adequate representation of its object. It never arrives at an absolute and final description of the universe. He used the term *fallibilism* to stress that scientific knowledge is limited. At the same time, however, he maintained that science is the best knowledge we have and that the method of science is the only reliable method of settling opinion. He did not distrust science: he placed great confidence in it, and he held that it does converge on truth, i.e., on an accurate description of reality.

In his attitude toward science, Peirce was close to the position taken by Achinstein, Shapere, Scheffler, and others who believe that the world-view position of the fourth phase went too far in historicizing and relativizing and, consequently, devaluing scientific achievement. These contemporary scholars hold that science, although it does not provide the certainty of knowledge which was the aim and the claim of the received view, does nevertheless provide knowledge which converges on truth. One of the reasons that Peirce's ideas are being reconsidered at this time is that the position he held, even though he wrote more than eighty years ago, is a source for ideas used by many present-day writers—those writers who belong to the fifth phase. A major issue for these writers and for other contemporary philosophers of science is how the matter of truth is to be settled if one cannot appeal to an absolute ground of certainty such as the sensa or logical operations. Peirce's answer to this question was that the locus for settling truth claims should be "the mind of the community." Habermas has shown particular interest in this idea as he has developed his own "discourse theory of truth."[66]

In Peirce's formulation, the method of the sciences produces a fallible result. Knowledge gained through scientific inquiry cannot be absolutely exact, absolutely universal, or absolutely certain.[67] Although the scientific method gradually converges on truth, it never really achieves a final and completely certain statement of truth. The closure is not final: genuine doubt may open the same questions again and start new processes of inquiry. There is always the possibility of error in the process. What science produces, then, is confidence or belief in its results. It is on the basis of our beliefs in what the world is like that we act, and since there is a difference between what the world is "really" like and our beliefs concerning what it is like, our activity may be misdirected and may not achieve the desired results. Then doubt about our beliefs arises, and this in turn leads to activity designed to revise the beliefs so that they will more closely resemble the real world. Science is the method which provides the best alternative for bringing belief into closer conformity with reality. Peirce used Kant's term *pragmatic* to describe his theory that it is our belief system of the world in which meaning is located. Meaning is not located in a direct reference between word and world, Peirce said, and he quoted from Kant's *Critique of Pure Reason*: "Contingent belief, which yet forms the ground for the actual employment of means to certain actions, I entitle 'pragmatic belief.'"[68]

Peirce held that science is concerned with real things which exist outside the mind and are independent of any individual's knowledge of them:

> I define the "real" as that which holds its characters on such a tenure that it makes not the slightest difference what any man or men may have thought them to be, or ever will have "thought" them to be, here using thought to include imagining, opining, and willing (as long as forcible "means" are not used); but the real thing's characters will remain absolutely untouched.[69]

Science is realistic, rather than nominalistic—that is, it is concerned to develop knowledge about real classes of objects. These classes are real; they are not merely the invention of the knower. Reality affects the knower (in this, Peirce is at odds with Kant's concept of *noumena* which in inaccessible to the mind), and it is knowable through its effect on the knower. "Experience supposes," Peirce said, "that its object reacts upon us with some strength, much or little, so that it has a certain grade of reality or independence of our cognitive exertion."[70] The object is independent of the knower, and yet it influences the knower. If reality were so unrelated to thought as to be incognizable, then all methods for attempting to know, including science, would be useless.

Peirce maintained that thought approaches a greater knowledge of the real through the means of public investigation and cooperative reasoning. (This view stands directly opposite the Cartesian view that individual consciousness is the test of certainty.) Because the object of knowledge exists independently of the knower, it remains the same when viewed by various individuals, although each individual view is limited. The object is knowable, however, and thus the various views and reasoning about the object over time are corrected by the manner in which reality responds to the activity we engage in, activity which is based on our beliefs.

> The real, then, is that which, sooner or later, information and reasoning would finally result in, and which is therefore independent of the vagaries of me and you. Thus, the very origin of the conception of reality shows that this conception essentially involves the notion of a COMMUNITY, without definite limits, and capable of a definite increase of knowledge. And so those two series of cognition—the real and the unreal—consist of those which, at a time sufficiently future, the community will always continue to re-affirm; and of those which under the same conditions, will ever after be denied.[71]

So the state of complete knowledge is an ideal which represents the goal toward which science strains, although the goal is never actually attained. In such an idealized state, thought about reality would actually describe reality, and this perfect knowledge would be reflected in the common understanding of the community. In such an idealized state, there would be no difference between the real and the community's thought about it.

The real world would then be the object of ultimate public agreement. If a proposed reality is truly real, investigators would, in the end, agree on it. Although the condition "if public agreement is ultimately reached" is counterfactual, it provides a meaningful way of understanding the condition which is not this perfection, for it is the never-achieved condition which gives meaning to the present attempts at arriving at knowledge. The real is not the result of investigation, it is the object which investigation continually strives to represent. And because reality is independent of mind, truth cannot be different to different people. Truth must be public. It may be that some false propositions are held as true for many generations, but such "ignorance cannot affect what would be the result of sufficient experience and reasoning. And this it is which is meant by the final settled opinion, . . . and it directly satisfies the definition of reality."[72]

In the nonideal state in which we exist, then, scientific activity converges toward truth. There is no final grasp of the ultimate and exact state of reality. Our methods of knowing do not provide direct access to reality, and so we have to continue to refine our knowledge. Our methods have the limitations of inductive reasoning, and thus, while our observations can continually grow in accuracy, the inductive inferences made from the observations are open to error. More fundamental than the limits to inductive inferences is the fallibility of perceptual judgment which provides the basic observations and correctives to the abductive inferences. Although we cannot doubt a perception at will, it is reformable; something we have always perceived as being in a particular class may be noticed differently on some occasion, and we discover that we have been wrong about what we have conceived it to be. Consequently, no series of perceptual judgments can be regarded as certain and beyond any further change.

There is no hope of eliminating all error, Peirce said. Yet the method of science does settle public arguments over belief. And since it is a method of self-correction, the beliefs it produces approach accuracy of description over time. The goal of a complete agreement between belief and reality, although never achieved, can be approached over time through the community's use of the scientific method.

Gerard Radnitzky

Gerard Radnitzky is one of the important figures in the development of the renewed effort to view science as a legitimate approach to knowledge, an approach that provides cognitive progress through the reasonable comparison of rival theories. While working in Sweden, Radnitzky produced the three-volume *Contemporary Schools of Metascience* (1968–1973). He has since taught at the University of Trier in West Germany, and his more recent thought is contained in a paper titled "Disappointment and Changes in the Conception of Rationality: Wittgenstein and Popper."[73]

Both instrumentalists and realists hold that theories are instruments for producing predictions and explanations, but instrumentalists claim that theories do not represent certain aspects of reality (or if they do, we cannot know it)—that, instead, theories are merely mental concepts which are useful in making predictions; while realists hold that theories consist of true or false statements referring to "real" or "existing" entities. By abandoning the postulate of realism, the proponents of instrumentalism give up truth as a regulative principle of scientific inquiry. In the historicist or world-view approach to science, this can lead—as it did in the case of Feyerabend—to a denial of the possibility of any methodology of research and to the dismissal of the problem of rational theory appraisal. If there is no standard of truth or reference to reality, then there is no way to judge reasonably the adequacy of a theory other than that it produces accurate predictions.

Radnitzky maintained that the pessimism and relativism of the instrumentalist approach is too strong and that realism is a more accurate way to understand scientific theory. Science works to solve problems by providing a real description of the world.

> I would claim that (1) insofar as a large proportion of scientific research exemplifies rational problem solving, . . . [and insofar as] our aim is to improve our theories about empirical reality and thereby also our world picture, then all research enterprises indeed share some common features . . . "conjecturing and criticizing." (2) The researcher has to act as methodologist on his own, whether he knows it or not. He certainly has to take the final decision himself and on his own responsibility.[74]

He goes on to propose that the researcher, by articulating his methodology, has a chance to be criticized and consequently to be improved. This does not mean that there is an authoritarian, approved methodology; it means that the research approach can be judged according to rational considerations without being expected to conform to an "approved" model.

Radnitzky chooses Popper's criticist attitude—that is, an approach which provides a rationale for provisionally preferring a theory over its rival(s), or a particular course of practical action over other possible moves or ways of conduct. Radnitzky opposes the *Weltanschauungen* claim that we are prisoners of intellectual frameworks and can make, at best, only an irrational leap from one framework to another. The philosopher of science, in that case, can do no more than describe the various language games.[75] Popper has shown why this approach, which he calls "the myth of the framework," is mistaken. He holds that we can sometimes—or even often—eliminate errors and make cognitive progress by participating in other "frameworks" and by subjecting our own language games to critical examination—that is, by holding all of our views, theories, and standards, in principle, open to criticism and by demonstrating a willingness to learn from our errors.

Radnitzky supports the critical attitude for providing a realistic conception of the human capacity to know. It takes the place of the overoptimistic conception that there are absolute foundations (sense and formal logic) upon which knowledge can be based and the overpessimistic conception of the relativist-historicist proponents. He believes that the relativist-historicist position and the foundationalist position share a common conception with Descartes that only certain knowledge is genuine knowledge (*epistēmē*).[76] The third way, the criticalist approach, offered in the fifth phase, holds that it is nonetheless possible to attain cognitive progress, even though human knowledge about empirical reality is, in principle, fallible. It was Peirce who introduced the term *fallibilism* and developed a criticalist approach, but Popper has improved the approach and is now its chief advocate in the philosophy of science. Fallibilism is concerned with the procedures which may be used for determining whether there are good reasons for conjecturing that one theory is more truthlike than another. It recognizes the fundamental historicity (the time-boundness) of all reports of empirical testing, but it also recognizes the concept of timeless truth in its attitude toward error and empirical testing.[77]

Criticism needs to be distinguished from justification. In justification, a particular statement is established as having a certain degree of probability. The idea of confirmation or inductive support on the basis of certain observations is a type of ampliative inference that provides a probability index of the extent to which the observations might be logically derived from the hypothesis. In criticism, there is no attempt to prove a theory to be true or to provide it with a degree of confirmation. There is no objective procedure within criticism for determining that a particular theory has a specific degree of probability or inductive support. Probability confirmation is based on the idea that the regularities described by the theory will hold for the future. In criticism, it is considered rational to adopt a belief in the theory and to act upon it because the theory has been severely tested, not because there is a high degree of inductive probability. The theory is believed in because it has better stood up to empirical testing than its competitors have; therefore it is conjectured that the theory is superior to its rivals in truthlikeness.

Radnitzky summarizes the critical approach of rational appraisal in regard to two competing theories:

> The methodologically most interesting situation in theory appraisal is the situation in which a *rational preference* has to be established *between two rival theories both of which* are not free from "difficulties"—i.e., which *have, strictly speaking, to be considered false* or, more accurately, *discorroborated for the time being*. Therefore, in practice, the concept of "being more truthlike than the competing theory or theories" serves as regulative principle. . . . The intuitive idea of one theory being a more accurate or less accurate description than a rival theory is absolutely indispensable in methodology as it is in daily life.[78]

Comparative corroboration of a theory rests on whether the theory has weathered criticism better than its rival(s), not on whether it has a higher degree of confirmation. Degree of confirmation is strictly a logical process and does not depend on rational decision. The belief that one statement is more truthlike than another does not mean that it is epistemologically certain. Criticism is not grounded in epistemological givens; it operates at the level of rational decision. To equate individual commitments based on rational criticism with statements relating to "truth" or epistemologically grounded statements would be to perpetrate a psychologistic fallacy; to regard consensus, the conviction of the majority, as equivalent to "truth" would be to perpetrate a sociologic fallacy.[79]

Evolutionary Epistemology

The analogy between biological evolution and the growth (evolution) of knowledge has been used by those who emphasize rational choice, rather than pure logic, as the essence of science. Peirce, who was strongly influenced by evolutionism, held that scientific knowledge has evolved through trial and error. Donald T. Campbell has proposed a natural selection model of conceptual evolution and has termed his approach "evolutionary epistemology."[80] Karl Popper has also described his approach as evolutionary (as in *Objective Knowledge: An Evolutionary Approach*), and Stephen Toulmin, in *Human Understanding* (1972), has used an evolutionary metaphor in his analysis of the historical development of concepts.

In scientific research, as in general human problem-solving activity, there are conjectures and innovative steps which correspond to variations and mutations at the biological level. The variations are the changes in human concepts. These changes, however, are not random; they comply with the requirements of minimal logic (for example, the requirement of internal consistency), and they are influenced by our background knowledge, our expectations, our world outlooks, our ideals for science, and so on. Corresponding to the pressures of natural selection are the attempts at criticism, including attempts at falsification. Survival value corresponds to the ability of a concept or theory to weather attempts of rival theories to replace older ones because it is held to be more truthlike after critical appraisal. (However, past survival does not guarantee future survival.) The selection process is the rational theory preference process in which conjectures interact with criticism in the form of severe empirical testing.

So long as the evolutionary idea is retained as a metaphor for scientific development, it is an appropriate model for historical realism. At times, however, the metaphor has slipped out of control and has been used to suggest that scientific development is necessary for biological survival and the evolution of the human species.[81] Toulmin speaks to this point:

> It will not be necessary to assume . . . that intellectual evolution has something "biological" about it, or even that the process of conceptual change in the sciences displays any substantial resemblance to the process of organic change. We shall be committed only to a more modest hypothesis, namely, that Darwin's populational theory of "variation and natural selection" is one illustration of a more general form of historical explanation.[82]

In the evolutionary analogy, concepts of science are not primarily statements judged by the criteria of an abstract logical system. Instead, they are conjectures about reality which are submitted to test by the rationality involved in practical human judgments. According to Toulmin:

> Rationality is an attribute, not of logical or conceptual systems as such, but of the human activities or enterprises of which particular sets of concepts are the temporary cross-sections: specifically, of the procedures by which the concepts, judgments, and formal systems currently accepted in those enterprises are criticized and changed.[83]

Toulmin criticizes Kuhn's presentation of evolutionary change because it does not account for the continuity in change. Kuhn's presentation treats conceptual change as a sequence of radical switches between rationally incommensurable positions.[84] The necessity for acknowledging both change and continuity in the history of science requires acknowledging the possibility of conceptual variation and rational critique of the variations available.

Summary

Historical realism understands science as a rational process in which reason is presumed to be a practical problem-solving action. This notion of reason comprises much more than deductive inference, for science is a human activity in which we seek to understand our world through conjecture and refutation. We are not able to prove that a conjecture is certain; all conjectures are fallible and subject to rejection in competition with other hypotheses. The choice between which conjectures are kept and which are rejected is influenced by the external history of science and by the internal history of empirical testing. This view of science is far removed from the kind of Cartesian science that held knowledge up to the standard of absolute certainty. The original debate as to the nature of a methodology for human science was framed within the context of the Cartesian model and the Humean, Kantian, and Machian versions of that model; however, that model itself has become problematic.

The reformulation of science that is being developed in historical realism is attempting to overcome the relativism and pessimism of the *Weltanschauung* reaction to logical positivism. The recent renewal of the human science debate has heralded the "new paradigm" notion of the *Weltanschauung* position. Because this approach is basically an anti-science and nonmethod stance, however, it does not provide a new methodological position for human science. The historical realism attempt seems to offer a more realistic comprehension of the human acquisition of knowledge and understanding. It provides a new template for cooperative discussions between the supposed "two cultures," the "sciences" and the "humanities," in which we might find that knowing about human phenomena is not so different from knowing in general. Historical realism does not place science into a deductive-sensation position, it opens up knowing to the whole human repertoire of judgment and action.

The next three chapters will take up other systems of inquiry that have developed since 1950 outside the mainstream of the philosophy of science. The field of linguistics has provided a system of structuralism which has been taken up by anthropology and literature. Biology and engineering have prepared an organic or systems approach. The philosophical thought in Wittgenstein's later work has stimulated the system-of-action theory. And the renewal of hermeneutic theory in Europe has brought into being renewed efforts toward an interpretive system of inquiry.

4

Systems and Structures

The last two chapters have focused on the discussion that has been concerned with the relationship between scientific findings and "reality," a discussion that has revolved around the question: Does science give trustworthy information about the world? Of additional interest for the construction of a methodology for human science are the parallel conceptual developments that have been concerned with ways in which to approach the objects and processes that science studies. This chapter deals with the idea that complex objects or systems are best approached as wholes with interacting parts, rather than through an analysis of the constituent parts.

Holism was first advocated for the study of organic systems, but the concept was later taken over for the study of linguistic and other social systems. This approach gives its attention to the organization or structure of a system and to the modes of information exchange that occur within the system and/or take place between it and its environment. We will begin with a review of the origins and the historical development of the holistic or systems approach.

Systems

There are examples in Greek and Roman literature where society is compared to a living body,[1] and an organic analogy was one of the emphases of the Romantic movement (for Herder and Rousseau, for instance), but it was Hegel's transformation of the analogy into a logical principle that strengthened the concept of holism. The idea was presented in Hegel's *Philosophy of Mind* (1817) and further developed in his *Philosophy of History*, published after his death in 1831.

Hegel was concerned with a principle of "internal relations," through which he sought to correct our common-sense conceptual framework. Hegel held that no particular constitutes a self-sufficient independent unit, that any particular is what it is only because it stands in relationship to other units, each of which to some degree modifies its nature, just as these are themselves modified in the process. Common-sense and scientific thinking make use of an analytic or mechanical type of thinking in which entities are understood to be unchanged by the relationships into which they enter. Hegel maintained that this type of thinking is incapable of recognizing internal relations in which entities *are* altered by the relationships into which they enter. He also spoke of another type of thinking that he called "reason," which is necessary for the comprehension of internal relations. He contrasted "reason" (*Vernunft*) or dialectical thinking with "understanding" (*Verstand*) or analysis. "Understanding," he said, is a more elementary stage of thought in which entities are placed in fixed categories, while "reason" moves toward completeness and considers entities to be fluid and constantly self-amending.[2]

The sort of thinking required for comprehending systems demands a different kind of logic than is used for understanding classes and relations between classes. Both deductive and inductive logic are based on the notion of classifying—that is, they use concepts as definitions that bind together entities that possess the characteristics of the concepts and exclude all others. For example, in regard to the concept "apple," one classifies all objects either as "apple" or as "nonapple." Concepts are then related to one another so that if an entity is an "apple," it is also a "fruit." This relating is accomplished through the use of Aristotle's logic of classification. The relating might also be done according to Russell's logic by observing that if an entity is an "apple," it is larger than an entity which is a "pea." Or it might be done using causal relation in which an entity is necessary and sufficient for the production of another entity. In all of these instances, the logic deals with relations between classes and entities. Writers concerned with comprehending the nature of organized wholes find that this traditional analytic logic is unable to deal with an entity whose nature is formed in relationship to a whole rather than in relationship to other entities.

Applying the various traditional types of logic to the example of an athletic team, analytic thinking would view the team as "nothing else than a collocation, mixture, heap, or the like."[3] The team would be defined as an adding-together of independent parts, and thus it would be assumed that the team could be understood by examining its parts. By contrast, the concept of internal relations recognizes that the team is more than a collection of parts. A new property— a new characteristic—appears as a result of the relationship of the parts which is created when the parts come together to form a team. In forming a team, the members of the team do not remain the same as they were when they existed in isolation; one of each member's new characteristics is a characteristic which is shared with each other team member, "team membership." Thus, a particular member of the team—Jim—is different from what he was before he became a team member, and if he leaves the team, he will not be the same as he is as long as he remains a member. Comprehension of the concept "team" requires the use of dialectical thinking, which recognizes the new form of wholeness and understands that it consists of more than the sum of the parts which make it up. The nature of the team cannot be deduced from the character of the individual parts, and the properties of the team can be discovered only by studying the team as a whole.

Another example which is often used to illustrate the concept that the whole is more than its parts—the concept of emergence—is water. A molecule of water is made up two parts of hydrogen and one part of oxygen. Studying the hydrogen atoms and the oxygen atom in isolation would not allow one to deduce what new property is formed when the atoms are combined. The hydrogen and the oxygen in combination produce a colorless, odorless, and tasteless liquid. The properties of this combination can be discovered only by studying the whole. By breaking down the whole into its parts and then examining these parts (analysis), one loses the qualities which are characteristic of the whole.

The logic of deduction is unable to account for emergent properties. The valid conclusion of a deductive argument cannot contain an expression that does not appear in the premises. Deduction, therefore, commits one to a static view of the universe since the tautological character of its logic assumes a realm of timeless truth. The structure of deductive argument prohibits its use in dealing with radical, deep change, mutation and discontinuous leaps. As described in chapter 2, scientific laws which provide the explanation of past events and the prediction of future events should be in the form of deductions. Emergent properties, however, cannot be deduced from premises that do not contain references to these properties. Through the scientific laws of deductive form, it would not be possible to conclude (predict) from premises that refer only to the properties of the gaseous elements hydrogen and oxygen that these elements will produce the colorless liquid—that is, that a new property will emerge. The study of emergent properties requires the use of a nondeductive logic—specifically, the logic of dialectic in which the parts are comprehended from the point of view of the whole.

A problem which arises with the use of dialectical thinking—focusing on the whole—is how to place boundaries around wholes. The extreme position holds that everything is part of the whole; this position has been held by the neo-Hegelians in England and the United States, particularly from 1890 to 1920 by Francis H. Bradley, Alfred E. Taylor, Bernard Bosanquet, and many others.[4] For adherents of this position, all relations are internal—that is, in the "universe"—and thus any treatment of an entity misses the emergent qualities which are present in the "all"; since parts cannot be comprehended when isolated from the whole, then all knowledge derived from a single aspect of reality is defective. Although this extreme position is no longer influential, it demonstrates the difficulties which arise when an attempt is made to establish boundaries around the wholes that are selected for study.

Organic Wholes

During the last quarter of the nineteenth century, the analytic approach to science was under attack from three directions: neo-Hegelian philosophers argued that the comprehension of the internal relations of wholes required the use of dialectical reason; neo-Kantian philosophers held that understanding human expression and meaning required the use of *Verstehen* (comprehension); and biologists maintained that the analytic approach was inadequate for dealing with organic entities and that holistic concepts must be used instead. All three of these attacks argued for the use of a kind of reason that could comprehend qualities which result from the interaction of elements—qualities that are not in the elements themselves but are present in the relations among the elements. For example, the new qualities of compounds emerge from the interaction pattern of chemicals; meaning emerges from the patterns or structures that exist between and among words; life emerges from the interaction of physical entities. In this climate emerged the notion of organicism, which is the precursor of systems theory.

The analytic approach was unable to explain the theory of evolution at the time of its introduction during the last half of the nineteenth century. Later, with the rediscovery of Mendel's work, the analytic approach was able to give an account of spontaneous variations in species by means of the changing combinations of elements in genes. Lacking such an explanation, biologists such as Hans Driesch held that there was a "life force" or a "creative urge" within individual organisms which produced variations. But the analytic approach was unable to account for this force, and doubts were raised about its effectiveness in explaining other phenomena. For instance, cells were discovered to be very complex entities, and this discovery came at a time when the analytic approach could not account for the way in which cells worked. Moreover, experiments carried out on developing embryos showed that when an embryo had a section removed, its development was altered from its normal course in such a way as to nullify, as far as possible, the effects of the damage from the sectioning. The question raised by these experiments concerned whether each cell was the unit of life or whether in some way the whole organism constituted a unit. Supporters of the analytic approach were not able to deal with the concept that the organism was a whole and that the cells engaged in a "cooperative" activity which served the whole.

The notion of qualities of the whole organism—qualities that were not accounted for by an analysis of its parts—implied several additions to ordinary science. Hans Driesch[5] called the quality of the whole "entelechy," a term taken from Aristotle's notion of "end" or "fullness"; it was this quality or vital force which "urged" the organism toward self-fulfillment and unified its activity. Entelechies are conceived as goal-directed nonphysical agents which affect the course of physiological events in such a way as to restore an organism to a more or less normal state. Henri Bergson and Samuel Butler[6] held a similar position. There were forces within living organisms which could not be accounted for by examining the various parts, they said, and these forces drove organisms onward toward developing new forms. They called their theory "creative evolution." In contrast to the theory of natural selection, which held that evolution was the result of forces in the environment, creative evolution placed the cause of evolution within the organism itself.

The concept that the organism possesses qualities in addition to the sum of its parts also raised questions about the traditional notion of cause and effect. The brothers R. B. and J. S. Haldane wrote in 1883:

> The physicochemical description of the vital processes does not exhaust them. . . . It would thus appear that the parts of an organism cannot be considered simply as so many independent units, which happen to be aggregated in a system in which each determines the other. It is on the contrary the essential feature of each part that it is a member of an ideal whole, which can only be defined by saying that it realized

itself in its parts, and that the parts are only what they are insofar as they realize it.[7]

The Haldanes maintained that "the ordinary conceptions of physical science are insufficient when applied to the phenomena of life, and that other conceptions must be substituted."[8] The nineteenth century analytic notion of cause and effect is inadequate for explaining living systems. In living organisms, it is not a matter of a prior event producing another event; instead, the parts reciprocally determine each other. Each part of an organic system is determined by its interaction with other parts of the whole. It should be noted, however, that the word *determined*, as used here, is altogether different from the *determinism* used in analytic thinking.

The organistic view also maintained that the organic whole is "prior" to its constituent parts. The whole is not the result of the joining together of the discrete and independent parts; it is the pattern which joins the parts together in a particular way. "The organic whole is not a multiple of ultimate units, but is, on the contrary, itself one single individuality."[9] Consequently, the organicists held that living things need to be understood by considering the features of the whole. The organism, they said, is a functioning unit, and it is the unit which determines the characteristics of the constituent parts; it is not the characteristics of the parts which determine the qualities of the whole.

Social Systems as Wholes

In applying to human phenomena the holistic idea that the characteristics of the parts of a system are "determined" by the qualities of the system, a question arises regarding the relationship between the individuals who make up the group and the properties which emerge from the group itself. Can the characteristics of a mob be determined by the characteristics of the individuals who make up the mob, or are the actions of the members of a mob determined by the characteristics of "mobness"? It seems easier to understand that the activities of cells are determined by the group in which they are individual members. Cells seem to have no self-direction, and thus it is easy to believe that they receive direction from the organism, but to extend the analogy to human groups presents difficulties. The use of the ideas derived from organistic theory for social entities has created a controversy in the human sciences—the argument over holistic versus individualistic methodology.

Emile Durkheim, who held an organistic view of human groups, proposed the concept of "social facts" in *The Rules of Sociological Method* (1895).[10] Groups have characteristics that individuals do not, Durkheim said, and social facts refer to qualities which groups possess. Social facts are the characteristics of the unity which is referred to in such terms as *family, crowd, army,* and *mob.* They are also the characteristics of the unity which is referred to in larger human collectivities—such as "the economic system," "the law," and "moral customs"—and in historical collectivities—such as "the Inquisition," "the Reformation," and "the 1960s." "Society," Durkheim wrote, is not "merely an extension of the individual being."[11] For him, the collective terms refer to some unity which is not definable in terms of individual behavior. A social fact is external to the individuals who make it up, and it exerts constraint over them.

Durkheim's position is called "holism." The opposite view is called "individualism," and it holds that all collective terms are analyzable and that they refer to the complex patterns of behavior, beliefs, and attitudes of various people in certain situations. The "individualist" would define a mob as a collection of individuals who are behaving in a certain way. In this view, it is not a mob that terrorizes a community; it is individuals who are animated by certain feelings and desires and are together conducting themselves in a certain way. And it was not the Inquisition that did something; it was an individual who lit a fire at the feet of another individual, and he did so from certain personal motives in a certain situation.

The issue in this controversy is whether human phenomena consist of qualities which emerge in collectivities and are not merely the sum of the qualities of individual members, or whether there is something more and other than those individuals. Do social groups have emergent properties on the model of organisms?

If there are social entities that are greater than the sum of their individual members, how are they related to each other and to the members who make up the social entities? One answer to the first part of this question is that social entities are related by laws in the same manner that physical objects are related by laws. According to Durkheim, social facts can be treated like the facts of observation which make up the data of physical laws. For example, the law that says that inflation is caused by full employment is equivalent in form to the law that says that the movement of the second ball is caused by the force of the first ball which has struck it. This position supposes that there can be a comprehensive social theory which explains and predicts social facts by subsuming them under social laws. In other words, a deductive system of science can be applied to entities which are social groups. This theory accounts for the actions of groups in terms of other groups. Individuals have no part to play, for their actions are determined by their participation as parts of the group. This was precisely Durkheim's point of view, and if we extend it we can say that individuals do not choose their styles of houses or their styles of clothing, for these things are imposed by the external coercive power of the unity which is the group.

One aspect of the holistic approach to human phenomena is role theory. A role is a position occupied by a person in a group relative to other persons in that group. It carries with it certain expected regularities regarding the individual's behavior toward other members of the group and their behavior toward him or her. Thus the group entity controls the behavior of its parts by defining roles, much in the same way as an organism defines the activities of its cells. And if group behavior is determined only by the roles of its members and by its environment, then specific personalities, or even personality types, need not be mentioned in laws concerning the social process.

By contrast, individualists maintain that the behavior of the group can be described in terms of its individuals. Consequently, there is no necessity to propose additional emergent qualities to account for the action of the group, because one needs only to add together the individual behaviors. (The question of whether individual behavior can be explained and predicted by means of psychological laws or whether it is, in part, open to "free choice" is discussed in chapter 5.) Individualists usually hold that laws of the complex can be derived from laws about the elements and laws about how the elements combine, and so social laws are not emergent qualities; they can be reduced to laws which explain and predict individual behavior.

One solution to the holism versus individualism controversy has been to propose a psychosociological theory in which individual choices are said to affect the qualities of the group, and at the same time the qualities of the group are said to affect individual choices. This solution does not allow for a comprehensive social theory, since group action is not a necessary consequence of the premises that make up social laws. Group action and individual action are influenced by each other, but they do not causally determine each other.[12] Such a solution lacks precision, and it makes the prediction of both individual action and group action impossible. The theory holds that neither the individual nor the group is the basic unit of human reality, claiming, as it does, that the human realm consists of both of these units in interaction.

General Systems Theory

Ludwig von Bertalanffy, an early architect of general systems theory, was trained as a biologist, and he was an advocate of the "organismic viewpoint." In *Modern Theories of Development* (1928), he said:

> Mechanism . . . provides us with no grasp of the specific characteristics of organisms, of the organization of organic processes among one another, of organic "wholeness," of the problem of the origin of organic "teleology," or of the historical character of organisms. . . . We must therefore try to establish a new standpoint which—as opposed to mechanism—takes account of organic wholeness, but . . . treats it in a manner which admits of scientific investigation.[13]

In 1968, Bertalanffy expanded the notion of holism in relationship to organisms into a general theory about any whole and any system. There was a need for such a general theory, he claimed:

> Similar general conceptions and viewpoints have evolved in various disciplines of modern science. While in the past, science has tried to explain observable phenomena by reducing them to an interplay of elementary units investigable independently of each other, conceptions appear in contemporary science that are concerned with what is somewhat vaguely termed "wholeness," i.e., problems of organization, phenomena not resolvable into local events, dynamic interactions manifest in the difference of behavior of parts when isolated or in a higher configuration, etc.; in short, "systems" of various orders not understandable by investigation of their respective parts in isolation.[14]

Bertalanffy maintained that systems—organized wholes—exist in the most diverse fields and are not limited to organic or social entities. From physics and engineering to life insurance statistics and information, the data are arranged in systems as well as in mere aggregates of relationships.

Instead of studying a specific system, general systems theory studies the properties that hold for systems in general, whether they appear in the biological, the linguistic, the social, or the physical sciences. The idea behind general systems theory is that there is a general, ideal form which is isomorphic to all systems. This general form is the object of inquiry, and the level of inquiry is the properties of systems, not specific systems themselves. Since the philosophy of science had limited inquiry into the logic of relationships to relationships between entities—that is, to the study of correlational and causal relations (the "if . . . then" statements) and to the study of comparative relations based on identity, diversity, and similarity—there was a need to develop a similar study of the logic of systems. This logic could then be used by the various disciplines in the study of their subject areas, just as they had used the relational logic for explaining and predicting relationships within these areas.

Before we proceed, a distinction needs to be made between two separate uses of the word *whole*. Sometimes a concrete organized object, such as a body or a mob, is called a whole, while at other times the "organization" of the object is called a whole. For example, the organizational pattern of a circle consists of a designated center point with all other points equidistant from it. In the present discussion, the word *whole* will refer only to organized objects, and the organization itself—the way the parts are arranged—will be called *system*. A circle, whether red or green or large or small, would be called a *whole*; the pattern, the arrangement of the parts that is "circle," would be called *system*.

The logic of systems is concerned with organizational patterns in systems. General systems theory is concerned to investigate the various systems and their patterns of organization (also called "structures"), rather than specific wholes. It is also concerned to make clear the nature of organizational patterns that comprise systems—that is, what the properties and combinations of organizing patterns are and how they can be understood.

General systems theory has been more successful in describing how organizing patterns differ from relational patterns than in developing in a precise way a logic that describes the behavior of the constituents of a whole. To understand a whole, one needs to look at how the parts are arranged, for the system is an independent framework in which the parts are placed. The pattern or system is independent of the parts which make it up. An example used earlier, the pattern of a particular melody, is independent of any particular sound; the melodic pattern can arrange the sounds in various keys and it can obtain them from various instruments. But not just any entity can function in the system. The parts may need to have certain attributes which will enable them to fill the positions which are required for the system. For example, in the geometric arrangement that is a triangle, the parts must be lines. The lines may extend beyond the intersections which make up the system of the triangle, but these extensions are not relevant to the pattern, even though they are included in the constituent parts. In another instance, the pattern of a circle may not have enough parts to fill it in, or some of the parts may be out of position. In this case, the pattern of the circle may be missing some of its points, or some of the points may be slightly inside or outside the pattern.

The organistic principle "The whole is greater than the sum of its parts" can be misinterpreted, even though it points to a characteristic of patterns, because of the use of the term *sum*. One incorrect interpretation would be that the whole is made up of its parts, plus an additional factor. Wholes cannot be compared to additive aggregations—ever. In an aggregate, the parts function because of their own qualities; for example, in linear distances, part A is additively connected to part B to get part A + B. The important characteristic of entities formed out of summation is that the quality of the element determines whether it can be part of the aggregate entity. The old adage "One cannot add apples and oranges" means that the key to inclusion in an aggregate of apples is that the element to be added must have the property of "apple." But when the elements constitute a whole—as opposed to an aggregate—it is not the inherent quality of the element which is significant; it is the position or meaning or significance in the system. The formation of wholes is of a different order than the formation of aggregates: in an aggregate, the parts are added; in a whole, the parts are arranged.[15]

As we have already mentioned, one of the problems for general systems theory is the question of how to separate out from the rest of the universe a particular viable system for study. Hegel held that everything is a subsystem of the "All"; thus, a thing cannot be known unless one knows the All. Although Hegel attempted to develop a system for knowing the All, his answer to the question has not found general acceptance. As a consequence, systems thinking has focused on subsystems within the "universe."

This approach began with the recognition that certain principles hold for material systems, despite the similarities and/or differences between the component parts. The system properties or structures regulate the behavior of the components of the whole and thus the behavior of the whole itself. It was considered that the subsystems, in themselves, are isolated from their environments—that is, no substances can enter a system from outside it, and no substances from inside it can leave it. The boundaries of these closed systems are impermeable. In such systems, the initial order will randomize over time toward a maximum randomness or equilibrium; it will follow, in short, the second law of thermodynamics. In a simple closed physical system, then—such as a gas in a closed container—

the initial order—variations in pressure and temperature—will move to a system of equilibrium where the pressure and temperature will be the same throughout the container. The initial pattern of organization will dissipate into disorganization. At one time the vitalists, still considering the living organism to be a closed system, argued that living systems "disobey" the second law of thermodynamics because they retain the patterns which organize the parts and even in their developmental stages become more organized instead of randomized.

In a classic 1950 paper, Bertalanffy restated the notion of "open systems." From this restatement arose a movement of thought which has become central for general systems theory. The open-systems approach accounts for the continuing differentiation within living systems without contradicting the second law of thermodynamics. An open system receives substances from its environment and discharges substances into its environment. Unlike a closed system, an open system does not depend on its initial condition as the sole determinant of its final state. The final state will depend on the properties of the system itself—that is, organizational structures which are independent of the initial conditions imposed on the system. For example, if a change occurs to affect the motion of a planet, such as the close approach of a large comet, the planet will not end up in the same place it would have been if there had been no environmental disturbance. Living systems, however, show a different behavior; they may reach the same place (state) from different initial conditions and in different ways. This is called *equifinal behavior*: the final state can be attained in various ways. Systems with equifinal behavior appear to have "goals of their own," and they manifest quasi-purposive behavior. Open-systems theory applies not only to living systems but to all open systems. Computers and machines with feedback systems are open systems. (The relationship between purposive behavior and the concepts of open systems will be examined in the next chapter.)[16]

In a 1962 paper, Bertalanffy repeated a distinction that W. Ross Ashby had made between two methods of general systems research. He quoted from Ashby:

Two main lines are readily distinguished. One, already well developed in the hands of von Bertalanffy and his co-workers, takes the world as we find it, examines the various systems that occur in it—zoological, physiological, and so on—and then draws up statements about the regularities that have been observed to hold. This method is essentially empirical. The second method is to start at the other end. Instead of studying first one system, then a second, then a third, and so on, it goes to the other extreme, considers the set of all conceivable systems and then reduces the set to a more reasonable size.[17]

The search for the general organizational processes of systems can be carried out, then, through empirico-intuitive methods in which various existing systems are compared, so that the common features which hold across systems can be differentiated from the accidental features of each system. The result of this type of research has been the identification of the principles of "wholeness, sum, centralization, differentiation, leading part, closed and open system, finality, equifinality, growth in time, relative growth, [and] competition."[18]

The other approach to identifying the characteristics of systems—the approach used by Ashby—uses deduction. This approach begins with questions about what is essential for a system to operate. The answers to these questions are given in the form of axiomatically organized theories that are akin to the deductive system of laws which has been described in chapter 2. The axiomatic approach has led to the discovery of the theory of probability, the theory of non-Euclidean geometries, and (more recently) the information and game theory.

Bertalanffy encouraged both the empirico-intuitive and the axiomatic approaches, although he warned that it is too early for the theoretical model to be considered closed and definitive. He concluded his discussion on the research methods appropriate for the discovery of systems principles by saying that the investigation needs to remain open:

> [These remarks] only emphasize that there is no royal road to General Systems Theory. As every other scientific field, it will have to develop by an interplay of empirical, intuitive, and deductive procedures. If the intuitive approach leaves much to be desired in logical rigor and completeness, the deductive approach faces the difficulty of whether the fundamental terms are correctly chosen. This is not a particular fault of the theory or of the workers concerned but a rather common phenomenon in the history of science.[19]

Functionalism

Whether individuals or groups are seen as systems, it is understood that the constituents of each system are organized so that the parts function in relation to the whole. In general systems theory, *function* refers to the role that the various elements of a system perform in maintaining the system in a persisting state—or, in the case of machines, in maintaining the efficiency of the system for the purpose for which it has been set up. There are differences, however, in the ways the functions of the parts of a system are to be treated in social systems and in machine systems or biological systems. The differences hang on the question of whether social systems are wholes or aggregates—that is, whether they are to be treated by a holistic methodology or by an individualistic methodology. If a society is to be accepted as a single integrated system, then the various parts can be viewed as functioning for the "end" of the social system, whether that end is merely the maintenance of the system as a whole in its environment or whether it is the achievement of some other goal, such as increasing the power of the system in relation to other social systems. If social systems are aggregates, then they may be so diversified that the various subsystems work in opposition or in competition to obtain their own maintenance or other ends.

Functional notions were used earlier by Emile Durkheim and W. Robertson Smith,[20] but the term *functionalism* was first put forward as the name for a special method and approach by Bronislaw Malinowski in 1926.[21] According to Malinowski, functional analysis was to be:

> Explanation of . . . facts . . . by the part they play within the integral system of culture, by the manner in which they are related to each other within the system, and by the manner in which this system is related to the physical surroundings. . . . The functional view . . . insists therefore upon the principle that in every type of civilization, every custom, material object, idea and belief fulfills some vital function, has some task, to accomplish, represents an indispensable part within a working whole.[22]

Thus, the function of magic in a social system is, for example, to remedy maladjustments and mental conflicts which culture has created by allowing humans to transcend their biological equipment; myth may function by strengthening the traditions which maintain the culture. Malinowski maintained that every cultural item plays a functional role, that none are irrelevant extended parts or merely random occurrences in the social system. The practices in the society, he said, are functional for the biological and psychological needs of its members and do not primarily serve as contributions to the total social system.

A. R. Radcliffe-Brown took a view from the other side.[23] He held that the practices should be understood in relation to the contributions they make to the system instead of in terms of how they serve the members' needs. Radcliffe-Brown regarded a social system as a set of interconnected patterns of recurrent sets of relationships described by social roles. It is the patterns of structures of relationships which are functional, he said, not separate cultural items. This "structural-functional" concept "became, for some three decades, the preeminent, if never an unrivalled, stream of social theory within American sociology."[24] In this approach, a social system is analogous to a biological system. The structure (patterns of relationship) serves the survival of the social system in the same manner that the structure of an organism serves its survival.

Robert Merton's *Social Theory and Social Structure* (1949) offered critiques of both Malinowski and Radcliffe-Brown and contained proposals for futher developments in functionalism. Merton noted that the term *function* needs to be precisely defined. *Function*, he said, should be reserved for observable objective consequences and should not be used for the subjective aims or purposes of individuals. What people intend to achieve may not coincide with the actual functional roles which their actions play in the social system. For example, the saying of prayers in a group may be motivated by a desire for salvation, but the act itself may function to unify the members of the group.

Merton believed that Radcliffe-Brown's idea that society always has a functional unity ought to be abandoned. It should be noted, he said, that societies vary in their degrees of integration. Moreover, it is not specific institutions—such as religion or myths—that are necessary for society; what is necessary is the performance of certain functions in social groups, and these functions may be carried out by different institutions. Once it is recognized that it is not the specific institutions that are required for the survival of a social system, i.e., when it is recognized that there are many different institutions that can perform the same function, the inherent "conservative" approach in the old functional theory is no longer appropriate. For example, religion need not be preserved in order to meet a system's need for integration; new institutions, such as nationalism, could arise to provide integration. Merton contrasted function with dysfunction by contrasting "those observed consequences [of standardized practices or items] which make for the adaptation or adjustment of a given system" with those consequences which act against adaptation or adjustment.[25] A particular social practice, he said, may be functional on certain levels of the system and dysfunctional on other levels.

One of Merton's more important distinctions was the one he made between "manifest functions" and "latent functions." Manifest functions are "those objective consequences contributing to the adjustment or adaptation of the system which are intended and recognized

by participants in the system"; latent functions are those consequences which are not intended and recognized. Activities performed
with particular intention by the participants can have consequences
unanticipated by them, and it may be the unanticipated consequences
that are functional and will contribute to meeting the system's needs.
An example of the latent function of a religious practice can be
found in Weber's analysis of the "function" of Calvinism: a moral
outlook that emphasized diligence, thrift, and abstinence promoted
moneymaking which, in turn, contributed to the survival of the social
system.

Another of Merton's additions to functional theory was the understanding that, even though various practices can perform the
same function for a system, the range of the variety is limited by
the "structural constraints" that derive from "the interdependence
of the elements of a social structure."

Functionalism draws on the implications of organismic and systems
theory for comprehending social practices. It provides a form of
explanation which accounts for a practice by relating it to its role
in a system. Functionalism holds that the practice cannot be explained
in deductive or inductive terms because its meaning is derived from
the role it performs to serve the "end" of the whole. Thus, functional
analysis does not provide an explanation of a practice by the covering-
law approach.

Merton's distinction between latent and manifest functions clarifies
the differences between purposes and functions. Individuals may
have their own manifest purposes and may also—in their daily jobs,
for instance—serve the purposes of others. Their actions serve a
purpose, but the actions may also have functions. Tools and machines
have only functions, for they can have no conscious purposes. *Purpose*
is sometimes used interchangeably with *function* in reference to
artifacts—as when one says "The purpose or function of a saw is
to cut wood"—but what is referred to in this statement is the human
purpose the saw serves. *Purpose* and *function* can also sometimes be
used interchangeably in referring to human actions—as when one's
purpose or intention is to provide leadership, which is a functional
need of the group—but an individual's act may have a function
which is different from his or her purpose in performing the act.

Generally, the term *function* is best used when the end served is
not consciously intended by whomever or whatever is a means to
that end. The function—not the purpose—of the heart is to circulate
blood. The function of marriage for the group is conceivably quite
different from the purposes or intentions of the people who marry.
People do not normally marry, for example, to promote social

stability. People behave purposively when they do things that they believe will bring them certain ends. Purposive action may also be functional for the social system, but it need not be. (The distinction between purposive and purposeful action is discussed in chapter 5.) When natural processes or social institutions are said to have "purposes," what is meant is that they have functions, not that they have conscious ends toward which they are striving.

By restricting the meaning in this way, one can "interpret" function. Merton used the term *interpretation* instead of *explanation* because comprehending function is not the same as subsuming an event under a law. In this usage, the function of the heart is "interpreted" by describing its contribution to the organism, and the function of a political machine is "interpreted" by showing how it serves the system of business.

In a 1959 article, "The Logic of Functional Analysis," Hempel, writing from the viewpoint of the deductive system of methodology, criticized functional analysis for failing "to meet the minimum scientific requirement of empirical testability." Hempel asked: How can one make observations which will confirm or refute a functional "explanation"? For instance, there is no way to confirm or refute the statement "The function of the political boss is to provide leadership for the political system, and this leadership does not develop readily in other ways within the structure of the system."[26] Hempel proposed that functional analysis can perform a suggestive or heuristic role in empirical research by suggesting hypotheses which can be reformulated into "if . . . then" statements from which observational statements can be deduced and then tested.

Hempel's article represented the received-view position,[27] which maintains that the deductive system is the only "truly" scientific approach to knowledge, and that if statements are to describe knowledge they must fit into the format of deductive statements. The systems approach to knowledge holds that functional knowledge fits into an alternative logical format. In the systems "interpretive" format, the procedure for testing a proposed explanation is closer to the procedure of judicial argument in which the position proposed is considered to be the best of the possible alternative ways of organizing the information. Through the use of suggested interpretation, the information is structured in a way which is meaningful and reasonable. An argument for a particular interpretation uses the expanded definition of reason which has been described in the section on historical realism in chapter 4. The results of this approach does not produce the certainty of knowledge that Hempel argued for, but it does produce a level of nondemonstrative understanding which moves beyond a purely relativistic "All interpretations are of equal value."

Structuralism and Human Systems

Thus far, the discussion of systems has been limited to what Ervin Laszlo has termed "natural systems."[28] These include physical, biological, and social systems, and so they are more inclusive than wholes composed only of material elements. But there are other events that can also be explored for systemic properties, and these Laszlo describes as the "events which can only be observed by introspection and which make up the immediate, felt experience of each of us." He calls them "mental events."

The remainder of this chapter will explore the systemic characteristics of the realms of cognition and language. The exploration of cognitive systems has taken the rubric *structuralism*. Structuralism is concerned with describing the structures—the organizing patterns—of cognition, language, consciousness and unconsciousness, and such human expressions as novels, poetry, paintings, and so on. Experience is understood to be a whole that is best comprehended through the use of a systems approach.

Gestalt theorists had pointed out that perception does not consist of independently existing objects whose concrete features can be perceived clearly and individually and whose nature can be classified accordingly. We construct our experience in organized patterns of relationships, the Gestalt theorists said, and thus the nature of the elements of experience has no significance by itself; each element has significance only through its relationship to other elements in the pattern. The full significance of an entity of experience can be known by understanding the structural pattern in which it is a member. Experience is a whole that consists of organized or structured parts. It is the structure—the arrangement of the parts—that defines the parts and their role in the whole.

The word *structure* comes from the Latin verb *struere*, which means "to construct." The word was used exclusively in an architectural context until the seventeenth century when its use was extended to the study of anatomy and grammar. The arrangement of the organs of the body came to be viewed as a kind of construction, and language was understood to be the arrangement of words in speech having a "structured" character. The term always designated a whole—the parts of a whole and their interrelations—and it was on this basis that the term was borrowed by the human sciences.[29]

The "structures" of structuralism are parallel to the "wholes" of systems theory. The term *structure* is used to refer both to the whole and to the system or organization which makes up the whole. In *Structuralism* (1968), Jean Piaget defines a structure as an arrangement of entities which embodies the properties of wholes, the properties of transformation, and the properties of self-regulation.[30] An arrangement is a system if it has a sense of wholeness or internal coherence. An arrangement is not simply a composite or aggregate of independent elements; it is a system in which a set of patterns, intrinsic to the system, confer on the constituent parts properties that are larger than those they possess outside the system. The whole (structure) is not static; it is an open system. The organizational patterns are capable of processing new elements and transforming them into members of the system, thereby giving them characteristics they lack outside the system. For example, the marks *s*, *a*, and *y*, when brought into the system of the English language, are transformed and become a meaningful word.

Wholes or structures are self-regulating in the sense that they make no appeals beyond their boundaries to validate their organizing or transforming procedures. The procedure which transforms marks on paper into meaningful words is not drawn from a reality outside the whole; the meaning is created in relationship to other patterns within the whole. The combination of letters *s*, *a*, *y* has meaning because it is different from the other patterns of letters in the language system, not because of an inherent connection to something outside the system.

It can be seen from Piaget's description that *structure* is used in a more restrictive sense than *whole*. While *whole* pertains to any organized system, including closed systems (such as gas in a closed jar or mechanical systems like pendulums), *structure* pertains to those systems which are open and self-regulating. Although mechanical self-regulating systems and feedback systems are sometimes used as analogies in structuralist literature, structuralism is actually concerned with the systemic characteristics of human systems.

The Linguistic Model

The structuralist approach to the study of language is usually said to have begun with the work of Ferdinand de Saussure, in particular with the three series of lectures on general linguistics which he gave from 1907 to 1911. Notes from the lectures were published in 1915 under the title *Course in General Linguistics*.[31] In these lectures, Saussure rejected the atomism of classical grammar and emphasized, instead, the underlying system of relations within language through which words receive their meanings. Words are not meaningful in isolation, he said, but receive their meanings because of their differences from other words of the same systems. Claude Lévi-Strauss is perhaps the best-known of the social scientists who pay homage to Saussure as the person who laid the foundations for the proper conception of the human sciences.[32]

Nikolai Trubetzkoy, in *Principles of Phonology* (1939), outlined the methodological implications of the study of relationships for the social sciences.[33] Trubetzkoy held that the social and human sciences, since they are concerned with the social use of material objects, must distinguish between the objects themselves and the system of distinctive or differential features which gives them meaning and value.

Structuralism is important for human science if we recognize that the human realm cannot be treated merely as a series of events that are similar to events in the physical world. Discourse about events in the physical world can take place without attention being paid to people's impressions or ideas about these matters. But in the human realm, events have meaning, and discourse about a particular event needs to include, in addition to a physical description with space–time coordinates, the meaningful interpretation that people give to the event. For example, there is a human gesture in which a person raises the middle finger of his hand and shows it to another person; this gesture cannot be understood or explained with physical description alone. The meaning of the gesture must be included.

Human science needs to be concerned, not with events themselves, but with events that have meaning. Meaningful events—that is, social facts—are understood by focusing primarily on the functions which these events have within the general social framework. The search for any underlying system which gives meaning to events requires a different kind of system of inquiry than is used to search for the historical causes of those events. It was Saussure, in his investigations of language, who spelled out the issues involved in the search for meaning-bestowing structures. His question was: How and why do physical events (markings on paper, sound waves, facial expressions, etc.) have meaning? Clearly, then, his work has direct bearing on the fundamental problems of the human sciences and their attempt to deal with the world of meaningful objects and actions.

Before Saussure, language had been studied as if it was analogous to a biological organism. It was seen as evolving and changing through history: the roots of words could be traced back to earlier forms of the language, and the influences of one language on another could be explained. Saussure, by the time he gave his noted lectures, had developed a new approach to the study of language. He proposed that instead of studying the development of language—that is, engaging in diachronic studies—we study language itself so that we can understand its nature. In order to do this, we need to focus on language as it stands, to take a cross-sectional view and try to understand what language is composed of—that is, engage in synchronic studies.

Language, Saussure said, is a system of signs. Noises count as language only when they serve to express and communicate ideas. In order for noises to communicate ideas, they must be part of a system of conventions which relate noises to ideas. A noise is part of a linguistic system when that noise is linked to an idea. The noise is called the *signifier*, and the idea is called the *signified*.

Which noises are linked to which ideas is arbitrary. There is no natural or inevitable link between a particular noise and the idea to which it gives expression. In English, we use the sequence of noises "dog" to signify the idea of an animal of a particular species, but the sequence of noises making up "dog" is not better suited to the idea of dog than "lod" or "tet" or "bloop." If the members of a community would accept it, then one could utter the sounds making up "lod" and they would signify the concept of "dog." The concepts to which the sequences of sounds refer do not have an independent existence in some Platonic-like realm. If they did have, then each language would merely assign arbitrary sounds as the names for the various concepts which exist before language and independently of any language. Moreover, it would be a simple matter to translate from one language to another: we could merely replace an English word with, for instance, a French word which signifies the same concept. There is a catch, however. Each language articulates and organizes the world differently, and the concepts shift and change their boundaries within each language. The meaning concepts signified by the various arbitrary sound sequences are language-dependent. There is no fixed conceptual scheme to which languages must conform; the concepts are arbitrary in the same way that noises which are meaningful are arbitrary. Both are conventions of the groups which use them.

If the signifiers and the ideas signified are arbitrary, how are they defined? Saussure's answer to this question was that they are defined in relation to other concepts and noises. Language can divide the spectrum of conceptual possibilities and the signifiers in any number of ways. The signifier–signified system in English seems to work as well as the French system, although the sequences of sounds recognized as signifiers and the conceptual apparatus are different. Saussure's conclusion from this situation is that the signifiers and the signified are not autonomous entities defined by some kind of Platonic essence. They are, instead, members of a system and are defined by their relations to the other members of that system. The concept of "stream," for instance, receives its meaning in relation to its differences from the concepts of "river," "brook," and "creek." To learn a word—that is, to know what sequence of sounds signifies what concept—one must learn the place of the word in the system of the language. The word does not mean anything by itself; it means something only in relation to other words and concepts. "Concepts," Saussure said, "are purely differential, not positively defined by their content but negatively defined by their relations with other terms of the system."[34] Thus, "red" is what is not "green" or "yellow" or "blue" or some other color.

One of the consequences of Saussure's notion of definition through difference is that the signifier and the signified occupy a breadth in the spectrum of sound and meaning, not a precise point. For example, when someone from the southern region of the United States says the word *creek* it sounds like "krik," and when someone from New England says the same word it sounds like "kreek." Even the same person may at different times use different sound sequences for the same word, according to instruments which measure the sound waves produced. And we all realize that what we hear on the telephone is different from what we hear when we hear in person the voice of someone we know; yet we recognize both the words which are spoken and the identity of the speaker.

It is clear, then, that different noises produce the same signifier. The signifier does not equal a particular sequence of sounds; it is, instead, an abstract unit which consists of a limited range of noises. The noises can vary considerably, as long as they do not become confused with the noises of contrasting signifiers. The noises making up a particular signifier have no intrinsic significances of their own. What is significant are the distinctions between various possible noises. There is considerable latitude in the range of noises used to utter such a word as *bed*, as long as these noises are not confused with the ranges of noises used to signify other similar words, such as *bad, bud, bid, bode, bread, bled, dead, fed, head, led, red, said, wed, beck, bell,* and *bet*.[35]

It is the distinctions within a system that are important. Linguistic units, both the signifiers and the signified, have a purely relational identity. To make this point about identity by relation, Saussure used the example of the pieces used in chess games. The actual physical shape and the material from which the king, the queen, the rook, the knight, the bishop, and the pawn are made are of no importance. These may vary considerably, as long as there are ways of distinguishing the pieces from one another.

> Take a knight, for instance. By itself is it an element in the game? Certainly not, for by its material make-up—outside its square and the other conditions of the game—it means nothing to the player; it becomes a real, concrete element only when endowed with value and wedded to it. Suppose that the piece happens to be destroyed or lost during a game. Can it be replaced by an equivalent piece? Certainly. Not only another knight but even a figure shorn of any resemblance to a knight can be declared identical, provided the same value is attributed to it.[36]

Saussure's point is that the units of the chess game have no material identity; there are no physical properties which in themselves make up a king or a pawn. The identity of each chess piece is a function of the differences within a system. Thus, "pawn" is not a physical manifestation (the particular thing sitting on the chessboard); it is an abstract form defined by its relationship to other forms. The "difference" is not a difference between two objects of physical realizations. The "difference" that marks off a concept within the conceptual field or a word in the sound spectrum is what distinguishes these forms from the other forms in the system.

Given the distinctions among the actual manifestations, the speaking of words, and the system of forms, Saussure pointed out, the system of a language (*la langue*) needs to be treated differently than is the actual speech of the people who use the language (*parole*). *La langue* is a social product which is transmitted to the members of the linguistic community, and it comes to exist "in the mind" of each speaker as the community's conceptual system through which the world is understood. *Parole* involves both "the combinations by which the speaker uses the code of the linguistic system in order to express his own thoughts" and "the psychophysical mechanisms which permit him to externalize these combinations."[37] In *parole*, the speaker selects and combines elements of the linguistic system to engage in conversation. For Saussure, it was not the speech acts of *parole* that should be the focus of the linguist, but rather the system of language itself, *la langue*. The actual carrying on of conversation is an individual act which varies according to circumstances; in this sense, it is accidental. The language system, however, provides the underlying social form in which these individual speech acts take place. Saussure was interested in giving attention to the distinctions to be made between the abstract units of the system as a whole.

The clarification of the difference between the language system and the speech acts allowed Saussure to show that there are two kinds of meaning. One kind of meaning is relational and is based on the linguistic system; this kind is called "value." The other kind of meaning is reference, and it involves the use of the linguistic units in actual situations of utterance; this kind is called "signification." It was the second kind of meaning that was employed by Russell and the logical positivists in their attempt to relate statements about reality to the real world. The difference between these two kinds of meaning is illustrated by the use of the sentence "I am going home" when it is spoken by a particular person at a particular time. As *parole*, the "I" of the sentence refers to "me," a particular person. In *la langue*, however, the "I" does not refer to anyone; its meaning is the result of the distinctions that are made between "I" and "you," "he," "she," "it," "we," and "they." In *la langue* (the language system), "I" means the speaker in general as opposed to anyone else. In *parole* (the speech act), "I" refers to a particular person and takes on a specific reference.

This difference between *la langue* and *parole* is of first importance in structuralism because it is the difference between institution and event, between the underlying system which contains the forms of behavior and the actual instances of behavior. The distinction clarifies two objects of inquiry for the human sciences—the study of the underlying systems and the study of actual behavior or events. The study of the system in which events take place requires an inquiry which leads to an understanding of the forms by means of which the spectrum of concepts is broken up and of the differences that determine how these forms are related to one another. The study of actual events can focus on the particular reasons for the action carried out or on the overall probabilities that an action will occur under various circumstances. In the study of language, investigations aimed at understanding *la langue* consist of inventories of the distinctions which create signs as well as inventories of rules of combination; investigations aimed at understanding *parole* focus on who says what and when.

Language—that is, language (*la langue*) as distinct from speaking (*parole*), and language synchronically considered—is essentially a system for differentiating words and concepts. Saussure asserted that the differentiation takes place within two kinds of relationships, paradigmatic and syntagmatic. The patterns which organize a language are of these two basic kinds. The syntagmatic relationships are those that a word has with other words in a sentence. In the sentence "John runs," the word *John* has a syntagmatic relationship with the word *runs*. The relationship is the relationship of a subject to a verb. Such a relationship does not exist between two nouns or two verbs; the constructions "Dog river" and "flow throws" are not transformed into meaning. Syntagmatic relationships do not exist between every noun (or pronoun) and every verb, however: the sequence "The river bites" and "The dog flows" do not normally make sense. The syntagmatic patterns determine how words need to relate to other words in a sentence so that the sound can become meaningful. Should a word lose some of these relationships, or should it gain others, it would also lose the particular meaning it has held. Saussure maintained that the differences between a word and those other words with which it occurs in recognized "syntagms" are crucial to the definition of the word. "In the syntagm," he said, "a term acquires its value only because it stands in opposition to everything that precedes or follows it, or both."[38]

The paradigmatic relationships were less clearly defined by Saussure. They include all of the essential relationships which a word has that are not syntagmatic relationships. The paradigmatic relationships are those that the word has with words which are close to it in meaning. For example, the verb *force* is related to the words *compel, coerce, constrain,* and *oblige* in such a way that the meaning of *force* is determined by its difference from these words. Should it lose some of these relationships, or should it gain others, its meaning would become subtly different. It is usual to think of the paradigmatic relationships of a word as those that it has with words which may replace it in a sentence without making the sentence syntagmatically unacceptable. For example, in the sentence "John forced Jerry," *forced* could be replaced by *coerced* to render the sentence "John coerced Jerry." In sum, the meaning of a particular word is structured by its relationships to the other words with which it may be used in a sentence.

Language, synchronically considered, is a system for differentiating words. It does this by organizing them according to syntagmatic and paradigmatic patterns of relationship within which the words are marked off from other words and receive their meanings. Like many other realities, "language is a system of interdependent terms in which the value of each term results solely from the simultaneous presence of the others."[39] This system is not the product of the conscious mind (as are some formally constructed languages meant for use in logic). The patterns are unconscious, and the whole system of language "is a complex mechanism that can be grasped only through reflection; the very ones who use it daily are ignorant of it."[40]

Structuralism and the Human Sciences

Saussure's work has significantly influenced the way the human realm is conceptualized by contributors to the various human sciences. The primary categories of meaning are not reflections from an autonomous natural realm; they are divisions created by the organizational patterns of a language. Various languages divide the conceptual scheme into different classifications. The communication and the expression of experience are given through one's linguistic system, and thus the comprehension of communication and expression requires an appreciation of the system in which they are given. Saussure's linguistic model has been used to analyze a variety of human expressions, from cooking procedures to novels. The remainder of this section will mention briefly the uses to which the linguistic model has been put in linguistics, anthropology, and psychology since Saussure developed it.

Linguistics. The synchronic approach to language was developed independently by two other linguists at about the same time that Saussure was delivering his lectures in Switzerland. In the United States, Franz Boas's *Handbook of American Indian Languages* (1911) was based on a descriptivist approach to language. Boas held that there are certain obligatory categories which differ from language to language but which are necessary for the expression of meaning.[41] In Czechoslovakia, Vilem Mathesius issued a call (also in 1911) for a new, nonhistorical approach to language study. There subsequently came into being around Mathesius a circle of linguists who, beginning in 1926, held regular discussions. This group came to be known as the Prague school of linguists.

The Prague linguists studied language in terms of function, and they analyzed a given language with a view to showing the respective functions played by the various structural components in the entire language. They sought to do more than describe the structures of a language, however; they wanted to give functional "explanations" as to why the language was structured in the way that it was. An example, which came from Mathesius's own work, was a concept that was later called "functional sentence perspective." Many sentences are uttered in order to give the hearer some information. But we do not produce pieces of information that are merely unrelated and random. We produce statements that are tailored not only to tell the hearer what we want him or her to learn, but also to say something that fits in with what he or she already knows and something that is appropriate for the context of the discourse which has already been developed. Continuity in a discourse is necessary, and it requires that a sentence have two parts: a "theme" that refers to something the hearer already knows, and a "rheme" that states some new fact about the topic being discussed. Sentences, then, can be analyzed to show which part functions as a theme and which part functions as a rheme.

An important member of the Prague school was Roman Jakobson, who moved to the United States just before the Nazi occupation of Czechoslovakia. In 1949, Jakobson was at Harvard, and since 1957 he has been associated with the Massachusetts Institute of Technology, which has become the center of the modern revolution in linguistics. In Jakobson's approach to phonology, there is a relatively simple, orderly, universal "psychological system" of sounds which underlie the wide variety of observed sounds which are used when a language is spoken. Despite surface appearances, Jakobson claims, there are only very few sound differences which are used to differentiate words. Each of these sounds is a two-value type of sound. The reason that only these sounds, of all the possible sounds that humans can make, are used for language has to do with innate features in the human mind. Jakobson is thus at odds with the position taken by Saussure (and Boas), which holds that the sounds that are noted in a language vary unpredictably from language to language. According to Jakobson, it is because of deep psychological (not organic) principles that the variations used by languages are limited in number, that they have a basic form which is the form of two-valued logic.[42]

Noam Chomsky worked within Jakobson's sphere of influence, first at Harvard and then at MIT. While Jakobson holds that the organizational patterns which differentiate sounds into words are small in number, exist at a deep level, and are the same for all languages because of the human psychological system, Chomsky maintains that the syntax of sentences—that is, the ways in which words are put together to form sentences—is also limited, exists at a deep level, and is the same for all languages and people. In *Syntactic Structures* (1957), Chomsky proposed that the reason the words "The cat is on the mat" have meaning in English while the words "Mat the on is cat the" do not, is that the first sequence is ordered according to patterns of relationship which operate for English and the second sequence is not so ordered. The first sequence is thus "grammatical" or "well formed." In communication, one (usually without awareness) organizes words into sequences that produce meaning, and the hearer, who shares the same language, deciphers the sequence as meaningful because the words all participate in the same structural system.

The structures have the form of rules. If a sentence does not fit one of the rules, it is not heard or read as meaningful. An infinite number of sentences can conform or be generated by the rules, but it is clear when a sequence of words does not conform to the rules. Chomsky also takes up the question of how a child learns the rules for generating sentences. The reinforcement theory of learning cannot explain a child's mastery of syntax or grammar, he says, for the child not only can utter what he overhears but can also speak new sentences that have never been heard by anyone before. The inductive model will not account for the mastery of rules, either, for a large number of possible grammars or rule sets are compatible with what is actually said in front of the child. Chomsky proposed that children are born with an innate ability to infer the correct set of rules. Children are able to pick up the rules of any language community in which they are reared. Chomsky postulates that children innately possess the grammars of all languages. He holds that all languages share a single underlying structure and that children are born with a disposition to follow this basic structure as they reconstruct an actual language on the basis of what is said around them.

> Man has a species-specific capacity, a unique type of intellectual organization which cannot be attributed to peripheral organs or related to general intelligence and which manifests itself in what we may refer to as the "creative aspect" of language use.[43]

Linguistics has moved from the description of the structures which differentiate sounds, concepts, and syntax to an attempt to understand the origin of the organizational patterns of language. Jakobson and Chomsky maintain that these patterns of relationship are part of the psychological makeup of human beings and are thus universal across all linguistic systems. Whether or not this is so, the approach to language as a system in which the parts (sounds and words) receive characteristics (meaning) from the organizational patterns of the whole (the linguistic system) has renewed language study during this century. The approach has also provided a number of suggestions for theories of learning and language acquisition.

Anthropology. Claude Lévi-Strauss has acknowledged his debt to structural linguistics in his book *Structural Anthropology* (1958). In addition to Saussure, he cites Trubetzkoy, a member of the Prague school, and calls him the "illustrious founder of structural linguistics."[44] Lévi-Strauss quotes from Trubetzkoy, who described the structural method as four basic operations:

First, structural linguistics shifts from the study of "conscious" linguistic phenomena to the study of their "unconscious" infrastructure; second, it does not treat "terms" as independent entities, taking instead as its basis of analysis the "relations" between terms; third, it introduces the concept of "system"—"modern phonemics does not merely proclaim that phonemes are always part of a system; it 'shows' concrete phonemic systems and elucidates their structure"; finally, linguistics aims at discovering "general laws," either by induction "or . . . by logical deduction, which would give them absolute character."[45]

Although language is the predominant means of communication among human beings, nonverbal means of communication are also used. Messages can be sent in forms other than linguistic forms. The study of sign systems in general is called "semiology" in the United States and "semiotics" in Europe.[46] (These terms come from the Greek word *semeion*, "sign.") An example of a nonlinguistic sign might be a bunch of roses, used to signify passion. When used as a sign, the bunch of roses is not merely a horticultural entity; it is filled with signification which is a combination of the giver's intent and organizational patterns of meaning in the society.

Lévi-Strauss has explored garments, food, furniture, and architectural systems as sign systems which communicate meaning. The garment system, for example, consists of the pieces, parts, or details of garments. The juxtaposition of various skirts, blouses, and jackets is held to be equivalent to a syntagmatic organizational pattern, and the variation in pieces which are worn on the same part of the body (wearing a bonnet or a hood or a toque, for instance) is held to be equivalent to a paradigmatic organizational pattern. The structure in which meaning is given becomes evident only when the relationships between elements are considered. A systems view must be adopted, and the whole set of relations between elements must be studied in order to discover the relational patterns. The structure is not an observable fact, and it is not derived through probability inference. The elements—the variation in the clothing worn—change, but the relations or structures remain.

Lévi-Strauss has also applied the structural approach to the reading of myths and to kinship systems. The variations in these systems can be reduced to a small number of simple types or structures. Although the specific myths and kinship systems change, the basic patterns of relations remain the same, in the same manner that the individual, historical statements of *parole* vary, but the structure or *la langue* which allows words to take on meaning is relatively static.

Jakobson and Chomsky hold that the structuring patterns for phonics and syntax are unchanging and are part of the universal human psychological makeup. Lévi-Strauss holds a similar position in regard to the patterning of signs. In Lévi-Strauss's view, the changes brought about by history do not affect the human mind itself or its deep-organizing structures. It is as if the brain is prewired to devise meaning patterns of a particular style. For Lévi-Strauss, as for Jakobson, this style is binary and is similar to Boolean algebra.

The structures are not simple theoretical constructs which give a pattern to the observations. They also exist as part of the researcher and are the "source" of the relations observed. For Lévi-Strauss, they are not transcendent essences (essential patterns or principles shaping the experience of phenomena) correlated to the meaning bestowing process of a transcendental subject, but are a really existing part of the psyche as a natural reality. The structures emanate from the human mind and are always the same. Thus, they exist before the social system and are not derivative from it (as Durkheim held), and so they cannot be explained through a functional analysis.

> In anthropology as in linguistics . . . it is not comparison that supports generalization, but the other way around. If as we believe to be the case, the unconscious activity of the mind consists in imposing form upon content, and if these forms are fundamentally the same for all minds—ancient or modern, primitive or civilized (as the study of the symbolic function, as expressed in language, so strikingly indicates)—it is necessary and sufficient to grasp the unconscious structure underlying each institution and each custom in order to obtain a principle of interpretation valid for other institutions and other customs, provided, of course, that the analysis is carried far enough.[47]

Moreover, the structural organizational activity does not serve the needs of the social system, rather the reverse; the structures are patterns which precede all social systems, although they are the basic patterns which construct social meaning.

Dilthey (see chapter 1) also held that human experience is "structured" or organized by the life categories. For Dilthey, however, these categories change through history and are affected by historical circumstances. For Jakobson, Chomsky, and Lévi-Strauss, the particular expression of structures—the surface structures—changes in history, but the primary form of the organizing activity of human phenomena—the depth structures—is the same for all human beings at all times.

Psychology. The cognitive realm, conscious and unconscious, and the neural realm have been understood and modeled as systems. The linguistic and anthropological turn to universal structures has implied that the psychological nature of human beings is an open system with preestablished organizing procedures which take in sense data from the environment and construct them into organized patterns which make up experience.

Jean Piaget's approach to cognitive development draws upon his early training as a biologist and upon Saussure's work in linguistics. Piaget believes that the mind is made up of organizing structures which he has called "schemata." These cognitive schemata exist to organize stimuli by constructing holistic gestalts from partial information. The schemata are organized as wholes—that is, "every schema is . . . coordinate with all other schemata and itself constitutes a totality with differentiated parts."[48] The schemata, however, change over time, becoming more differentiated, less sensory, and more numerous, and the network they form becomes increasingly complex. Piaget's approach is a genetic approach to the organizing structures in that the general form of the schemata changes in stages that are linked to the chronological age of the maturing child, and he holds that particular schemata are formed through the processes of assimilation of and accommodation to stimuli.

Henri Ey's *Consciousness* (1963) reports on recent theory of neural organization. "The organization of the brain," Ey says, "corresponds neither to a reflex chain (not even a vertical one), nor to a mosaic of centers, nor to a homogeneous mass without localization."[49] Instead, he sees neural activity as a whole, a system which transforms the character of independent parts through the organization of the total system. Ey uses such terms as *transanatomical wholes, anatomical-functional configurations,* and *patterns of connection,* and he says that his viewpoint coincides "with the very notions of 'emergence' and of 'autonomy' ('boundary conditions') in the general theory of open systems (K. E. Boulding, L. von Bertalanffy, A. Koestler, K. Menninger, etc.)." Ey suggests an isomorphism between the structures of neural activity and the structures of consciousness. He uses the term *destructuralization* to describe his notion of the erosion of structure of the field of consciousness in acute psychoses.

Jason Brown presents a similar view of the neuropsychology of cognition in *Mind, Brain, and Consciousness* (1977). Brown expands the notion of destructuralization, which has been developed primarily in relation to disorders of language, to all of cognition. He proposes that the comprehension of the diversity of systems in patients with functional or organic brain disorders requires a structural approach to the cognitive process.[50]

Systems Inquiry and Methodology

These few examples of the use of the "systems and structures" system of inquiry, although brief and not discussed in detail, serve as illustrations of the application of this system of inquiry in human science research. Examples could be multiplied in each of the disciplinary areas mentioned, and they could be expanded to include literary criticism and philosophy.[51]

The research methods used in this system of inquiry differ considerably from the methods—hypothesis testing, rigorous control of experimental variables, and treatment of data with sophisticated statistical procedures—used in the nomothetical-deductive system. For example, Piaget's research is based on a clinical-descriptive technique he developed which involved asking individual children carefully selected questions and noting their responses. In some of his work, his data were based on observations of infant behavior. He frequently followed his "intuition" when he was interviewing children, and so it might be charged that, in effect, no two children received the same experimental treatment. His sample sizes were small, and the main source of his early data was his own three children, scarcely an unbiased sample.

The hypothetical-deductive model of logical positivism distinguished between description and explanation. Description was observation statements without interpretation, and explanation was the subsuming of these descriptions under lawlike statements. Because of the link between descriptions and laws, the prediction of future descriptions of events was possible. As we have seen, this separation of purely descriptive statements from law statements was severely criticized during the third and fourth phases in the recent development of the philosophy of science.

Structuralism, however, does not value the distinction between description and explanation. In the structural system of inquiry, explanation essentially refers to synchronic "causation" in which an event is explained by describing its role in the system of which it is a part. The answer to any "why" question is given by locating the event within the system. The deductive system explained an event by giving an "if . . . then" statement, noting that if the event in the "if" clause had occurred, then the event in the "then" clause must necessarily occur. But a systemic explanation ends in a description of the structure behind the event.

Scientific activity for the "systems" system of inquiry involves conceptualizing the phenomenon under investigation as a totality by defining its specific organizing principles, by showing that the events are the result of the interaction of these principles, and then by defining the part-whole relationships with the structures behind the event. Generalizations and regularities are explained by referring to the underlying structural activity through which they occur and through which they receive their qualities or characteristics. To describe the structure is to explain the event.

Research using the systems approach suggests that human beings are systemically organized, that they are not simply aggregates of independent parts. In this research, the organic, experiential base of the human realm is systemic, and so are its individual, social, and historical expressions. Individual entities can of course, be abstracted from their systemic environments and analyzed to discover the lawlike relations which hold among them. Although these procedures allow for a degree of accuracy and demonstrative logical treatment, they lose the connectedness which is part of their full characterization in the human realm.

Walter Buckley has described the tension that exists between these systems of inquiry:

> Behavioral scientists can be roughly divided into two groups: those who aspire to the scientific status of physical scientists and, in consequence, tend to select research problems that yield to the analytic method; and those who are moved by a need to "understand man." The former stand in danger of trivializing the study of man. . . . The latter stand in danger of obscuring the study of man in free-wheeling speculations without sufficient anchorage in facts or testable hypotheses.[52]

The systems approach uses a logic that is different from the logic used by the deductive and inductive systems. It represents a more open use of reason, and it shares the problem-solving goal of practical reason. The historical realism of the third chapter and the systems approach of this chapter both call for an expanded notion of reason. The systems system of inquiry is an effort to grasp an understanding of wholes while adhering to the principles of disciplined generalization and rigorous reflection.

5

Human Action

Human action is one of the subjects which divides the humanities from the physical sciences. The humanities study human expressions and actions, implicitly accepting the notion that human beings are free to choose to do various things and that they will, at times, freely produce exceptional and creative expressions. The sciences, on the other hand, assume that the universe is ordered and that events are causally related. Human science methodology looks toward both the humanities and the sciences as sources of knowledge about human phenomena, and it is therefore a crossing point for the two perspectives. Human science also views science itself as a human action, and the results of these investigations relate to the notion of scientific activity itself. Is human action, then, part of the causal nexus of the universe, as seen from the perspective of science, or is it freely determined by human agents, as seen from the perspective of the humanities? Are human actions significantly different from the rest of the changes that occur in nature, and if they are, in what ways are they different?

The renewed debate over the nature of human action received its impetus from Carl Hempel's classic paper "The Function of General Laws in History," published in 1942.[1] Hempel proposed that the explanation of human action in history should conform to the format of deductive-nomological explanation used in the natural sciences. It willl be remembered from chapter 3 that Hempel was the moving force behind the adoption by logical positivism of the deductively related theoretical network concept and the deductive format for explanation and prediction. His article had an impact on the methodology of history[2] and, through Donald Davidson, on action theory.[3]

Hempel's position was that human actions can be accounted for by the same "species" of causal explanation that is used in the

169

physical sciences, and there were, through the years, a number of energetic responses. Historian William Dray, in *Laws and Explanation in History* (1957), countered that historical explanations (which concern human actions) do not rely on general laws at all.[4] Also in the 1950s, Richard Taylor defended the view that human actions are not caused by antecedent events; people, he said, are agents of their own actions.[5] And Charles Taylor, in *The Explanation of Behavior* (1964), declared that human actions cannot be explained by causal laws of the deductive-nomological form (as Hempel had insisted) and proposed that human actions require a teleological form of explanation.[6]

A parallel development during this period grew out of Wittgenstein's later work. It was a reaction to the idea that statements about human action can be treated as references to mental events—that is, that what happens inside a person's head can cause bodily movement. The Wittgenstein group asserted that these statements are part of the language game which provides justifications or accounts of human actions. The statements about actions, they said, are not meant to convey information about mental events; instead they are statements which concern the rules of social interaction.

A third course of development concerned the nature of logic and its relationship to human action. Formal logical systems used in practical thought, including decision theory and deontic logic, were refined, and work was begun on uncovering the processes of the nonformal style of personal argumentation that is used by individuals and groups in making decisions. This nonformal approach is called "practical reasoning," and it shows promise as a means for helping to clarify the entire enterprise of science by treating it as an endeavor which engages in practical reasoning rather than in a formal system of demonstrative logic.

The Nature of Human Action

Wittgenstein, in his *Philosophical Investigations*, put the question about the nature of human action in this way:

> Let us not forget this: "When I raise my arm," my arm goes up. And the problem arises: What is left over if I subtract the fact that my arm goes up from the fact that I raise my arm?[7]

In other words: How are human actions significantly different from the rest of the changes that occur in nature—if at all?

In an example used by Weber, a description is given of a man who is in a forest gathering materials for a fire. The action of the man is contrasted with the pieces of wood that are lying on the forest floor and that the man is picking up. The pieces of wood are natural objects, and they have arrived in their present place and their present situation through the regular operations of nature as it has proceeded from the formulation of the nebulae, to the cooling of the earth, to the evolution of the plants, to the action of the winds carrying seeds from place to place, to the generative activity of moisture and the earth, and so on. The man reaches and picks up the pieces of wood, carries them to his home, and burns them to heat his house and provide his comfort.

In this comparison, the action of the man is different from the action of the wood because it involves movement. Human beings, like the other higher animals, can move about from place to place "on their own," and they can move and carry other things from one location to another as well. The pieces of wood lack the capacity for locomotion and self-movement. Thus, a characteristic of action is that it is the result of creatures who can initiate and direct their own movements. But self-movement, although it may be a necessary characteristic of action, is not sufficient in itself to define action. Self-movement is also a characteristic of other animals and of various self-propelled inanimate things. Some natural events are self-propelling (volcanic eruptions, for instance), and so are some artifacts (such as rockets). Consequently, other characteristics besides self-movement are needed to define action.

One additional characteristic can be discovered if we look at the man in the forest again. It is purposiveness. The man is picking up the wood *in order to* warm his house and bring comfort to himself. This characteristic, however, even though it is necessary, may not be sufficient to define human action, either. A guided missile, an artifact, is purposeful in its movement as it alters direction in response to information given to it. And the activity of an animal is purposeful when it responds to signals in its environment as it hunts for food or seeks protection for itself.

In addition to self-locomotion and purposiveness, human action has the characteristic of intention. Intention exists when somebody does something with an awareness of an action-plan. The guided missile does not act from awareness or from a plan of its own; what it does is the result of mechanical changes which are part of a complex causal network of events. And here a distinction must be made: the term *purposeful* is used to describe the goal-directed events of cybernetic systems; the term *purposive* is reserved for the intentional experience which characterizes human action.[8] The characteristic of intentional awareness consists of the experience of wanting something and believing that a particular movement will achieve what is wanted. Whether intentional mental events are to be considered as part of the natural order, causally linked to antecedent physical and mental events, is a central question within action theory.

The definition developed thus far states that human action is intentional, purposive, self-propelled movement. But this definition is too simple; exceptions to these characteristics can be found. For instance, there are some things which seem to be human actions and yet do not involve self-generated movement. Are mental activities—such as conjuring up a memory or imagining some future event—to be considered human action? What about intentional omissions—such as refusing to move when ordered to do so? At the same time, there are some human activities that have become habitual and no longer involve intentional awareness. For example, when one is learning to play tennis, one is very much aware of the intention to use a particular motion of the arm to toss the ball for the serve, but after one has played tennis for many years one moves the arm and tosses the ball without any intentional planning. The motion and the toss have become habit, even though they can return to conscious action if the serve repeatedly misses and one is obliged to pay more attention.

Human beings "do" many things which are not actions. We are born, and we die. We bleed, and we tremble. We stumble, and we fall. These are unintended, inadvertent, unknowing, accidental, reflex "happenings," and thus they are not actions. Thoughts and memories "come" to us; dreams appear in consciousness; fear and anxiety manifest themselves in us. These events are not intentional, either, and so they are not actions.

Human action concerns intended activity. As such it includes communication acts as well as bodily movements. Communication acts leave traces: literature, art, artifacts, and organizational and social systems. The subject matter of human science is the realm of human action and its traces. The recent thought about how this action can be accounted for and explained is of central importance for the renewed methodological debate.

The remainder of this chapter will be concerned with explanations of human action. We will consider first the approaches that hold that explanation of human action should be of the causal type—that is, the type used by the physical sciences. Next we will look at the objections of William Dray, Richard Taylor, and Charles Taylor to this type of explanation, and we will give particular consideration to Charles Taylor's position that human action should be accounted for by using the teleological type of explanation. Because of clarifications about the concept of teleology which have been made through the development of cybernetics, the use of teleological accounts needs to distinguish "purposeful" behaviors programmed to achieve end points and "purposive" actions freely chosen as means to obtain goals. Following that discussion, we will look at the language-analysis approach to human action that has been encouraged by Wittgenstein's later work. Finally, we will summarize the development of practical reasoning.

Explanations and Accounts of Human Action: Causal Explanations

Hempel's 1942 paper was concerned with the methodology of history. Historians from Saint Augustine to R. G. Collingwood had sought to account for historical events by investigating individual human choices, and they had used teleological explanations. Hempel wanted to clarify historical methods, and he proposed that historians could become more "scientific" by consciously applying the methodology developed in the physical sciences. He suggested that the difference between history and the physical sciences was merely programmatic. The deductive-nomological model of scientific explanation was applicable to history as well as to the physical sciences, he said, and it was therefore unnecessary to devise alternative accounts of the way explanation proceeds in history.

Hempel recognized that history had a long way to go before its finished products would conform visibly and in detail to the proposed model of explanation in the same way that the products of the "more mature" physical sciences already did. The reason that the full formulation of general laws was missing from past historical research was primarily that the laws were too complex and required a long chain of premises in order to allow historians to deduce particular events as conclusions. Historians had characteristically given elliptical or incomplete explanations, which were, strictly speaking, only explanatory sketches. Hempel suggested what a "scientific" history might be:

An explanatory account may suggest, perhaps quite vividly and persuasively, the general outline of what, it is hoped, can eventually be supplemented so as to yield a more closely reasoned argument based on explanatory hypotheses which are indicated more fully.[9]

Those who follow Hempel's notion that human actions can be explained through deductive-nomological laws of a causal type can be divided into two groups: those who hold that only public observations can count as scientific data, and those who accept introspectively known mental events as part of causal explanations. The first group is composed of two subgroups: those who limit discussion to observable behavior, and those who infer internal variables (such as attitudes and beliefs) from behavior. The second group accepts mental events (such as wanting to achieve something and holding a belief that a particular act will achieve that something) as part of the causal chain; this group also accepts the data of self-reports regarding the occurrence of mental events.

Explanations in Terms of Public Observations

Behaviorism. Defining human action as intentional behavior creates difficulties for those systems of science which are committed to admitting only sensed observations as data. The verification theory of truth, with its correspondence rules, can include only those concepts which are linked to direct observations. This approach is often called "objectivism" in reference to the fact that only intersubjectively agreed-upon observations are accepted as admissible data.[10] The mental states of people—their thoughts, feelings, wishes, and hopes—are not directly accessible to public inspection, and thus hypotheses about these states cannot be tested by appeal to observational data in the way that a hypothesis about a liquid's acidity can be tested by appeal to the intersubjectively observable change in color of a piece of litmus paper. Although we are frequently correct in our everyday inferences about other people's mental states, all we have to go on is what they choose to tell us or what we can observe of their behavior and expressions. There is no way of independently testing the accuracy of our inferences about the mental states of other people, and so a science committed to using only observational data has to refrain from appeal to mental events in accounting for human action.[11] Nevertheless, there are those who maintain that the exclusive use of observational data provides a legitimate (for some, a complete) description.

A causal explanation[12] can be given, in principle, by means of terms that, like those in the physical sciences, have reference only to objectively observable properties of physical objects. In this approach to human action, the material objects are human bodies in motion. The event of a bodily movement can be related to another event in the environment in the same way that any two physical events can be related. A lawlike statement or hypothesis can be tested by deducing a sample of the events which would hold if the hypothesis is correct. The hypothesis "If stimulus type A, then response type B" can be tested by sampling the occurrence of some type A events to see if type B events also occur. Through experimental design, the researcher can test whether the relationship between the type A event and the type B event is necessary and sufficient sequential relationship. If so, then the law "If type A, then type B" is a "causal" law. It is also possible to conduct purely inductive research in which the researcher examines the occurrence of pairs of multiple events and from these observations induces a probability of relationship between or among them.

In these systems of inquiry about human action, such mentalistic terms as *purpose* and *thought* are left out by the definition of what is admissible as data. In these systems, the behavioral scientist is a spectator of the human scene, noting its observable features and the connections among them. The researcher seeks regularities in human behavior, just as the physicist looks for regularities in inanimate behavior.

Neo-Behaviorism. Some researchers using these "causal" systems have moved far beyond the early behaviorists, who were unwilling to use mental concepts as part of the repertoire of explanatory categories. Mental concepts are now translated into observational terms by means of operational definitions that specify which observable behaviors represent a particular mental concept. For example, the mental concept of "intelligence" is translated into objective (that is, intersubjectively observable) behavioral responses to carefully constructed questions.

The validity of instruments constructed to measure these mental states or events is an evaluation of the successfulness of translating a mental state into a set of observable behaviors. In fact, the major thrust of psychological research during the past twenty years has been the investigation of mental or cognitive states and events through the method of translating these private and inaccessible events into publicly observable behaviors. Such mental areas as recognition, attention, memory, decision-making strategies, and language processing have been given attention by researchers using procedures which produce objective data held to represent mental events. Sociologists and social psychologists have investigated attitudes, values, "attribution processes," and other "subjective" characteristics, often using creatively designed instruments for translating the concepts into objectively acknowledged data.[13] Researchers have also investigated mental events through the use of electroencephalograms; the neurological electrical activity which is recorded by electrodes is stipulated to be a physiological correlate of mental activity.

This system of inquiry—which uses observational data to infer internal (mental or neurological) action—is now the primary approach used by academic psychology and sociology. Although its results are more often given as correlations than as causes, and although its research is concerned with empirical generalizations rather than with the testing of large theories, its logic is a species of Hempel's notion of lawlike generalizations, and its approach to human action shares the format of the physical sciences. It is assumed that action can be investigated in the same way that other regular occurrences in nature are investigated—through the comparison of scores along variables.

Mental Events as Causes of Action

Among the investigators who accept the general logic of regular relations among events, there is a group which also admits directly experienced mental events as data. In this approach, intentional actions are defined as movements which are caused by particular sorts of mental events or states.[14] The kinds of mental events that are involved in causing intentional acts are reason, decisions, choices, and resolve or determination that precedes movement or action.

In response to the question "Why did he turn out the light?" the answer is given: "He turned out the light because he thought it was unnecessary and wasteful to have the light on during the daytime." This answer mentions an antecedent of the action, a belief that is held by the person in question and has prompted him to take the action he has taken. The general category of explanations of intentional human action which refer to antecedent mental events or states is called "reason-explanations." "Reason," in this usage, refers to the mental events which would be described in answer to the question "What was your reason?" or "Why did you do that?"

When a human action is explained in terms of the agent's reason, what kind of explanation is it? Specifically, is this a species of causal explanation, or is it an explanation of quite a different sort? Donald Davidson and Alvin Goldman, following Hempel, hold that there is no radical difference between reason-explanations and ordinary causal explanations. Mental events, such as action-plans, they say, can cause physical events. If a person flips the switch in order to turn on the light, and if we want to explain the flipping of the switch (the explanandum), we can refer (as the explanans) to the mental event, the desire to have the light turn on, and to the action-plan or belief that flipping the switch will turn on the light. Thus, it is the person's action-plan that has caused the act of flipping the switch.

The notion of causation in this context serves as a reminder of the problems connected with the concept of "cause." Hume claimed that all that can be observed is a constant conjunction between objects. But the term *cause* commonly means more than just conjunction; it means a type of conjunction in which the occurrence of one event is a sufficient condition for the production of a second event—there is cause and effect. Consequently, the assertion that an event in the mental realm causes an event in the physical realm raises again the much-discussed philosophical issue concerning the relationship between the mind and the body.

The reason-explanation theory, as causal, is couched in traditional interactionist terms. As presented, it is incompatible with epiphenomenalism, which holds that there is only one-way causality which goes from body to mind, and with parallelism, which asserts that the mind and the body are much too different from each other to be able to interact causally. It is also incompatible with certain forms of materialism, which maintain that mental events are really nothing but physical events.[15]

Goldman believes that in discussing mental causes we must expand the notion of causes so that it goes beyond the kind of "mechanical" causation in which billiard balls are said to propel one another or levers are said to push and pull. According to Goldman, we need to admit the expanded notion of causality which appears in commonsense understanding:

> From a commonsense point of view, some of the clearest cases of causality involve intentionalistic states. Among the most certain causal propositions we know may be the proposition that S's desire for sleep was caused, at least in part, by his having stayed awake for 35 hours, and that S's thinking of Vienna was caused by his wife reminding him of their trip.[16]

In this view, intentional states (mental events) are sometimes causes of other events, including acts. But to say that one thing causes another is not to say what kind of cause is involved, and it certainly is not to say that the cause involved is the kind of mechanical cause that is described in nineteenth-century physics books. Reasons can be causes of actions without being mechanical causes; even in physics, such causes are no longer thought to be the only sorts of causes that exist. Our reasons can move us, even if they do not do so in the way that one billiard ball moves another or in the way that the moon moves the tides.

The kinds of mental events that are the causes of action are held to be sets of wants and beliefs—that is, the kinds of events we appeal to in order to find reasons for our actions. The mental cause theory holds that an intentional movement (an action) is one in which the person wants the movement (or its consequence) to occur and that the wanting causes the movement to occur. Where a volition (act of will) intervenes,[17] the wanting causes the volition which causes the occurrence. There are also more complex instances where the occurrence of one event is a means to accomplish the occurrence of a second event. Let us assume that I want to drive my car as a means of getting to my friend's house. If I want the second event to occur (arriving at my friend's house), and if I believe that the first event (driving the car) will produce the second event, and if the wanting and the belief cause me to get into the car, then—and only then—is the first act intentional.

During the late 1950s, as the deductive-nomological system began to come under attack for its internal logical inconsistencies (for example, its assumption that observation and theory statements could be independent of each other), it also came under attack for its treatment of mental phenomena and human action as explainable and predictable through subsumption under laws. The criticism appeared in various disciplines, increasing in volume during the 1960s. In general, this literature proposed that mental phenomena and human action require an explanatory scheme which acknowledges the acausal and nonrandom nature of these phenomena.

Arguments against the mental cause theory. The first argument against the causal position is called the "logical-connection" argument. An early presentation of the logical-connection argument was made by A. I. Melden in *Free Action* (1961).[18] This argument points out that in causal explanations the causes must be logically independent of each other in such a way that the existence or nonexistence of one event in no way logically entails the existence or nonexistence of the other event. In regard to human action, this means that the desire and the belief must be independent of the action. But in the mental cause explanation, the very reasons given for acting in a particular way must make mention of the action. That is, the reason for turning on the light (in the example given) is that the individual wanted to turn on the light. Consequently, one is left with an example of the same kind of supposed cause that is implied when the question "What is the cause of the drug putting someone to sleep?" is answered with the statement "The cause is the drug's soporific power." This is no explanation at all; it merely has the appearance of an explanation, because "soporific power" is only another way of saying "power to cause sleep."

Davidson, defending the mental cause theory, answers that there *is* independence, because when the action is mentioned in stating the causal reason there is no implication that the action will occur. The expectation that one will do something and the actual doing of that something are independent, then, of the existence or nonexistence of the other event.[19]

Another argument against the mental cause theory concerns the notion of causal laws in relation to actions. The causal explanation appeals either implicitly or explicitly to a lawlike generalization which links cause and effect by stating that whenever the prior mental event happens, the action effect must follow. The argument asserts that reasons and actions do not meet this condition. It is possible to have a belief and a desire to do something without actually doing it. A person may want to be at a friend's house, and may believe that driving his car will help him achieve that end, but if the car will not start, there is nothing that the mental events can do to bring about the desired result. It is clear, then, that reason-explanations are not supported by causal laws. In a causal law, the consequent can be deduced from the premises, and if the premises are true, then the conclusion will be true. "The statement that one person did something because, for example, another threatened him, carries no implication or covert assertion that if the circumstances were repeated the same action would follow."[20] Therefore, the relationship between mental events and actions is not causal; mental events and actions are related in another way.

Davidson, responding to this criticism, admits that generalizations connecting reasons and actions do not constitute the kinds of laws which can serve as the basis for accurate predictions, but this is so, he says, because of the complexity of human situations. A specific intentional action is determined by multiple causes; the actor's beliefs and wants are necessary but not sufficient to cause an action. Without the agent's reasons, the physical event might happen, but it would no longer be described as an action. It could conceivably happen that a person might be taken by force to a friend's house, and the physical event would be the same—arrival at the house—but it would not be the result of a human action by the person who was taken. Reasons are required to explain actions.

In Hempel's format for explanation, the law and initial conditions are required for predicting the consequent. In human action, the initial conditions are held to be complex. The generalization of the causal connection between the mental event and the action should include the initial conditions. The form of the generalization would thus read: "Whenever a person has such-and-such wants and beliefs and is in such-and-such circumstances, then he or she will act in such-and-such a way." Davidson also holds that the laws connecting reasons and actions are probably complex:

> Any serious theory for predicting action on the basis of reasons must find a way of evaluating the relative force of various desires and beliefs in the matrix of decision; it cannot take as its starting point the refinement of what is to be expected from a single desire.[22]

Moreover, these laws may ultimately be statistical laws and not, therefore, perfectible according to a deductive formulation. This would mean, assuming that all of the relevant information about the initial conditions was available, that the action would proceed from the matrix of desires and reasons only some of the time, although the ratio concerning how often could be given. Others have said (for example, Weber) that these causal laws hold only for rational action or for ideal cases where the action takes place in contexts free of irrational responses.

Dray has maintained that the specifications of the initial conditions which a general law would hold would require such an extensive description that the conditions would hold only for the specific case under consideration, thus making the notion of laws in the human situation trivial. Consequently, he says, the relationship between reasons and action should not be considered as a species of the causal law model.

A third criticism presented against the mental cause theory concerns the type of observations that are usually required to establish a causal law. Giving an answer to the question "Why did you do that?" does not require that people engage in a number of similar acts and then, through induction, come to the conclusion that they performed the acts because they wanted to perform them. The relationship between wants and beliefs and an action is not revealed by the examination of instances; it is known directly. We have knowledge of our own intentions without inference, and so this knowledge is not of the causal law type. Causal law knowledge requires the testing of sample deductions from the law to confirm the law.

Davidson counters this argument by asserting that induction is not the only way to learn the truth of a causal law. "In order to know that a singular causal statement is true," he says, "it is not necessary to know the truth of a law; it is necessary only to know that some law covering the events at hand exists."[22] One case is often enough to persuade us that a law exists, and we do not need to know the law itself.

The causal law theory of the relationship between reasons and action supports the notion that the investigation of human action can conform to the covering-law approach of the deductive system. Because it can, it is also susceptible to the general attacks which have been made on that model (described in chapter 3). Nevertheless, it provides the basic format for behavioral and social science research on human actions. Generally, the approach claims that the states and dispositions of people cause their particular beliefs and wants which, in turn, cause a particular action. For example, a person who has a general conservative disposition, it is believed, will want to elect a conservative candidate to public office; if the person believes that one candidate is more conservative than other candidates, he or she will vote for that candidate.

This approach assumes that people's beliefs cause them to act in predictable ways. That is, if we know what someone's beliefs and dispositions are, then we can predict (although only with probability) how that person will act in a given situation and we can explain why the person has acted the way he or she has acted in a particular situation in the past. For example, the mental state of "need for achievement" affects a person's actions. (Notice that the word *affects* is used; the word *causes* is avoided because there is difficulty in obtaining experimental control over mental events and because the word itself is controversial.) Thus, someone with a high need for achievement chooses tasks which are of only moderate difficulty, and someone with a high fear of failure chooses tasks of low difficulty. Some researchers have tried to create particular mental states—for instance, fear—so that they can observe the variance between actions based on "normal" reasons and actions based on "fearful" reasons.

Freedom and determinism. If reason-explanations are causal, then— insofar as we act for reasons—our behavior is caused. Causal explanations that conform to the deductive-nomological model explain action as instances of exceptionless laws. Reason-explanations derived from this interpretation are deterministic: they imply the inevitability of the actions explained in the light of the antecedent mental events and circumstances and in light of laws of nature (which include relationships between mental events and physical events). If the causal laws are held to be statistical in these cases, then particular actions are probable, given the preceding circumstances. A particular action is not inevitable, but the explanation that invokes the applicable statistical law shows that there is good reason to anticipate the action. One understanding of statistical laws holds that an underlying relationship is really an exceptionless relationship and that, if we had more information, the statistical law would be replaced by an absolute deductive law. Another understanding of statistical laws holds that the relationship itself is truly a relationship of some randomness and the probability index is a statement of the actual relationship. In either case, however, it is not usually maintained by this position that randomness is the result of the free choice of actors, but that it is, instead, situated in the bond between the intention and the action.

There are two positions regarding the link between intention (reason) and action. One position states that the link is lawful and determinate but that the intention itself is undetermined and derives from the will of the actor. The other position maintains that the intention is caused by yet other factors (such as disposition), and these, in turn, are caused by still other factors which link back to events outside the actor's control. The action, then, is simply an identified point in a chain of causally related events, and it is a cause of subsequent events. Thus, the chain of causal bonds reaches from outside the individual, through the bodily and psychic apparatuses, into conscious attention where it appears as wants and beliefs, and into the physical motion of the body, and it is the body which causes other events.

This second position is usually called *determinism*. In "hard determinism," all human actions and their antecedents are ultimately functions of features of their agents' initial genetic endowments, the environment(s) in which they have lived, and the interactions or experiences with which they have been connected. Richard Taylor says that such a determinism implies a "fatalistic" attitude because the individual cannot control "whether or when or where [an event] will occur" that will cause him to act in a certain way.[23]

The view traditionally called libertarian is incompatible with determinism. It maintains that people—at least most people—are autonomous in and responsible for much of what they do. Libertarians have often argued that we know this from our own experience of having to make decisions and act. In this view, the ultimate cause of a decision and an action is the agent. A person can actually do something other than what he does. This position might be called *nondeterminism*, and it should not be confused with *indeterminism*, which holds that nothing is caused regarding either physical or mental events. In libertarianism, the possibility of choice exists, and it is exercised at times when a person considers which of two or more actions is to be taken and makes a real choice between or among them.

Most of human activity is the result of habit or the tendency toward typical behavior which free people to concentrate on those choices which they consider deserving of attention. For example, a person does not choose to tense certain muscles so as to move the legs in order to walk. These actions are habitual, and they allow a person to decide to walk across a room. Some choice remains, however: a person can choose which leg muscles to tense in order to accomplish a particular goal, such as imitating a limp.[24]

Explanations and Accounts of Human Action: Acausal Explanations

A common feature of the recent nondeterministic theories of action is their insistence that special qualities are involved in the understanding of human action. This represents a more or less explicit reaction to behavioristic psychology, which has tended to accommodate explanation to the patterns provided by the behavior of inanimate objects. The nondeterministic theories maintain that human action requires a type of explanation that differs from the deductive-nomological and the causal kinds. In these views, human action stands out in a special way from the rest of the physical and biological world and possesses properties which have emerged in the reflective capacity of human beings.

In response to the causal explanation model for human action, the major effort has been made by the linguistic analysts. They assert that "reasons" given for actions are not references to antecedent mental events at all but are social communications. At the same time, there have been several criticisms of the causal explanation model that have maintained that human actions are susceptible to explanation in terms of "reasons," although the type of explanation cannot be the Hempelian deductive-nomological form.

Alternatives to the causal explanation model fall into two categories. In the first category is a theory that explains human action as autonomous acts of agents; William Dray and Richard Taylor have spoken for this position. In the second category is a theory, proposed by Charles Taylor, that human action can be explained according to the model of teleological explanation. Our description of the teleological model of explanation will require an excursion into recent theoretical developments which hold that teleology is simply a type of nomological explanation.

Action Explained by an Autonomous Agent

William Dray's *Laws and Explanation in History* (1957)[25] responded to the logical empiricist proposal for a "scientific" history by asserting that historical explanations do not rely on general laws. As an example, Dray used Louis XIV of France, who was unpopular because he pursued policies which were detrimental to French national interests. The deductive-nomological approach would hold that this "historical event" illustrates a general law that states that all rulers who commit acts that are detrimental to national interests become unpopular. The law would hold, however, only if so many limiting and qualifying initial conditions were added that in the end it would be equivalent to saying that all rulers who pursue similar policies to those of Louis XIV, under exactly similar conditions to those existing in France and the other countries affected by his policies, become unpopular. As Dray pointed out, what one ends up with is merely a restatement of the unique event, not a generic law which will hold in a general way.

To explain a historical action, Dray said, is to show that the action is the appropriate or rational thing to do on the occasion under consideration. He termed this a "rational explanation." The historian's task, he continued, is not to develop general laws; his task is to reconstruct "the agent's calculation of means to be adopted toward his chosen end and in the light of the circumstances in which he found himself; and to explain the action we need to know what considerations convinced him that he should act as he did."[26] The historian explains, then, by imputing to the agent an act of practical reasoning through which he or she has decided to do what he or she has done. For Dray, actions are unique events that are determined by the actor's considerations, and thus they cannot be instances subsumed under a "covering law." The answer to the question "Why have people acted the way they have acted?" is "They calculated what should be done in the situation, and they did it."

Following the reason-explanation mode of human action, research concerns itself with describing the reasons people give for their actions. If a person is available, he or she can be queried concerning why he or she has done something; if a person is a historical figure, then letters or documents can provide the answer. The rational agent becomes the final term in the explanation, and no further causes are sought beyond him.

During the 1950s, Richard Taylor proposed an agency model of explanation in several articles, and this notion was given extended treatment in his *Action and Purpose* (1966). Taylor asserted that agents can be "active"—that is, they can start chains of events in the world and need not function merely as links in chains already started. In other words, human beings are sometimes the cause of their own behavior; the action is caused by the agent who performs it. No antecedent conditions are sufficient to account for the fact that the person has performed precisely the action he or she has performed. Sometimes these actions are performed after the actor has intended to perform them, but at other times reasons are not consciously present before the act is performed, and in these instances the actor provides "rationalizations" when presented with the query, "Why did you do that?"

This conception fits what we assume ourselves to be. We see ourselves as beings who cause things to happen, not as beings whose behavior is merely the consequence of conditions which act upon us. And yet we are fully aware that we are not the cause of certain events in which we are intimately involved. For example, my pulse is regulated—which is to say caused, because it is purposeful in a cybernetic way—by certain conditions within me. It is not caused by me. It is not a human action, because I have nothing to do with it, do not serve as its agent. I do not intend its action, and I do not take control over it (except in rare instances when I purposively change its rate as part of meditative exercises).

Taylor has described his conception of an agent who causes activity in this way:

> [This conception] involves . . . rather strange metaphysical notions that are never applied elsewhere in nature. The [notion] is that of a "self" or "person" . . . who is not merely a collection of things or events, but a substance and self-moving being. For on this view it is a man himself, and not merely some part of him or something within him, that is the cause of his own activity. . . . Even though a man is a living being, of enormous complexity, there is nothing, apart from the requirements of this theory, to suggest that his behavior is so radically different in its origin from that of other physical objects, or that an understanding of it must be sought in some metaphysical realm wholly different from that appropriate to the understanding of nonliving things.[27]

This conception involves, in fact, a radically different notion of causation. The notion of causation, in which events are caused by beings that are not themselves events, but substances, is completely different from the usual notion of causation that lies in antecedent events which are sufficient to produce other events. Because of this difference, Taylor suggested that another word should be used to describe the relationship between agents and the events they bring about. Instead of the word *cause*, he said, it would be better to use such words as *originate*, *initiate*, and *perform*.[28]

Action Explained by Teleological Laws

In *The Explanation of Behavior* (1964), Charles Taylor proposed that human actions are instances of teleological laws instead of causal laws.[29] Teleological laws relate events to their intended consequences rather than to antecedent events. Actions occur because of their suitability for achieving the purposes of their agents.

Taylor held that human actions are goal oriented and are consciously purposive. Only a teleological explanation, in terms of Aristotle's final cause, would be valid for human action, he said. The adoption of the notion of final cause for human action requires some redefinition of the concept as used by Aristotle, so as not to introduce some obscure force or require a reversal of the temporal order of causality. In a teleological explanation, the explanatory principle is based on the form of a system in which the condition for the appearance of an event is that the appearance will bring about the proposed end. The form of a teleological law is such that an event is accounted for in terms of how it is required so that an end can be brought about. In sum, a teleological law reads: "Whenever an action of type A is most suitable of all the types in the agent's repertoire for achieving the agent's purpose, an action of type A occurs."[30] Thus, one can account for—explain—a human action by using a teleological law.

Joseph Rychlak, in *The Psychology of Rigorous Humanism* (1977), proposed a psychology based on teleological understanding.[31] Rychlak coined the term *telosponse* to differentiate "response" in human action from the "response" mode of stimulus–response: "Human beings do not 'learn' to telospond. It is an aspect of their very nature, a description of what mind 'is' rather than how it has been molded into performing from some other innate condition."[32] He called for the inclusion of teleological laws in psychological theory and asked that this theory be submitted to the same control-and-prediction methods of testing that have been used in nonteleological hypotheses. In this way, he said, a "rigorous" testing of teleological laws would be achieved.

Teleological explanations have long been a part of biological and human science. There have been, however, recent developments in cybernetic systems which seem to display teleological activity, and these developments have caused a reexamination of teleology which has resulted in a proposal that teleological laws are merely complex connections among causal laws.

The word *teleology* is derived from the Greek word *telos*, which means "completion" or "end." One of Aristotle's four causes was the final cause—that is, "that, for the sake of which" something happens. According to Aristotle's explanation, the reason that a rock fell to the ground was that the essence of a rock was "earth," and the rock moved toward the earth in order to arrive at its appropriate resting place. The final cause was the end toward which the object moved. With the rise of modern science, the concept of a final cause was found unnecessary to account for motion. Galileo could account fully for the motion of the planets by appealing to preexistent laws of motion; he did not need the idea that the planets were moving in order to achieve some end. By the seventeenth century, the concept of a teleological explanation was rarely used by physical science. William Harvey's studies of blood circulation, Boyles's studies of gases, and Huygens's conception of centrifugal force did not need the notion of "for the sake of" for comprehending the events.

But even though teleological explanations had been discarded in the physical sciences, some biologists and human scientists continued to use them. Certain biologists, while agreeing that the physico-chemical explanations of life did not require a teleological approach, argued that life itself was more than a physicochemical entity, that it was an emergent property, and it therefore could not be comprehended by studying only its components. These were biologists who held the organistic position, who studied an organism as interrelated parts which contribute to the maintenance of the organism as a whole.

As we have noted, Carl Hempel's 1942 paper "The Function of General Laws in History" proposed that all explanation, including explanation of historical events, could use the same deductive-nomological model. In this model, events are subsumed under general laws. The point of Hempel's paper was that history (human science) used—or should use—the logic of explanation used in the physical sciences. In the physical sciences, observations are made with a view toward establishing laws which are then used to make predictions; in history, laws are used to explain "observations"—although the laws do conform to the same logical type.

In 1943, Arturo Rosenblueth, Norbert Wiener, and Julian Bigelow published an article titled "Behavior, Purpose, and Teleology."[33] These authors wrote independently of Hempel, but they had a similar intention of extending the deductive system of explanation to biology and the behavioral sciences. They proposed a "deductivist" account of "teleology" through the concept of "negative feedback." This concept came from the development of a technology based on feedback control during World War II. With the advent of bomber aircraft, the antiaircraft gun became a major weapon of defense. Since an airplane moved so rapidly, the gun could not be aimed at the present position of the target, for the target would have changed position by the time the bullet reached it. Information about speed, angle of descent or ascent, and so on had to be taken on successively observed positions, and then extremely rapid calculations had to be made before the gun could be aimed. Wartime technology created a device which had a goal programmed into it; the goal was to have a bullet strike an airplane. The device received information about the path of an airplane and made a "decision" about where to aim the gun and when to fire it. Other devices of a similar type operated on the principle of corrected performance; information was fed back to the device concerning its previous action, and the device automatically "adjusted" itself by calculating the difference between its goal and its previous performance.

These devices exhibit the principle of "equifinality"—that is, they can choose various paths to the same goal—and this action resembles the "purposive" behavior of living organisms. Another example is the ordinary thermostat, which operates through information feedback to maintain a predetermined temperature. It is a self-regulating or homeostatic system similar to those which operate within biological systems to maintain a constant body temperature. The general study of "self-correcting" machines designed to achieve programmed goals became known as cybernetics, a term coined by Norbert Wiener in 1948 from the Greek word for "steersman." The development of the field of cybernetics has had a revolutionizing effect on technology, but it has also had a major impact on the philosophy of science. Cybernetics provides an illustration of how the laws of the physical realm can account for "goal-directed" behavior, eliminating any need to employ teleological explanations.

The analysis of teleology proposed by Rosenblueth, Wiener, and Bigelow appears to agree with Hempel's proposal that all scientific explanation can adhere to the deductive-nomological model. Various other proposals have been made that support the contention that teleological explanations are reducible to forms of the causal type of deductive-nomological explanations. For example, such proposals have been made by Richard Braithwaite in Scientific Explanation (1953) and by Ernest Nagel in The Structure of Science (1961).[34] A question remains concerning the extent of the behavior that can be explained by the cybernetics model. Georg H. von Wright has maintained that cybernetic explanations lack the idea of intentionality which is central to the understanding of human actions.[35]

Purpose and Function. The domain traditionally considered for teleology needs to be divided between purposeful activity and functional activity. When this distinction is not made, confusion about the nature of human actions results. The summary which follows carries the assumption that human action is something more than purpose and function. Later sections of this chapter will propose that human action includes the actor's intention and may also include conscious deliberation. The terms *purpose* and *function* as used here can apply to artifacts and organic systems as well as to some of the behavior of humans.

Purposeful activity is activity which exhibits persistence toward a goal under varying conditions. Such activity requires that a goal be identified and that both persistence toward it and sensitivity to varying conditions which affect the attainment of it be in evidence. These criteria for identifying purposeful action hold not only for human beings but also for other animals and for such artifacts as self-guided missiles.[36]

Critics of this definition point out that a river is persistent in reaching the sea and is sensitive to the conditions necessary for reaching the sea—it detours around all obstacles—but one could not call the flowing of a river purposeful, and one could not call reaching the sea the river's goal. In response to this type of criticism, George Sommerhoff has offered a more extensive analysis of purpose.[37] Sommerhoff defines *purpose* by using a concept that he calls "directive correlation," which he also uses to define *sensitivity* and *persistence toward a goal.* Directive correlation occurs when two variables—one a steering variable and the other the goal state—are independent in the sense that the value of one is compatible with any value of the other. For example, a target-tracking mechanism exhibits purposeful behavior because the two variables—the position of the target (the goal variable) and the direction of the mechanism (the steering variable)—are independent; they are, however, related so that the correlated variables are sufficient for the realization of the goal, the striking of the target. Sommerhoff's definition of purposeful activity, then, is activity that exhibits sensitivity and persistence toward a goal as a result of directive correlation.

In the analyses of Sommerhoff and Braithwaite, purposeful behavior does not involve a special kind of causality; it involves only a special organization of ordinary causal processes. According to these writers, both living organisms and machines are capable of purposeful activity, and consequently special concepts or patterns of description and explanation are not needed for it. Still at issue, however, is a question of whether human actions are fully accounted for by this description of purpose. Those who have followed Hempel and Braithwaite tend to answer yes, but others have held that this description of purpose does not account for the actions of agents who act deliberately for the sake of consciously envisioned ends. It may be that the acts of agents are, in principle, unpredictable and can be accounted for only after the event. We will return to this matter in the next section after discussing function.

Functional activities are those activities which contribute to a *fundamental* process of a whole, while purposeful activities, as we have seen, are persistent, flexible patterns of directively correlated behavior which seeks a goal. Some functional activities may be purposeful, but others are not. We ordinarily attribute functions to two sorts of systems, artifacts and organisms. Let us consider the simple artifact of a cooking pan. First, we ascribe a function to the pan as a whole; in this case, the function of the pan is to cook. Next, we ascribe functions to the parts and properties of the pan, insofar as they "contribute" to the function of the pan as a whole— that is, their usefulness in cooking. The function of the handle is to provide a grip, and within the subsystem of the handle the function of the rivets is to attach the handle, and so on. The function of the metal of which the pan is made is to conduct heat. We can see, then, that functions are hierarchical. The whole has a function, and each subordinate part has a function which contributes to the next level above it and, ultimately, to the function of the whole.

Since an artifact is an object produced or shaped by human workmanship as an aid to our own activities, the function usually ascribed to it is its contribution to the human activity for which it has been designed. However, the concept of "artifact" may be interpreted quite broadly to include not only things like cooking pans and tools but all cultural products—for example, works of art, language, and legal systems. Within this broad interpretation, one can ask such questions as "What is the function of Mary Tyrone in Eugene O'Neill's play *Long Day's Journey into Night?*" or "What is the function of prepositions in German?"

In assigning functions to living organisms, the whole can be considered to be the species, and its fundamental process of function can be considered to be maintenance. A step down in the hierarchical process is then considered to be the individual member whose fundamental functions are maintenance and reproduction. These functions of individual members contribute to the function of the maintenance of the species as a whole. Within the single organism, the functions of the various parts are understood as contributions to survival and reproduction. For example, the heart contributes to survival by pumping blood, the valves of the heart contribute to the function of pumping blood, and so on. A functional analysis would locate the particular activity in the hierarchy and demonstrate how the activity serves functions in relationship to the system of which it is a part. The various systems within the whole, of course, do not function in a purely hierarchical manner, but these systems are completely interrelated so that they contribute to various elements in the hierarchy.

The controversy over holistic and individualistic definitions of social systems (discussed in chapter 4) may be understood in light of this definition of function. At issue in the controversy is whether the social system is an artifact constructed by its members, so that it is a subsystem contributing to the maintenance function of their survival, or whether the social system itself is the primary system, so that its fundamental function is not survival of the species, but survival of itself.

In this understanding of function, function in itself is not purposeful. Purposeful activities may be functional, however. Within the hierarchy of activities contributing to the fundamental process of the whole, some of the contributing subsystems may be activities directed toward a goal—such as the maintenance of a constant temperature in an organic system—while others may not—such as the excretion of urine by the kidneys.[38] Thus, an activity can be both purposeful and functional—as in the system of temperature regulation. But sometimes a purposeful activity which, under normal circumstances, is functional (that is, contributing to the fundamental process of the whole) may be dysfunctional under other circumstances. For example, the male moth engages in purposeful activity when he responds to the attractant secreted by the female moth; in normal functioning, he is contributing to reproduction. But when the attractant is used by farmers to bring moths into contact with insecticides, the purposeful behavior is dysfunctional. Or, in Freud's conception purposeful patterns are developed to deal with libidinal impulses, and in a child they are functional because they protect him or her from damaging behavior. But the same system of purposeful behavior becomes dysfunctional in adults.

The concept of living organisms as organized functional hierarchies is an essential part of evolutionary theory, and it stands in opposition to the concept of organisms as aggregates of individual parts. Hierarchical functioning has become the mainstay of physiology and morphology,[39] and it supports the medical view of disease as a derangement of function. In the first decades of this century, it was also the guiding view of the functional psychology of James Angell, John Dewey, and Harvey Carr at the University of Chicago. A functional approach to mental operations was developed, described in terms of their contribution to the fundamental function of the organism and its adaptation to its environment.[40]

Explanations and Accounts of Human Action: Linguistic Accounts

A number of contemporary philosophers, influenced by Wittgenstein, have proposed a different sort of conception for the understanding of human action. These philosophers—among them A. I. Melden, Anthony Kenny, and Elizabeth Anscombe—hold that it is a mistake to think that a reason-explanation specifies the process that has led up to an action or that, indeed, it specifies anything which has actually existed in the spatiotemporal environment of the action.[41] They suggest, instead, that human action can be best approached by bringing out how the agent conceives, or would conceive, the action. The exchange in which the question "Why did you do that?" is answered by "Because I wanted to," they say, does not refer to a psychological event that has existed just before the action. Moreover, the notion of some internal "will" which surveys a variety of options and then chooses to do something is a result of the illusion that all words function according to a model of designation and object. The terms *will* and *wants* and *beliefs* need not refer to objects or events within the person.

This group of thinkers maintains that the difficulties in comprehending the nature of human action follow from the confusion brought on by using an inappropriate language game for talking about action. The language game of science constructs a world of entities and things which interact to produce changes. In this language game, "deciding," "wanting," and "believing" show up as antecedent processes which cause an action. In *The Concept of Mind* (1949), Gilbert Ryle states that it is the misuse of terms referring to reasons or motives for doing something that leads to postulating that there is something inside us ("the ghost") which directs our activities.

> Liking and disliking, joy and grief, desire and aversions are, then, not "internal" episodes which their owner witnesses, but his associates do

not witness. They are not episodes and so are not the sorts of things which can be witnessed or unwitnessed.[42]

In place of the introspective or inferential study of internal events, Ryle suggests that one should study the concrete circumstances in which these expressions are ordinarily used. When this is done, it can be seen that when a person says "I did it because I wanted to," the expression is part of a social interaction in which the speaker is explaining or accounting for an action—that is, giving reasons for the action. The statement, "I did it because I wanted to" becomes meaningful in a social context; it is a type of justification communicated to others, not a statement about a series of internal and private events.

Statements concerning reasons for human action are not to be understood as explanations in the way that statements about the occurrence of natural events are understood as explanations. Because statements about reasons for human action are used in the language game of justification, they refer to rules and not to things. For example, a move is made by a chess player. Someone who does not know about chess would see only that one piece of wood is transferred by hand from one square on a board to another square on the board. In order to answer the question "Why did you do that?" the player would need to give an account of the rules of the game. The explanation is given in terms of the rules of action, not in terms of antecedent causes. Explanations in terms of rules are implicitly references to evaluation. One of the rules of chess is to play to win. Thus, the reason for a move—for example, to capture the queen— can be evaluated as good, bad, or indifferent on the basis of the overall goal of winning the game. Another illustration of the linguistic analysis of human action is the act of signaling for a left turn. The reason for the signal refers to the rules of the road, not to a causal chain of inner events.

A bodily movement is a human action when one can justify it to others. But if one has a facial tic, the answer to "Why did you do that?" does not involve a justification of the sort that maintains that twitching is appropriate to the setting—that is, it does not need to refer to rules. Actions which are not accountable in terms of rules are not held to be intentional or human actions; they are merely happenings.

This interpretation of "intentional" acts as acts which a person is prepared to defend in the context of justification represents an acausal account of human action. In this interpretation, statements about why something has been done are not understood as references to inner events; they are understood as a kind of interaction between people that exists within their language game. An explanation, then, should not be read as an assertion or as a piece of information about a factual state of affairs. It is the performance of an act— namely, the act of justifying. And so, despite the grammatical appearances, the primary purpose of the statement "I did it because I wanted to" is not to give factual information. The person who answers the question "Why did you do that?" is engaging in a social ritual, and the ritual is defined by rules that state that the person must accept responsibility or liability for the act.

✓ Proponents of linguistic analysis of human actions hold that to treat statements giving reasons for human action as if they are statements referring to physical or mental events is to misunderstand the nature of these statements. And it is this misunderstanding, they say, that has led to arguments about what causes human action. Those who argue for a causal rendering of human action related to antecedent physical and/or mental events—for instance, Charles Taylor, who argues that human actions need teleological explanations, and Richard Taylor, who appeals to the self as the agent which causes actions—all err because they assume that reason-explanations are references to events. A linguistic approach analyzes how statements accounting for the reason or motive for doing something are used in social interaction. From this analysis, those who follow a linguistic approach conclude that what defines a happening as a human action is a person's willingness to give an account of the action and take responsibility for it.

An additional insight into human action is given by speech-act theory. J. L. Austin developed the notion language can also be a way of doing something or of acting.[43] Speech-act theory recognizes that in addition to other types of actions, humans can also act through the use of statements. Statements can be used not only to state something (the locutionary act) but also to do something (the illocutionary act). The actor can bind himself or herself with a pledge. In a speech-act, the statements imply specific commitments by the speakers who "do" what they say in the act of saying it. For example, the statement "I apologize" is not a description of a state of affairs, and thus it is not true or false. It is an action itself, the act of apologizing. In a similar way, the statement "I promise" is an act of promising, an act of putting oneself under the obligation to do what one says will be done. Austin presented this theory in connection with problems in the theory of knowledge. He suggested that the statement "I know" is not a description of a psychological state; it is, instead, a performative statement which has the effect of "I guarantee" or "I stake my reputation" and assures accuracy. Following these ideas, P. F. Strawson holds that to say "It is true" is not to make an assertion about a proposition but to perform an act of endorsing or accepting the proposition.[44]

According to performative theory, the statement "He did it intentionally" (or "for a reason") is not a report about a person or his inner processes; it is an act of assigning responsibility or liability to the person for the act. When a person says that he or she did something intentionally, he or she is acting to take responsibility for the action.

Practical Reasoning

Another development in the consideration of human action has been work with the theory of practical discourse. Practical discourse is a systematic study of the notions, propositions, and rational processes that relate to human action. The work in this area has concerned the particular case in which a decision is made among various alternative actions. The brief description which follows is meant to provide the context for practical reasoning, and it deals mainly with formal or theoretical developments concerned with decision making.

Decision theory is formal in the mathematical sense of the term—that is, it constitutes a body of theorems deduced from a set of axioms, and it therefore in no way represents an investigation into actual reasoning as employed in real action. In situations of certainty, where it is possible to list all of the elements of a problem, one can deduce the correct answer. When the problem does not lead to *the* correct answer, however, one needs to establish an order of preferences in which probabilities intervene. The logic of probability is held to be the essential instrument in all reasoning that involves uncertainty. The use of this logic provides a "rational" approach for deciding among alternative answers to a problem and for acting "rationally" on the basis of these answers.

Decision theory thus presupposes a rational actor—that is, an actor whose choices of action can be completely defended on the basis of what the theory proves should be the preferred outcomes. Game theory introduces the notion of two or more actors in a situation of conflict. In zero-sum games, the winnings of one player equal the losses of the other. In negotiated (or cooperative) games, the idea of collective rationality is introduced; the advantage is increased for all players as one strategy is preferred to another. In some games—chess, for instance—the solution is purely based on strategy, since the outcome depends solely on a series of foreseeable actions. In this situation, there exists a best strategy for each player, and game theory consists in conceptualizing the pattern of pure strategy solutions. In another kind of game—such as bridge—finesse and bluffing are added to the logic of choice. In theory, however, the actors are defined without any reference to psychological traits. They are defined solely by their positions as players—that is, by the rules of succession and the range of permissible choices. Game theory considers only the logicomathematical structure of games; it is not concerned with the individual psychological peculiarities of the players.[45]

Another approach to the formal study of the choice of actions is called "the logic of practical discourse" by G. H. von Wright.[46] This field covers the logic of the uses of languages which do not refer to assertions about events. Such assertions are covered by the deductive and inductive logics. Deontic logic studies the formal relations between languages used to describe obligations. Other nondescriptive uses of language about which logics have been developed are imperatives ("Do this," "Do that") and value judgments ("This is good," "This is better"). These logics are purely formal in that they are developed from systems of axiomatic givens. They also do not account for differences in persons—the agent of the action—or in their attitudes or intentions or decisions.

In practical reasoning as opposed to practical logic, the concern is no longer with a formal system of logic applied to action, as is the case with decision theory and deontic logic. Practical reasoning—also called the "theory of argumentation"—concerns itself with what justifies a decision. Unlike the formal approach, however, this approach holds that the decision depends on the person making it, and thus formal rules of decision making cannot be abstracted from persons and their actions into a system of demonstration modeled on deductive logic. In the theory of practical reasoning, the word *reasoning* refers to a discussion technique for convincing or refuting an adversary and for coming to an agreement with others about the legitimacy of a decision. It will be recalled that in the "historical realism" phase of the philosophy of science (discussed in chapter 4) Radnitzky maintained that decisions about scientific theory are the result of practical reasoning and argument rather than of demonstrative logic.

Practical reasoning stands between the logic of demonstration and theories of motivation. "Reasons," in the context of practical reasoning, are motives which have undergone the test of argumentation.

Argumentation is a logic to the extent that "the motives for a decision are treated as reasons which validate and legitimize it, and which are therefore eminently communicable, comprehensible, capable of being recognized, assented to, adopted."[47]

To differentiate practical reasoning from theories of motivation, four contemporary views of motivation can be noted. (1) The current view of motivation in academic psychology is that motives ("reasons") for decision making are an extremely complex form of the stimulus–response pattern that is extended to include a large number of intermediate variables, both conscious and unconscious.[48] (2) Another approach to motivation is the psychology of personality, in which it is understood that it is the function within the personality system that accounts for "why" people choose to do what they do. (3) In psychoanalysis, the "reasons" given when asked "why" one has done something are treated as rationalizations—that is, as one of the ways in which repression deforms unconscious representations and affects. (4) In the sociology of cognition, the reasons put forward by people as part of a discourse on what to do are merely expressions made under various disguises of conflicts of social forces in which they are caught up.

In contrast to these theories of motivation—which deny the validity of the reasons people give for their actions—practical reasoning takes the argument for a particular action at its face value. It treats the argument at the actual level it adopts, criticizing it and justifying it within its own reference frame, thus making it possible for the decision itself to be approved or rejected. An argument as to whether theory A or theory B should be accepted and used as the basis for actions is judged on the merits of the evidence in the case as presented; it is not viewed as a mere acting out of forces existing within the psychological or sociological contexts of the parties in the debate.

Practical reasoning as developed here regards the positions put forward to justify actions as norms or values. They are seen as propositions which imply that the acts are good and should have been performed. Practical reasoning takes into account, however, the conditions under which agents in real life accept these implied norms as meaningful and commit themselves to them personally. When seeking a decision on which action is to be taken, an argument using practical reasoning begins with the norms to which the participants in the argument are committed and then seeks, by means of the techniques of argument, to ground the decision on them. Practical reasoning cannot originate in a field of discussion in which there are no normative commitments. This does not mean that these norms are universal and eternal; all that is required in practical reasoning is that the norms be recognized by an audience which may vary in size but is always limited to those to whom the discourse is addressed at the specific time of the argument.

Practical reasoning always takes place among individuals or groups in a historical time. Just as the notion of timelessness is essential for deductive reasoning, the notion of temporalness is essential for practical reasoning. Practical reasoning is based on related decisions that serve as precedents while a decision is made about the action under consideration. The argument itself takes time and is time-limited. The argument precedes the action, and after the action has taken place, new information is available for use in the next discourse about what to do. Temporality is a particular feature of action, and it provides the basic feature of practical reasoning. In this characteristic, practical reasoning finds "an echo and support" both in the theory of orthopractic reasoning (the reasoning concerned with the appropriate thing to do in a context of ends and means) and in the "tense-logic" used by A. N. Prior in his analysis of the function of indicative propositions involving time copulas (verbs such as *is*, *was*, and *will be*).[49]

The theory of argumentation—practical reasoning—is thus applicable to situations in which people are already committed to values and norms, since otherwise there would be no basis for reasoning. It presupposes a situation in which these values are conflicting or the system of norms (what should be done) is incomplete or no decision has yet been made (because the situation is new, and it is not yet known what should be done). The order in which practical reasoning operates is not a harmonious, perfect, and intangible order; it is an imperfect order in which decisions need to be made over conflicting notions.

Two models have been proposed for the theory of argumentation, the juristic model and the rhetorical model. Legal reasoning offers an exemplifying case of practical reasoning. Chaim Perelman and Stephen Toulmin suggest that an analysis of legal reasoning will provide fresh insights into the process of practical reasoning.[50] Both judicial proceedings, including the arguments of counsel and the decisions of judges, and legislative decisions regarding the formation of laws provide forms of practical reasoning, and the examination of these forms will clarify principles of argument. Rhetoric is a model in the sense that it provides procedures and techniques for argumentation. In this respect, the theory of argumentation is a "new rhetoric" that is based on an attempt to bring together understandings of argumentation and persuasion and develop them so that they will produce a fuller theory of practical reasoning.[51]

The theory of practical reasoning has been used by Habermas in his attempt to overcome the relativism of the *Weltanschauungen* approach to knowledge without falling into the error of assuming a deductively demonstrable truth. Habermas outlines the problem:

> The "unity of argumentative reasoning" is compatible with this "differential meaning-constitution of object domains." In all sciences argumentation is subject to the same conditions for the discursive redemption of truth claims. These conditions of a rationality that is not scientifically restricted can be elucidated within the framework of a logic of theoretical discourse.[52]

Habermas defines the logic of theoretical discourse as an analysis of the structure and conditions of the form of communication in which hypotheses of truth claims are examined through argumentation and then rejected, revised, or accepted. (The notion of argumentation in human science will be taken up more fully in chapter 7.)

Human action is of interest to human science both because of the insights it affords into the nature of the human realm as activity and because the attempt to understand the human and physical realms is itself a human action. The nature of the human science enterprise requires the use of practical reason in deciding among various interpretations of its subject matter and its activity. As a human product, science is more akin to the judicial-rhetorical projects than to the project of demonstrative logic.

6

Existential–Phenomenological
and Hermeneutic Systems

The reason-explanation system discussed in the last chapter was developed primarily in England, and it is part of what Gerard Radnitzky has called the "Anglo-Saxon schools of metascience."[1] The two systems described in this chapter were developed within the framework of the "Continental schools of metascience," and they focus on the lifeworld—that is, on human experience as it is lived. The movement includes Dilthey, Husserl, Heidegger, Merleau-Ponty, Gadamer, Ricoeur, and Habermas. The development of the Continental schools is complex, and this chapter must overlook some of the nuances of the movement and some of the variations on its themes in order to concentrate on the major themes themselves. The two major themes are existential-phenomenology and hermeneutics. In many respects, these systems of inquiry overlap previous systems, but their foundations and their vocabularies are different.

In 1973, Joseph Kockelmans identified the three main possibilities in the human sciences: the empirical, the descriptive, and the hermeneutic.[2] Each of these three approaches to the human realm employs its own set of methods and proceeds on its own assumptions. From its particular system of inquiry, each approach is able to develop a kind of knowledge about human beings. This chapter focuses on two of these approaches, the phenomenological or descriptive approach and the hermeneutic or interpretive approach. But before we turn to them, let us briefly review the empirical point of view.

The empirical approach is represented by the deductive and pragmatic systems of inquiry described in chapters 2 and 3. Kockelmans describes it from both a logic of science perspective and a philosophy of science perspective. From the logical perspective, a science is considered to be empirical if it satisfies five conditions. Kockelmans lists these conditions as follows:

1. It approaches its subject matter by formulating hypotheses which must fulfill specific conditions.
2. It tests its hypotheses by means of procedures which are guided by certain criteria.
3. It explains its hypotheses by relating them to laws or lawlike statements.
4. It verifies its explanations by using a principle of verification which must fulfill certain specific conditions.
5. It follows certain rules in formulating the definitions of its basic concepts.[3]

From the philosophy of science perspective, the empirical approach treats the statements of the human sciences in such a way as to relate them systematically to one another in a determinate fashion. The empirical approach produces knowledge which is theoretical, formal, functional, and quantitative. The knowledge is *theoretical* in that it excludes forms of understanding which are found at the level of "concernful dealing with things and careful dealing with our fellow man." This theoretical knowledge is derived from observing the world in such a way that the observer is no longer completely engaged with it and involved in it. Acquiring the knowledge requires a point of view which is outside the everyday lifeworld, and this point of view is achieved through the use of methods which distance the researcher from personal concern for the object of inquiry and attempt to overcome personal perspective and personal bias. The knowledge is systematic, and it is derived from the observation of facts.

Knowledge obtained through the empirical approach is *formal* in that it describes events or facts in terms of formal properties. The method abstracts elements from the whole, according to the formal characteristics which are its particular object of investigation. The knowledge is mathematically *functional* in that it relates the abstracted elements in terms of their functional relationships—that is, in terms of the functional scheme "If P then Q."[4] The formal and functional qualities together lead to descriptions of general laws of relationship between the formal qualities. For example, to arrive at the descriptive statement "Greater IQ scores are positively correlated with academic performance," the formal characteristics of IQ, human life involvement, and academic performance are abstracted and connected to each other in terms of their functional relationships.

Knowledge obtained through the empirical approach is *quantitative* in that the formalizations are categorized and described in numerical relationships. For example, from the full interaction and experience among a group of students in a classroom, a characteristic such as performance in mathematics is abstracted (or isolated), and the performances of the students in mathematics are related in a rank order so that it is possible to produce the "fact" that Johnny ranks twelfth in a class of nineteen in mathematics.

Kockelmans demonstrates that an empirical science of the human realm is logically possible and that statements of the human sciences can by systematically related to one another in a mathematically functional way. However, this requires an abstraction of the human realm in respect to formal properties, and necessarily implies that an important part of the meaning of human phenomena must be left out of consideration. Formalization gives statements that are relatively poor in content compared to the fullness of human experience which it is presumed to explain. Consequently, other approaches are required in addition, approaches which can compensate for the losses "which the limitations essentially connected with the empirical approach necessarily entail."[5] The phenomenological and hermeneutic systems provide two other contexts of knowledge. The phenomenological (descriptive) approach focuses on the structures of experience, the organizing principles that give form and meaning to the lifeworld, while the hermeneutic (interpretive) approach concentrates on the historical meaning of experience and its developmental and cumulative effects at both the individual and social levels.

The Existential–Phenomenological System of Inquiry

The term *descriptive* is used to refer to a group of research endeavors in the human sciences which focus on describing the basic structures of lived experience. Included in this group are phenomenological sociology,[6] ethnomethodology,[7] phenomenological psychology,[8] and existential-phenomenology.[9] These movements trace some of their roots to Alfred Schutz or Maurice Merleau-Ponty and, through them, to Husserl.[10] This section will take up again (see chapter 1) Husserl's method for gaining rigorous descriptions of the structures of consciousness, followed by the existential critique of his position. Then the descriptive methods of Schutz for sociology and Giorgi for psychology will be discussed.

Husserl had developed the phenomenological method as a means to gain knowledge of invariant structures of consciousness. He had focused on pure consciousness, as experientially given (rather than as it appears in some theory, e.g., a theoretical account of the relation of neurophysiological structures to consciousness), and had treated consciousness as an independent realm. Within the realm of consciousness various "objects" are constituted. In a manner that is reminiscent of Saussure's proposal that language organizes the spectrum of possible meaningfulness into various concepts, Husserl maintained that experience is not a buzzing flux but a constituted meaningful and ordered understanding. The constitutive process may be termed a synthesizing activity of consciousness. This, however, does not refer to an additive operation supposedly "gluing together" atomistic "sensa" (which are not given in direct experience, but presupposed by the theory in which they appear). Instead, it refers to the way in which the spectrum of experience is organized into units and recognizable wholes. To take an example from perception, let us say we experience an apple on the table. The apple may be seen from this side or that side, but these perspectives are already perspectival views *of* an object constituted as "the same" apple; the various views are caught up in the synthesizing operations by which the experiential object "apple" is constituted. Furthermore, the apple is experienced *as* an instance of the type or *eidos* "apple." However, it may also be experienced as a "piece of fruit," as "something to eat," as an example of a "physical thing extended in space," and so on. Similarly, the lines on a sheet of paper (a drawing of a Necker cube) may be perceived as a cube with either one or the other of two surfaces appearing as nearest because of the constituting work of consciousness.[11] Thus for Husserl experience is not at all a matter of a thing called "consciousness" automatically reacting to "stimuli" whose ultimate cause is supposed to be a given physical reality unequivocally present "out there." Rather, experience is built up through an activity of constitution along the lines of types (*eidē*) or "essential structures."

Husserl proposed two basic approaches to the study of human experience. One, the method of free variation, leads to the description of invariant or essential structures; the other, intentional analysis, focuses on a concrete experience itself and describes how that particular experience has been constructed. In the first method, the free variation leads—to return to our example—to a description of the structure of the essence of "appleness"—that is, it disengages the idea of apples from all accidental aspects manifested in a particular apple. A particular apple may be red, but redness is not part of the essence of "appleness," for there are also yellow and green apples. The structure of "appleness" includes a particular skin texture, seeds, stem, and so on. However, the search for essential structures differs from the process through which biologists establish taxonomic categories based on anatomical similarities. According to Husserl, the structures of experience are the organizing principles making sense of experience in the first place; the "facts" (this particular apple is green and is three inches in diameter, etc.) presuppose the *eidos* "apple." Thus free variation differs from induction; the latter examines actually existing cases and proposes generalizations, the former sifts out the essential features of such an experience "in principle" (for any apple, real or imaginary, here before me or eaten yesterday, and so on).[12]

In the second method, intentional analysis, attention is given to a particular experience in which the various structures and modes of consciousness that have been synthesized to constitute it are analyzed and descriptively explained. In writing about the example of the apple above, the apple was not, in fact, in front of me, but was constituted in the imaginative mode. It was not a perceptual or remembered actual event. It took place in a constituted horizon, the writing of a book, and fulfilled a need for an illustration. In this method the operations of conscious activity are described as various synthesizing processes occurring together to create a unique experiential moment.

Husserl had investigated consciousness as a pure "region" that could be considered in a way essentially separate from the "facts" of the empirical realm. However, in *Being and Time* (1927), Martin Heidegger proposed that consciousness was not separate from the world and instead was a formation of historically lived human existence. He called for an existential correction to Husserl that would understand the essential structures as the basic categories of being-in-the-world rather than pure consciousness. In *Phenomenology of Perception* (1945), Merleau-Ponty extended Heidegger's correction to include an emphasis on the relationship between the structures of experience and the embodied condition of human existence. The existential turn moved Husserl's realm of pure consciousness into the realm of the contingencies of history and embodiment. In existentialism, the structures of consciousness do not resemble the structures of logical and mathematical operations; they are made up of strata of transactions which have been constructed into meaningful human experience so that sense can be made of existence.[13] The existential-phenomenological (descriptive) system of inquiry investigates the various structures of orientation toward the world which make up human experience.

Two of the basic existential structures are space–time and embodiment. Experience is constituted as spatial and temporal. We say "It occurred there, at that time" or "I expect it to happen tomorrow." It is also formed through a physical, organic being. It derives from a person's sensory apparatus, and it has an orientational center that is a living, experiencing body. An object is experienced to the left or right of another object, because it is experienced from an embodied point of view.[14] For Merleau-Ponty, these basic structures of experience are an expression of the embodiment of experience. Other structures include "fearfulness," "love," "anxiety," "evil," "truth," and so forth. Although one can look to a limited number of structures of the basic strata of existence—Brentano identified three basic classes (first, representations, second, judgments, and third, love and hate or desires and feelings)—as these are divided into finer and finer nuances, the structures seem to have no limit.[15]

An area of inquiry that has yielded significant results to existential-phenomenological investigation has been the destructuration of the lifeworld of persons experiencing mental "illness." Richard Zaner notes that in these cases what is revealed is the *absence* of the phenomenon in question (e.g., spatial coherence and temporal orientation). The lack of the normal structuring process helps show how these structures operate in normal circumstances. Merleau-Ponty also used examples of the perceptual experience of brain injured patients to show the presence of the structuring processes in normal experience.[16] Eugène Minkowski has developed a description of the changes in the structural experience of time in depressive patients.[17] He has found that openness to the future, which is a feature of the usual organization of time experience, has been closed off. Erwin Straus investigated the differences between the structural modes of normal consciousness and of hallucinatory consciousness.[18] He described the way in which structural boundaries, which normally hold between motor phenomena and sensory experience, are broken down so that action is more automatic and less controlled. This breakdown also affects the structures of interpersonal relatedness. In hallucination, the structures of experience become deformed. V. E. von Gebsattel has investigated the "world of the compulsive."[19] And Ernest Keen has proposed a reorganization of diagnostic categories on the basis of the basic life structures—being a body in space, being with others, and being a self in time.[20] Instead of classifying according to symptoms, this existential-phenomenological approach attends to the life structures through which experience is organized and made meaningful.

Alfred Schutz

In Alfred Schutz's major work, *The Phenomenology of the Social World* (1932), he brought a version of Husserl's phenomenology to bear on the problems of sociology as Weber had defined them. Schutz was born in Vienna in 1899 and lived there until he came to the United States in 1939. He studied at the University of Vienna, and quite early he became interested in Weber's attempt to establish a consistent methodological foundation for the social sciences. After Schutz's death in 1959, three volumes of his papers were published from 1962 to 1966, increasing the accessibility and the impact of his thought. *The Structures of the Life-World* was published in 1973; it contains the manuscript, edited by Thomas Luckmann, that Schutz was preparing as a final systematic statement of his position at the time of his death.[21]

Schutz stood in the tradition of human science, and he addressed the problem of objectivity and subjectivity in the study of people. With Weber, he maintained that the subject matter of sociology is human action, and he believed that action cannot be understood without reference to the meaning the action has for the actor. If the subjective side of the person is to be left out of the investigative system (as proposed by Watson's behaviorist manifesto in 1927), he said, then the researcher does not have access to the personal meaning which creates the action. Schutz, however, wanted to study the subjective realm in an "objective" manner. He agreed with Weber that Dilthey's early approach to the realm of the other's lived experience—that is, by projecting oneself into the other's experience and then reading into it one's own experience—was "unscientific" because it was not intersubjectively observable. Weber's answer to the problem was to treat subjective experience according to ideal types, which he introduced in order to pass from prescientific to scientific observation. By assuming what the subjective experience of people would be if they were completely rational, so that the subjectively experienced reason for action was that the act was a means to achieve a goal, one could, Weber believed, construct an "objective" science of the subjective experience. It was here that Schutz disagreed with Weber. He found Weber's account lacking because he saw it as an external and mechanical account of action in which subjective meaning is somehow attached to a behavior.

Schutz did agree with Weber, however, that action is defined through meaning, and he held that the first step in developing a methodology for this kind of social science was to formulate a concept of meaning. As he worked out his theory of meaning, he turned to Husserl and Bergson.

What is first given to consciousness is an unbroken stream of lived experiences. The contents of this stream are said to be divided into two types, passive and active. An example of the passive type is a sensation of red, and an example of the active type is a turning of attention to the sensation of red or the recognition of the sensation as something experienced before. At the time we are actually living through experiences, the contents—whether passive or active—are not separate and distinct, and they are not experienced as meaningful. After the contents have receded a slight distance into the past, however, they can be reflected upon and recognized and identified. The ego may lift an experience out from the stream, and in this lifting out the experience becomes a discrete entity that is clear and distinct. For Schutz it is in the lifting out and in the examination of an experience that it acquires meaning. In the lifting out, the dimension of being in the flow of experience, its concreteness, is lost, but it becomes an object of awareness.

Thus, the ego does not ascribe meaning to its experiences while they are happening. Some experiences—those closest to one's personality—may never have meaning ascribed to them, but most experiences are available in retrospect. Important in Schutz's work is the notion that we can also ascribe meaning prospectively—that is, to future experiences. The lifting out of a future event and ascribing a meaning to it is a complex matter, because in order for an experience to be discrete it must have an element of pastness. Schutz used the concept of "future perfect tense" from grammar to describe the process of ascribing meaning to a future experience. The goal or experience is to be pictured as over and done with, even while it is still anticipated. The picturing of what it will mean to have a future experience is essential for action. Action is behavior directed toward accomplishing a future goal. "What is projected," Schutz said, "is the act which is the goal of the action and which is brought into being by the action."[22]

For example, I picture being at a friend's house. To get there, I must walk along a sidewalk. The action of walking acquires meaning in the context of the goal of being at my friend's house. If I am asked "Why are you walking along the sidewalk?" my answer is "In order to get to my friend's house." Schutz distinguished this kind of answer to a "why" question, in which the reason for the action is related to accomplishing the goal, from the kind of answer which explains what in my past has led me to the project of going to my friend's house. The first kind of answer Schutz called the "in-order-to motive"; it relates a phase of total event (the walking) to the goal. The second kind of answer Schutz called the "because motive"; Schutz pictured it as an answer in the pluperfect tense. If I open my umbrella as it begins to rain, my "in-order-to motive" is to keep dry. My "because motive" is the perception of the rain and my knowledge from previous experiences of the effect of rain on my clothes. Or, there are two answers to the question "Why is he reading the book?" The answers are "In order to learn the material in the book" and "Because he has a need to get good grades." Schutz's distinction between the two types of motives offers an interesting approach to the problem of determinism and freedom (presented in chapter 6 in the discussion of action theory).

In regard to the matter of understanding the experience of another person, Schutz developed a continuum that ranged from direct experience of the other person to indirect experience of the other person. In this conception, genuine understanding of another person is a concrete type of perception. We do not directly intuit another person's subjective experiences, but we intentionally (in the phenomenological sense) grasp them because we assume that facial expressions and gestures are a "field of expression" of inner life. In face-to-face interaction, we sense that the other person's stream of consciousness is flowing in a manner temporally parallel with our own, and as we interact with the other person our experiences become interlocked. In these "we-relationships," one person comprehends (*versteht*) the other person's subjective meaning. Such comprehension is different from the comprehension of objective meaning, which focuses only on the meaning of the content of what is said instead of on why this particular person has made this particular statement at this particular time.

Only by comprehending the motives of the actor do we grasp the subjective meaning. And according to Schutz, it is the grasping of subjective meaning which is the goal of social science. When I am not face-to-face with other persons, I cannot have direct access to their experience. My knowledge of my contemporaries—with whom I am not in direct relationship, even though such direct relationship is possible—and of my predecessors and successors must be closer to the indirect end of the continuum. For knowledge of their subjective experience, one needs to revert to ideal types—either understood as course-of-action types such as social roles, or personal or personality types. The ideal types are arranged on a scale of increasing anonymity. George Walsh has offered some examples based on this scale:

> There [are] my absent friend, his brother whom he has described to me, the professor whose books I have read, the postal clerk, the Canadian Parliament, abstract entities like Canada itself, the rules of English grammar, or the basic principles of jurisprudence.[23]

As the types get farther away from the direct experience and grasping of the subjective meaning of individuals, more and more objective categories are used to refer to subjective experience. These objective ideal types are—as Weber claimed—a fundamental tool of social science. They are, however, only one tool; social science also uses the direct understanding of immediate subjective experience. Schutz maintains there is a complex of hierarchically arranged concepts from direct subjective knowing to completely objective knowledge for use in social science.

Duquesne Studies in Phenomenological Pyschology

Amedeo Giorgi, who has helped develop the methods used at Duquesne University in Pittsburgh for describing psychological meanings or human structures,[24] has said that "the challenge facing a human scientific psychology is that of trying to establish concepts, categories, techniques, and methods that will enable us to work with the dialectic 'perceived situation-work.'"[25] Giorgi is drawing on Merleau-Ponty's identification of three orders of structure—physical structure, vital structure, and human structure. Merleau-Ponty understood that each order of structure interacted with the environment in a different way. The dialectic or interaction between the world and a physical structure is that of stimulus setting off a reflex reaction by the structure; vital structures act instinctively to their understanding of the environment as a specific situation for them; and human structures respond with planned activity or work to the environment as they perceive it as a personally meaningful situation.[26]

Merleau-Ponty's analysis of structure owes much to Gestalt theory, although he does not relate the three orders to a physiological base. He relates them, instead, to the lifeworld, and so human science remains within the human order. The origin of the data for human science is the structures of experience. Investigations, however, should move from these structures to psychological meaning—that is, from basic and universal description to description of the unique and individual experiences of people in the world. An inverse movement is also necessary—that is, from the lifeworld of individuals to the invariant phenomenological structures.

The method developed by Giorgi to obtain descriptions of phenomenological structures begins with individual descriptions of an experience, and from these descriptions comes the more general description of a phenomenological structure. Giorgi has called this method "empirical phenomenological analysis." The researcher first gathers empirical or objective data in the form of written descriptions or transcribed interviews from subjects on the topic that is the object of the investigation (the phenomenon whose essential structure is sought). The researcher then goes through the following steps, as summarized by Giorgi in a 1974 article:

(1) The researcher reads the entire description . . . straight through to get a sense of the whole.
(2) Next, the researcher reads the same description more slowly and delineates each time that a transition in meaning is perceived with respect to the [phenomenologically] intentional discovering [of the experience].
(3) The researcher then eliminates redundancies and clarifies or elaborates to himself the meaning of the units just constituted by relating them to each other and to the sense of the whole.
(4) The researcher reflects on the given units, still expressed essentially in the concrete language of the subject, and comes up with the essence of that situation for the subject with respect to the phenomena [under consideration]. Each unit is systematically interrogated for what it reveals about the [phenomena] for that subject. The researcher transforms each unit, when relevant, into the language of psychological science.
(5) The researcher synthesizes and integrates the insights achieved into a consistent description of the structure of [the phenomena].[27]

Giorgi distinguishes among structure, type, and level. *Structure* is the more basic term, and it describes primary organizing principles of consciousness. "A structure," Giorgi says, "is a network of relations that is lived through rather than known . . . thus to be aware of a structure is to be present to the very organization of the world as one lives and thinks it."[28] In other words, structure is normally the "how" of experience rather than a separate "object" of experience. Types and levels are ways of orienting oneself with respect to the structure. *Level* refers to the degree of presence of a structure, and *type* refers to changes in appearance of the structure. If the structure, for example, is a color, then a change of type would involve a change from, say, red to yellow, and a change of level would involve a change from, say, a dull red to a bright red. Consequently, when one is doing research involving descriptions of structures of the lifeworld, one needs to differentiate among type and level as well as structure itself.

In Giorgi's research on the general structure of learning, a description that included all of the dimensions of learning would be very abstract and removed from individual instances of learning. With the inclusion of type in the investigation—such as the type involved in learning to drive an automobile, learning to do mathematical problems, or learning how to behave in certain situations—

the descriptions become variations within a type; they are more specific than a more general investigation of the basic structure itself.

Giorgi has described the type of reasoning used in developing the descriptions of the lifeworld structures:

> The relationship is not empirical observation—idealized model—verification or lack of verification as in the logical style so much as it is empirical description—eidetic intuition and description—empirical embellishment—eidetic synthesis.[29]

The descriptions are developed out of a dialectical approach in which one describes the phenomenon and then penetrates it with a deeper description until a structure is clarified. This clarification does not necessarily conform to the rules of formal logic. The regularities of the lifeworld are not always organized into deductively arranged relationships, and the more inclusive is not always determinate over the less inclusive.

An example of a fundamental description of a structure of the lifeworld is the research on anger carried out by Emily Stevick while she was a student at Duquesne.[30] To establish her data base, she interviewed 30 women aged 15 to 18. She began each interview with the request "Try to remember the last time you were angry and tell me anything you can about the situation, about what you felt, did, or said." After a response was received, she asked for clarification and a fuller description, and when this information had been obtained, she asked specific questions about issues which her earlier research and interviews had suggested. The interviews were recorded, and transcriptions were made. Stevick then explicated and organized each interview by the use of two methods of qualitative content analysis.

Stevick offers considerable detail about her process of integration. First, she listed the meanings which occurred to her as she read through each transcription. These meanings were then combined into essential descriptions of the experience of anger as described by each informant, and as she reflected on these descriptions she produced fundamental descriptions or a "total gestalt" of the experience. Next, she condensed each protocol into "meaning expressions." This analysis showed that the variations in the informants' descriptions displayed three aspects of the experience: an essential prerequisite for anger, the essential components of anger itself, and the termination of anger. Continuing to use the variations in the subjects' descriptions, Stevick worked to deepen her grasp of the ingredients in the essence of anger. This final process of gaining insight into the essential components is described by her as one which "involves the investigator's understanding, extracting meanings, relating, synthesizing—human activities which at least to this point defy complete explanation." She concludes with her description of the essence—the structure—of anger:

> Anger is the pre-reflective experience of being made unable by another who prevents us, and it is the counteraction of this sense of inability by an affective transformation of the other and of the relationship with the other. The body is experienced as bursting forth, and expresses itself, publicly or privately as each person's pre-reflective restrictions allow, in expansive, explosive, nontypical behavior.[31]

Stevick's description illustrates the kind of results that empirical-phenomenological research leads to. It emphasizes structure as a way of interacting with the world, and it thus falls within the existential-phenomenological tradition. Anger, instead of being located in an isolated individual, is a "mode of lived consciousness which emerges out of an interpersonal situation in which an important other prevents one's being." In addition, "it is a pre-reflective presence and a response to a situation in which the lived-body is pulled into the world to protect its very being." The person, as embodied consciousness, becomes "permeated through and through with anger so that it bursts forth to preserve its ability which is its very being in the world."

Other members of the Duquesne group have investigated anxiety, decision making, privacy, at-homeness, serial learning, being criminally victimized, envy, and so on. The sources of the data can be written descriptions (such as those Stevick used), interviews, observations of human action, and personal imagination; these sources can also be used in combination. The method involves collecting statements from subjects, particularly their descriptions of the experience being investigated, and then "systematically and rigorously interrogating these descriptions step by step to arrive at the structure of the experience."[32] One of the goals of the method is to produce descriptions which lead to a general, if not universal, intersubjective agreement.

Descriptive or existential-phenomenological human science aims to uncover the basic structures of human existence. It seeks to describe the schemata or themes that constitute experience. In this sense it continues Dilthey's search for descriptions of the life-categories or existentials (as Heidegger called them). This search is roughly analogous to Saussure's project of describing the structures of language, or to uncovering the architectural plans which lay out the basic structure of a home. Hermeneutics supplements the descriptive approach by seeking to understand human actions and expressions. Because the meanings of actions are not always immediately apparent, interpretive techniques are required to make the meanings clear. In doing the work of interpretation it is often necessary to call upon information about the basic structures uncovered by descriptive methods. Interpreting the meaning of a particular conversation (*parole*) often requires knowledge of the structure of the language (*la langue*) in which the conversation is taking place. Descriptive and hermeneutic methods supplement each other, the first focusing beneath the surface of individual events in order to describe patterns, the second focusing on the linguistic and nonlinguistic actions in order to penetrate to the meaning of these events.

The question of the difference in these two approaches is raised directly in volume 3 of the *Duquesne Studies*: "How does a hermeneutical-phenomenological psychology in the strict sense differ from the standard empirical-phenomenological research conducted at Duquesne University for the past twenty years?"[33] In answer to this query the editors of the *Studies* propose that there are differences in data base and in the procedures for arriving at conclusions. The Duquesne group collects protocols from subjects about the structures they are investigating, while hermeneutic studies usually focus on literary texts. However, Dilthey held that all human expression is open to hermeneutic interpretation, and more recently Paul Ricoeur has proposed that human action in general can be interpreted as if it were a text. The Duquesne group also questions the procedures used in hermeneutics. They ask, "Does a hermeneutic work . . . depend solely upon the singular talents of the individual author, or can the hermeneutical procedure be in some way specified and standardized so that it can be communicated to others for reduplication?"[34] E. D. Hirsch proposes a method of validation for hermeneutic studies that may answer the Duquesne group's concern.

The next section describes the hermeneutic approach in its various forms. Hermeneutics has passed through three phases in this century. Its earliest phase followed Dilthey's proposal that the interpreter should attempt to "take the author's place" through a sympathic move in order to grasp the meaning of a text. The sympathic move was necessary for a true and objective understanding of an expression. The second phase, which resembled the skeptical and relativistic position of Wittgenstein's language games, centered in the work of

Heidegger and Gadamer. Akin to the recent historical realism position in the philosophy of science, the third phase of hermeneutic theory proposes to overcome the second position through a method of probability assessment of various interpretive attempts. This last position has been developed by Emilio Betti, E. D. Hirsch, and Paul Ricoeur. Before presenting these three phases in the development of hermeneutics, the next section will address the notion of understanding or *Verstehen*.

Hermeneutics (Interpretation)

Verstehen

Max Weber believed that the object of the human sciences is meaningfully oriented behavior. What is to be investigated is the meaning of human actions. Actions include linguistic and nonlinguistic expressions as well as other bodily movements. Access to the meaning of actions is different in kind from access to the mere presence of actions. Ordinary perception provides the data base for the investigation of action as a mere physical occurrence. And in order to provide greater surety to one's own knowledge of an action, the support of others' perceptions can be called on. However, the meaning of actions is not directly present in ordinary perception. The awareness of what an action or speech-act means, requires another kind of "perception" that allows meaning to be known. This second kind of "perception" has been called "Understanding" or *verstehen*. The human realm is primarily the realm of meaning, and meaning fills human experience.

In everyday experience, objects and other people appear in a context of meaningfulness. I anticipate the results of my actions, and I feel my embodiment, which locates me in space and time. I am in this room, sitting at a desk, working at the typewriter in order to express in coherent writing the thoughts and words that are in my awareness. Upon careful reflection, a brief moment of experience holds seemingly endless information which lies throughout different strata of awareness. Aron Gurwitsch,[35] drawing on the concepts of Gestalt theory, has produced an extraordinary description of the organizational outline of the everyday experience. He clarifies the fieldlike quality of awareness and meaningfulness, wherein various figures and meanings are brought into focus against an always-present background of awareness. The field of awareness needs to be a primary realm of human science investigation.

The problem is: How do researchers gain access to this realm, and what conceptual tools do they use to explore it, once having gained access? The realm of experience is of a different order than the realm of physical space–time objects. In Gestalt and system–language theories, the realm of experience is an emergent quality which is the result of interaction patterns of activity which take place in an organic entity. This realm is an information system rather than a system of forces, and its patterns of interaction involve interpretation of codes rather than the push-and-pull of forces. The realm of experience is not static, formed once and for all; it is interactive with its environment, drawing from it conceptual organizing patterns, information from persons and nature, and resistance to its efforts to express itself through bodily activity. The realm of experience also acts upon its environment through linguistic and nonlinguistic expression. It is open to the world—that is, it is "intentional," in the phenomenological sense, and it is filled with sights and sounds originating in that world. The realm of experience has access to itself through the reflective experience of itself. It is deliberative and decisive, and it has concern for its effect on others and the natural world and for the effect that others and the natural world have on it.

In gaining access to the physical world, researchers can gather a group of people together and place an object before them and ask that they describe the object. If there is agreement among the various observers, researchers (assuming that they use a physicalist approach) understand that the description is true. Although some objects are not directly observable, they leave traces (for example, in cloud chambers), and thus they fit the model of things that can be grasped. This common-sense notion of how science operates is no longer accurate for describing contemporary research concerned with force fields and interactive systems, but it points to the common-sense difficulty in conducting research into a realm which one cannot literally get a hold on or grasp. For if the actors act in terms of meanings—in their definitions of the situations—these meanings are never, as far as physicalistically oriented researchers are concerned, directly observable. Yet the researchers must refer to these meanings if they are to account for the actions—which are observable.

In ordinary life (as it is distinguished from the role of the researcher), the problem of access does not seem so difficult. Our own realms of experience are immediately available to us; they are made up of our own awareness. And the realms of experience of others are usually not a mystery to us, even though they are not available to us as our own are. We understand (*verstehen*) another person's world. At least we are able to grasp that aspect of the other person's life experience as he or she conveys it to us by gestures and facial expressions and through what he or she says or writes. This process of understanding is an ordinary or "natural" (that is, unreflected) form of human awareness of another person's life experience and meaning.

In addition to the ordinary use of the term, *understanding* has a technical meaning which refers to a method of inquiry used in the human sciences. The two senses of *understanding*, the commonplace and the technical, can be distinguished from each other but not entirely divorced. The term *understanding* (without a capital letter) is used to mean any type of comprehension, including the comprehension of physical relationships ("I understand why the ball falls") and mathematical relationships ("I understand that two and two make four"). The term *Understanding* (with a capital letter) does not have this broad connotation in the human sciences. It refers to a specific type of understanding, the comprehension of meaning ("Do you understand what she meant by that?"). The positivist approach to knowledge emphasized the sensa as its source, and the sensa, in itself, gives only a perceptual knowledge that, for instance, marks of particular shapes appear on a sheet of paper or that various sounds are given in experience. The kind of comprehension which recognizes the meaning carried by the various situations is Understanding. This kind of comprehension proves exceedingly resistant to purely logical analysis. It is not purely an inductive operation, and it is not a deductive mental process. It is a process which embodies all of the capacities of the mind operating together. It involves a to-and-fro movement from part to whole and back to part again. There are no simple elements which serve as the base from which Understanding is derived; there are no absolute starting points. The meaning which one seeks to Understand is first understood in a tacit sense before it is known in the fullest sense.

In ordinary interaction, one Understands and responds to another person without reflecting on the meaning which is understand. When Understanding is used as a method in human science, researchers, after grasping a meaning, need to translate it into a form of data which can serve their research. The researchers abstract the "flow of meaning" from what is Understood and form it into concepts which can be represented. Researchers must communicate what it is that they have Understood, and so they must conceptualize and signify the meaning which has been the object of their inquiry. While ordinary Understanding may proceed at a nondiscursive level between two people, Understanding as a data-gathering tool for human science requires that the translation be directed toward valid representation. Representations, however, are to be derivatives of the experienced meaning; they are not to be conceptual impositions.

Dilthey and Weber held that Understanding is a vital part of human science, and H. P. Rickman has written:

> Understanding is the grasping of some mental content to which an expression points; it is, therefore, the primary cognitive process through which the subject matter of the human studies is given to us; it pervades these disciplines and is indispensable to them; its successful conclusion on the highest possible level is the goal of the human studies. The orientation towards understanding thus characterizes the disciplines concerned with man and distinguishes them from the physical sciences.[36]

The underside of Understanding is misunderstanding. How do researchers know that they have Understood the mental content and have not misinterpreted the expression? What if two researchers observe the same action or read the same manuscript but then arrive at different interpretations of what is meant? What is needed is a discipline or a method that regulates and consequently improves the act of comprehending meaning. Dilthey called upon the discipline of hermeneutics to serve as a guide for improving the Understanding efforts of researchers in the human sciences.

Hermeneutics is the science of correct Understanding or interpretation. It provides an exposition of rules to guide successful Understanding so that the interpretive effort is more efficient and so that the validity of its results is safeguarded from the intrusion of arbitrariness and subjective misunderstanding. Hermeneutics is a method of systematization of formal procedures which is designed to assist researchers in the task of Understanding and attaining a goal of correct interpretation.

Hermeneutics had a long history before Dilthey's adoption of it as a guide for gaining objectively valid Understanding. The term comes from the Greek word *hermeneuein* which means "to interpret." Some writers have held, although not without challenge, that the word is related to the name Hermes. Hermes was the god of Greek mythology who served as messenger and herald for the other gods. He not only bridged the spatial distance between gods and humans but also translated for humans the meaning and intention of the messages he brought.

Although the term "hermeneutics" dates from the seventeenth century,[37] the activity of text interpretation dates back to antiquity. Dilthey, in his important essay "The Rise of Hermeneutics" (1900)[38] traces the development of modern hermeneutics to the period after the Renaissance. The Council of Trent which sat from 1545 to 1563 in response to the Protestant movement held that the biblical text was not open to direct understanding and the Church's tradition was necessary for the scriptures to be made intelligible. In opposition to this position, the Protestants called for a return to the text itself. However, if the extrinsic source of tradition were not used to clarify the meaning of the scriptures, then principles of interpretation intrinsic to the text (hermeneutics) would have to be clarified to aid in understanding the scriptures. Flacius (1567) was the first to develop such principles; he proposed that a portion of the text should be understood as it related to the intention and composition of the whole scripture. Flacius believed that the whole by which the part was to be understood was the entire New Testament. Later the whole was understood to be individual texts and the notion of a unified New Testament was questioned. Thus Dilthey attributes the need of Protestants to understand the biblical text without using the dogma of tradition as the important impetus for the development of rules of interpretation.

In addition to the heightened need to understand anew the bibical texts, the desire to understand the texts of classical antiquity was increased during the post-Renaissance period. The humanist movement accepted the classical period as exemplary for human culture. In order to understand and assimilate the classical period it was necessary to return to its texts. Through its texts the classical period could be opened up to the 16th century readers. However, the understanding of these texts of a culture separated from them by language, custom, and time required a method of interpretation that would render an accurate understanding. Eventually, the hermeneutic procedures developed to interpret the bibical and classical texts were brought together into a general theory of interpretation applicable to any text, sacred or secular.

Parallel to the development of canons for the interpretation of texts was the tradition of interpretation in the legal realm. Applying laws to particular cases made it necessary to understand what the writers of the laws had intended when the laws were written. It was the task of court officials to make clear the meaning of a law and to apply the valid juridical interpretation to the case before them.

Dilthey credits Friedrich Schleiermacher with the development of a truly effective hermeneutics. In 1819, Schleiermacher wrote that "hermeneutics as the art of Understanding does not exist as a general field, only as a plurality of specialized hermeneutics,"[39] and he therefore sought to consolidate the various hermeneutic techniques into a general field. He proposed that there were basic principles that held for all interpretive work, whether the text was a legal document, a piece of religious scripture, or a work of literature. The general system of interpretation which he developed consisted of two parts, grammatical interpretation and psychological interpretation. The grammatical part contained twenty-four canons, the first two of which read:

[1] Everything that needs a fuller determination in a given text may only be determined in reference to the field of language shared by the author and his original public.

[2] The meaning of every word in a given passage has to be determined in reference to its coexistence with the words surrounding it.[40]

The psychological canons centered around the requirement that the interpretation of a text take into account the totality of thought of the author, not merely the immediate text. In addition to bringing together into a general system the various interpretive enterprises, Schleiermacher attempted to analyze the process of Understanding and to inquire into its possibilities and limitations.[41]

Dilthey

It was Dilthey, in his 1900 essay, who changed the meaning of *hermeneutics* from a discipline for interpreting an author's meaning into a general method of comprehension through which the data basic for the human sciences are given. Dilthey worked to develop a "criticism of historical reason" which would supplement Kant's "critique of pure reason." Hume's skepticism had raised questions as to whether Newton's science provided certain knowledge about the world. Hume had held that we cannot know about relations between events, such as whether one event causes another; knowledge (*epistēmē*), he said, is limited to the experience of single events and does not involve connections between them. Kant had attempted to provide a base for the causal understanding of science through an analysis of connecting patterns or categories which organize knowledge. Kant's approach produced a knowledge that was nonhistorical—that is, a knowledge that did not change. The law of gravity, he pointed out, was true in all places and at all times.

While not denying the adequacy of Kant's analysis for providing a foundation for the knowledge of natural objects, Dilthey asserted that it was not adequate for accounting for the knowledge we have of human phenomena—our understanding of life and other persons, as this understanding is expressed in conversations, poetry, and our informal "life-philosophy." Unlike unchanging natural laws, he said, the organizing patterns of the human realm are historical; they undergo change and development.

Dilthey took the mental operations that produced the understanding of texts—as described in the hermeneutic canons—to be the mental operations which produce knowledge of the human realm. He proposed, therefore, that knowledge of the hermeneutic type is the kind of knowledge that is fundamental for human science. He also extended this kind of knowing beyond its original textual locus so that it could encompass other forms of meaning, particularly nonverbal forms. Hermeneutic knowing, he maintained, applies to cultural systems, social organizations, and systems of scientific or philosophical concepts:

> A rigorous hermeneutic of social organizations is needed in addition to single textual works. . . . Hermeneutics is possible here because between a people and a state, between believers and a church, between scientific life and the university there stands a relation in which a general outlook and unitary form of life find a structural coherence in which they express themselves. There is here the relation of parts to the whole, in which the parts receive meaning from the whole and the whole receives sense from the parts; these categories of interpretation have their correlate in the structural coherence of the organization, by which it realizes its goal teleologically.[42]

Dilthey thus took the step that moved him from the problems of understanding arguments and texts to the problem of understanding in general.

Hermeneutic knowledge reveals the meaning of human expression. This kind of knowledge is different from Kant's pure knowledge. For example, hermeneutic knowledge deals with "structures of interactive forces"[43] where a singular event is understood by reference to whatever it is part of, so that its meaning and purpose can be defined. Pure knowledge, on the other hand, understands a singular event by subsuming it under a general law.

One of the difficulties with hermeneutic knowledge is that it is hard to attain a degree of intersubjective agreement and certainty that one has Understood an expression accurately. Some statements lend themselves to rather clear interpretation. For instance, the statement "Bring the book to me" yields a high degree of intersubjective agreement about what is meant. Other statements, however, do not produce the same easy agreement—as, for instance, this statement by Wittgenstein: "Like everything metaphysical, the harmony between thought and reality is to be found in the grammar of language."[44]

Russell had attempted to solve the problem of meaning by maintaining that in science only words that have ostensive, concrete meaning should be used. Since the human realm is much vaster than objects, Russell's limitation of meaning to objects that can be pointed to is inadequate to communicate and disclose such human phenomena as desire, purpose, care, and so forth. Moreover, the human realm does not consist of discrete parts; it is a blend in flux in which various aspects show up as focal points within a context. Wheelwright has proposed that a language which conveys this interconnectedness and complexity of human phenomena is more appropriate for the human realm than is the precisely and operationally defined language used in descriptions for physical science. He calls the first language "poeto-language" and the second language "steno-language."[45] The human realm is made up of meanings which have soft boundaries as well as depth. The metaphors in our language come closer to reflecting the kind of phenomena in this realm than do highly precise, clearly bounded terms.

Yet Dilthey considered himself to be a "stubborn empiricist"[46] and sought a science of the human realm that would produce a certain and objective (intersubjectively verifiable) knowledge. He wanted the human sciences to produce the kind of knowledge that could be counted upon as the base for social and political decisions. In the hope of producing knowledge equivalent in certainty to that produced by the physical sciences, Dilthey eventually turned away from the interpretation of one's own realm through introspection.[47] He maintained that introspection is inevitably predisposed and biased. "Only under very restricted circumstances," he said "does experience remain present to inner observation."[48] He did not believe that the problems of introspection could be overcome:

> I experience something which by its intensity stands out in my consciousness. That which took place previously is also there. I am pained by the death of my nephew; I remain localized in space and the temporal process. Through introspection I now make this process an object of my observation. Can I base a science on this?[49]

The more carefully we examine our own experience, the more susceptible the experience becomes to our interference, for the interference changes the experience itself. Moreover, our very use of language to describe our experience transforms the experience:

If I want to express this observation in words, I find that they belong to a linguistic usage which is conditioned by the questions which I pose. [For example,] if I ask myself or another person whether the aesthetic impression of a mountain scene contains an element of sympathy, then this feeling is immediately put there [by suggestion].[50]

Dilthey suggested that, instead of examining one's own experience and using it as the basis for knowing the life-categories, we should examine the expressions of life—literature and art, social life, and the course of history—and use them as the objects for investigation in the human sciences. These carriers of the human realm, he said, are more susceptible to correct interpretation than is one's own conscious experience.

Dilthey recognized that the human realm can never be fully known because it is historical and still in process, and he was aware that the tools of knowledge are also part of this changing human realm. The human sciences, like the physical sciences, he said, are human phenomena themselves, and thus there is no final perspective outside the realm from which to view the totality of life:

Every cognitive effort is conditioned by the relation of a knowing subject and his historical horizion to a specific group of facts which is also conditioned in scope according to a specific horizon. For every attempt at understanding, the object is there only from a specific standpoint. Therefore, it is a specifically relative way of seeing and knowing its object.[51]

Although Dilthey understood the perspectival nature of hermeneutic knowledge, he held that one could move from a limited personal perspective toward a broadened and more "objective" knowledge. There could be no objectivity of certainty, he believed, but there could be an objectivity of approximation in which there are degrees of truth which move closer to a sure understanding. For Dilthey, then, Understanding, even though relative and approximate, provides genuine knowledge of the human realm. He drew upon Schleiermacher's hermeneutic canons as the method of investigation which could yield interpretations which would be better approximations of the truth. Schleiermacher had held that to obtain an accurate understanding of a text one had to reexperience and reconstruct the author's experience in writing the original document. The act of interpretation is analogous to the original act of creating the document.

Philosophical Hermeneutics: Heidegger and Gadamer

Martin Heidegger's *Being and Time* (1927) marks the beginning of a significant challenge to the assumptions underlying Western science. Descartes had sought to establish an indubitable foundation upon which knowledge could be based. He located this foundation in human consciousness which "mirrored" the world.[52] The self or ego examined the reflections in the mirror of the mind, seeking those clear and exact images which accurately reflected the reality that we seek to know. Science became a method for "getting more accurate representations by inspecting, repairing, and polishing the mirror, . . ."[53] Heidegger called into question this basic image of human knowledge. He used the concept of interpretation as the tool for challenging the mirror metaphor of epistemology that pervades Western culture. Thus the concept of hermeneutics is used for a different purpose by Heidegger. Whereas Dilthey had seen hermeneutics as a method for providing an objective understanding of the expressions of life, Heidegger proposed that understanding was the basic form of human existence. It is not a way we know the world, he said; it is the way we are. For Heidegger, hermeneutics was not a method which, once designed, could be learned and employed by researchers concerned with the human realm, and he did not address the issue of why one interpretation is better than another. He maintained that to be human is to be interpretive, for the very nature of the human realm is interpretive. Interpretation, then, is not a tool for knowledge; it is the way human beings are. All cognitive attempts to develop knowledge are but expressions of interpretation, and experience itself is formed through interpretation of the world. Being human is a laying-open of what is hidden: we are beings who approach ourselves with the hermeneutic question "What does it mean to be?"

According to Heidegger, truth is not something that we construct by using methods which supposedly distance us from what is to be known, thereby assuring an objective knowledge untinged by personal bias and personal perspective. Truth, he said, occurs in our engagement with the world. Certain convictions—that true knowledge is free from presupposition, that human passions and concerns blind us to "things as they really are," that only purity of thought can lead to truth—are our undoing. True understanding is the result of human engagement, for there is no "pure truth" that lies outside human engagement with the world. In Heidegger's view, then, the attempts by Dilthey and Husserl to develop methods which would guarantee a truth undistorted by human desire and perspective were misdirected. He condemned as "abstraction" any attempt to distance oneself from an object of inquiry in order to know it better. We *know* through interaction and engagement, he said. Our existence, in its nature, has been "tuned" to become a specific existence—this existence here, "thrown into" the world. Consequently, the task of hermeneutic theory is not to develop the appropriate canons which can lead to accurate description. Understanding is already performed for us by the world in which we exist, through the social meanings contained in language. The only task for hermeneutics is to explore how this understanding has come about.[54]

In 1960, Hans-Georg Gadamer published a book with the somewhat ironic title *Truth and Method*. The book extended and applied the main concepts developed by Heidegger regarding the historical and interactive conditions of human understanding. Gadamer agrees that the Western search for knowledge unconditioned by culture or context is misdirected. Thus he is skeptical of Dilthey's plan for obtaining an objective understanding of the meaning of a text or other expression of life. He maintains that we cannot escape the historically conditioned character of our own understanding of texts, laws, rites, and other objects of hermeneutical study. We cannot approach objects in a value-free, undistorted context as proposed by the methods of an "objective" science. Instead we want to know what is useful, how to act in this situation, and how what we are learning fits into what we have already understood. Western philosophy has been mistaken in its hope to develop methods that would provide it with "pure" truth and sharp representations of the world in the mirror of one's mind.

Consciousness is not a historically neutral medium as Descartes held. Rather it (or we) is historically built up and is given with shaped ways of seeing, with attitudes and concepts already embedded in our languages, and with cultural norms and styles. Knowledge can never overcome the way of being human, it can not appear outside the conditions of our nature as historical beings. Gadamer is not opposed to the use of methods to increase our level of understanding and to overcome limited perspectives. However, he does not believe that methods will ever carry us beyond our culturally shaped context to some ultimately free standpoint from which we can see the things-in-themselves.

Gadamer's views are situated somewhere between the relativism that was implied in Winch's application of Wittgenstein's ideas to the social sciences (see chapter 5) and the objectivism of the Dilthey tradition. In Winch's point of view, beliefs and actions must always be understood in the context of the language game or the form of life in which they are located. In other words, one must adopt the rules of the game in order to understand the plays. They cannot be understood from outside, because the boundaries between systems are not permeable, will not allow understanding to pass through. Winch and Wittgenstein used the easiest case of Understanding, the learning of one's primary language, as the model. In this model, the everyday understanding of others within one's own language community provides an explanation of how we understand and find meaning in expressions. Gadamer maintained that a better model for Understanding could—and should—be drawn from cases where it is particularly difficult to Understand, for the study of these interpretive occasions would provide better clues to the process whereby comprehension is achieved. Gadamer chose for his model translation from one language to another.

If the way that the human realm is known is related to the way in which we translate from one language to another, then it is not enough merely to recreate, even assuming it is possible, what was in the mind of an author when a text was written. The interpreter gains understanding by grasping the meanings carried by the linguistic articulation of the text. He or she does not approach the text as a blank page, but has expectations, and approaches the text with prejudgments about what will be found there. These expectations are the beliefs and practices, concepts and values, that make up the interpreter's own lifeworld. Interpretation, then, involves a "fusion of horizons," a dialectical interaction between the expectations of the interpreter and the meanings in the text. From this point of view, there is no such thing as *the* correct interpretation. Interpretation is a mediation or construction between each interpreter's own language and the language of the text. The text continues to speak in various ways as it is approached by various translators, each of whom has his own lifeworld language.

In this kind of interpretation, the entire process has a hypothetical and circular character. From the context available to an interpreter from within his or her own lifeworld, he or she makes a preliminary projection of the sense of the text as a whole; thus one begins with a preapprehension or preliminary perception of the whole. This prejudgment is always vague, since it is by necessity without parts and is unarticulated. "A close analogy is the dim adumbration of an answer that we must project in order to ask a question in the first place."[54a] The parts of the text are not a mere mechanical collection; they are a complex which hangs together in a unity which is the meaning of the text. The process of understanding is a movement from the first prejudgmental notion of the meaning of the whole, in which the parts are understood, to a change in the sense of the meaning of the whole because of the confrontation with the detailed parts of the text. Dilthey called this movement from whole to parts to whole the "hermeneutic circle." The movement is not really a circle, however; it is more of a spiral in which each movement from part to whole increases the depth of understanding. The experience of understanding—as proposed by the concept of the "hermeneutic circle"—is common. For example, when one starts to read a book, one comes to it with a set of expectations, including the cultural givens related to the genre, previous books by the author, one's own mood and interests, and so on. As one begins to read, the meaning of the book with which one began is altered; in the case of a novel, the change may come about because the characters behave differently than was originally expected. One's hunch about the meaning of the book must be revised, and the revised hunch informs one's interpetation of subsequent action in the book. This dialectic between the parts and the whole continues throughout the reading of the book and even afterward because various parts are known differently.

The philosophical hermeneutics of Heidegger and Gadamer raises questions abut the very character of knowledge. They accuse the romantic hermeneutic tradition of retaining a Cartesian idea of knowledge in which *epistēmē* is achieved by overcoming all doubt. The truth is not hidden and it is not something that can be revealed only through reason. Instead, it is our Understanding, which brings forth experience to begin with. Philosophical hermeneutics rejects the notion of objective science—physical science or human science—as the measure of knowledge. Heidegger wrote:

> With our question, we want neither to replace the sciences nor to reform them. On the other hand, we want to participate in the preparation of a decision; the decision: Is science the measure of knowledge, or is there a knowledge in which the ground and limit of science and thus its genuine effectiveness are determined? Is this authentic knowledge necessary for a historical people, or is it dispensable or replaceable by something else? However, with our question we stand outside the sciences, and the knowledge for which our question strives is neither better nor worse but totally different.[55]

Gadamer maintained a dichotomy of truth and method. Method, as manifested in objective science, he said, abstracts from the truth instead of making it known.

Gadamer's concern was not to develop a method for the human sciences in the way that both Schleiermacher and Dilthey had wanted to do. He wanted to clarify the conditions under which all understanding actually occurs. He did not want to replace methodological investigations, but he did want to explore the underlying dimensions in which interpretation takes place. He took from Heidegger the basic assumption that all human knowledge is ultimately interpretation because it is derived from a historical and cultural perspective. Although we cannot stand outside ourselves by using rational procedures or find an ultimate foundation—such as the sense data elements—we do create an understanding of ourselves, of others, and of our world. But this understanding, he said, is developed within the context of the tradition of the society to which we belong, and while standing in this tradition through interaction with other traditions, we are able to overcome its limitations and create new categories of knowledge organization. In Gadamer's view, the problem for our finite understanding is not that we must overcome the condition in which we find ourselves. What we must do is take up the tradition in such a way that we obtain access to the past and at the same time open up new possibilities for the future.

The primary objections to Gadamer's view are aimed at his basic thesis—that interpretation can never lead to science, if by science we mean a discipline which achieves objective and permanent knowledge.[56] Gadamer maintained that no method can lead to a complete transcendence of the observer's own understanding, and therefore an absolute truth cannot be achieved through methods. It is in this sense that the title of Gadamer's book, *Truth and Method*, is ironic.

Betti, Hirsch, and Ricoeur

The period of philosophical hermeneutics parallels the period of the "relativistic" rebellion against logical positivism. Without attempting to establish any connections between the two movements, we may still note that there are certain parallels which reflect the Zeitgeist of the 1960s. It was a period when there was a breaking of the restraints of authority and a questioning of the value of scientifically inspired technological achievements. The 1960s affirmed the significance of the individual and the fullness of immediate experience as they stood in opposition to abstracted knowledge. The person was seen as a historical being who views the world from within his or her own personally meaningful context.

The philosophical hermeneutics of Heidegger and Gadamer call into question the possibility of objective historical knowledge. Although they accept the notion of expanding the horizon within an inquiry takes place, they do not accept that the ideal of an objective knowledge of the author's meaning in a text is possible to achieve. What we can obtain is an understanding which is the result of the fusion of our horizon with the text. Emilio Betti and E. D. Hirsch assail the whole notion of philosophical hermeneutics; they hold that "objectivity" is possible and reaffirm that the study of history and human expression can leave behind the perspective of the inquirer. From Betti's point of view, "Heidegger and Gadamer are the destructive critics of objectivity who wish to plunge hermeneutics into a standardless morass of relativity."[57]

Beginning in the 1950s, Betti sought to bring the work in hermeneutics together and to justify it as a valid form of knowledge acquisition in the light of the logical-positivist reservations.[58] As Dilthey did in his later work, Betti reserved the possibility of Understanding for the interpretation of expressions of the human realm. These expressions are publicly accessible and can be treated as objects, even though each object carries an embodiment of the human realm. The crucial difference between the hermeneutic knowing of expressions and other forms of knowledge is that the object consists of objectivations of mind, and it is the task of the interpreter to recognize or reconstruct the ideas, messages, and intentions carried in them. The text object represents an appeal, a call on the observer to understand. The call is answered by a reconstruction of the meaning, with the help of our categories of thought, and by a fitting together of the various pieces of evidence; the purpose is to reconstruct the author's intended meaning. For Betti, Understanding *is* the reconstruction of the intentions of the author.

Betti opposes Gadamer's position of "fusion of horizons" between the interpreter and the text. In *Hermeneutics as the General Methodology of the Geisteswissenschaften* (1962), he writes:

> The obvious difficulty with the hermeneutical method proposed by Gadamer seems to lie, for me, in that it enables a substantive agreement between text and reader—i.e., between the apparently easily accessible meaning of a text and the subjective conception of the reader—to be formed without, however, guaranteeing the correctness of understanding; for that it would be necessary that the understanding arrived at correspond fully to the meaning underlying the text as an objectivation of mind. . . . It can easily be demonstrated that the proposed method [of Gadamer] cannot claim to achieve objectivity and that it is only concerned with the internal coherence and conclusiveness of the desired understanding.[59]

Betti believes that Understanding is a dialectical process between two subjects, the reader and writer, and that this process can lead to an objective interpretation. Such interpretation will provide the methodological ground for human science.

Hirsch, in *Validity in Interpretation* (1967), responded to the reservations of philosophical hermeneutics by asserting that interpretation does provide normative knowledge:

> At stake ultimately is the right of *any* humanistic discipline to claim genuine knowledge. Since all human studies, as Dilthey observed, are founded upon the interpretation of texts, valid interpretation is crucial to the validity of all subsequent inferences in those studies.[60]

Hirsch pointed out that "validity" is different from "certainty." The practical aim of scientific knowledge, he believed, should be an agreement that truth has probably been achieved, not that all doubt has been removed and "certainty" assured. "The fact that certainty is always unattainable," he said, "is a limitation which interpretation shares with many other disciplines."[61] And he maintained that there is no neat formulation of correct methods that leads to the assurance that one has developed the best possible interpretation.

Our preliminary interpretations of the meaning of a text need to be validated. In a division that is close to Reichenbach's "context of discovery" and "context of justification," Hirsch separated the process of proposing an adequate interpretation of a text from the process of validation. The "context of discovery," the initial understanding of a text, is a "probability judgment," and a probability judgment is an informed guess; it lacks certainty. The reality that the researcher seeks to describe is the meaning carried by the words. It is the words which are directly experienced, and they carry the meaning, which is what we seek to know. If the meaning is clear, there is no need to engage in the method of interpretation (hermeneutics), for the purpose of interpretation—making clear a meaning that is present in a confused, fragmentary, and cloudy form— has already been accomplished. For Hirsch, the hermeneutic process is a rational means of reaching conclusions in the absence of directly experienced certitude. He maintained that the process of interpretation is a particular variety of the general process of probability judgments as outlined by Keynes.[62]

One begins the hermeneutic enterprise with a first guess as to the meaning of a text. Based on the available evidence, this guess has a low probability of being correct. As more evidence is gathered, new guesses are made, each successive guess having a higher probability of being correct. Hirsch offered three criteria for judging the reliability of each guess: the narrowness of the class, the number of members in it, and the frequency of the trait among those members. The class of the text can be narrowed by determining the authorship, the date, the tradition, and so on. Interpreters have better chances of understanding the meaning of a text if they know who wrote it, when it was written, and whatever other information is available. For example, if the interpreter knows that a particular text is a transcription of a speech given by an American president who had a consistent conservative tradition and that the speech was given three days after a weekend of violence in several cities, then the probability is increased that an interpretation is better than if none of this information about the class of the text is known. If, in the speech, the words "we need to heal the cities" appear (and if there is no clarification of these words within the speech itself), the interpreter needs to make clear what these words mean. Do they mean providing more social services for the inhabitants of the cities? Or do they mean increasing the strength of the police forces? If these words were used in three speeches during the same week, their meaning might be clarified in the contexts of the other speeches. Perhaps the speaker had used these words ten times in previous speeches during the last ten years, and perhaps each previous time the words about healing the cities had carried a law-and-order connotation. Or perhaps the words had become known to newspaper editors and writers as "code words" referring to financial support for service agencies serving inner-city residents and this was a first example of their use in a speech by the president. All of this kind of information provides evidence so that the original guess is amended as more information is gathered. Conflicting interpretations can be judged according to which one most adequately takes account of the information. The one most probably correct (valid) is the one which the weight of available evidence supports.[63]

The norm of correct interpretation is the most probable intention of the author of a text (or act). The interpretation is not a certainty, however, for new evidence can be developed which may lend support to a different understanding of the author's intention or a new guess may be generated which more adequately integrates the evidence. Interpretation is never final or absolute. For example, what did Shakespeare mean in *Hamlet*? What is the meaning of a statement made by a person being interviewed? The hermeneutic process for determining which of the available guesses of the author's intention is most probable is a dialectical movement that goes from interpretive hypothesis to evidence, back to an altered hypothesis, back to evidence, and on and on.

Paul Ricoeur has summarized Hirsch's procedures for validation:

> I agree with E. D. Hirsch that [the procedures for validation] are closer to a logic of probability than to a logic of empirical verification. To show that an interpretation is more probable in the light of what we know is something other than showing that a conclusion is true. So in the relevant sense, validation is not verification. It is an argumentative discipline comparable to the juridical procedures used in legal interpretation, a logic of uncertainty and qualitative probablity.[64]

In the dialectical movement, guess and validation are, in a sense, circularly related. They are both a "subjective" and an "objective" approach to the text, and they provide a meaning for the concept of the hermeneutic circle which leads to understanding of greater probability.

Hirsch's approach provides a method by means of which various interpretations can be compared so that one can be judged more probable than another. Multiple interpretations of the author's intention can be compared, for an interpretation must not only be probable, it must also be more probable than another interpretation. The notion that all interpretations are of equal worth is challenged by Hirsch's procedures. The statement that is often used to question someone's credibility, "That's just your interpretation," would hold only if the person was unwilling to submit the interpretation to a validity process where it could be compared to other interpretations.

Hirsch, like Betti, is critical of Gadamer's dismissal of hermeneutics as a method that leads to knowledge. In "Gadamer's Theory of Interpretation" (1965), Hirsch writes:

> Gadamer protests that there can be no *Methodologie* of textual interpretation because interpretation is not, after all, a *Wissenschaft* whose aim is objective and permanent knowledge. [Gadamer maintains that] no method can transcend the interpreter's own historicity, and no truth can transcend this central truth.[65]

Against Gadamer's position, Hirsch proposes that hermeneutics goes beyond the historically conditioned first guess about the text's meaning through a self-critical test that uses "all the relevant data we can find . . . and the best hypothesis is the one that best explains all the relevant data."[66] The process of testing makes hermeneutics more than Gadamer's historically conditioned first encounter with the text. The interplay between guess and validation in interpretation "suggests that the much-advertised cleavage between thinking in the sciences and the humanities does not exist. The hypothetico-deductive process is fundamental in both of them, as it is in all thinking that aspires to knowledge."[67] Because the method of hermeneutics provides a means for testing interpretations, Hirsch holds that it can provide a foundational knowledge for a science of the human realm.

Betti and Hirsch's critique of philosophical hermeneutics is directed to a position different from the main thrust of Gadamer's work. Betti and Hirsch argue that the canons of hermeneutic method can lead to an objective knowledge of what an author meant in his or her text. Philosophical hermeneutics addresses the problem of what a text means for the interpreter. Gadamer holds that the text can change our pre-judgments, but only through a dialectic unfolding in which we engage the text with our historically given horizon of understanding. We cannot approach the text from outside this given condition; we cannot avoid our self in attempting to know the text as meant by the author. Gadamer is not opposed to the attempt to understand the author's intention as Betti and Hirsch seem to assume. Rather, he holds that there are limits to how far we can discard our own cultural context in identifying the author's intentions.

Paul Ricoeur is the most important contemporary writer proposing that hermeneutics is the appropriate methodological position for the human sciences. Ricoeur best exemplifies the approach to human science methodology developed in this book. He has drawn on the work in phenomenology, psychoanalysis, French structuralism, Saussurian linguistics, speech-act theory, action theory, and hermeneutics to construct a methodological position for the study of human phenomena. He does not end in an eclecticism, but in a unified position attuned to the special requirements of human science. His position appreciates and incorporates the achievements of the behavioral and social sciences, while presenting an enlarged notion of research that addresses meaningful human action. One of Ricoeur's important contributions is the extention of the notion of understanding the intention of an author of a text to understanding the author of an action. Ricoeur also recognizes the cultural and unconscious structures that make up the content of human expression.

Ricoeur participated in Gabriel Marcel's discussions while a student at the Sorbonne in the late 1930s. As a prisoner during World War II he was allowed to study the work of Husserl as well as Heidegger and Jaspers. After the war he translated Husserl's *Ideas I* and added an extensive commentary. As a teacher of philosophy he concentrated each year on the personal study of a major philosopher. His first major work was *Freedom and Nature: The Voluntary and the Involuntary* (1950).[68] Here he set forth his basic project, developing an approach to the underlying unity that connects the felt dualism of mind and body or the voluntary and involuntary. The voluntary consists of the will and is the subjective dimension of existence; the involuntary refers to the body and biological nature of existence. The two dimensions are combined in existence into the unity that is a person. Will without body or subject without object would be ethereal, the body without will would be mechanical. Ricoeur sought to investigate the unity that mediates and underlies these aspects of humanness. A mode that manifests the unity of human existence is meaningful human action. The investigation of action can lead to an understanding of the integrity which underlies human existence.

Ricoeur held that the investigation of human action cannot proceed as if the author of the action is fully aware of what his or her action means. His study of Freud[69] led him to suspect that consciousness can cover over or disguise a person's reasons for acting. Thus the data gathered by phenomenological and reflective studies are inadequate to provide a full understanding. Introspection must be supplemented by interpretation to provide the understanding of action.

Ricoeur proposes that the researcher is like the reader of a text. The problem is to understand the meaning of the text. Human action as well as literary works can be read as texts.[70] Such a reading calls on the insights developed by Austin and Searle in their theory of the speech-act. Unlike the sign system theory developed by Saussure, the understanding of speech-acts involves a subject speaking at a particular time, referring to the world, and addressing another person. Meaningful action needs to be objectified in order for it to become an object for a human science. As the spoken word is transformed into an object when it is converted to written form, in a similar way, human action can go through a kind of objectivation without losing its character of meaningfulness. Ricoeur speaks of actions as 'leaving their mark" on time, and as calling for a reading rather than a hearing. "An action leaves a 'trace', it makes its 'mark' when it contributes to the emergence of such patterns which become the documents of human action."[71]

The objective meaning of the action becomes separated from the intention of the actor and produces unintended consequences. Unlike Dilthey and Betti, Ricoeur holds that the right understanding of an action cannot be solved by returning to the alleged intention of the author. The meaning of an action is often not clear because, on the one hand, of the metaphorical dimensions of meaning that require deciphering to unfold its several layers, and, on the other, the circular character of relating parts and whole. This requires that texts and actions be interpreted in order to disclose their meaning.

Ricoeur calls on Hirsch's guess and validation as a proper approach to arriving at an accurate reading of the meaning of a human action. He holds that "the procedures of validation have a polemical character," and relates the process of deciding among the conflict of interpretations to juridical reasoning. It is through a process of argumentation that agreement is reached about a proposed interpretation. However, there is no final arbitration, and an accepted interpretation is always open to further argument.

Interpretation leads to the understanding of the meaning of human action, the object of human science. However, meaning takes place in a social context. A structural investigation deepens the interpretive approach to single events by providing an understanding of the broader system. Ricoeur calls for a dialectical movement between looking at the uniqueness of an event and at the social context which forms it.

> If . . . we consider structural analysis as a stage—and a necessary one—between naive interpretation and a critical interpretation, between a surface interpretation and a depth interpretation, then it would be possible to locate explanation and understanding at two different stages of a unique hermeneutic arc. It is this depth semantics which situates the genuine object of understanding and which requires a specific affinity between the reader and the kinds of things the text is about.[72]

Interpretation as the methodology of human science accounts for the unity of the will and body or voluntary and involuntary which forms action as meaningful. It provides a level of objectivity appropriate to the kind of plurivocity that belongs to the values of meaningful human action. It also draws on the science of linguistics rather than on a science developed to study nonhuman phenomena.

Several social scientists have attempted to provide a more specific description of how Ricoeur's hermeneutic methodology would be applied in anthropology and sociology. Clifford Geertz, in "Thick Description: Toward an Interpretive Theory of Culture" (1973), remarks: "Doing ethnography is like trying to read (in the sense of 'construct a reading of') a manuscript—foreign, faded, full of ellipses, suspicious emendation, and tendentious commentaries, but written not in conventionalized graphs of sound but in transient examples of shaped behavior."[73] Paul Rabinow and William M. Sullivan have collected a series of essays "exemplary of the interpretative or hermeneutic approach to the study of human society," including a paper by Geertz.[74] In addition, Joseph Kockelmans in a 1975 article titled "Toward an Interpretative or Hermeneutic Social Science" has developed an outline for the approach a hermeneutically-based social science might take. These attempts are an indication that the hermeneutic approach being developed by Ricoeur is moving from philosophic exploration to methodological specification. Kockelmans said that the subject matter of a hermeneutic social science would consist of "the totality of all social phenomena which function in a meaningful way in our society." This kind of social science would not be interested in the factual occurrence of these phenomena or in explaining them by determining how they are related to one another. It would also not be interested in discovering the invariable structures of these phenomena, because that is the task of "descriptive" or phenomenological social science. Interpretive social science would focus its attention on an attempt to understand the meaning which these phenomena have in a particular society. Kockelmans elaborates:

> It will be clear that interpretive social science is not interested in discovering the meaning which a private individual or a group of individuals who happen to be concerned with, or involved in, these phenomena may attach to them, nor in the meaning which social agents "deep in their hearts" may attach to certain social actions they perform. Interpretative social science is concerned only with discovering the "social" meaning which a "society" attaches to certain phenomena and certain patterns of social behavior.[75]

The subject matter would be the meaning intersubjectively shared by the members of a society—that is, the meaning of patterns of social behavior, types of action, the adherence to social institutions, and the institutions themselves.

In trying to understand this social meaning, interpretive social science would employ hermeneutic methods. Kockelmans listed five canons which would provide a guarantee of the intersubjective validity of an interpretation.

1. Interpretive research needs to accept the autonomy of the object. The source of the articulated meaning is the phenomena themselves. The phenomena should not be forced into preconceived interpretive schemes, such as psychoanalytic or Marxian formats.

2. The researcher should search for an interpretation which makes the phenomena maximally reasonable or human. "Many social phenomena are so complex and so richly structured, so deeply rooted in the past of a society, that their genuine meaning often cannot be made explicit." The meanings have been covered over by secondary and tertiary layers of meaning so that their original significance is not longer available. The researcher must try to understand

the phenomena in a more profound way than those who are involved in them or confronted with them.

3. The researcher must try to achieve the greatest possible familiarity with the phenomena—with the historical origin, with the various components of meaning which have been gradually attached to the original meaning, and with the various traditions which have influenced the origin and the future development of the phenomena.

4. This canon—which Kockelmans notes is the most important—is the hermeneutic circle. This is the process of knowledge development that moves back and forth from understanding the parts to understanding the whole. The process is quasi-infinite on both sides, the parts and the wholes. Nevertheless, in most instances an interpretation can be reached which is adequate for the phenomena under consideration.

5. The researcher must try to show the meaning the phenomena have for the present situation. After the researcher has tried to understand the phenomena in their historical origin and further development, he or she must look at them to determine their meaning for the present situation. This act involves a fusion of the researcher's situation and the phenomena.

Interpretation and the Human Sciences

Within the tradition of Mill, the behavioral and social sciences must be grounded on "brute data," the validity of which cannot be questioned by offering alternative interpretations and the credibility of which cannot be confounded or undermined by further reasoning. This approach to science requires uninterpretable data as the base upon which to build explanations.[76] If the data lend themselves to various interpretations, then these interpretations must be distinguished from the basic, brute data from which they are inferred. Millian science, then, tries to reconstruct the human realm so that it consists of brute data alone. Human behavior (the acts of people) is identified beyond interpretation by using either physical descriptions or operationally defined (that is, based on brute data) descriptions of a phenomena. The subjective realm—the lived world of people, consisting of their beliefs, attutides, and values—is translated into brute data by collecting the words and marks of people given in response to questionnaires and constructed interviews or, in some cases, by recording their overt nonverbal behavior.

The task is to reduce the vagueness and multileveled meaning, as it appears in the flux of experience, to a precise and manageable piece of information that contains one ostensive statement. For example, the answers to a question, sometimes addressed to women, "Do you want to register for the draft?" must be limited to the kind of data which are usable in a science based on elements. The richness and ambivalence of experience involved in some of the possible answers to this question are too full of meaning to be of use to the research model. When the design calls for "yes" and "no" or a 1 to 7 Likert-scale designation as the only options, the complexity and variety of meaning in need of interpretation are left out—and they are left out deliberately so that unambiguous brute data can be developed. A model of science which cannot include ambiguous and interpretable statements gains precision in analysis, but it loses the character of the experienced world.

The data of the hermeneutic sciences remain open to further interpretation, and thus they cannot meet the criteria of complete intersubjective agreement. This means, of course, that the hermeneutic sciences have plurivocal data. They must rely on readings as the means of analysis, and they move in an uncompleted hermeneutic circle. The data have no meaning in isolation from the whole, and they require looking from the whole to the parts to the whole again. The "seeing" of the pattern which gives meaning to the text requires insight; the seeing is not a result of precise procedures as is, for instance, a mathematical result. In mathematics, the design and choice of procedures can require considerable creative work, but the analysis of the data follows directly from the application of the procedures. In the hermeneutic sciences, this is not so. Seeing the meaning is an insightful event supported by evidence, but the evidence is ambivalent and takes on its own meaning from its place in the interpretation proposed. The seeing is ultimately unformalizable, and thus its demonstration is not absolute. "This is what is meant by that speech" is a different kind of statement from "The correlation between yes answers to 'Do you want to register for the draft?' and socioeconomic status is 0.45." A science which makes the first kind of statement cannot achieve the degree of fine exactitude which is represented by the second kind of statement. The data behind the second kind of statement allow measurement to virtually any degree of exactitude.

Prediction, which is a primary goal of the behavioral and social sciences, cannot be supported by the evidence and conclusions of a hermeneutic science. As Charles Taylor has pointed out, "if the epistemological views underlying the science of interpretation are right, such exact prediction is radically impossible."[77] Taylor gives three reasons for this statement. First, we cannot shield the domain of human experience from external interference; it is an intentional system, open to interaction with other systems. Second, interpretation does not allow for exactitude, and the nuances of difference in meaning can lead to very different predictions in some circumstances. Third and most fundamental, human beings are self-defining, and with changes in self-definition go changes in what the categories of experience are. Taylor says that for the human sciences "it is much easier to understand after the fact than it is to predict."[78] And human science is largely *ex post facto* understanding. The very concepts which will form the experience in the future are not available to the researcher of the present, and to predict on the basis of one's present understanding what the future understanding will be is impossible because one lacks the vocabulary. "Human science looks backward," Taylor says. "It is inescapably historical." He concludes:

> There are . . . good grounds both in epistemological arguments and in their greater fruitfulness for opting for hermeneutical sciences of man. But we cannot hide from ourselves how greatly this option breaks with certain commonly held notions about our scientific tradition. We cannot measure such sciences against the requirements of a science of verification; we cannot judge them by their predictive capacity.[79]

Taylor makes one other point about the human sciences—that what meaning one can see in a text is founded on the interpreter's own meaning. Interpretation is founded on intuitions which all do not share. Successful interpretation requires "a high degree of self-knowledge, a freedom from illusion." Successful understanding may involve more than a sharpening of one's intuitions about organizing principles; it may involve a change in one's orientation. But Taylor adds: "It may . . . be that to understand a certain explanation one . . . has to change one's orientation—if not in adopting another orientation, at least in living one's own in a way which allows for greater comprehension of others."[80]

The descriptive and hermeneutic systems are aimed at describing and clarifying the nature of the experience which people live through and in which they plan and carry out actions. The human realm (the lived world, the everyday world, the common-sense world, the world of the natural attitude) is available through its various expressions—through direct communication that people have with each other, through written and artistic communications, through institutional forms and cultural belief systems. The character of the human realm appears to be organized by structural relationships rather than by the deductively ordered relationships of a formal logic.

The descriptive existential-phenomenological approaches have provided refined and discriminating portrayals of various aspects and forms in which the lifeworld organizes and expresses itself, and they have made careful analysis of how the lifeworld can be made accessible for study. The hermeneutic system of inquiry is especially sensitive to the circular nature of understanding the human realm, which is studied from within itself because hermeneutics maintains that there is no way for the knower to stand outside the lifeworld to observe it.

The nature of the lifeworld, experienced as the stream of consciousness, makes it difficult to provide precise statements about its contents and structures. As a reality originating in interacting patterns, it does not show up with clear outlines as physical objects do, and thus the researcher finds it difficult to produce the kind of knowledge that gains complete intersubjective agreement. Nevertheless, the descriptive and hermeneutic systems take the lifeworld itself as their subject matter. The methodology which has emerged from their efforts provides a more direct access to the central concern of human science, the human realm.

7

Human Science Research

The previous chapters in this book have presented a review of developments in the philosophy of science during the past few decades. The purpose of this review has been to place in context the controversy over a proper methodology for human science. The original debate was formulated before the recent reevaluation and study of scientific method had taken place, and so it did not include all of the later developments in pragmatic science, systems theory, linguistics, hermeneutics, and action theory. Even now, when existential-phenomenological and new hermeneutic approaches have been adopted by human scientists, these approaches have been seen by some merely as alternative paradigms to the received view, rather than as challenges to the notion of a science that gives statements that truly describe an independent reality. It should be emphasized that the new developments do not point toward mere alternative ways of achieving certain knowledge. Instead, they call for considerations of how one searches for knowledge when the results of that search are limited to conditioned and incomplete conclusions. In the present context, working in human science calls for procedures that allow the researcher to decide among alternatives. No longer does following the correct method guarantee that the results of the study are "true." Different systems of inquiry and different studies within these systems provide candidates for adoption by the community as the best we know at the present time.

I have found in my experience that doing effective human science research within a postpositive context requires, in addition to competence to operate within various systems of inquiry, two important conceptual tools. These are a clear understanding of what it means for the researcher to develop new knowledge and an appreciation of the peculiar and complex characteristics of the linguistic data type. Knowledge is that which the researcher creates in an endeavor

241

to provide the community information and understanding upon which it can base actions. In addition to use of the numeric data type, human science research uses the linguistic data type. Linguistic data is more sensitive to the meaningfulness of the human realm than the more abstract and limited numeric type. However, linguistic data is pliable and resilient, and thus work with it requires care and a grasp of its special characteristics. This final chapter explores these two important conceptual tools and their use in human science research.

The Nature of Knowledge

Several common themes have been developed in this book concerning the character of knowledge in which postpositivist human studies need to be carried out. The first theme has to do with the standard for acceptability of a knowledge statement. The requirement that the statement must meet the criterion of absolute certainty is too stringent. Criticism of the received view has shown that those who attempt to adhere to it cannot meet this requirement themselves, because the ground of pure observation, untainted by theoretical assumptions, is unobtainable and because the deductive links between theoretical concepts are diluted by the contextual variability of conceptual definitions. What is acceptable as "knowledge," then, is what has withstood the tests of experience and experiment; it has simply provided better solutions to problems than have competing proposals. Consequently, "knowledge" is no longer what is certain. "Knowledge" is fallible. It merely represents the best explanations available, and these are the explanations in which we trust enough to act.

A second theme concerns a new awareness that science is a human activity in which the subject as knower is central. Knowledge is developed in a historical and cultural context, and it is subject to the limitations of the conceptual and technical tools of its situation. Science is not progressive in the sense that knowledge can be accumulative and additive, each previous certainty merely incorporated into later processes of discovery, but it is progressive in the sense that later historical epochs have available, through literature and artifacts, the understanding developed in previous periods. Although this cultural heritage can be a conservative influence on subsequent inquiry, it provides a base for critiques and new attempts. Historical development appears not to be as revolutionary and discontinuous as Kuhn originally proposed; it is more of an evolutionary process in which research programs and problem solutions survive through competition.

A third theme has to do with the intellectual tools that are used to develop and justify knowledge. They are much more varied than those previously in use, sense experience and demonstrative logic. In the new understanding of science, an expanded notion of reason is proposed which includes the reasoning operations of systems logic, hermeneutic logic, and pragmatic logic. The understanding and explanation of field theory, organic systems, linguistic statements, and consciousness require orders of reason which are different from those that are based on clearly delineated, closed concepts and demonstrative relationships. These logics are not as precise in their conclusions as relational logic is, and thus there is a tension between their openness to vague and fuzzy categories and the need for clarity in demonstrating the processes which lead to their conclusions.

A fourth theme has to do with the operations through which knowledge is developed. These operations include the personal creative activity of proposing hypotheses, the testing of proposals, and the rhetorical communication of results to others in the scientific community.

The dissolution of the consensus that science produces certain knowledge has required a change in methodological understanding. No longer can a researcher assume the consensus as a given and merely apply the rules and recipes which have been previously formulated to guarantee certainty.

When the guarantee that following a particular method will lead to truth is removed, a search for a way to decide among fallible alternative results is needed. Not all knowledge claims are understood to rest on equally persuasive warrants; not every claim is worthy of acceptance by the community. Acceptance of a research result by the community—agreement that it is worthy as a knowledge claim— comes through the process of practical reasoning rather than through the process of demonstrative reasoning. The scientist needs to be concerned with the way in which worthy decisions are arrived at through argument. In a postpositive science, the problem for the scientist is making a decision about how to accept a hypothesis as a worthy knowledge claim.

The ultimate question which science attempts to address is: What is reality? The positivists maintained that we can answer this question because we have direct access to reality through our senses. It was this notion of direct access that was the point of the attack on positivism. The *Weltanschauungen* position, Quine's attack on the assumption that synthetic and analytic statements could be separated, and psychological investigations of perception all demonstrated that our sense experience is a construction, an interaction of culturally given conceptual schemes, cognitive structures, and linguistic apparatuses with the world. Thus, what is immediately available in experience does not correspond to the world as a thing-in-itself. What is available in experience is a creation composed of organizing patterns and sensation. Experience is analogous to a Picasso painting in two ways: (1) The object to be portrayed did not merely appear to Picasso; it was the result of a search for something that would fulfill his idea about what he wanted to paint. (2) The portrait did not correspond to the object; it was an interpretation that was held together by its own coherence and structures. The final portrait is a creation, then, not a photograph, and it is judged by its own standards—such as elegance, simplicity, and coherence—not merely by its likeness to the object itself.

If experience does not provide a direct opening to reality, how can we know what reality is? The positivists' first answer to this question was phenomenalism, which held that by focusing on the sensa in experience the subjective bias resulting from the constructive aspects of experience could be penetrated so that access to reality could be provided. This attempt was problematic because, even if the sensa reflect reality, one must overcome solipsism and communicate the experience of these sensa. And in order to do that, one must translate them into language, and language, even it its simplest ostensive reference, does not correspond directly to the thing named, for language is theory-laden. The problem of separating out the "subjective" aspects of experience—that is, overcoming experimenter bias—has been given much attention in research design; multiple observers, double-blind designs, and various instruments have been used in an attempt to provide "objective" data. But the criticism of the received view is aimed not only at removing individual bias. Its other charge is that members of a culture, a community, a theoretical network, or a research group share organizing structures through which their experience is given its basic form.

A postpositive human science is still confronted with the question: How can we decide among knowledge claims? Since the positivist answer cannot be accepted, how is the question to be answered? Three basic overlapping answers are offered below—through innate and universal reasonableness, through a universal trial-and-error learning, and through the use of pluralistic epistemologies.

Reasonableness

The first answer, an appeal to a universal pragmatic reason, assumes that human beings possess a kind of reasonableness to which an appeal can be made for judging between and among possibilities. This position, while recognizing the impact of culture and the differences in language games which separate the lifeworlds of various people, finds a reasonableness which runs through all cultures and is common to all people. Support for the position draws on Piaget's picture of common cognitive structures and Chomsky's concept of innate deep linguistic structures. It shares with Kant, without the superstructure of his transcendental descriptions, the notion that there is a universal reasonableness which cuts across all cultural perspectives. E. D. Hirsch assumes such a reasonableness in his development of probability justification, and Jürgen Habermas attempts to ground the reasonableness in a communicative competence that resembles Chomsky's universal linguistic competence. The syncretic position, described later in this chapter, also appeals to the notion of a universal reasonableness.

In *Validity in Interpretation* (1967), Hirsch describes reasonableness as the ability to make use of "probability judgments" in reaching conclusions "in the absence of directly experienced certitude."[1] Hirsch holds that "correctness" is the goal of interpretation and may in fact be achieved, even though we can never know that we have achieved it. "We can have the truth without being certain that we have it," he says, "and in the absence of certainty, we can nevertheless have knowledge—knowledge of the probable." He proposes a process of adjudication based on "objective" and "well-established" principles.

Hirsch takes Keynes's notion of probability as a format in which decisions can be made. Keynes asserted that probabilities can be qualitative as well as quantitative, that vague concepts like "more," "less," "very," and "slightly" can be used in connection with knowledge proposals. In Hirsch's approach, a hypothesis is understood to be a probability judgment or an informed guess. Although he does not offer any rules for making good guesses, he believes that the probability-judgment method provides a way to decide among the guesses. Judgments are uncertain by nature, he says, because they refer to reality that is partly unknown and may never be known with certainty.

The decision is based on all of the available evidence about an object or a structure. The process of decision requires construing from this evidence the most probable description or interpretation of the object of inquiry. Hirsch holds that it is on the basis of evidence that a decision is made between interpretations:

> The objectivity of interpretation as a discipline depends upon our being able to make an objectively grounded choice between two disparate probability judgments on the basis of the common evidence which supports them.[2]

The only certain method of choosing between two hypotheses is to prove that one of them is false. Following Popper's theory of falsifiability, Hirsch maintains that when we cannot prove one hypothesis false we must choose the hypothesis that is most probable.

Ricoeur agrees with Hirsch's position and considers that his approach is appropriate for deciding among intepretations of texts. "As concerns the procedures for validation by which we test our guesses," Ricoeur says, "I agree with E. D. Hirsch that they are closer to a logic of probability than to a logic of empirical verification."[3] But Ricoeur differs from Hirsch in believing that the text stands apart from its author and that the goal of interpretation is thus not merely "re-cognition of what an author meant."[4]

Habermas hopes to ground knowledge in an appeal to the conditions of discourse which are assumed by anyone who participates in an argument where the sole purpose is to judge the truth claim of assumed or proposed knowledge.[5] Although different inquiry systems use different procedures for acquiring data, forming concepts, and testing theories, the "unity of reason" is retained at the level of discourse for ascertaining the veracity of their truth claims. Habermas investigates the logic of discourse in which hypothetical truth claims are argumentatively examined and then rejected, revised, or accepted. He holds that there can be no separation of the criteria for truth from the criteria for the argumentative settlement of truth claims. Although there is some confusion in Habermas's writings about the meaning of *truth* in this context, the term will be interpreted here to mean our understanding of or commitment to a statement as the most accurate available description of the reality it purports to describe.[6] Thus, the outcome of argumentative discourse is an agreement about a statement, not "truth" itself. For Habermas, the settlement of knowledge claims depends on argumentative reasoning and not on experiences of certainty or correspondence with "reality as it is in itself." The goal of discourse is to reach a discursively realized, rational agreement.

Habermas examines how we can tell when the agreement is a "correct" consensus as opposed to an "incorrect" consensus. His basic point is that a consensus is rationally motivated, and thus it is "correct" if it has been brought about solely through the cogency of the arguments given. These arguments consist of speech-acts, not logical propositions, and the move from one stage to another cannot be explicated in purely formal logical terms. The modality of the discourse is not logical necessity and noncontradiction; it is cogency. In analyzing cogency, Habermas borrows from Toulmin's *Uses of Argument*.[7] Thomas McCarthy summarizes Habermas's description:

> Habermas analyzes the structure of an argument into the conclusion that is to be grounded, that data that is put forward for this purpose, the warrant that establishes the connection between the data, and the conclusion (for example, a general law or principle) and the backing for the warrant itself (for example, observational and experimental backing for a hypothesis).[8]

On the basis of Toulmin's description, Habermas gives a general characterization of the conditions under which an argument can lead to a rational consensus. McCarthy continues:

> His central thesis is that these conditions must permit a progressive radicalization of the arguments; there must be the freedom to move from a given level of discourse to increasingly reflected levels. More particularly there must be the freedom not only to enter into a critical discussion, to seek discursive justification of problematic claims, and to offer and evaluate various arguments and explanations but also to call into question and (if necessary) to modify an originally accepted conceptual framework.[9]

Habermas maintains that the possibility of reaching understanding in ordinary language communication by rational argument is a fundamental and universal competence akin to the linguistic competence postulated by Chomsky. This competence, however, is not related to the construction of linguistically meaningful sentences; it is related to the construction of a practical communication situation in which agreement between competing claims can be settled. The study of competence in discourse is part of Habermas's general study of universal pragmatics; he asserts that general structures appear in every possible speech situation and are themselves produced through the performance of specific types of linguistic expressions. He also considers that discourse can be the source of rationally decided norms and values.

Rational discourse is held to be an ideal toward which communication can strive. In the "ideal speech situation," the decision is to be a product of a "rational will"; the only permissible force is the "peculiarly unforced force of the better argument," and the only permissible motive is the cooperative search for truth. Domination, restraint on a participant's speech, and extraneous motives interfere with producing a rational consensus. Habermas believes that the ideal can be more or less adequately approximated, that it can serve as a guide for the institutionalization of discourse, and that it can function as a critical standard against which an actually achieved consensus can be measured.[10]

Trial-and-Error Learning

A second position, which is represented by Peirce, maintains that decisions about which knowledge claims are to be accepted are based on the common human trait of learning from experience. According to this view, concepts and techniques are improved and perfected through trial and error. For example, plowing implements improve because new techniques are suggested and tried; if the new techniques are found to be less good than the old techniques, they are abandoned, but if they are found to be better than the old techniques, they are retained. Eventually, improvements will be suggested for the new techniques, and they in turn will be replaced. The cycle of invention and trial is a format which holds for all cultures; it is also the model according to which all knowledge is improved—at the conceptual and theoretical levels as well as at the technical level. Toulmin and Donald Campbell present a similar outline for scientific development.[11]

This position can be merged with the reasonableness position if reasonableness is described as the ability to learn from mistakes. Most of those human scientists identified with the reasonableness position, however, maintain that even though reasonableness may include learning from mistakes, it also includes the ability to assess evidence—that is, the ability to decide whether the evidence supports or contradicts a generalization—and the ability to plan so as to select appropriate means that will lead to desired ends. The ability to plan, they point out, requires more than merely remembering what has worked in previous trials.

For Peirce, the knowledge of science is not "the truth"; it is an approximation which moves toward "truth."[12] "Truth" is not what is believed or what works. "Truth," in the sense of what is, stands over against our knowledge of it. In the view of the pragmatists, when we act on the basis of a knowledge belief, the effectiveness of our knowledge belief is demonstrated by the effectiveness of our action. For if the action does not produce the results we have expected from the belief, then the belief is probably wrong. It is the response to actions based on knowledge that provides evidence for or against the particular knowledge. For example, if one has a knowledge belief that a leather sack will hold water without leaking, the belief is tested when the leather sack either leaks or does not leak.

In the pragmatic model, science does not develop "truths." It develops knowledge upon which choices are made. "Truth" (things as they really are), while not knowable, provides the test for belief. But the test of knowledge about the human realm is more difficult than the test of knowledge about the physical realm because human phenomena are affected by our beliefs about them. When a man understands that his friend is angry, the man's experience of the friend's anger is affected because the context in which the anger is experienced is altered. Nevertheless, a proposal about a human phenomenon will still receive a response that is concerned with "what's really there" when a person acts on the proposal. In a very elementary way, one's knowledge belief that another person is angry can receive some validation when one asks the person "Are you angry?" and receives an affirmative response. In a therapist-client relationship, interpretations offered by the therapist sometimes bring the response "Yes, that makes sense, and that is why I did what I did." Generally, however, interpretations concerning a person's feelings of joy, happiness, shame, or guilt are tested through the person's comments and actions.

Peirce's position does not claim that knowledge is a "true" grasp of reality. Instead, knowledge is the community's attempt to understand the world. Method does not give truth; it corrects guesses. These guesses are revised and, over time, come to a closer approximation of the reality which always remains beyond the reach of human awareness.

Peirce held that the effort of proposing and testing against "nature" will lead in a cumulative manner to knowledge which over time will approach an accurate description of reality itself. The corrective power of trying out knowledge claims will continue to eliminate the parts of the knowledge claims that are in error until very little error will remain. This winnowing-away of mistakes in knowledge proposals will require the work of generations of scientists who, working together as the "ultimate community of inquirers," will at last be able to separate "truth" from "error."

Pluralistic Epistemologies

The third position is presented by James Ogilvy in *Many Dimensional Man* (1977).[13] Ogilvy holds that Peirce's notion of the historical continuity of a single community of inquirers misrepresents the way knowledge is actually developed. Science, Ogilvy says, calls for communities of interpreters rather than "a single Peircean community of inquirers." He maintains that the fact that communities do not accept all interpretations as equally valid does not imply that knowledge in general is converging toward a single, ultimate truth; the notion that all descriptions converge "like ever more accurate measurements" is mistaken.

The loci of truth claims, according to Ogilvy, are various communities of like-minded interpreters. We cannot escape our contexts, and so the limits of knowledge are contained in these communities. This, we should notice, is the position taken by Winch, who argues that the idea of what is reasonable varies from community to community. Ogilvy does not accept an individual nihilism in which "any illusion at random can put forth the same claim to validity,"[14] but he does observe that knowledge claims are nonetheless submitted to validation tests within various separate communities and what is accepted as knowledge by each community is what agrees with the standards that exists within that community.

Discussing the relationship between multiple values and multiple epistemologies, Ogilvy says:

> To put the point in language that the Apollonian mind might appreciate, pluralism of values can survive only if nourished upon an "epistemological" pluralism. Only if knowledge itself admits the plurality of many truths can many corresponding patterns of valuation be confirmed. Again, this does not mean that anything anyone says is therefore true, else "truth" would have no meaning. Marginal differentiations between truth and error and mutual confirmations made by communities of inquirers guarantee implicit universality to the concept of truth. But just as those marginal differentiations do not necessarily proceed toward a Reality to which they supposedly correspond, so the several communities of inquirers need not be bound to a faith in their coalescence in one community of agreement in order that the concept of truth makes sense.[15]

Ogilvy's argument is that there is not *one truth* which corresponds to *reality*. Instead, there are *some truths* which hold within communities. "Objectivity" is a construction; it is a kind of commitment in which an ultimate ground is hoped for. But the ground does not exist outside of a particular perspective; it is the "multiplicity" of various perspectives itself. "Truth" is a construct which, under examination, reveals itself to be something like an onion; the layers of perspectival understanding can be peeled away until there is nothing left at the core. "Reality" is views; it is not a thing which lies behind views and causes them.

The view taken in this book is that each of the various systems of inquiry is a context or "community" and represents an epistemological position. In this sense, an epistemological pluralism is proposed. It should be noted, however, that the comparison and interaction of contexts or systems of inquiry allow for an understanding that is greater than the understanding of any one point of view. The notion of comparison and interaction assumes a kind of reasonableness which emerges when a person is confronted with differences. The very acceptance of a possible alternative places one's own assumptions in question. One's point of view is transformed from *the* way of knowing into *one* way of knowing—a context— when alternatives are admitted. Out of the syncretic interaction of various positions, a fuller understanding arises. Because knowledge is not automatically the result of direct experience, but is a human construct, the comparison of various constructs can lead to an increase in the depth of understanding.

Tacit Knowledge as a Criterion

Because the human sciences propose knowledge claims about topics that are part of the human realm itself, we usually have some prior understanding of a topic. This tacit knowledge can function as a criterion by means of which various proposed knowledge claims can be judged. As Chomsky has put it, knowledge in the human realm is "neither presented for direct observation nor extractable by inductive procedures of any known sort." A knowledge claim "must be tested for adequacy by measuring it against the standard provided by the tacit knowledge that it attempts to specify and describe," and it must "meet the empirical conditions of conforming, in a mass of crucial and clear cases, to the . . . intuition" people have about the structure. The ultimate standard for determining the accuracy of the researcher's proposals is the intuition that people have about their everyday experiences.[16]

The relevant tacit knowledge is not always immediately available to the subject, and it has to be drawn out by questioning the subject with the aid of examples. The relationship of scientific knowledge of the human realm to the everyday knowledge of that realm differs from the comparable relationship in the sciences that study objects.

The sciences of objects normally refute and replace our pretheoretical knowledge with provisionally correct theoretical accounts. The human sciences, in contrast, make pretheoretical knowledge explicit; they do not falsify it. In this respect, the relationship of the human sciences to their object domain resembles the relationship of *explicans* (statements which make explicit what is unclear) to *explicandum* (what is to be explicated) instead of the relationship of *explanans* (laws and covering conditions) to *explanandum* (what is to be explained).

Syncretic Research

As the community considers various knowledge claims, it can deepen and clarify its understanding of a topic through the integration of the results derived by the various systems of inquiry described in this book. In the case of competing claims, the capacity of the community to integrate one of the claims more thoroughly and fruitfully with those derived from alternative modes of inquiry can be used as a criterion for accepting one over the other. The integration of the various claims does more than merely provide a means for judging among proposed hypotheses, however. The integration itself can produce a deeper appreciation and understanding of the topic under consideration.

This section suggests that human science research can reap significant methodological benefits from using multiple procedures for its research designs. A single topic—anxiety, for example—might be approached with the hermeneutic, the systemic, the phenomenological, and the statistically linked measurement systems of inquiry. Anxiety might be studied by using instruments that measure the degree of anxiety in relation to settings and actions, by using intensive interviews and gathering descriptions of exemplars for phenomenological analysis, by gathering interpretive descriptions of actions or accounts of feelings of anxiety, and by using a systemic approach to the functional and dysfunctional roles of anxiety in relation to the other parts of personality and to personality as a whole. Each of these systems of inquiry is able to detect and describe some aspects of anxiety, but each of them also misses parts of the full experience. It is as if one is looking at a drop of water through a microscope. As the focus of the microscope is varied, different aspects of the contents of the drop of water can be seen. One can also stain the drop of water so that still other aspects, previously hidden, show up, but when this done, some aspects, previously seen, will no longer be seen. By using all of the information gained from the different procedures, the researcher can learn more than he can learn from any one procedure alone. Some of the same things will appear in all of the systems of inquiry; some will show up in only one; and some will show up in several approaches.

In addition to integrating knowledge gleaned through various systems of inquiry, it is also necessary to assure that knowledge claims developed for varying uses are integrated. As Habermas has made clear, the particular use we will make of the knowledge about a topic influences the kind of knowledge that is developed. Knowledge of anxiety developed for use in propaganda films and knowledge of anxiety developed by a therapist concerned to ease a patient's stress differ in regard to the purpose and the proposed use of the information. Various knowledge claims about the same topic, each in the context of a particular use, can be brought together and utilized to increase the fullness of our understanding of the topic.

The use of multiple methods to study the same problem has been termed *triangulation*, a word that comes from the geological survey and navigational technique of locating an unknown point by forming a triangle that has the unknown point and two known points as vertices. Norman Denzin, although he does not emphasize the various contexts of inquiry and use through which knowledge claims are developed (an emphasis of this book), has described various kinds of triangulation in his source book *Sociological Methods* (1978). According to Denzin:

> No single method is uniformly superior; each has its own special strengths and weaknesses. It is time for sociologists to recognize this fact and to move on to a position that permits them to approach their problems with all relevant and appropriate methods, to move on to the strategy of methodological triangulation.[17]

Denzin lists four varieties of triangulation: theoretical triangulation, data triangulation, investigator triangulation, and the use of multiple methods. In theoretical triangulation, several different theoretical perspectives are used in the analysis of the same set of data. In data triangulation, multiple sampling strategies are used in gathering data; data collections varying in time, social situations, and social interaction situations can be used. In investigator triangulation, more than one observer is used in a field situation; by combining the results of independent observers and interviewers, observer bias and the reliability of single observations can be detected.

Methodological triangulation is subdivided into "within-method" and "between-method." In within-method, an investigator employs varieties of the same method, using, for example, three different scales to measure the same variable. In between-method, several methods—for example, survey, field, and experimental methods—are used to investigate the same problem.

When all of these various approaches are combined into the study of one problem, the process is called "multiple triangulation." Here multiple methods, data types, observers, and theories are combined in the same investigation. Such an effort may be difficult to achieve in a single investigation, but it can be achieved by combining the present study with the results of previous investigations conducted by other researchers.

It is proposed here that the very nature of the subject matter of human science suggests the value of combining the results of several systems of inquiry in order to gain a fuller understanding of topics under investigation. Gregory Bateson has made the point that the combination of information from various systems of inquiry produces a kind of knowledge that differs from the simple accumulation or addition of information.[18] Bateson uses the analogy of vision to show that a new order of understanding achieved. Vision is not merely the adding together of information obtained by the left and right eyes; information from both eyes is syncretized into a single three-dimensional picture. The combination of information from different systems produces a new dimension of understanding, the dimension of depth. By combining and integrating the knowledge gained through the various systems, an understanding of a topic becomes available which is deeper than the understanding gained from any one system or from merely placing information side by side. The use of multiple approaches requires—in addition to carrying out the various investigations—a final syncretic integration of the results into a new statement that combines the various dimensions of the topic.

To emphasize that this final activity is more than a matter of collating results, it is called *syncretism* rather than *synthesis*. *Syncretism* denotes the uniting or combining of differences, a meaning which *synthesis* does not carry. This approach proposes something more than the use of multiple systems of inquiry: it proposes the additional step of syncretizing the results of the multiple inquiries into a unified and integral result.

An example of the syncretic use of multiple methods is provided by a study of introversion that was made by Kenneth Shapiro and Irving Alexander in 1975 at Duke University.[19] Shapiro and Alexander used the Thematic Apperception Test (TAT), personal phenomenological reflection, and a Jungian theoretical framework. Although they considered the use of the Myers-Briggs Test as an instrument for producing quantifiable data, they rejected it on the grounds that the questions used to measure introversion imply a theoretical definition of the very concept which they were questioning. Thus, they used the "softer" TAT, which produced stories from their subjects. These stories were then graded by independent observers. Scores relating to the overall introversion or extroversion of each story were given, and then elements of all of the stories were scored. The scores of the elements and the overall descriptions were correlated to determine if different elements were related to introversion and to extroversion. The phenomenological study was based on Eugene Gendlin's focusing technique[20] and produced structural descriptions of experiences of introversion and extroversion. The TAT results and the phenomenological descriptions were then combined, using Jung's descriptions of introversion and extroversion as the theoretical guide, so that a final statement about introversion and extroversion was produced.

A different approach to syncretic research is described by Karl-Otto Apel in *An Analytic Philosophy of Language and the "Geisteswissenschaften"* (1965).[21] Apel's approach is called "tacking" or "zig-zagging" and is drawn from the process of psychoanalysis. The tacking procedure first involves an engagement and participation by the researcher with the person or group which is the focus of the investigation. The researcher next distances himself from the situation by changing the point of view and analyzing what has been experienced in the earlier phase. Then the researcher returns to the situation as participant, but he now experiences it with the understanding he has gained from the distancing perspective. This movement from participation to analysis continues through various stages, and with each tacking the researcher gains greater understanding of the situation. Suggestions made by Apel have been used by Habermas in his proposal for combining hermeneutic and empirical sciences to create guidelines for the logic of a critical science.[22] Hermeneutic interpretation, although it provides access to a person's understanding of his world, lacks the logic for uncovering the operation of lawlike causality in social structures and life history. The tacking approach to syncretic research combines the hermeneutic and empirical analyses in a dialectical progression so that it successively builds up greater and greater understanding.

The syncretic process requires the use of systems logic and hermeneutic understanding procedures because the process involves identifying similarities in differences and because it also involves identifying an organizing pattern which fits the order of the topic of investigation.

In a previous paper,[23] this author has identified five principles of syncretization:

1. The syncretic process does not force an artificial unity on the results of the various systems of inquiry.

2. The work is synoptic. It looks at the manifestations of the subject of inquiry as they have appeared in various approaches in order to identify underlying patterns which will account for the manifestations.

3. The integrity of the results of the initial inquiries needs to be maintained. The original studies need to be examined in terms of their own systems of inquiry for rigor and accuracy before they are admitted into the syncretic analysis.

4. In the syncretic process, the information becomes a part of a new whole, and its meaning can be transformed by its relationship to the integrated whole.

5. The syncretic process does not end with a finished product. As all knowledge forms, it remains fallible and open to improvement, either through a more thorough and deeper integration of the present studies or through the admission of new information and studies into the integration.

Arguing for a Knowledge Claim

As already stated, the current revised understanding of science is that the results of research activity are knowledge claims that compete to gain the community's acceptance. No longer is it asserted that knowledge is based on a sure foundation and that correctly following the prescribed method will assure results that are true. The scholarly community, through the use of the process of practical reasoning, commits itself to a particular proposal as the best available claim to the understanding of the topic under consideration. A model for describing the process of consideration is a judicial proceeding in which two counselors argue before a jury, each proposing that his or her position is the one to be upheld. The evidence for one position is usually not so strong as to dismiss the alternative; proposed knowledge is not usually of the "smoking gun" type. In human science, the case to be decided more often resembles the case in court where the jury is asked to decide whether the crime was committed under diminished capacity or whether there was prior motivation for the act. Neither side can present conclusive evidence to defend its position, and so the jury must decide which position is most likely correct in view of the available evidence.

Because so much of the human realm is imprecise, because it is defined by historical and situational contexts, the arguments used to defend a proposed understanding as an improvement over those understandings previously offered will not compel assent from all—or even, sometimes, from most—qualified judges. The lack of exactness and uniformity in the structures of the lifeworld means that not all judges will weigh the import of the evidence in the same way. In some instances, given the proposed options of understanding in a particular situation, no one option may so clearly outshine the others in clarifying the lifeworld as to solicit unanimous consent. In other instances, however, a proposed hypothesis may so neatly fit and order the evidence that it gains full assent. At times, the acceptance of one proposal as more probable than others cannot wait until full assent has been obtained. Under the necessity to act, a decision regarding one proposal over another must be made, even though questions about the adequacy of both proposals remain. The subject matter and the logics used in human science often do not provide results upon which there is full agreement, but a lack of certainty about proposals does not mean that these proposals are less "scientific" than physical science proposals or that they should be refused admission to the fund of knowledge.

The argument for a position needs to include consideration of alternative positions. It should point out how they are lacking, and it should provide evidence to show why the present proposal is more likely to be correct. For example, if a researcher is arguing for a particular description of why a person has acted as he or she has, he needs to offer a full range of evidence, such as previous statements, actions which preceded and followed, facial expressions which accompanied the action, and so on. The researcher must also show how alternative interpretations are not able to account for some of the evidence with the same fullness that the proposed description does. What can count as evidence in support of a position is often part of a tradition concerning the type of question under consideration, but sometimes the researcher needs to argue for the acceptance of a new type of evidence to support his proposal.

An accepted proposal is always open to reconsideration in the light of a new proposal, new evidence, or new techniques of argument. Consequently, many of the knowledge proposals in human science resemble proposed interpretations in the humanities. Shakespeare's in *Hamlet*, for instance, continues to attract new proposals. The acceptance of a new proposal as an improvement over previous proposals does not mean that it is considered to be the final statement about the meaning of *Hamlet*. Similarly, descriptions of the structure of "anxiety" or "love" can be improved on, and agreement in the community about a description does not mean that members of the community believe that no further work is necessary on the topic.

Because of the vague boundaries and the contextual variability of much of the human realm, the arguments given and the pragmatic tests will not provide precise answers to the question of whether a proposed knowledge claim should be admitted. Frequently, the logic used in presenting the argument requires a systemic and hermeneutic understanding. At times, even the most rigorous attempts at defending a position fail to convince because they lack an integrative and unifying quality which would allow the judges to understand the evidence in a deeper and broader way. To point out what mistakes have been made in an argument or how new evidence would reinforce a position is insufficient, for the problem may lie more in the researcher's lack of comprehension of the organizing structure of a phenomenon than in the misapplication of a particular method. The expectation that the new science will have the precision and clarity of a deductive logic is inappropriate. Creating research designs, analyzing data and describing results, and arguing for one's knowledge claim are now understood to be events in the human realm and in history. Thus the vagaries and the sagacity of human action will be part of scientific work.

Use of Linguistic Data

In the context in which the debate concerning appropriate methods for human science is argued, the most important change, then, is the change in the understanding of science. We have abandoned the notion that science is an activity that provides us with an accurate description of reality about which we can be sure, and we have come to see that science is a human and historical activity which uses various logics and systems of inquiry to develop useful knowledge. This knowledge is fallible; it can be argued for or against, and it can change in various cultural and historical periods. Knowledge becomes less pretentious; it no longer makes a claim to be truth because of its use of deductively derived methods grounded in an indubitable foundation. The kind of science which struggles to understand is not bound to any "correct" method that is guaranteed to give truth. Instead, methods are viewed as tools to be used in the struggle to answer the questions that are put forth. Methods are judged for their usefulness and for their success in producing meaningful understanding about the objects of inquiry; they are not judged according to a standard of tautological statements and deductive logic.

The question the debate addresses is: What methods are appropriate for human science? It can be answered with the statement: Human science should use those methods which provide the fullest answer possible to the questions asked about topics concerning the human realm and which produce knowledge claims whose defense before the community is convincing enough to bring about assent. This answer assumes that the community is committed to engagement in the argument without the restrictions imposed by a closed position. Members of the community are willing to be convinced if the argument for the knowledge claim is cogent. The argument is forceful if the methods and procedures used in the research have uncovered sufficient reliable indications that the knowledge claim is the best of the available alternatives. The argument is not called upon to produce an irrefutable claim to knowledge; it needs only to convince sufficiently to bring about belief in its understanding and a willingness to act on the basis of that belief.

With science opened up to the kinds of methods which are most productive of understanding, many methods that were excluded by the former standard—which called for them to assure that the results were certain—have been admitted, and consequently human science researchers have a larger repertoire of methodological approaches available to them. The methods to be used are those which provide the greatest access to the subject matter of human science, the human realm. There are special characteristics of the human realm that require for their fullest disclosure the use of particular data types and particular data-gathering approaches.

Special Characteristics of the Human Realm

Research strategies are based on the nature of the subject matter under investigation. The subject matter of human science is the human realm, and the special characteristics of this realm inform the researcher which of the various approaches to gathering data, which data types, and which kinds of data analysis are appropriate.

The human realm consists of the special strata of reality that have emerged with the appearance of the complex system of human life. Although the human realm includes physical and biological orders, it is only because of their characteristics as parts of a person or parts of a social system that they are included in the subject matter of human science. For instance, the investigation of germs in isolation from the human realm is not part of human science, but germs affect the functions and experiences of a person or a social group, and so they may come to be included in particular ways in human science investigations. Perhaps what makes the human realm most difficult to investigate is its unique character: it is a sphere of awareness. It is consciousness, and consciousness permeates experience with meaning which, in turn, creates a second-order, nonphysical reality of ideas. Consciousness searches for and interprets perceptual interaction with the environment, and this gives a multilayered depth to experience and provides a context in which action takes place.

Of the various characteristics of the human realm, five call for special attention by the researcher. These are its systemic character, its lack of clear definitions and boundaries, its unfinished quality and its continuing development, its composition which involves a knowing subject as well as a known object, and its special problem of access.

Systemic character. The realm of human phenomena that is the subject matter of human science has a systemic organization, and for this reason it is difficult to investigate it by looking at parts in isolation from the whole. Essential characteristics of the parts of the human realm are missed if they are investigated without consideration of their context and their relationship to the whole. The pattern of the human realm has been investigated in the work of Aron Gurwitsch, Richard Zaner, Paul Ricoeur, and Jason Brown, among others. Gurwitsch suggests that investigation in this realm is a matter of focusing on some aspect of it and giving attention specifically to this aspect against its own background (horizon), following the model of the perceptual concept of figure and ground.[24] Zaner, in *The Context of Self*, describes the subject matter of human science as embodied consciousness or "self," the nature of which is the nature of a contexture. This particular contexture is a "complex of 'parts,' 'functions,' 'members,' 'systems,' 'performances' involving at once the unique interconnections of what Plügge terms [the] bodily physical and the bodily live, such [that] they form a 'single event,' or what I [Zaner] have called a living 'integrity.'"[25] Ricoeur reports that in metaphor the context changes the meaning of a word while at the same time it retains the nuances of understanding that are connected with it in other contexts.[26] And Brown describes experience as vertically, horizontally, and isomorphically connected with the complex interconnections within the brain.[27]

In *Phenomenology of Feeling* (1977), Stephan Strasser summarizes the approach to the human realm which understands it to be organized hierarchically in strata.[28] He describes the principles of this approach with four theses:

1. Every level has its peculiar nature which corresponds to a definite ontological rank. . . .
2. The peculiar nature of the higher level is independent of the peculiar nature of the lower level; it displays eidetic autonomy.
3. The factual being of the lower levels constitutes the necessary, but not sufficient, condition for the factual being of the higher level. . . .
4. The subordination of the lower to the higher life-functions is an activity of the living individual and not that of one particular level.

The higher levels arise from the lower, and so the strata approach must be supplemented by a genetic approach. Yet there is a unity in which all of the levels participate; in Strasser's words, it is a "unity of conglomerate." The development of a higher level is governed by the same set of organizing structures which govern the development of each level preceding it. "This means," Strasser says, "that an intimate principle of life and of order, which functions as norm in the genesis of all the levels of the living whole, must be at work."

When the human scientist investigates the human realm, he examines the language, the thought, and the action of various social communities. These communities already have structures of meaning by means of which they have ordered their experience. The human scientist attempts to "order these orderings." Schutz has described the task:

[The researcher's] observational field, the social world, is not essentially structureless. It has a particular meaning and relevance structure for the human beings living, thinking, and acting therein. They have preselected and preinterpreted this world by a series of commonsense constructs of the reality of daily life, and it is these thought objects which determine their behavior, define the goal of their action, the means available for their attaining them—in brief, which help them to find their bearings within their natural and socio-cultural environment and to come to terms with it. The thought objects constructed by the social scientist refer to and are founded upon the thought objects constructed by the commonsense thought of man living his everyday life among his fellow men. Thus, the constructs used by the social scientist are, so to speak, constructs of the second degree, namely constructs of the constructs made by the actors on the social scene, whose behavior the scientist observes and tries to explain in accordance with the procedural rules of his science.[29]

In sum, the area of study for human science is the organizing patterns of experience which form the "objects" to be investigated. Since the goal of human science is the study of the structures which underlie the everyday experience, it seeks more than a mere paraphrase or a translation of an unclear meaning; it seeks an explicit knowledge of the organizing principles which construct the ongoing flow of daily experience.

Unclear boundaries. The systemic character of human phenomena makes it difficult to describe their aspects with concepts that have clearly delineated boundaries and still capture the relationships among the phenomena that are pointed to by the concepts and by other phenomena. The characteristics of the concepts change within the systemic context. The central meaning may remain the same, but the boundary region is often fuzzy. The problem has been described by Ulric Neisser in *Cognitive Psychology* (1967):

> Ill-defined categories are the rule, not the exception, in daily life. The visual distinctions between dogs and cats, or between beauty and ugliness, are ill-defined, just like the conceptual differences between creative science and hack work, or health and neurosis. So are the EEG patterns which indicate a particular stage of sleep, the X-ray shadows which suggest a tumor, the style of painting which identifies a Picasso, or the features which continue to characterize the face of a friend through the years.[30]

Meanings have the characteristics of prototypically organized categories; they do not have the characteristics of the kind of clearly delineated categories that are often used for scientific clarity. A. Attneave[31] has made the first major study of prototype learning in which a category is defined by a prototype or exemplar which represents the central tendency of the category. For example, the category "bird" is often represented in consciousness by a prototypical robin. As instances approach the characteristics of the prototype, they are more readily held to be instances of the category.

Technical definitions are usually formulated by defining attributes, not prototypes.[32] In applying technical definitions to meanings, we gain a fake precision which is not a part of the vagueness of experience. For example, a researcher who is studying anxiety can develop an operational definition and gradations on an "anxiety" variable scale which show much finer shades of precision than a person would ever attach to the meaning of his or her feelings. But imprecision in subject matter, it should be noted, is not limited to studies in human science. Other sciences, such as contemporary physics and biology, also investigate subject matters that are imprecise.[33]

Wittgenstein proposed that instances of a category are tied together by the principle of family resemblance. As a category organization, family resemblance is of a different sort than either prototypical organization or technical organization. In a category organized by family resemblance, it is the successive overlap in the attributes of instances that holds the instances together as a category. For example, members of a family often "sort of look alike" in various ways. The sister may look a bit like the brother, and the brother may look like the father, but the sister may also look like the cousin, and the cousin and the father may not look alike at all. If only the cousin and the father were compared, they would not be seen to belong to the same family, and the same sort of thing can happen in other categories defined by family resemblance.

Abstract categories—such as "beauty," "truth," "justice," and "fairness"—have no real perceptual attributes and seem extremely vague, and yet they are among the most significant categories for the understanding of the human realm. Various highly significant activities—waging a world war, directing one's life efforts—are carried out in relation to these categories. They are part of the second-order-meaning realm that human science investigates. Because of the vagueness of meaning, the investigator needs to be aware of the level of precision inherent in these research categories as he or she sets out to organize human experience.

Unfinished quality. The human realm is unfinished. It continues to develop by creating new patterns of integration and then incorporating them as structures which will form still newer patterns. This process of continued development is not random; it is built up out of itself, and its own past accomplishments are used as the images out of which further developments can emerge. The human realm is in flux, but it never begins over. Its change is continuous with its past, and the past continues as a developmental trend. The realm is not static; it evolves historically. The future, however, is open-ended, and the change is not teleologically drawn toward a single fixed goal set in advance.[34]

Composition. Another difficulty in investigating the human realm is that the activity of knowing is itself a human phenomenon. Strasser calls this problem the "anthropological dilemma,"[35] and he expresses it thus: "How can man as a person make man as a person the object of an empirical inquiry?" In short, our organizing categories are used to organize our organizing categories. There is no absolute point outside human phenomena from which to investigate. Moreover, the knowledge gained in the investigation changes the character of what has been investigated. For example, people will generally choose canned goods with red labels instead of blue labels, but when the purchaser of canned goods knows that this is, the knowledge itself changes the way in which the purchaser interprets the red label. When we investigate the physical realm—rocks or planets, for instance—in itself the knowledge we gain does not affect the object of investigation, but when we investigate the human realm, our knowledge of it as it exists at present is incorporated into the realm itself and changes the mode of its organization.

Access. The human realm is not directly accessible to perceptual observation. It is a realm of meaning, and because of its nonphysical nature, its phenomena must be approached indirectly—that is, through such publicly accessible manifestations as bodily movements and linguistic expressions. From these manifestations, characteristics of the human realm are inferred. Although direct access is available through personal introspective reflection, unconscious distortions and cultural structures that are part of the realm are difficult to know through introspection.[36] Consequently, researchers usually have to approach the human realm through its expressions in cultural objects, literature, and linguistic and nonlinguistic actions. Expressions can be developed by researchers through the use of questionnaires and interviews.

These five characteristics influence which strategies and approaches are appropriate for investigating the human realm. In particular, they determine which data types are most revealing of human phenomena and which methods of data treatment uncover the themes within these data.

Data Types for Human Science

Access to the human realm is gained through its expressions. The principal form of expression is linguistic, although facial expressions and bodily gestures (including dancing) are also sources. In addition, nonliterary artifacts—such as machinery, art objects, and architectural constructions—are data sources. But the richest source of information is linguistic expressions, and these can be oral or written in form. Before the recent development of technology for storing oral communications through voice recordings, oral communication could not be preserved in its original form; it would vanish in a moment, and it was therefore inaccessible after the fact, except through the memories of those who had heard the original speeches. The usual means of recording oral communications was to transpose them into written form, a practice which continues as recordings are transcribed.

The most exact and accessible form of expression is written linguistic expression. Written expressions can be created in response to a researcher's queries, or they can be collected by the researcher in the form of personal or public documents. Most present-day behavioral and sociological research derives data through queries in the form of questionnaires and recorded interviews. Anthropological and historical research, because of the nature of the subject matter, must often use data from historical documents and/or artifacts.

The basic form of the linguistic data of human science is discourse. Whether the discourse consists of affirmation or denial of statements on a questionnaire or whether it consists of statements volunteered in open-ended interviews, the data are the result of a speech event. Linguistic data are of a special nature, and understanding the particular features of the data type is important for the human science researcher because these features affect the modes of data collection and data analysis.

As we saw in chapter 5, Saussure has distinguished between *la langue* and *parole*: *la langue* is the code of a language, and *parole* consists of speech events and particular messages given by speakers. The data of human science are the *parole* of a language; they are the spoken events communicated at a specific time in a specific place. The basic unit of *parole* is the sentence, not the individual word. In *la langue*, the words obtain meaning only in reference to each other in the same way that the definitions in a dictionary refer to the other words in the dictionary. In *parole* (discourse), the sentence makes a reference that goes beyond the linguistic system to experience. The sentence ascribes a predicate to a subject. The subject picks out something particular—I, San Francisco, this desk, the fall of Rome—and the predicate picks out something universal—a kind of quality, a class of things, a type of relationship, a type of action. The speech event intertwines and interplays these two polarities, the particular and the universal. The speaker means something about the world when the sentence is spoken; the sentence refers to something in the world. In the speech event, the speaker applies words to reality. Ricoeur has written:

> Language is not a world of its own. It is not even a world. But because we are in the world, because we are affected by situations, and because we orient ourselves comprehensively in those situations, we have something to say, we have experience to bring to language.[37]

The form in which something is said about the world is the sentence; it is not individual words. The sentence conveys a message from the speaker about something which is not merely language itself.

The fundamental structure of discourse is the subject intertwined with a predicate. This structure is not the structure of *la langue* and structuralism—that is, it is not an analytic structure in which discrete units based on oppositions are combined—but a synthetic structure in which the functions of identification and predication are brought together in the same sentence. On this manifestation of meaning are grounded the oral and written actualizations of discourse. Jacques Derrida holds that writing has a root distinct from speech and that we have misunderstood writing's distinctiveness because of having paid too much attention to speech.[38] Ricoeur, however, maintains that both expressions have a common ground, which is discourse.

The message of discourse, then, can be contained in either an oral or written medium. Nevertheless, the nature of the medium has a significance for the researcher. In the written form, an inscription is substituted for the immediate vocal, physiognomic, or gestural expression, and the immediate connection with the human source of the discourse disappears. In the document, marks on paper convey the message in place of the personal voice. What writing fixes is not the event of speaking, but the meaning of the speech-act, the locutionary act.[39] We are not as sensitive to the other dimensions of the speech-act, the illocutionary and the perlocutionary aspects, when they are conveyed in writing. Through the use of grammatical paradigms and procedures expressive of its "force," the illocutionary act can be inscribed. But to the extent that in spoken discourse the illocutionary force depends upon the nonverbal aspects of discourse—mimicry and gesture—it is less inscribable than the propositional meaning. The perlocutionary act is the least inscribable aspect of discourse. The responses of fear, seduction, and conviction, for example, are sometimes difficult to evoke from a reader with the same intensity with which they are invoked from a hearer in the presence of a speaker. Writing also poses special problems when it is not the fixation of previous oral discourse. In this case, thought is brought directly to writing without passing through a stage of oral discourse.

The written text is addressed to an unknown reader, potentially to whoever knows how to read. The relationships between the speaker and the message and between the hearer and the message are transformed when they become relationships between the writer and the message and between the reader and the message. The face-to-face relationship is replaced by a more complex and different kind of interaction. In oral discourse, the sentence designates the speaker by using personal pronouns, and the tenses of the verbs in the sentences are determined by the present moment of the conversation. The context of the statements is shared by those who are speaking together. It is the same thing to understand what the speaker means and to understand the statements. The double reference of the English word *meaning* and the German word *meinen* holds in face-to-face conversation; what the speaker "means" or intends to say and what the sentence "means" are close together.[40] With written discourse, the author's intention cannot be directly clarified by questions and answers. The text begins to take on an independence, and its meaning becomes dissociated from the intention of the author. In inscription, the meaning of the text becomes autonomous; it is not continuous with the author's meaning. The text's career escapes from the finite situation in which it has been written.

In face-to-face discourse, a primitive possibility for clarifying what the speaker means is to point out an object or to gesture. References in a conversation rely on demonstrations which depend upon the situation perceived in common by the participants, and the references are thus situational. The type of text which merely restructures the conditions of a situation—such as a letter, a diary, or a description—can allow the reader to be present in an "as if" way. It is "as if" the reader is present with the writer when the writer is writing. Such is usually the approach that a researcher takes to transcriptions of face-to-face discourse. But this approach is not possible with historical texts and various kinds of contemporary texts. We should notice, however, that the notion of the separation of the meaning of the text from the author's intention stands in disagreement with the approach used by Dilthey and Betti. In their approach, the whole point of the interpretation of a text is to recreate an author's meaning and discover his or her reasons for writing the text.

The exemplar of data collection in human science is the face-to-face interview. Written questionnaires, documents, artifacts, and other forms of expression are species of the interaction between speakers and hearers, but as we have already seen, there is a difference between the situation in a face-to-face interview and the situation that exists between a text and a reader. The face-to-face encounter provides the richest data source for the human science researcher seeking to understand human structures of experience.

This interaction takes place in the context of a relationship. The more comfortable and trusting a person feels with the researcher, the more open and giving he or she will be concerning his or her own experiences. As we all know, we are able not only to reveal our experiences to another person but also to hold back those experiences or disguise them. The subject can deceive. He can assume a role in which he offers what he believes the researcher wants to hear or what he believes is socially desirable. Usually the researcher is interested in obtaining descriptions of experience from the subject and is not interested in witnessing a performance. Professional distance and lack of interest on the part of the researcher do not produce unbiased data; they bring forth, instead, skewed information that has been filtered through roles or expectations. Sidney Jourard's research on interviewing[41] suggests that the more self-revealing the researcher is in the discourse, the more probable it is that the subject will give undisguised information. A researcher needs to do more than simply ask questions in a proper way; he needs to establish a relational context in which the subject will feel free and will be encouraged to reveal his experiences as they have appeared to him.

Because the human realm is a realm of meaning, data of the linguistic type have the characteristics most appropriate for holding the meaning of the realm. The nature of linguistic data is meaning, and thus they are most adequate for dealing with the realm of meaning. Linguistic data, like the human realm, are held in vehicles of expression. The data are not the container—the marks on the paper or the sounds on the tape. The data are the meanings themselves. Linguistic data are fragile, and they are affected by the transformation of the mode of their expression. Thus the researcher needs to take care and understand when linguistic data are transferred from the oral mode to the written mode.

Since the linguistic data type shares the form of meaningful structures with the human realm, it is usually the most appropriate data type for research concerning this realm. In addition or as an alternative, the numerical data type can be used as a mode in which to organize the evidence derived from the human realm. The numerical data type is used to describe the extent to which the quality or qualities under investigation hold. The advantage of this data type is that there are many statistical tools available for organizing it. However, because of the meaningful character of the human realm, it is usually necessary to translate the evidence that appears in the form of the linguistic order into the form of the numerical order. This translation is accomplished through the use of scales that allow subjects to indicate, either directly (Likert-type scales) or indirectly (for example, the Minnesota Multiphasic Personality Inventory scales), to what extent a quality or experience exists. Subjects do not need to respond with such general statements as "I am very angry"; instead, they can rate the extent of their anger on a scale of 1 to 10. From these ratings, scores can be developed.

Measurement theory in human science research is concerned with how to translate the linguistic characteristic of one's experience in the human realm into a numerical form. Data of the numerical type give quantitative descriptions (or scores) of the extent to which the subject possesses the characteristic. Quantitative descriptions imply a qualitative category. They require a qualitative understanding of the category before the extent to which the category is present can be determined. For instance, the answer to the question "How much dexterity does a person have?" depends upon an understanding of the nature of the concept or structure of "dexterity." The additional information gained from knowing the extent of the category present at a particular time opens up the investigation, for it represents an advance far beyond the limits of the two-valued logic which indicates only the presence or absence of the category. A structure which varies in extent is called a variable. The variation in two or more categories can be correlated to determine the relationship between the change in one variable and the change in others.

Often measurements are made on specific physical movements, physiological changes, or words rather than on the meanings of expressions, and the meaning structure is defined in terms of these "objective" criteria. The resulting definition is at least once removed from the experience which is the focus of the investigation. This "objectivized" definition is thus subject to validation in terms of the experiential construct it is supposed to measure.

One of the problems with "objectivized" definitions stems from the imprecision and the vague boundaries of many experiential categories. The precision of the objective measure is greater than precision of the experience itself. This leads to what Michael Scriven has called the "precision fallacy."[42] For example, to hold the difference between 7 and 9 units on an interval scale as equivalent to the difference between 3 and 5 units on the same scale is often to create more information than was present in the experience.

The numerical data type is more useful for sciences that deal with objects that are susceptible to exact differentiation and that respond to finely tuned physical instruments. However, data about the human realm translated into this type can provide indications and dimensions of correlation which, when synthesized with other data types, contribute to greater understanding of human phenomena. Where analysis of data of the linguistic type can err on the side of less precision than the experience and where the analysis of data of the numerical type can err on the side of more precision than the structure can bear, the two analyses can supplement one another, and their combined use can produce a syncretic result which is fuller than the result gained from either data type when used by itself. Whether the researcher uses linguistic data, numerical data, or a combination should be determined by which data type is most likely to provide the kind of information that would answer the question he or she is asking about the human realm.

Various data types can serve as vehicles for information, but the understanding that science is a form of pragmatic and historical action, rather than a form of deductive logic, also allows various approaches to gathering data. In addition to the sampling or data-gathering model, devised to enable the researcher to draw inductive conclusions from data of a numerical type, other nonstatistically based models are possible.

Statistical sampling theory is based on ideas of probability. It is used for the induction of the mean and variation of a population from the examination of a random sample of the population. Those studies which seek descriptions of relationships between populations require random sampling,[43] but those studies of human phenomena which focus on descriptions of organizing structures, rather than on relationships of extensiveness among structures, require other approaches to choosing the sources of data which are to be treated. Sampling for descriptions of structures is based on the examination of exemplar cases rather than on random cases. Several examples and analogies may help to clarify the difference between these two sampling approaches.

(1) If a researcher is investigating the structure of the human hand, he will be able to identify the basic organization of the hand by examining one person. If the researcher is interested, however, in the average size of the adult human hand or in the correlation between the size of the human hand and the size of the human foot, then he will need a random sample of people so that he can generalize the findings to the entire population.

(2) If an investigator wishes to describe a game of chess and he is concerned with the underlying structures upon which various moves are based, he must select for study moves which are examples of the rules that describe how various pieces are moved. A move which demonstrates a new rule is more important for observation than a move which repeats a rule that has already been studied. It may take several observations before the investigator understands the rule which the player is following as he moves the chess piece. But if the investigator's question is concerned with the percentage of times games are opened with the king's pawn moved forward two places, then he needs to observe a random sample of games.

(3) If an investigator is interested in the structure of "triangleness," he looks at various examples (kinds) of triangles—equilateral, isosceles, scalene, and right triangles—in order to determine the pattern which makes all of these examples triangles. A useful sample is one which offers a new variety that provides an insight into the pattern. If, however, the investigator is interested in the mean and variation of the sizes of the sides of triangles in a series drawn in a book, then he must measure a random sample of the sides of the triangles in the series so that the mean size of the sides in the entire series can be induced from the sample.

The choice of sample for descriptive studies of an organizing structure is based on the usefulness of a particular example in uncovering the pattern. Unusual examples often offer the most important clues to the pattern. How close an example is to the mean manifestation of the pattern is not the point of this kind of investigation. The researcher of structures seeks to collect those expressions which test the proposed description. The selection is not completed in advance of the study as is so when random selections are made. As the description is being formed, examples are sought which raise questions about it. There is a dialectical interaction between the development of the description and the selection of interviewees.

The human science researcher approaches the research question as a problem to be solved through the use of whatever methods of data gathering and whatever types of data are helpful in developing a defendable and arguable position. The strategy for answering the question needs to be understood as a whole, as the various parts interact together to give an integrated design. Data of the linguistic type are not susceptible to statistical analysis unless they are first translated into the numerical type. Thus, the processes used in analyzing or examining the data to be used in presenting knowledge claims should be related to the data type and to data-gathering practices. If the data have been gathered in the form of the numerical data type, then the kinds of statistical procedures that are applied to evidence about physical objects and processes gathered in numerical form can be used. But data gathered in the linguistic type require other processes for analysis. In working with linguistic data, the researcher is primarily seeking to identify patterns which appear across the examples. The mental process of pattern recognition is like the mental process that is required for solving the problems in the Miller Analogies Test. Two examples from this test are:

"Line" is to "draw" as "music" is to "face," "song," "ears," or "act."

"Love" is to "kiss," "heart," "sex," or "hug" as "fatigue" is to "yawn."[44]

Pattern identification involves a review of the various examples, and this review is followed by a guess about the pattern that runs through the examples. The tentative pattern is tested by reexamining the examples to see if the pattern holds for all of them—that is, to see if each of the examples can be built up by using the pattern as a "skeleton" or generating organizational structure.

The linguistic data that the researcher collects consist of descriptions of instances of meanings or organizing patterns. For example, if the investigation aims to provide a description of "care," the subjects are asked to give accounts of experiences of care. These examples are then compared with each other, and the common elements are drawn from the collection in order to produce a description of the organizing pattern which lies underneath many single instances. The description is a description of a structural pattern, and thus it includes the relations among the parts as well as an outline of the whole pattern. Usually the researcher also describes the relationships between and among the pattern under investigation and other basic organizing structures, such as spatial and temporal patterns, embodiment, and interpersonal systems.

After the various patterns have been identified, the research moves to a search for a more basic "pattern in the patterns." If an overall pattern or unity to the examples is not discovered, then the analysis has to be reviewed for the possibility that there is more than one structure which underlies the descriptive data. The examples need to be examined in regard to levels and types of structure.[45]

The treatment process continues with a movement between the proposed structural description and the examples until an account can be given which clarifies the data in the fullest manner. The final description, of course, is the ideal toward which the researcher works, although he must necessarily stop somewhere before this ideal is attained. The researcher decides when the description is ready for presentation, and he is prepared to argue for it over other alternatives. This is a judgment he makes after his further searches do not produce clearer structural descriptions.

If the researcher is using a syncretic or multiple-methods approach, the analyses from the several methods are examined and combined to produce a description which integrates the results from the various studies. At this point, the researcher often presents the findings to the subjects who have given the original descriptive examples. The subjects are asked to judge the structural description's accuracy in terms of their own experiences. Sometimes their critique forces the researcher to rework the data-treatment process because the findings have seemed inadequate to the subjects. Finally, however, the researcher is ready to argue for the results before the "community of scholars." It is the task of this group to scrutinize the results in the light of the data and the arguments.

Methods are no longer considered correct or right in themselves. They are appropriate only in relationship to the kind of question being addressed. The researcher chooses the data type, the model of sampling, and the process of treatment as part of an overall strategy to make a knowledge claim that improves on the present state of understanding of some aspect of the human realm as seen from the perspective of a particular need that requires the increased understanding. The results of the attempt and the reasons for believing that the results are an improvement in understanding (that is, how the things the researcher did will lead the community to accept the conclusions) argue for their acceptance.

Presented here are summaries of two studies in human science which are examples of how the research strategies and methods are integrated to form a total design that develops evidence that will argue for the acceptance of the results by appealing to the procedures of practical reasoning.

Edward S. Casey's investigation, reported, in *Imagining: A Phenomenological Study*, is an expression of his concern with a comparative phenomenology of mental activity.[46] He believes that the various modes of mental activity—perception, imagination, memory, hallucination, fantasy, and reflective thought—have been inadequately distinguished from each other in Western psychology and philosophy. In *Imagining*, Casey provides a detailed analysis of imagination and compares and contrasts imagination with perception. Elsewhere[47] he has distinguished acts of imagining from acts of memory, hallucination, and fantasy.

Casey describes how he selected examples at the start of his investigation:

These examples will be taken from my own experiences of imagining, and this will be done despite the merit of Husserl's [admonition to use historical examples]. It may be admitted that examples taken from history and literature possess a complexity and subtlety often lacking in everyday, garden-variety acts of imagining. But by the same token, it would be naive to regard such examples as unadulterated reports of their authors' imaginative experiences, for they have almost invariably undergone significant modification. . . . What is needed in a scrupulous descriptive account of imagination is the reporting of examples in an

unmodified form and precisely as they present themselves to the imaginer. The examples to be [used] . . . meet this demand insofar as
they represent direct descriptions which were written down immediately
after the experience took place.[48]

Casey's analysis of the essence or *eidos* (Husserl's term) of the
activity of imagining begins with descriptions of three firsthand
experiences of imagining. The first is an imaginative sequence which
arises spontaneously: a school of dolphins appears at different lo-
cations, swimming playfully. The second is a self-willed imagining
of several instances of auditory experiences. The third is the imagining of a scene which could possibly occur later in the same day
at a seminar he is to attend.

From these basic examples, Casey's free variations lead him to an
understanding that what is imagined (the content) affects and is
affected by the components of the activity (the act) of imagining.
He also derives from the variations three dimensions which make
up the essence of imagination—spontaneity and controlledness, self-
containedness and self-evidence, and indeterminacy and pure possibility. He then explores each of these dimensions in detail.

Casey understands that both the act and the content of imagining
can occur either spontaneously or through effort and control. At
times, imaginative activity appears without any effort on our part,
takes us by surprise, and explodes all at once. It is instantaneous,
and it generates itself. At other times, we call forth the act and its
contents.

It appears to Casey that all aspects of the imagining experience
are characterized by both self-containedness and self-evidence. Although a perceptual object always presents itself as open to further
exploration if a different standpoint is assumed, in imagining "there
is no such displaceability of standpoint."[49] The object of imagination
presents a "frontality" and offers no other profiles. Moreover, there
is no need to gather additional evidence to correct what appears.
"Imagining is not subject to untruth or falsehood of any sort,"[50]
for there is no "object out there" to which imagination aspires to
present a correct view. Imagining presents only appearance and
nothing but appearance. Casey says:

Self-contained and self-evident, imaginative experience respects a self-
sufficing experience, an experience that takes place exclusively within
the psychical interface lying between the imaginer and his own autonomous activity. Such an activity suffices for itself, being contained within
its own self-prescribed boundaries and showing itself with pellucid self-
evidence. As self-determining and self-aware, this activity fully discloses

itself in its self-enclosed and self-enclosing character. As self-transparent, what is imagined on any given occasion is at one with the mind of the imaginer. Nowhere else within the spectrum of mental acts do we discover such complete concrescence of mind with the products of its own activity.[51]

Indeterminacy and pure possibility, the remaining pair of eidetic traits (imagining), are "mutually facilitating."[52] What we imagine possesses an intrinsic background vagueness that is not shared by the objects of perception. The lack of perceptually determined detail allows what we imagine to be free from the constrictions imposed on perceived objects and therefore to remain essentially open in character.[53] The objects of imagination, as differentiated from the objects of hallucination, are not believed to be either real or unreal. We suppose that what is given in the imagination is "free from either overt or covert connection with what is actual."[54] In imagination, the object can be posited and contemplated for its own sake, "not for the sake of anything external to, or more ultimate than, itself."[55] Because of its trait of pure possibility—that is, because it need serve no other end than its own appearance—"imagination's basic operations continually engender variety . . . [and give] rise to multiple options, directions, and routes. . . . It is the primary way in which the mind diversifies itself and its contents."[56]

Casey's variations led him to a recognition of the multiplicity of the mental. It is "a multiplicity borne out . . . by the existence of eidetic differences between various kinds of mental acts." Thus, there are plural possibilities for cognition, each possibility contributing to the "teeming pluralism of psychical phenomena."[57] Each kind of mental activity adds its particular contents and structural assumptions to the full experience of the person. Imagination's contribution is to provide a freedom of mind that allows for the pure possibility and for the indeterminate, thereby creating the variation and multiplicity which lifts us out of complete adherence to the determinate and the necessary.

After discussing the phenomenological investigation and presenting his essential description of imagination, Casey addresses the question of how this structure is placed in human experience. He focuses on three domains—art, psychology, and philosophy—and describes the way that imagination manifests itself in these activities and bestows on them its various powers for creating experience that is released from the limits of pure perception.[58]

Another area of study for human science research is the structure of the phenomenon "perception of physical objects." Unlike the objects which appear in memory or imagination, the objects of perception are believed to be "real"—that is, they are believed to stand physically before us. Previous investigations of "real perceptual objects"—by Husserl and Gurwitsch—have shown that although these objects appear only in various profiles, depending on the perspective of the viewer, partial appearances are experienced as belonging to single, stable objects. The perceptual profiles are ordered into univocal experiences of physical objects which the viewer believes to be really there. This operation is basic to our "objective attitude," and it provides the structure of our normal perceptual experience.

Two kinds of experience—the experience of unfamiliar real objects and the experience of mistaken identities—show this structuring process in relief. When we confront an unfamiliar object, the univocal, stable object does not at first appear. If we continue to explore the object, however, we experience a promise of resolution of the profiles into a determinate object. In the experience of mistaken identity, the original perception of the object is, upon further examination, re-cognized into a different "appearance-system in its entirety," and this happens instantly, not gradually. Paul Richer offers an illustration of this phenomenon—the experience of seeing a diamond which, upon closer scrutiny, turns out to be a drop of water—in "A Phenomenological Analysis of the Perception of Geometric Illusions."[59]

Studying the perception of objects which fail to stabilize into univocal objects provides an additional guide to understanding the perceptual mode of consciousness. The habitual process of forming appearances into single, stable objects is thwarted by those objects which are illusory. Although these objects call forth a univocal perception, they are essentially duplicitous. They cannot be brought beyond a bivocal organization, and so they fail to elicit a belief in their reality as true objects—a belief which accompanies the accomplishment of a univocal perception.

Richer's research is directed at the perceptual experiences that fail to coalesce into singular objects. He studies the abnormal perceptual experience "to elucidate the normal," and he investigates the perception of geometric illusions which are a particular example of the general experience of unstabilizing perceptual objects. Although he acknowledges the artificiality of geometric illusions, he does not believe that the artificiality diminishes their significance in providing an entry into understanding the perception of bivocal objects.[60]

One of Richer's objectives is to demonstrate that the experience of bivocal objects is different in kind from the experience of univocal objects. This difference is not commonly understood. The usual definition of an illusion as "that which appears real but is not genuinely real" assumes only one kind of perceptual experience, Richer says, and he hypothesizes that the perception of an illusory curve, for example, is not identical to the perception of a real curve, the difference being that the illusory curve is perceived as having a "fault."[61] It cannot be made to stop being two objects and allow itself, as happens with nonillusions, to be formed into a single object. Thus, in addition to adding to our understanding of general perceptual operations, Richer's study undercuts the commonly held theoretical presuppositions upon which most "objective" studies on the perception of illusions have been based.

In order to obtain examples that would provide an opening into the essence of perceiving illusory objects, Richer created experiences of this phenomenon for thirty people. He presented participants in his research with cards on which were drawn geometric figures. He recorded their verbal and bodily response while each participant was presented with three four-by-six-inch cards. On the cards were figures of the Orbison illusion and Herring's illusion, and there was one card with a nonillusory figure. The cards were given one at a time to each participant, and after receiving the card the participant was asked to describe the figure on the card in detail so that the researcher, who was not looking at the figure, "would know exactly how it looks." The verbal response was recorded in writing by the researcher as the participant talked. The researcher also recorded "any body movements that were obviously aimed at changing the subject's perspective and . . . any manipulations of the inspected card itself." Richer varied the order of the presentation of the cards so that half of the participants received the nonillusory card first while the other half received it last. This was done to see what effect the "set" to see illusory aspects might have on the perception of the nonillusory figure.[62]

The written protocols provided instances of the bivocal phenomenon which enriched the variations Richer could have gained from his own experiences. He did not use the results of the participants' experiences as a basis for empirical generalization, which should provide a description of what in fact was present. Instead, he used the various examples of perceiving an illusory object as a means to arrive at the essential structure of the phenomenon. The examples provided variations that led him to intuit the necessary characteristics of the perceptual act in which illusory objects are present to consciousness. Part of his process of variation involved a comparison of the responses to the illusory figures with the responses to the nonillusory figures. He found that the participants, as they described the figures, picked up and maneuvered the illusory figures much more than the nonillusory figures. "A vast majority of observers recognized some unusual character in the illusory figures," Richer says.[63]

> In summary, results of this study demonstrate that if subjects viewing two-dimensional geometric illusions are allowed freedom of movement and freedom of expression, they usually report being directly aware of the figure's peculiar character. This character reveals itself perceptually in the following ways:
>
> 1. The figure is unstable and can be seen as two different shapes.
>
> 2. Changes in distance, angle, or focus of an observer's point of view result in changes in the figure's shape.
>
> 3. In any particular point of view, the illusory portion can appear to fluctuate or vibrate.
>
> 4. Forces are sometimes perceived as maintaining the illusory portion in a state of tension.[64]

Richer concludes that "there is an overall difference in the way observers react to illusory as compared to nonillusory figures."[65] He then draws out the implications of these results for the commonly held definition of illusory phenomena:

> The results of this research point to a revision of the usual understanding of an illusory phenomenon as "that which appears real but is not genuine real." The illusory figures in this study usually did not appear real— they distinguished themselves perceptually as peculiar.[66]

He also uses his description to explore the relationships between the normal univocal perception of objects—as described by previous phenomenological researchers—and the perception of bivocal objects:

> The character of the peculiarity proved to involve a perceptual duplicity in which the figure strangely appeared two ways at once, caught, sometimes, even vibrating between them, in a state of tension. The figure's refusal to gel was magnified by attempts to gain a privileged perspective which under ordinary circumstances (with real perceptual objects) would solve the perceptual dilemma.[67]

These two examples of human science research show how the various parts of a research project are brought together and how they affect each other.[68] The selection of linguistic or numerical data type or the combination of the two, the selection of sources from which the expressions of the human realm are gathered, and the procedures by means of which this evidence is examined for conclusions and answers to the research question are all determined within the context of practical decisions made by the researcher. No longer are there recipes which, if followed, will produce the correct answers. Each project calls for creative solutions to strategic problems related to the kind of question asked and the special properties of the human realm.

Concluding Remarks

Developments in the philosophy of science during the past two decades have shattered the consensus which was achieved during the period from the 1930s to the 1950s by logical positivism. Research is now conducted in what has come to be known as the "postpositivist" period.[69]

This central feature of the change that has been occurring is a release from the requirement that science (knowledge) must be able to withstand all skeptical criticism. According to logical positivism, methodology had to produce absolutely certain (apodictic) knowledge—that is, *epistēmē.* Knowledge was indubitable or it was not knowledge. Scientific statements were judged from within a two-valued logic: knowledge was either true—that is, it was certain—or it was problematic—that is, it lacked certainty. Within this commitment to certainty, methodology required a demonstrative or deductive logic at its base, because only deduction leads to necessary conclusions.

The postpositivist period begins with the acceptance—by Popper, Laudan, Shapere, Radnitzky, and Toulmin (in his later work)[70]—that scientific knowledge is part of the realm of assertoric knowledge. In assertoric knowledge, some knowledge claims are better than others, but none is beyond doubt. This is a more common-sense understanding of knowledge, for it means that one can have more confidence in some knowledge claims than in others and need not make a final choice between truth and falsity. Knowledge statements are judged along a continuum that ranges from completely reliable to completely unreliable extremes. Statements can move on the continuum in either direction as more experience is gained with them.

The logic for justifying assertoric knowledge is different from the deductive logic required for attaining absolute certainty. Assertoric knowledge uses practical reasoning and argumentation. It requires a decision among alternatives, none of which provides certainty. A supporter of a knowledge claim is expected to argue cogently before the appropriate community, providing evidence pertinent to his or her proposal and defending his or her position as the most likely correct position among various alternatives. Assertoric knowledge is time-bound. It is knowledge that one (or a group) decides for—a particular alternative—in order to act in a given situation. This kind of knowledge is not considered true for all times and for all places, but it does serve as the basis for action. A researcher who strives for assertoric knowledge must bring to bear all of his or her powers of argumentation and reasoning, for he or she is asked to take a stand and to act without the assurance of certainty.

A researcher needs more than a kit of tools or a set of directions about how to perform methodological operations. He or she needs to develop a strategy that will indicate which systems to use and how to use them in a particular investigation. Research results are not obtained merely by using a method correctly. A project must be designed, and design problems are compounded in a science of multiple logics and methodological tools.

There is no one method which is the correct method for conducting human science research. The point of view taken in this book is pluralistic in regard to methods and logics. There are various systems of inquiry that the researcher can use. Instead of trying to adapt one tool—whether it be statistical induction or existential-phenomenological description or something else—the researcher must try to select the research system that is appropriate for answering the particular questions he or she is addressing. The availability of various systems also means that many more kinds of questions can be addressed by the researcher. These increased possibilities place greater responsibility on researchers, requiring that they become something more than mere technicians, that they become, in fact, methodologists. They need to concern themselves with the various approaches to the creation of knowledge and the ways in which these approaches use different logics to relate statements and meanings.

Science has changed and expanded during the past several decades, but it continues to differentiate between knowledge proposals, finding some acceptable and rejecting others. Various systems of inquiry have matured, and they offer alternative contexts for treating and understanding our world. Human science seeks to know the reality which is particularly our own, the reality of our experience, actions, and expressions. This realm is closest to us, yet it is most resistant to our attempt to grasp it with undestanding. Because of the success we have had in knowing the world around us, the human realm has expanded its power to such an extent that we can act to create well-being and physical security and comfort and to inflict untold suffering and destruction. Serious and rigorous re-searching of the human realm is required. This book is an attempt to describe the present state of the art in human science methodology. The disjoining of the tightly organized parts of the received view provides a more favorable environment within the politics of knowledge for renewed growth. The renewal in human science methodology, after its dormancy for six decades, is just beginning. What is required for growth beyond this beginning is research programs positively supporting trials with various methodological systems. Graduate programs and the editorial policies of scholarly journals need to encourage variety in approaches and to offer critiques based on the significance of the questions addressed and the fruitfulness of the answers given, as well as on the persuasiveness of the evidence and the arguments.

What is called for is getting on with the development of a science without certainty that deepens our understanding of human existence. And what is needed for this development is dissertations and research studies that engage in serious exploration of the human realm.

Appendix: The Term "Human Science"

Geisteswissenschaften

John Stuart Mill, writing in 1843, used the term "moral sciences" to describe the sciences of human nature and proposed that they employ the methods recently developed in the physical sciences. Said Mill:

> Although several other sciences have emerged from this state [i.e., a state still abandoned to the uncertainties of vague and popular discussion] at a comparatively recent date, none now remain in it except those which relate to man himself, the most complex and most difficult subject of study on which the human mind can be engaged.[1]

These sciences of human nature—"moral sciences"—were in a state of confusion, according to Mill. "The backward state of the moral sciences," he said, "can only be remedied by applying to them the methods of physical science, duly extended and generalized."[2] When Schiel translated *System of Logic*, the book in which these passages appear, into German in 1849, he used the term *Geisteswissenschaften* to mean "moral sciences." Although *Geisteswissenschaften* as a term had appeared briefly before,[3] it first became generally recognized in this context.

The meaning of the term was extended by Wilhelm Dilthey,[4] and it appeared in the title of his *Introduction to the Human Sciences* (*Einleitung in die Geisteswissenschaften*) (1883). The term has since become associated with Dilthey's position that the "moral sciences" (extended from Mill's definition to include disciplines such as philology and aesthetics, as well as psychology, anthropology, political economy, law, and history) or human sciences should not be modeled

283

on the natural sciences as Mill had proposed. The methodology of the "moral sciences," Dilthey said, must be different from the methodology of the natural sciences. (Dilthey's position is described in more detail in chapter 1.)

Wissenschaften. If we attempt to translate Dilthey's term, *Geisteswissenschaften,* back into contemporary English, we encounter certain problems. The original term "moral sciences" is no longer available, because the word *moral* has acquired a more limited meaning and applies to ethics rather than to human action in general. The term *sciences* has also come to connote a particular approach to knowledge that is modeled on the physical sciences and makes use of experimentation and quantified data.

Geisteswissenschaften is a combination of two words—*Geist* and *Wissenschaften.* *Wissen* means "to know" (*epistēmē*), and *Wissenschaft* (*Wissenschaften* is the plural) refers to a disciplined study that aims at knowledge or to scholarship in general. Thus, *Wissenschaft* carries a broader meaning than the English word *science.* Because of this limitation of the English word, *Wissenschaften* is usually translated as "studies." *Natur-wissenschaften,* however, is translated as "natural sciences." The word chosen to translate *Wissenschaften* into English implies a choice as to whether knowledge is limited to statements confirmed within a logical-empirical epistemological framework or whether it includes statements derived with frameworks other than the logical-empirical one.

It was Dilthey's contention that the human realm could be studied "objectively" and that certainty was possible. He proposed, however, that the methods used for the *Geisteswissenschaften* should include additional approaches (such as *verstehen* or understanding) that were inappropriate for the natural sciences.

Three major interpreters of Dilthey have used "studies" for the translation of *Wissenschaften.* Hodges, Rickman, and Makkreel, writing from 1944 to 1979, all translate *Geisteswissenschaften* as "human studies."[5] However, in a recent book about Dilthey, Michael Ermarth comments about the problem of translating *Geisteswissenschaften:*

> The rather flaccid "human studies" fails to convey Dilthey's concern for methodical rigor, general validity, and critical self-consciousness; thus it perpetuates the notion of this group of disciplines as somehow edifying and worthwhile but largely inchoate and vague in character. Indeed, "human studies" seems more appropriate for describing the condition of these disciplines before Dilthey set about his task of providing their theoretical-critical foundation. The German Wissenschaft is certainly broader than the English "science," but it is decidedly more adamant than the looser term "study."[6]

Thus writers who have wished to imply an enlarged base of scientific knowledge have often translated *Wissenschaften* as "science," thus rendering *Geisteswissenschaften* as "human science." Giorgi titled his book *Psychology as a Human Science*, Strasser titled his book *Phenomenology and the Human Sciences*, and Ricoeur's recent collection is titled in English, *Hermeneutics and the Human Sciences.*[7] Those authors who have recently written about hermeneutics have also used the translation "human science"—for example, Palmer, Bleicher, and Thompson.[8] French writers use the phrase *des sciences humaines*— for example, Foucault in *The Order of Things: An Archaeology of the Human Sciences.*[9]

In this book, *Wissenschaften* is translated as "sciences," because I hold the view that the human realm can be investigated with methodological rigor, general validity, and critical examination—although not with absolute certainty. It is my position, as well, that recent developments in the philosophy of science have shown that the natural sciences are also limited to assertoric knowledge. Consequently, both the study of the human realm and the study of the natural realm operate within the same kinds of limits—and both produce, at best, assertoric knowledge.

Geist. The more problematic term in *Geisteswissenschaften* is not *Wissenschaften* but the prefix *Geistes*. While the various interpreters of Dilthey disagree about how to translate *Wissenschaften*, they are in full agreement in translating *Geist* as "human." *Geist*, however, has a long history and varied meanings. Its usual translation is "spirit," but in English "spirit" often refers to something religious or something unreal. Rickman suggests that a more apt translation would be "the cultural world,"[10] as in *Zeitgeist*. Often "mind" is given as the translation of *Geist*, but Dilthey distinguished the products of the mind from the psychological processes that produce those products. He called the psychological or mental processes *seelisch*.

Dilthey found *Geisteswissenschaften* to be the "least inappropriate" term, and he at times used such alternatives as "sciences of society," "sciences of culture," and "moral sciences." He wanted to emphasize his conviction that human experience does not take place in a vacuum but is formed in and integrated into the psychophysical existence of persons. The term *Geist*, with its connotation of a disembodied spirit, did not convey his sense of the object of the human sciences, but with these reservations voiced he settled on *Geisteswissenschaften*.

Geist refers to whatever is produced or shaped by the intellectual and creative capacity for abstract thinking, conceptualizing, and logical reasoning. It specifies the objectifications of the mind—i.e., languages, religions, codes of law, the sciences, and the shaping of physical objects into human productions, such as tools, houses, machines, and decorations.

The world of the mind is a third and distinct sphere which stands separate from the physical sphere and the sphere of psychological or mental processes. Recognition of this sphere is necessary if we are to describe the facts and relationships that both shape our experiences and activities and are created by our experiences and activities. The sphere of *Geist* and its contents is the area that human science investigates and seeks to clarify. Human science attempts to understand the relationships and connections between and among the meanings, institutions, and other cultural products that are objectifications of mind or *Geist*. The rules of a chess game or of grammar, ideologies and social systems, the meanings of gestures and words, and our conceptual apparatus are all part of the *Geist* sphere.

Dilthey proposed that because the *Geist* sphere differs from the physical sphere it requires a methodology that differs from the methodology required by the physical sphere. And because this sphere also differs from the sphere of psychological or mental processes, the methodology it requires will not be the same as the methodology required by a cognitive psychology.

Throughout the nineteenth century, the question of how to approach and study the *Geist* sphere was usually answered by employing the methods used for the physical sphere. But idealists in the social sciences and romanticists in literature in their various guises maintained their distance from intellectual standpoints fostered by the natural sciences, and in most instances expressed deep hostility toward the spread of machine technology. Authors in these fields were generally skeptical of the possibility of creating a science of society based on the methods used in the natural sciences. However, their views served as no more than a critical foil to the much more influential writings of those authors who sought to use natural science methods to study the *Geist* sphere. In the 1850s, Comte formulated the idea of a science of society based on the methods used to study nature. The use of these methods, Comte thought, would reproduce in the study of human social life (*Geist*) the same kind of impressive illumination and explanatory power that had then already been yielded up by the sciences of nature.[11]

The wish to establish a natural science of society that possesses the same sort of logical structure and pursues the same objectives as the science of nature probably remains—in the English-speaking world, at least—the dominant standpoint. Although the certainties of natural science itself have been heavily assaulted in the twentieth century, there continues to be a sustained attempt to claim that natural science knowledge—or a particular characterization of it—should be regarded as the exemplar for everything which can be legitimately declared "knowledge."

Behavioral, Social or Human Sciences

Various terms have come into use to describe the studies of the human realm. In addition to *human sciences*, the words *social sciences* and *behavioral sciences* have been suggested as the generic term for these sciences. Distinctions among these terms have been offered by Fred Kerlinger, René Maheu, and Jean Piaget.

In *Behavioral Research: A Conceptual Approach*, Fred Kerlinger discusses the concepts of science and research and argues for the use of "behavioral sciences" as the inclusive term:

> The behavioral sciences are those sciences that study and seek to understand man, human institutions, and human actions and behaviors: sociology, psychology, anthropology, economics, political science. The term "social sciences" is also used, but "behavioral sciences" appears to be a more general, more inclusive term. This definition is only in general correct. Although the behavioral disciplines can be fairly clearly defined, the distinctions have often been blurred in actual theory and research. Sociologists and psychologists, for instance, often borrow from each others' fields. Moreover, some behavioral scientists, despite the definition of behavioral research, study animals, sometimes with considerable impact on scientific knowledge of behavior.[12]

In spite of Kerlinger's support for *behavioral sciences* as the inclusive term for studies of human phenomena, the term retains the specter of behaviorism and its prohibition against including consciousness as a part of scientific study.

In the late 1960s, UNESCO undertook a large study called *Main Trends of Research in the Social and Human Sciences*.[13] The study was divided into two parts, *The Social Sciences* and *The Human Sciences*. René Maheu, writing in the "Preface" to Part 1 of the study, distinguishes between the two sciences:

> A first part of the vast range of sciences aimed at promoting the knowledge of man, his social life and his individual existence, is constituted by a body of disciplines—those that are the subject of the present volume [*Social Science*]—which seek to identify laws and are motivated by the ideal of a learning as objective, as assured, as independent of human opinions, attitudes and situations as that which characterizes the natural sciences. In other sectors of scientific activity—those to which a second volume is to be devoted—references to the

order of values, norms and objectives, the demand for reflection and the concern for man's free self-determination at both the community and individual levels, dominate, without on that account departing from the pursuit of rigorous and objectively based knowledge.[14]

Maheu describes the social sciences as those sciences of the human realm which seek a knowledge characteristic of the natural sciences, and he describes the human sciences as those sciences "whose ideal of knowledge and truth is hardest to formulate and which remain profoundly linked to . . . the fundamental choices to which they commit themselves."[15]

In the "Introduction" to the same volume, Jean Piaget states that the distinction between the social sciences and the human sciences is no longer a clear one:

We shall confine ourselves here to pointing out that no distinction can be drawn between the disciplines frequently referred to as the "social sciences" and those known as the "human sciences." . . . Such a distinction could only make sense . . . if it were possible to dissociate in man what pertains to the particular society in which he lives from what is common to the whole of humanity. . . . There is a growing trend towards doing away with any distinction between the sciences known as "social" and those known as "human."[16]

Later on in the "Introduction," however, Piaget does distinguish between the "nomothetic" or "law-seeking" sciences and those sciences that do not set themselves such a task. The law-explanation system of inquiry is but one approach to the understanding of human phenomena. In this book, the disciplines are neither divided into law-explanation versus other explanation systems nor into individual versus group studies; the term *human science* is used to refer to an inclusive approach to human phenomena that uses multiple systems of inquiry, including but not limited to the identification of "laws."

Each of these terms is inclusive of the various sciences of the human realm, yet they come to have attached to them shades of meaning related to epistemological assumptions. *Behavior* and *social science* imply a commitment to a unified science based on the methods developed for exploration of the physical realm. Dilthey's proposed expanded epistemology has become attached to the term *human sciences*. The term *human sciences* is used in this book as the generic term for studies of the human realm, since I am proposing the employment of multiple systems of inquiry for the study of human phenomena.

At times the term *human science* (in the singular) is used to refer to the methodological approach described in this book. Thus *human science*, as distinguished from *natural* or *behavioral science*, is a science which approaches questions about the human realm with an openness to its special characteristics and a willingness to let the questions inform which methods are appropriate.

At the broadest level, the *human sciences* investigate all of the experiences, activities, constructs, and artifacts that would not now exist, or would not ever have existed, if human beings had not existed. Human phenomena constitute a milieu that consists of individual experience in an environment, and this environment is made up of social structures, values, language, physical objects, and such human constructions as buildings, highways, and automobiles. The object of human science is the elucidation and understanding of this world. Thus the object of inquiry is broad, and it includes the study of personal consciousness and experience, as well as social, political, and economic systems. But the context in which these activities and experiences are viewed is that of human achievement and construction. There is an essential link between the appearance of human beings and these expressions, and consequently the expressions—including personal consciousness—are viewed as human-related entities rather than as things in themselves. The human sciences explore the realm of the human.

Notes

Introduction (*Pages 1–13*)

1. Abraham Kaplan, *The Conduct of Inquiry: Methodology for Behavioral Science* (Scranton, Pa.: Chandler, 1964). In describing the approach of his book Kaplan wrote: "With regard to the widely differing and often mutually hostile schools and approaches in behavioral science, my position can be regarded, I suppose, as neutralist, and will therefore be condemned, no doubt, by both sides—not rigorous enough for one, and too demanding for the other. My aim has not been compromise, however, nor my ideal a golden mean. What seems to me important is yielding, not to demands externally imposed, but rather to those intrinsic to our own aspirations" (p. xv).

2. Amedeo Giorgi, *Psychology as a Human Science: A Phenomenologically Based Approach* (New York: Harper & Row, 1970). "To be human, [psychology] must have as its subject matter the human person and he must be approached within a frame of reference that is also human, i.e., one that does not do violence to the phenomenon of man as a person. . . . [This] does not necessarily imply a lack of rigor or discipline" (pp. 224–225). "For a human scientific psychology the more proper question to put to behavioral phenomena . . . [is] precisely to ask about their meaning and not their measurement" (p. 232).

Anthony Giddens, *New Rules of Sociological Method: A Positive Critique of Interpretive Sociologies* (New York: Basic Books, 1976). "The themes of this study are that social theory must incorporate a treatment of action as rationalized conduct ordered reflexively by human agents, and must grasp the significance of language as the practical medium whereby this is made possible" (p. 8).

3. Thomas S. Kuhn, *The Structure of Scientific Revolutions*, 2nd ed. (Chicago: University of Chicago Press, 1970), p. 36.

4. Larry Laudan, *Progress and Its Problems: Toward a Theory of Scientific Growth* (Berkeley: University of California Press, 1977). "I propose that the rationality and progressiveness of a theory are most closely linked—not with

its confirmation or its falsification—but rather with its *problem solving effectiveness"* (p. 5).

5. The concept of the researcher's toolbox comes from Charles Hampden-Turner, *Radical Man* (Cambridge, Mass.: Schenkman, 1970), pp. 1–17.

6. Mario Bunge, *Causality and Modern Science*, 3rd rev. ed. (Cleveland: World, 1963; reprint, New York: Dover, 1979). "Philosophers of cultural sciences should also grant that our comparative ignorance of the laws of society and history is due . . . to the very prejudice that there 'are' no laws of history. . . . People who are able to take the social mechanism apart in theory may wish to change it in practice, and—what is more dangerous for those who live on the persistence of fossil social forms—such men may even succeed in their attempt. This is essentially why the pragmatic view of science, summarized in the positivistic maxim 'To know is to foresee; to foresee is to control', which enjoys such wide acceptance in connection with the science of nature, is so often forgotten in the sphere of the social sciences, where it is found more desirable to hold that human society is rationally unknowable, hence unpredictable, hence incurable" (p. 273).

Also May Brodbeck, "General Introduction," in May Brodbeck, ed., *Readings in the Philosophy of the Social Sciences* (New York: Macmillan, 1968): "Does knowledge of man imply control of man? Some fear that it does, but even if they are right, it is a 'non sequitur' to argue that knowledge, because fearful, must be impossible" (p. 3).

7. Donald T. Campbell and Julian C. Stanley, *Experimental and Quasi-Experimental Designs for Research* (Chicago: Rand McNally, 1963).

8. Thomas D. Cook and Donald T. Campbell, *Quasi-Experimentation: Design and Analysis Issues for Field Settings* (Chicago: Rand McNally, 1979).

9. Compare Kuhn, *Structure of Scientific Revolutions*, chapter 3, "The Nature of Normal Science," in which he describes normal science as "mopping up operations" within a paradigm or accepted model or pattern of doing science.

10. See Alfred Schutz and Thomas Luckmann, *The Structures of the Life-World*, trans. Richard M. Zaner and H. Tristram Engelhardt, Jr. (Evanston, Ill.: Northwestern University Press, 1973), chapter 3, "Knowledge of the Life-World," for a discussion of the development of a person's stock of knowledge.

11. Compare Harmon M. Chapman, *Sensations and Phenomenology* (Bloomington: Indiana University Press, 1966), where he describes the impact of the apodictic standard for truth on Descartes, empiricism, and rationalism. Chapman proposes an "assertoric" standard in place of the apodictic one. See p. 54.

12. Ludwig Wittgenstein, *Philosophical Investigations*, 3d ed., trans. G. E. M. Anscombe (New York: Macmillan, 1968); Peter Winch, *The Idea of a Social Science and Its Relation to Philosophy* (London: Routledge & Kegan Paul, 1958); Benjamin L. Whorf, *Language, Thought, and Reality: Selected Writings of Benjamin Lee Whorf*, ed. J. B. Carroll (Cambridge, Mass.: MIT Press, 1956); Hans-Georg Gadamer, *Truth and Method*, trans. Garren Burden and John Cumming (New York: Seabury Press, 1975).

13. Sigmund Koch, "A Possible Psychology for a Possible Postpositivist World," paper read at the symposium on "Psychology in a Postpositivist World: Three Perspectives" at the American Psychological Association 88th Annual Convention, Montreal, September 1980.

Chapter One: The Original Debate (Pages 15–57)

1. See John Losee, A Historical Introduction to the Philosophy of Science, 2nd ed. (Oxford: Oxford University Press, 1980), pp. 60–69.

2. Thomas S. Kuhn, "Mathematical versus Experimental Traditions in the Development of Physical Science," Journal of Interdisciplinary History 7 (1976): 1–31, reprinted in Thomas S. Kuhn, The Essential Tension: Selected Studies in Scientific Tradition and Change (Chicago: University of Chicago Press, 1977), pp. 31–65. Kuhn distinguishes between the mathematical tradition with roots in classical Greece and the experimental tradition developed in the medieval guilds. Kuhn holds that Bacon was distrustful, not only of mathematics, but of the quasi-deductive structure of classical science. "Galileo's dominant attitude toward that aspect of science remained within the classical mode" (p. 49). It was Newton who combined the experimental design publicized by Francis Bacon with the mathematical and theoretical approach of classical science.

3. See Edwin A. Burtt, The Metaphysical Foundations of Modern Physical Science (Garden City, N.Y.: Anchor Books, 1954), pp. 207–302.

4. Michel Foucault, The Order of Things: An Archaeology of the Human Sciences (New York: Pantheon Books, 1971). "Among all the mutations that have affected the knowledge of things and their order . . . only one, that which began a century and a half ago and is now perhaps drawing to a close, has made it possible for the figure of man to appear. . . . As the archaeology of our thought easily shows, man is an invention of recent date. And one perhaps nearing its end" (p. 387).

5. Thomas Hobbes, Leviathan, 1651 (New York: Collier Books, 1962). "For seeing life is but a motion of limbs . . . why may we not say, that all 'automata' . . . have an artificial life? For what is the 'heart', but a spring; and the 'nerves', but so many strings; and the joints, but so many 'wheels', giving motion to the whole body." Quoted in Thomas H. Leahey, A History of Psychology: Main Currents in Psychological Thought (Englewood Cliffs, N.J.: Prentice-Hall, 1980), p. 99.

6. See Maurice Mandelbaum, History, Man, and Reason: A Study in Nineteenth-Century Thought (Baltimore: Johns Hopkins University Press, 1971). Mandelbaum distinguishes between the "systematic positivism" of Comte and Spencer and the "critical positivism" of Mach. Comte was the first to transform philosophy into a synthesis of the sciences. He held that the intellectual life of a society was the organization around which all other elements were formed. He also allowed "directional laws" in which the development of social forms could be predicted. Mach did not accept these laws and held that only "functional laws" were valid as descriptions.

7. John Stuart Mill, *A System of Logic*, selections in Philip P. Weiner, *Readings in Philosophy of Science* (New York: Scribner's, 1953). Mill emphasized the individual's psychological activity as the base of experience. Comte, on the other hand, proposed that the social context was responsible for variations in experience. Thus Comte placed sociology at the apex of his hierarchy of the sciences, and excluded psychology as a basic science.

8. See Michael Ermarth, *Wilhelm Dilthey: The Critique of Historical Reason* (Chicago: University of Chicago Press, 1978), p. 72.

9. Fred N. Kerlinger, *Behavioral Research: A Conceptual Approach* (New York: Holt, Rinehart & Winston, 1979), p. 2.

10. Giambattista Vico, *The New Science*, rev. trans. of 3rd ed., Thomas Goddard Bergin and Max Harold Fisch (Ithaca, N.Y.: Cornell University Press, 1968), quoted in Josef Bleicher, *Contemporary Hermeneutics: Hermeneutics as Method, Philosophy and Critique* (London: Routledge & Kegan Paul, 1980), p. 87.

11. See Georg Henrik von Wright, *Explanation and Understanding* (Ithaca, N.Y.: Cornell University Press, 1971), p. 5.

12. See *Encyclopedia of Philosophy*, 1967 ed., s.v. "Windelband, Wilhelm," by Hayden V. White.

13. *Encyclopedia of Philosophy*, 1967 ed., s.v. "Rickert, Heinrich," by Robert Anchor.

14. See Rudolph H. Weingartner, *Experience and Culture: The Philosophy of Georg Simmel* (Middletown, Conn.: Wesleyan University Press, 1962).

15. Wilhelm Dilthey, Manuscripts from the Berlin Nachlass. Literatur-Archiv der deutschen Akademie der Wissenschaften, Berlin, quoted in Ermarth, *Wilhelm Dilthey*, pp. 108–109.

16. Dilthey, *Introduction to the Human Sciences*, quoted in Ermarth, *Wilhelm Dilthey*, p. 121.

17. Dilthey, Manuscripts, quoted in Ermarth, *Wilhelm Dilthey*, p. 220.

18. H. P. Rickman, *Wilhelm Dilthey: Pioneer of the Human Studies* (Berkeley: University of California Press, 1979), p. 170.

19. Edwin G. Boring, *A History of Experimental Psychology*, 2nd ed. (New York: Appleton-Century-Crofts, 1950).

20. Kurt Danziger, "The Positivist Repudiation of Wundt," *Journal of the History of the Behavioral Sciences* 15 (July 1979): 205–230, esp. p. 210.

21. David E. Leary, "Wundt and After: Psychology's Shifting Relations with the Natural Sciences, Social Sciences, and Philosophy," *Journal of the History of the Behavioral Sciences* 15 (July 1979): 231–241, esp. p. 235.

22. Herbert Spiegelberg, *The Phenomenological Movement: A Historical Introduction*, 2 vols., 2nd ed. (The Hague: Martinus Nijhoff, 1976), pp. 35–36.

23. Franz Brentano, *Psychology from an Empirical Standpoint*, ed. Linda L. McAlister, trans. Antos C. Rancurello, D. B. Terrell, and Linda L. McAlister (New York: Humanities Press, 1973), p. 77.

24. Ibid., p. 80.

25. Ibid., p. 79.

26. See Spiegelberg, *The Phenomenological Movement*, pp. 42–43.

27. Brentano, *Psychology*, p. 78.

28. Quoted in Spiegelberg, *The Phenomenological Movement*, p. 84.

29. Ernest Keen, "Doing Psychology Phenomenologically: Methodological Considerations," mimeograph (Lewisberg, Penn., 1975), pp. 70–73.

30. See Gabriel Marcel, *Being and Having*, 1935, trans. K. Farrer (London: Collins, 1965).

31. Max Weber, *The Theory of Social and Economic Organization*, 1925, ed. Talcott Parsons (New York: Free Press, 1964), p. 88.

32. Weber, *Theory*, p. 106.

33. Ibid., p. 92.

34. Max Weber, *Economy and Society*, ed. Guenther Roth and Claus Wittich (New York: Bedminster Press, 1968), in Fred R. Dallmayr and Thomas A. McCarthy, *Understanding and Social Inquiry* (Notre Dame, Ind.: University of Notre Dame Press, 1977), pp. 38–55.

35. Weber, *Theory*, p. 109.

36. Ibid., p. 104.

37. Ibid., p. 103.

38. William James, *Essays in Radical Empiricism* (New York: Longmans, Green, 1940), p. 42.

39. Kurt Danziger, "The Social Origins of Modern Psychology," in Allan R. Buss, ed., *Psychology in Social Context* (New York: Irvington, 1979), pp. 35, 42.

40. Seymour B. Sarason, *Psychology Misdirected* (New York: Free Press, 1981), p. 4; see also chapter 8, "A New Psychology Need Be Born."

41. Kurt Koffka, *Principles of Gestalt Psychology* (New York: Harcourt, Brace, 1935), p. 684. See Martin Leichtman, "Gestalt Theory and the Revolt against Positivism," in Buss, *Psychology*.

42. Quoted in Leahey, *A History of Psychology*, p. 209.

43. Norman K. Denzin, "The Research Act," in Jerome G. Manis and Bernard N. Meltzer, eds., *Symbolic Interaction: A Reader in Social Psychology*, 3rd ed. (Boston: Allyn & Bacon, 1978), pp. 58–68.

44. T. W. Wann, ed., *Behaviorism and Phenomenology: Contrasting Bases for Modern Psychology* (Chicago: University of Chicago Press, 1964).

45. John B. P. Shaffer, *Humanistic Psychology* (Englewood Cliffs, N.J.: Prentice-Hall, 1978).

Chapter Two: The Received View of Science (*Pages 59–91*)

1. Frederick Suppe, "The Search for Philosophic Understanding of Scientific Theories," in Frederick Suppe, ed., *The Structure of Scientific Theories*, 2nd ed. (Urbana: University of Illinois Press, 1977), pp. 3–232.

2. Dalia Ducker, "Survey of Dissertations in Clinical and Professional Psychology Programs," paper read at the American Psychological Association 88th Annual Convention, Montreal, September 1980. Ducker surveyed 144 programs in clinical and professional psychology with a return from 78

programs. Although 81 percent did not have specific policies limiting methods considered acceptable for dissertations, the most common designs used were the laboratory experiment (41 percent) and the field experiment (28 percent). The least common were phenomenological (1 percent), descriptive (1 percent), and case studies (1 percent).

Robert A. Baron, Donn Byrne, and Barry H. Kantowitz, *Psychology: Understanding Behavior* (Philadelphia: W. B. Saunders, 1977), a standard psychology textbook, reads, in describing research on motivation: "in research, . . . psychologists have learned that neither set of philosophical assumptions [rationalism and mechanism] is necessary in the task of building a science of behavior. Empirical determinism [the approach used in psychology] simply assumes that behavior is a natural phenomenon and that it is predictable. The question asked in behavioral research is not really 'why' behavior occurs but rather 'how' and 'when.' Most often, those conducting research are trying to determine the conditions under which behavior occurs rather than to discover some ultimate explanation of behavior. The goal is to be able to make accurate predictions" (p. 223).

3. Oswald Hanfling, *Logical Positivism* (New York: Columbia University Press, 1981).

4. The basic texts for the original logical positivism and its subsequent refinements are contained in several collections: see A. J. Ayer, ed., *Logical Positivism* (New York: Free Press, 1959); Herbert Feigl and May Brodbeck, eds., *Readings in the Philosophy of Science* (New York: Appleton-Century-Crofts, 1953).

5. The name "the received view" was first introduced in Hilary Putnam, "What Theories Are Not," in E. P. Nagel, P. Suppes, and A. Tarski, eds., *Logic, Methodology, and Philosophy of Science: Proceedings of the 1960 International Congress* (Stanford, Calif.: Stanford University Press, 1962).

6. Rudolf Carnap, *An Introduction to the Philosophy of Science*, ed. Martin Gardner (New York: Basic Books, 1966), p. 3.

7. Bertrand Russell, "Descriptions," 1919, reprinted in Jay F. Rosenberg and Charles Travis, eds., *Readings in the Philosophy of Language* (Englewood Cliffs, N.J.: Prentice-Hall, 1971), pp. 161, 175. See Ian Hacking, *Why Does Language Matter to Philosophy?* (Cambridge: Cambridge University Press, 1975), pp. 82–92.

8. "Phenomenalism" and "phenomenalists" is not the same as "phenomenology" and "phenomenologists." "Phenomenalism" refers to the attempt to ground knowledge in the bits of sensa that appear in consciousness. "Phenomenology" is the method developed by Husserl to study the full contents of consciousness. These contents include those constituted by the various modes of awareness including imagination, remembrance and perception, as well as various types of "objects" such as logical forms, numbers, and physical things. Phenomenology is a method to investigate the invariant structures in which these modes present their contents and the essential forms in which various singular presentations are experienced as unified and the same. (See chapter 6.)

9. "It was the original opinion of Carnap and Schlick that these [protocol] sentences constitute a special class of empirical statements whose validity is guaranteed by their simple reproduction of experience." John B. Thompson, *Critical Hermeneutics: A Study in the Thought of Paul Ricoeur and Jürgen Habermas* (Cambridge: Cambridge University Press, 1981), p. 13.

10. Attempts to save the derived statements about physical objects and laws were undertaken by Kant with his transcendental subjective-idealist framework which allowed for synthetic a priori statements, Hegel's dialectical unfolding of *Geist*, and the nineteenth-century empiricist attempts of Mill to vindicate induction.

11. William Barrett, "Positivism" in *Philosophy in the Twentieth Century*, vol. 2 (New York: Harper & Row, 1962), p. 472.

12. Rudolf Carnap, "Testability and Meaning," 1937, reprinted in Feigl and Brodbeck, *Readings*, pp. 47–92.

13. Interest in the "truth conditions" of a sentence has been renewed since Russell's quote. See especially A. Tarski, "The Semantic Conception of Truth and the Foundations of Semantics," 1944, reprinted in Herbert Feigl and W. Sellars, *Readings in Philosophical Analysis* (New York: Appleton-Century-Crofts, 1949), pp. 52–84.

14. Bertrand Russell, *Our Knowledge of the External World* (Chicago: Open Court, 1929), pp. 45–48.

15. Ibid., pp. 45–48.

16. Philip Brian Bell and Phillip James Stains, *Reasoning and Argument in Psychology* (London: Routledge & Kegan Paul, 1981). The example used by Bell and Stains provides an illustration of the difficulty of relating deductive forms of argument to the human realm. The form of the argument is indeed an illustration of the modus ponens and modus tollens, and the same example used earlier is in the form of the fallacy of denying the antecedent ("If P, then Q. Not P. Therefore Not Q"). However, the structure of the human realm is systemic rather than deductively organized; often explanation takes the form of part–whole and mutual interaction relationships rather than instances of general classes. Thus the example does not ring true to experience, yet nevertheless is correct as a form of deductive logic.

17. Gödel later showed Russell was in error that mathematics was a completely axiomaticized system.

18. Richard S. Rudner, *Philosophy of Social Science* (Englewood Cliffs, N.J.: Prentice-Hall, 1966), p. 11.

19. See chapter 4, where Skinner's proposal to return to a pretheoretical positivism is discussed.

20. "Protasis" is the term used to refer to the subordinate clause in the conditional sentence; "apodosis" refers to the clause stating the conclusion or consequence of a conditional sentence.

21. Hempel's contributions to explanation theory began with a 1942 paper on general laws in history (see note 42). His first general presentation of the nomological-deductive explanation was in Carl G. Hempel and Paul Oppenheim, "Studies in the Logic of Explanation," 1948, reprinted in

Baruch A. Brody, ed., *Readings in the Philosophy of Science* (Englewood Cliffs, N.J.: Prentice-Hall, 1970), pp. 8–27. In 1959 in "The Logic of Functional Analysis," reprinted in May Brodbeck, *Readings in the Philosophy of Social Science* (New York: Macmillan, 1968), pp. 179–210, he introduced a distinction between deductive and another type of explanation which he has variously termed "inductive," "statistical," "probabilistic," and "inductive-statistical."

May Brodbeck, "Explanation, Prediction, and 'Imperfect' Knowledge," in Herbert Feigl and Grover Maxwell, eds., *Minnesota Studies in the Philosophy of Science*, vol. 3 (Minneapolis: University of Minnesota Press, 1962), reprinted in Feigl and Brodbeck, *Readings*, pp. 363–398, argues that "the use of statistical hypotheses does not . . . require abandoning deduction" (p. 378). She holds that a statistical generalization is as "universal" as a so-called deterministic or nonstatistical law. In both cases the law goes beyond the evidence and is more than a summary of observations. The deterministic law, given the initial conditions, can be used to predict an individual event. The statistical law and its initial conditions can be used only to predict a so-called mass event, that is, the frequency with which an attribute will be distributed in the given class. With statistical laws one explains deductively why more of one thing occurs than another, and thus both types of law use deduction as the form of argument for explaining and predicting.

22. Hempel and Oppenheim, "Studies," p. 323.

23. Carl G. Hempel, *Aspects of Scientific Explanation and Other Essays in the Philosophy of Science* (New York: Free Press, 1965); Richard B. Braithwaite, *Scientific Explanation: A Study of the Function of Theory, Probability and Law in Science* (Cambridge: Cambridge University Press, 1955); Ernest Nagel, *The Structure of Science: Problems in the Logic of Scientific Explanation* (New York: Harcourt, Brace & World, 1961); Karl Popper, *The Logic of Scientific Discovery*, 1934 (New York: Basic Books, 1959).

24. Hempel and Oppenheim, "Studies," write: "These two expressions derived from the Latin *explanare*, were adopted in preference to the perhaps more customary terms "explicandum" and "explicans" in order to reserve the latter for use in the context of explication of meaning, or analysis" (p. 23, note 1).

25. Example from *Encyclopedia of Philosophy*, 1967 ed., s.v. "Explanation in Science," by Jaegwon Kim.

26. Carl G. Hempel, *Philosophy of Natural Science* (Englewood Cliffs, N.J.: Prentice-Hall, 1966), p. 51.

27. From Bell and Stains, *Reasoning*, p. 32.

28. Fred N. Kerlinger, *Foundations of Behavioral Research*, 2nd ed. (New York: Holt, Rinehart & Winston, 1973), p. 8.

29. Hempel, *Aspects*, p. 54.

30. Carnap, *Introduction*, p. 3.

31. Hempel and Oppenheim, "Studies," p. 338.

32. Reported in Abraham Kaplan, *The Conduct of Inquiry: Methodology for Behavioral Science* (Scranton, Pa.: Chandler, 1964), pp. 91–92.

33. Carnap, *Introduction*, p. 212.

34. Mario Bunge, *Causality and Modern Science*, 3rd rev. ed. (New York: Dover, 1979), p. 289.

35. Ibid., p. 289.

36. Carnap, *Introduction*, p. 189.

37. Norman R. Campbell, *What Is Science?*, 1921 (New York: Dover, 1953), pp. 51–57.

38. Hans Reichenbach, *Experience and Prediction* (Chicago: University of Chicago Press, 1938).

39. The importance of the "context of discovery" is emphasized and explored by Michael Polanyi, *Personal Knowledge: Toward a Post-Critical Philosophy* (Chicago: University of Chicago Press, 1958; reprint, New York: Harper & Row, 1964), and Norwood R. Hanson, *Patterns of Discovery: An Inquiry into the Conceptual Foundations of Science* (Cambridge: Cambridge University Press, 1958; reprint, 1969).

40. Carl G. Hempel, *Fundamentals of Concept Formation in Empirical Science*, vol. 2, no. 7, International Encyclopedia of Unified Science (Chicago: University of Chicago Press, 1952), p. 36.

41. Campbell, *What Is Science?*, p. 96.

42. Carl G. Hempel, "The Function of General Laws in History," 1942, reprinted in P. Gadiner, ed., *Theories of History* (Urbana: University of Illinois Press, 1959), pp. 349–350. See R. F. Atkinson, *Knowledge and Explanation in History: An Introduction to the Philosophy of History* (Ithaca, N.Y.: Cornell University Press, 1978). Atkinson posed two questions for the deductive intepretation of historical inquiry: "whether historical explanations so conceived can ever be complete and whether there are available for history laws, regularities, or generalizations of the appropriate type" (p. 106). Commenting on the first question, he said that law explanations found in history are never "deductively watertight"; in regard to the second question, he held that historical study gives summaries, not laws (pp. 110–115). Atkinson was reacting to the deductivist demand that historical explanation fit the law theory, because law explanation is the only possible theory of explanation. According to such deductivists as Brodbeck, the explanations provided in history that do not meet the deductive criteria are radically defective.

43. Peter L. Berger and Hansfried Kellner, *Sociology Reinterpreted: An Essay on Method and Vocation* (Garden City, N.Y.: Anchor Books, 1981), p. 42.

44. Anthony Giddens, *Central Problems in Social Theory: Action, Structure and Contradiction in Social Analysis* (Berkeley: University of California Press, 1979), p. 238.

45. Thomas A. Leahey, *A History of Psychology: Main Currents in Psychological Thought* (Englewood Cliffs, N.J.: Prentice-Hall, 1980), p. 308.

46. Duane Schultz, *A History of Modern Psychology*, 2nd ed. (New York: Academic Press, 1975), p. 241.

47. David Thomas, *Naturalism and Social Science: A Post-Empiricist Philosophy of Social Science* (Cambridge: Cambridge University Press, 1979), p. 7.

Chapter Three: Pragmatic Science (*Pages 93–133*)

1. Emile Durkheim, *Suicide: A Study in Sociology*, trans. John A. Spaulding and George Simpson (Glencoe, Ill.: Free Press, 1951).

2. Stephen Toulmin, *The Philosophy of Science: An Introduction* (London: Hutchinson, 1953; reprint, New York: Harper & Row, 1960). See also his influential *Foresight and Understanding: An Enquiry into the Aims of Science* (Bloomington: Indiana University Press, 1961; reprint, New York: Harper & Row, 1963).

Michael Polanyi, *Personal Knowledge: Toward a Post-Critical Philosophy* (Chicago: University of Chicago Press, 1958; reprint, New York: Harper & Row, 1964).

3. Frederick Suppe, "The Search for Philosophic Understanding of Scientific Theories," in Frederick Suppe, ed., *The Structure of Scientific Theories*, 2nd ed. (Urbana: University of Illinois Press, 1977), p. 116.

4. Ibid., p. 117.

5. Peter Achinstein, *Concepts of Science* (Baltimore: Johns Hopkins University Press, 1968), pp. 160–172; Willard van Orman Quine, "Two Dogmas of Empiricism," in *From a Logical Point of View* (Cambridge: Harvard University Press, 1953).

6. Pierre Duhem, *Aim and Structure of Physical Theory*, 1906 (New York: Atheneum, 1962).

7. Mary Hesse, "Is There an Independent Observation Language?," 1970, reprinted as "Theory and Observation," in Mary Hesse, *Revolutions and Reconstructions in the Philosophy of Science* (Bloomington: Indiana University Press, 1980), p. 83.

8. Suppe, "Search for Philosophic Understanding," pp. 221–230.

9. Ibid., p. 230. Semantic discussions concern the relation of signs to their reference; syntactic discussions concern the relation of signs to one another.

10. Richard S. Rudner, *Philosophy of Social Science* (Englewood Cliffs, N.J.: Prentice-Hall, 1966), pp. 47–53.

11. Rom Harré, *The Philosophies of Science: An Introductory Survey* (Oxford: Oxford University Press, 1972), p. 170.

12. B. F. Skinner, *The Behavior of Organisms* (Englewood Cliffs, N.J.: Prentice-Hall, 1938).

13. David Walsh, "Varieties of Positivism," in Paul Filmer et al., eds., *New Directions in Sociological Theory* (London: Collier-Macmillan, 1972), p. 41; Anthony Giddens, *New Rules of Sociological Method: A Positive Critique of Interpretative Sociologies* (New York: Basic Books, 1976), p. 132.

14. Robert K. Merton, *Social Theory and Social Structure*, rev. ed. (Glencoe, Ill.: Free Press, 1957), p. 96.

15. Ernest Nagel, *The Structure of Science: Problems in the Logic of Scientific Explanation* (New York: Harcourt, Brace & World, 1961), pp. 86–87.

16. James L. Kinneavy, in *A Theory of Discourse: The Aims of Discourse* (New York: W. W. Norton, 1971), pp. 111–113, identifies four kinds of gener-

alization from particulars or inductive inferences: (1) perfect or complete induction—the unusual case in which the sample equals the population, i.e., every member of the population or set is examined and thus the generalization is a summary induction; (2) intuitive or philosophic induction—where one generalizes to the universal from the *nature* of the particular, i.e., by examining the structure of one heart one can generalize that this same structure holds for all hearts since it is the nature of the heart to have this structure; (3) mathematical induction—where a property that belongs to the first member of a series and to its successors belongs to all members of the series, i.e., from the members of a series "1, 4, 9, 16" one can inductively infer that the next number is "25"; and (4) probability, ampliative, or problematic induction—where the characteristics of a population are inferred from the characteristics of a sample of that population. Probability induction is what is usually referred to when "induction" without qualification is used.

17. See Philip Brian Bell and Phillip James Staines, *Reasoning and Argument in Psychology* (London: Routledge & Kegan Paul, 1981), pp. 59–61.

18. John Stuart Mill's four inductive methods are discussed in his *System of Logic* (1843). John Losee, in *A Historical Introduction to the Philosophy of Science*, 2nd ed. (Oxford: Oxford University Press, 1980), pp. 148–151, describes the four methods. In the methods instances of antecedent circumstances are compared with the phenomena which appear, and from inductive inference the probable cause of the phenomena is inferred. (1) The method agreement: If ABEF produces abe, ACD produces acd, and ABCE produces afg, then it is probable that A is the cause of a, because A and a are the only aspects of the antecedent circumstances and phenomena which appear in all instances. (2) Method of difference: If ABC produces a, and BC does not produce a, then it is probable that A is an indispensable part of the cause of a. (3) Method of concomitant variations: If A + BC produces a + bc, A ° BC produces a ° b, and A − BC produces a − b, then A and a are causally related, because as A increases and decreases in intensity a also increases and decreases in a concomitant way. (4) Method of residues: If ABC produces abc, and B is the cause of b and C is the cause of c, then A is the cause of a.

19. Benjamin L. Whorf, *Language, Thought, and Reality: Selected Writings of Benjamin Lee Whorf*, ed. J. B. Carroll (Cambridge, Mass.: MIT Press, 1956). See also Geoffrey Sampson, *Schools of Linguistics: Competition and Evolution* (London: Hutchinson, 1980), pp. 81–102.

20. See Nicholas F. Gier, *Wittgenstein and Phenomenology: A Comparative Study of the Later Wittgenstein, Husserl, Heidegger, and Merleau-Ponty* (Albany: State University of New York Press, 1981), pp. 80–83, for a discussion of the term *Darstellung* in place of *Vorstellung*, Kant's term for "representation" or a mental image that stands for, or mirrors, things-in-themselves. The issue Wittgenstein addresses is the relationship between language and mental representation. For a further discussion of this issue see Stephen Toulmin, *Human Understanding: The Collective Use and Evolution of Concepts* (Princeton, N.J.: Princeton University Press, 1972), pp. 192–199.

21. Peter Winch, *The Idea of a Social Science and Its Relation to Philosophy* (London: Routledge & Kegan Paul, 1958), p. 31.

22. See Anthony Giddens, *Central Problems in Social Theory: Action, Structure and Contradiction in Social Analysis* (Berkeley: University of California Press, 1979), where he maintains that Wittgenstein's separation of meaning and reference is overly drawn, especially as interpreted by Winch, who translates the difference into a type of idealism (p. 31). Also Hilary Putnam, *Meaning and the Moral Sciences* (London: Routledge & Kegan Paul, 1978): "It seems to me that the account according to which understanding a language 'consists' in being able to use it (or to translate it into a language one 'can' use) is the only account now in the field. Perhaps Michael Dummett will succeed in developing an alternative account (I know he wants to); but at present I know of no alternative. Second, I don't think 'ability to use' a language has to be thought of as coming from the learning of separate little playlets of the kind Wittgenstein uses in the early pages of the *Investigations* to illustrate the notion of 'language game'. Some Wittgensteinians appear to think of language in this way—as consisting of 'disconnected' 'uses' (e.g. the expression 'that's a different language game' such persons sometimes use), but I don't think Wittgenstein is guilty of this; and, in any case, it is not essential to the doctrine" (p. 97).

23. For Wittgenstein's use of "grammar" see Gier, *Wittgenstein*, p. 206: "Wittgenstein admits that to call what he is doing 'grammar' is to 'express it badly' but he nonetheless goes on to defend his uncommon usage. He says that he is not worried about the agreement of verbs with their subjects because such mistakes are harmless. When he speaks of 'grammar' it means that we are asking 'Does it make any sense to say?' and if it doesn't make any sense, then it is a 'vicious' violation of the rules of grammar." A few pages later Gier quotes William Lawhead: "Any rule is a rule of 'grammar', for Wittgenstein uses 'language' to refer to all 'the various expressions and form-making activities through which persons project themselves toward the world in order to appropriate it, orient themselves toward it, and interact with the human community in ways that are personally and intersubjectively meaningful.'" (p. 209, Gier quoting Lawhead).

24. G. E. Moore, "A Defence of Common Sense," 1923, reprinted in William Barrett and Henry D. Aiken, eds., *Philosophy in the Twentieth Century*, vol. 2, *The Rise of the British Tradition and Contemporary Analytic Philosophy* (New York: Harper & Row, 1962), pp. 145–167.

25. Ludwig Wittgenstein, *On Certainty*, ed. G. E. M. Anscombe and G. H. von Wright, trans. Denis Paul and G. E. M. Anscombe (London: Basil Blackwell, 1969; reprint, New York: Harper & Row, 1972), p. 14e: "The propositions presenting what Moore 'knows' are all of such a kind that it is difficult to imagine 'why' anyone should believe the contrary. E.g. the proposition that Moore has spent his whole life in close proximity to the earth. . . . What could induce me to believe the opposite? Either a memory, or having been told.—Everything that I have seen or heard gives me the

conviction that no man has ever been far from the earth. Nothing in my picture of the world speaks in favour of the opposite."

26. Gerard Radnitzky, "Disappointment and Changes in the Conception of Rationality: Wittgenstein and Popper," paper read at the 10th International Conference on the Unity of the Sciences, Seoul, Korea, November 1981, p. 23.

27. See Paul Feyerabend, *Against Method: Outline of an Anarchistic Theory of Knowledge* (London: Redwood Barn, 1975; Verso Edition, 1978).

28. Gier, *Wittgenstein*, esp. chapter 3, "Life-Philosophy," traces Wittgenstein's links to the Continental tradition of life-philosophy. Life-philosophy held a central position in Wilhelm Dilthey's thought as described above in chapter 2.

29. Winch, *Idea of a Social Science*, pp. 24–25: "I must now attempt a more detailed picture of the way in which the epistemological discussion of man's understanding of reality throws light on the nature of human society and of social relations between men. To that end I propose to give some account of the light which has been shed on the epistemological issue by Wittgenstein's discussion of the concept of *following a rule* in the *Philosophical Investigations*."

30. Ibid., p. 45.

31. Ibid., p. 133.

32. Ibid., p. 121.

33. Peter Winch, "Understanding a Primitive Society," *American Philosophical Quarterly* 1 (1964): 307–324, reprinted in Fred R. Dallmayr and Thomas A. McCarthy, eds., *Understanding and Social Inquiry* (Notre Dame, Ind.: University of Notre Dame Press, 1977), p. 177.

34. See chapter 7 below for discussion of translation and hermeneutics.

35. Winch, "Understanding," p. 176.

36. I. C. Jarvie, "Understanding and Explanation in Sociology and Social Anthropology," in Robert Borger and Frank Cioffi, eds., *Explanation in the Behavioral Sciences* (Cambridge: Cambridge University Press, 1970), pp. 231–248, reprinted in Dallmayr and McCarthy, *Understanding and Social Inquiry*, p. 191.

37. Ibid., p. 195.

38. Hans Reichenbach, *Experience and Prediction* (Chicago: University of Chicago Press, 1938).

39. Toulmin, *Philosophy of Science*: "The adoption of a new theory involves a *language shift*, and one can distinguish between an account of the theory in the new terminology—in 'participant's language'—and an account in which the new terminology is not used but described—an account in 'onlooker's language'. 'Suppose', as Wittgenstein once said, 'that a physicist tells you that he has at last discovered how to see what people look like in the dark, which no one had ever before known. Then you should not be surprised. If he goes on to explain to you that he has discovered how to photograph by infra-red rays, then you have a right to be surprised if you feel like it. But then it is a different kind of surprise, not just a mental

whirl before he reveals to you the discovery of infra-red photography, you should not just gape at him; you should say, 'I don't know what you mean'" (p. 14). See also Toulmin, *Foresight and Understanding*, in which he points out that drastic conceptual changes often accompany the replacement of one inclusive theory by another, especially the changes in the "Ideals of Natural Order."

40. Thomas S. Kuhn, *The Structure of Scientific Revolutions* (Chicago: University of Chicago Press, 1st ed. 1962, 2nd ed. 1970).

41. Polanyi, *Personal Knowledge* (1958); Hanson, *Patterns of Discovery: An Inquiry into the Conceptual Foundations of Science* (Cambridge: Cambridge University Press, 1958; reprint, 1969); Feyerabend, *Against Method*.

42. See Hanson, *Patterns*, p. 13.

43. See Polanyi, *Personal Knowledge*, pp. 56–58.

44. See Percy W. Bridgman, *The Logic of Modern Physics* (New York: Macmillan, 1927), where he proposed that the problem of the meaning of theoretical terms could be solved by defining the terms according to the set of operations used to determine the concept. For example, "the concept of length is therefore fixed when the operations by which length is measured are fixed: that is, the concept of length involves as much as and nothing more than the set of operations by which length is determined. In general, we mean by any concept nothing more than a set of operations; *the concept is synonymous with the corresponding set of operations*" (p. 5). Carl G. Hempel, in "A Logical Appraisal of Operationalism," *Scientific Monthly* 79 (1954): 215–220, reprinted in Hempel (1965a), argued that operational definition is unsatisfactory as an analysis of the meaning of theoretical terms. Suppe, *Structure*, comments, "It seems to be characteristic, but unfortunate, of science to continue to holding philosophical positions long after they are discredited. Thus, for example, Skinner's radical behaviorism, which insists on operational definition, came into prominence and dominated behavioral psychology well after most philosophers had abandoned the doctrine of operational or explicit definitions" (p. 19).

45. Thomas Kuhn, "Second Thoughts on Paradigms," in Suppe, *Structure*, pp. 459–517. In the discussion period after Kuhn presented his paper, Shapere said to Kuhn, "You have got a private group view on your hands, and you thus get into the same kind of relativism that you had in your book" (p. 507). Kuhn's answer proposes an evolutionary theory similar to that described in the next section of this book (p. 508).

46. Dudley Shapere, "Scientific Theories and Their Domains," in Suppe, *Structure*, pp. 518–599; and "Discovery, Rationality, and Progress in Science: A Perspective in the Philosophy of Science," in K. F. Schaffner and R. Cohen, eds., *PSA 1972: Proceedings of the 1972 Biennial Meetings of the Philosophy of Science Association. Boston Studies in the Philosophy of Science*, vol. 20 (Dordrecht, Holland: D. Reidel, 1974). Gerard Radnitzky, *Contemporary Schools of Metascience* (Chicago: Henry Regnery, 1973); Larry Laudan, *Progress and Its Problems: Toward a Theory of Scientific Growth* (Berkeley: University of California Press, 1977); Stephen Toulmin, *Human Understanding: The Col-*

lective Use and Evolution of Concepts (Princeton, N.J.: Princeton University Press, 1972).

47. Suppe, "Afterword—1977," in *Structure*, p. 633.

48. Suppe, "Afterword," p. 657.

49. Karl Popper, *The Logic of Scientific Discovery*, 1934 (New York: Basic Books, 1959). The principle of falsifiability holds that hypotheses in the form of universal statements, such as "All swans are white," can*not* be verified or proved true by examining a sample of instances of swans. All this examination can accomplish is to corroborate the statement, i.e., to affirm that as yet no negative evidence has been found. On the other hand one negative instance, the discovery of a black swan, can disprove or falsify the statement.

50. Imre Lakatos, "Falsification and the Methodology of Scientific Research Programmes," in Imre Lakatos and Alan Musgrave, eds., *Criticism and the Growth of Knowledge: Proceedings of the International Colloquium in the Philosophy of Science, London, 1965*, vol. 4 (Cambridge: Cambridge University Press, 1970).

51. Toulmin, *Human Understanding*, pp. 479–503. As of July, 1982, volumes 2 and 3 have not yet appeared.

52. Dudley Shapere, "On the Introduction of New Hypotheses in Science, and on the Notion of Rationality in Science," unpublished manuscript, quoted in Suppe, "Afterword," p. 704.

53. Paul Ricoeur, "What Is a Text? Explanation and Understanding" in John B. Thompson, ed. and trans., *Hermeneutics and the Human Sciences* (Cambridge: Cambridge University Press, 1981); Jürgen Habermas, *Knowledge and Human Interests*, trans. Jeremy J. Shapiro (Boston: Beacon Press, 1971); Karl-Otto Apel, *Towards a Transformation of Philosophy*, trans. Glyn Adey and David Frisby (London: Routledge & Kegan Paul, 1980); Radnitzky, *Contemporary Schools*.

54. Charles S. Peirce, *Collected Papers of Charles Sanders Peirce*, 8 vols., ed. Charles Hartshorne, Paul Weiss, and Arthur W. Burks (Cambridge: Harvard University Press, 1931–1934, 1958), 1. 99. The convention in citing from this edition uses a number to the left of the decimal point to designate the volume of the *Collected Papers*; the number to the right of the decimal point to designate a numbered section of that volume.

55. Ibid., 6.3.

56. Ibid., 5.582.

57. Ibid., 6.428.

58. Fred N. Kerlinger, in *Foundations of Behavioral Research*, 2nd ed. (New York: Holt, Rinehart & Winston, 1973), refers to Peirce's four ways of knowing, pp. 5–6.

59. Peirce, *Collected Papers*, 1.238.

60. Ibid., 1.234.

61. Ibid., 2.776.

62. Gregory Bateson, in *Mind and Nature: A Necessary Unity* (New York: E. P. Dutton, 1979) notes the importance of the abductive process, pp. 84, 142–143.

63. Ibid., 1.46.

64. Ibid., 1.120.

65. Ibid., 7.198.

66. Jürgen Habermas, *Theory and Practice*, trans. John Viertel (Boston: Beacon Press, 1973), p. 14. See also chapter 7 below for an extended discussion of Habermas's theory of "truth."

67. Peirce, *Collected Papers*, 6.607.

68. See Francis E. Reilly, *Charles Peirce's Theory of Scientific Method* (New York: Fordham University Press, 1970), pp. 118–119.

69. Peirce, *Collected Papers*, 6.495.

70. Ibid., 2.605.

71. Ibid., 5.311.

72. Ibid., 7.336 (note).

73. Radnitzky, "Disappointment."

74. Ibid., p. 19.

75. See the section on Wittgenstein above.

76. I believe that Radnitzky has overstated the point he is making here when he accuses all historicist-relativists of holding to the value of a Cartesian apodictic knowledge. As described below in chapter 6, Heidegger and Gadamer challenge the epistemological assumptions that call for a search for sure foundations as a ground for knowledge. The search for foundations is understood by them to be a culturally conditioned way of coping in the world. Rather than presenting an alternative method of knowing, they call for a shift in the conversation. For a sympathetic presentation of hermeneutics as an alternative to epistemology rather than an alternative epistemology, see Richard Rorty, *Philosophy and the Mirror of Nature* (Princeton: Princeton University Press, 1979).

77. Karl Popper, "The Myth of the Framework," in E. Freeman, ed., *The Abdication of Philosophy: Philosophy and the Public Good. Essays in Honor of Paul Arthur Schilpp* (LaSalle, Ill.: Open Court, 1976); *Objective Knowledge: An Evolutionary Approach*, 5th rev. ed. (Oxford: Clarendon Press, 1979).

78. Radnitzky, "Disappointment," p. 28.

79. Ibid., p. 29.

80. Donald T. Campbell, "Evolutionary Epistemology," in P. Schilpp, ed., *The Philosophy of Karl R. Popper*, 2 vols. (LaSalle, Ill.: Open Court, 1974).

81. Sigmund Koch, "A Possible Psychology for a Possible Postpositivist World," paper read at the symposium on "Psychology in a Postpositivist World: Three Perspectives" at the American Psychological Association 88th Annual Convention, Montreal, September 1980, pp. 18–20.

82. Toulmin, *Human Understanding*, p. 135.

83. Ibid., p. 133.

84. Ibid., p. 134.

Chapter Four: Systems and Structures (*Pages 135–167*)

1. For example, Aristotle, *Politics* (1253a. 18–28): "The state is by nature clearly prior to the family and to the individual, since the whole is of necessity prior to the part; for example, if the whole body be destroyed, there will be no foot or hand, except in an equivocal sense, as we might speak of a stone hand; for when destroyed the hand will be no better than that. But things are defined by their working and power; and we ought not to say that they are the same when they no longer have their proper quality, but only that they have the same name. The proof that the state is a creation of nature and prior to the individual is that the individual, when isolated, is not self-sufficing; and therefore he is like a part in relation to the whole."

2. Hegel's concept of *Verstand* translated as "understanding" refers to an analytic kind of reason used to place entities into categories; this is to be differentiated from Dilthey's concept of *verstehen*, also translated as "understanding," which refers to the kind of knowledge a person has in grasping the meaning of a message spoken or written by another.

3. G. W. F. Hegel, *Science of Logic*, 1812, trans. W. H. Johnston and L. G. Struthers, 2 vols. (New York: Macmillan, 1929), II, p. 350. See also G. E. Moore, "External and Internal Relations," in *Philosophic Studies*, 1922 (London: Routledge & Kegan Paul, 1960).

4. Francis H. Bradley, *Appearance and Reality*, 1893 (Oxford: Oxford University Press, 1962); Alfred A. Taylor, *Elements of Metaphysics* (London: Methuen, 1903); Bernard Bosanquet, *Knowledge and Reality*, 1885 (St. Clair Shores, Mich.: Scholarly Press, 1976).

5. Hans Driesch, *The Science and Philosophy of the Organism*, 1908 (London: A. & C. Black, 1929).

6. Henri Bergson, *Creative Evolution*, 1907, trans. Arthur Mitchell (New York: Random House, 1944). See *Encyclopedia of Philosophy*, 1967 ed., s.v. "Butler, Samuel," by T. A. Goudge.

7. R. B. Haldane and J. S. Haldane, quoted in D. C. Phillips, *Holistic Thought in Social Science* (Stanford, Calif.: Stanford University Press, 1976), pp. 25–27. Phillips argues against holism or systems theory as a preferred approach to science: "The analytic or mechanistic method, in the form expounded by such writers as Madden, Hempel, and Nagel, is such a moderate and reasonable position that no scientist, not even a holist, can avoid putting it into practice. By contrast, holism—taken seriously—is an eminently unworkable doctrine" (p. 123).

8. J. S. Haldane, quoted in Phillips, *Holistic Thought*, p. 26.

9. Edmund Montgomery, "The Unity of the Organic Individual," in *Mind* 7 (1882), quoted in Phillips, *Holistic Thought*, p. 28.

10. Emile Durkheim, *The Rules of Sociological Method*, 1895, trans. Sarah A. Solovay and John H. Mueller, intro. George E. G. Catlin (Chicago: University of Chicago Press, 1938; reprint, New York: Macmillan, 1964). See Anthony Giddens, *Emile Durkheim* (New York: Penguin Books, 1978), pp. 40–41.

11. Durkheim, *Rules*, p. 102.

12. See R. Nevitt Sanford, *Self and Society* (New York: Atherton, 1966); D. Kretch, R. S. Crutchfield, and E. L. Ballachey, *Individual in Society* (New York: McGraw-Hill, 1962).

13. Ludwig von Bertalanffy, *Modern Theories of Development*, 1928 (New York: Harper & Row, 1962).

14. Ludwig von Bertalanffy, *General System Theory: Foundations, Development, Applications* (New York: George Braziller, 1968), p. 37.

15. A. Angyal, *Foundations for a Science of Personality* (Cambridge: Harvard University Press, 1941), excerpts from chapter 8 reprinted in F. E. Emery, ed., *Systems Thinking* (New York: Penguin Books, 1969), pp. 17–29.

16. V. I. Kremyanskiy, "Certain Peculiarities of Organisms as a 'System' from the Point of View of Physics, Cybernetics, and Biology," *General Systems* 5 (1960): 221–230.

17. Ludwig von Bertalanffy, "General System Theory: A Critical Review," in Walter Buckley, ed., *Modern Systems Research for the Behavioral Scientist* (Chicago: Aldine, 1968), pp. 11–30.

18. Ibid., p. 15.

19. Ibid., p. 17.

20. *Encyclopedia of Philosophy*, 1967 ed., s.v. "Functionalism in Sociology," by Dorothy M. Emmet. See also Dorothy M. Emmet, *Function, Purpose and Powers: Some Concepts in the Study of Individuals and Societies*, 1957 (Philadelphia: Temple University Press, 1972). In psychology, "functionalism" refers to a program that arose at the end of the nineteenth century in Chicago under John Dewey and James R. Angell. The "functionalist" program was opposed to the "structuralist" approach of Titchener in that it proposed that psychology should study the operations of the mind in their role of adapting the human organism to the environment rather than dissecting the mind into its structural components. Functionalism in sociology, anthropology, and psychology shares a concern with explaining social practices or mental operations by describing their role or contribution to the goal of the whole.

21. Bronislaw Malinowski, "Anthropology," in *Encyclopedia Britannica*, 13th ed., Supplement I (Chicago, 1926).

22. Ibid., pp. 132–133.

23. Malinowski's understanding that the role of social institutions was to fulfill specific needs of individual members of a society is called "instrumental functionalism." Radcliffe-Brown's understanding that institutions served the needs of the social system as a whole is called "structural-functionalism." See A. R. Radcliffe-Brown, *Structure and Function in Primitive Society* (Glencoe, Ill.: Free Press, 1952).

24. Anthony Giddens, *Studies in Social and Political Theory* (New York: Basic Books, 1977), p. 98.

25. Robert K. Merton, "Manifest and Latent Functions," in *Social Theory and Social Structure*, rev. ed. (Glencoe, Ill.: Free Press, 1957), p. 43.

26. Carl G. Hempel, "The Logic of Functional Analysis," 1959, reprinted in May Brodbeck, ed., *Readings in the Philosophy of Science* (New York: Macmillan, 1968), pp. 179–210.

27. See chapter 3 above.

28. Ervin Laszlo, *Introduction to Systems Philosophy: Toward a New Paradigm of Contemporary Thought* (New York: Gordon & Breach, 1972; reprint, New York: Harper & Row, 1973), p. 119. See also Jeffrey S. Stamps, *Holonomy: A Human Systems Theory* (Seaside, Calif.: Intersystems, 1980) for an application of systems theory to the human realm.

29. Miriam Glucksmann, *Structuralist Analysis in Contemporary Social Thought: A Comparison of the Theories of Claude Lévi-Strauss and Louis Althusser* (London: Routledge & Kegan Paul, 1974), p. 15.

30. Jean Piaget, *Structuralism*, 1968, ed. and trans. Chaninah Maschler (New York: Basic Books, 1970), pp. 5–16.

31. Ferdinand de Saussure, *Course in General Linguistics*, 1907–1911, ed. Charles Bally and Albert Sechehaye, trans. Wade Baskin (New York: McGraw-Hill, 1966).

32. Claude Lévi-Strauss, *Structural Anthropology*, 1958, trans. Claire Jacobson and Brooke G. Schoepf (New York: Basic Books, 1963).

33. See Jonathan Culler, *Ferdinand de Saussure* (New York: Penguin Books, 1977), p. 101.

34. Saussure, *Course*, p. 117.

35. Example from Culler, *Saussure*, p. 19.

36. Saussure, *Course*, p. 110.

37. Ibid., p. 14.

38. Ibid., p. 123.

39. Ibid., p. 114.

40. Ibid., p. 73.

41. See Geoffrey Sampson, *Schools of Linguistics: Competition and Evolution* (London: Hutchinson, 1980), pp. 57–80.

42. Roman O. Jakobson, C. G. M. Fant, and M. Halle, *Preliminaries to Speech Analysis*, 1952 (Cambridge, Mass.: MIT Press, 1965).

43. Noam Chomsky, *Cartesian Linguistics* (New York: Harper & Row, 1966), p. 67.

44. Lévi-Strauss, *Structural Anthropology*, p. 33.

45. Ibid., p. 33.

46. Compare Charles S. Peirce, the American founder of semiology, who proposed the notion of a triad of signs: the icon—for example, a painting or diagram which resembles the subject it represents (*Collected Papers*, 2.247); the index—for example, a knock on the door which is an index of someone's presence, or smoke as an index of fire—which has an actual, sequential relationship to the subject it represents (2.248); and the symbol—for example, language, where the word "tree" represents the object "tree"—in which the relationship between sign and referent is arbitrary (2.249).

47. Lévi-Strauss, *Structural Anthropology*, p. 21.

48. Jean Piaget, *The Origins of Intelligence in Children* (New York: International Universities Press, 1952), p. 7.

49. Henri Ey, *Consciousness: A Phenomenological Study of Being Conscious and Becoming Conscious*, 1963, trans. John H. Flodstrom (Bloomington: Indiana University Press, 1978), p. 123.

50. Jason Brown, *Mind, Brain, and Consciousness: The Neuropsychology of Cognition* (New York: Academic Press, 1977).

51. See Richard Macksey and Eugenio Donato, eds., *The Structuralist Controversy: The Languages of Criticism and the Sciences of Man* (Baltimore: Johns Hopkins University Press, 1970).

52. Walter Buckley, "Foreword," in Buckley, *Modern Systems Research*, p. xxii.

Chapter Five: Human Action *(Pages 169–199)*

1. Carl G. Hempel, "The Function of General Laws in History," 1942, reprinted in P. Gardiner, ed., *Theories of History* (Urbana: University of Illinois Press, 1959).

2. See Frederick A. Olafson, *The Dialectic of Action: A Philosophical Interpretation of History and the Humanities* (Chicago: University of Chicago Press, 1979), chapter 1.

3. Donald Davidson, "Actions, Reasons, and Causes," 1963, reprinted in Donald Davidson, *Essays on Actions and Events* (Oxford: Oxford University Press, 1980), pp. 3–19. See Davidson, "Hempel on Explaining Action," in Davidson, *Essays*, p. 262: "On one issue, my early paper ["Actions, Reasons, and Causes"] and Hempel's earlier one did differ. I emphasized the role of *causality* in our understanding of action, urging that an appropriate belief and desire could explain, and be the reasons for, an action only if they caused it. I don't think Hempel objects to this idea, and indeed in the expanded version of his A.P.A. address which appeared as part of the final essay in his 1965 book he explicitly says that 'the offer of a bribe . . . may be said, in everyday parlance, to have caused the explanandum event (treason)'. The difference in our accounts, if there really is one, concerns the exact way in which *laws* are involved when we explain actions by mentioning the agent's reasons."

4. William Dray, *Laws and Explanation in History* (Oxford: Oxford University Press, 1957).

5. Richard Taylor, "Comments on a Mechanistic Conception of Purposefulness," and "Purposeful and Non-Purposeful Behavior: A Rejoinder," *Philosophy of Science* 17 (1950), reprinted in Walter Buckley, ed., *Modern Systems Research for the Behavioral Scientist: A Sourcebook* (Chicago: Aldine, 1968), pp. 226–231, 238–242.

6. Charles Taylor, *The Explanation of Behavior* (London: Routledge & Kegan Paul, 1964).

7. Ludwig Wittgenstein, *Philosophical Investigations*, trans. G. E. M. Anscombe (New York: Macmillan, 1953; 3rd ed., 1968), p. 161.

8. Georg Henrik von Wright, *Explanation and Understanding* (Ithaca, N.Y.: Cornell University Press, 1971), pp. 59–60. The term "intentional" is used in this context to refer to the actor's volition or purpose. This use is to be distinguished from the phenomenological use of the term as the characteristic of consciousness to be open toward contents of some sort.

9. Carl G. Hempel, "Explanation in Science and History," 1962, reprinted in P. H. Nidditch, ed., *The Philosophy of Science* (Oxford University Press, 1968), p. 64.

10. See Frank Cunningham, *Objectivity in Social Science* (Toronto: University of Toronto Press, 1973), pp. 3–23.

11. See B. F. Skinner, *Science and Human Behavior* (New York: Macmillan, 1953): "An even more common practice is to explain behavior in terms of an inner agent which lacks physical dimensions and is called 'mental' or 'psychic.' The purest form of the psychic explanation is seen in the animism of primitive peoples. From the immobility of the body after death it is inferred that a spirit responsible for movement has departed. The *enthusiastic* person is, as the etymology of the word implies, energized by a 'god within.' It is only a modest refinement to attribute every feature of the behavior of the physical organism to a corresponding feature of the 'mind' or of some inner 'personality.' The inner man is regarded as driving the body very much as the man at the steering wheel drives a car. The inner man wills an action, the outer executes it. . . . The fictional nature of this form of inner cause is shown by the ease with which the mental process is discovered to have just the properties needed to account for the behavior. . . . In all this it is obvious that the mind and the ideas, together with their special characteristics, are being invented on the spot to provide spurious explanations. A science of behavior can hope to gain very little from so cavalier a practice. Since mental or psychic events are asserted to lack the dimensions of physical science, we have an additional reason for rejecting them" (pp. 29–31).

12. See chapter 2 for the nomological-deductive definition of "cause" as a relationship between two or more events that is sufficient, necessary, and sequential.

13. See Jonathan L. Freedman, David O. Sears, and J. Merrill Carlsmith, *Social Psychology*, 3rd ed. (Englewood Cliffs, N.J.: Prentice-Hall, 1978); Arnold L. Glass, Keith J. Holyoak, and John L. Santa, *Cognition* (Reading, Mass.: Addison-Wesley, 1979).

14. Lawrence H. Davis, *Theory of Action* (Englewood Cliffs, N.J.: Prentice-Hall, 1979), p. 11: "Actually philosophers disagree as to whether causes and effects are best thought of as events, states of affairs, conditions, or something else. John L. Mackie . . . seems to favor conditions. Donald Davidson is perhaps the leading exponent of causation as a relation strictly between events."

15. See Jerome A. Shaffer, *Philosophy of Mind* (Englewood Cliffs, N.J.: Prentice-Hall, 1968), pp. 37–76, for a discussion of the traditional approaches to the mind–body problem.

16. Alvin I. Goldman, *A Theory of Human Action* (Princeton, N.J.: Princeton University Press, 1970), p. 80.

17. See Gilbert Ryle, *The Concept of Mind* (New York: Barnes & Noble, 1949), pp. 62–69. Ryle maintains that the notion of "volition" is a holdover from the idea of a "ghost in the machine." Talk about "willing" something to happen is misinterpreted to refer to a mental act; instead such talk belongs to language games about responsibility and accountability for actions.

18. A. I. Melden, *Free Action* (London: Routledge & Kegan Paul, 1961).

19. Davidson, "Actions, Reasons, and Causes."

20. H. L. A. Hart and A. M. Honoré, *Causation in the Law* (Oxford: Oxford University Press, 1959), p. 52.

21. Davidson, "Actions, Reasons, and Causes," p. 16.

22. Ibid., p. 18.

23. Richard Taylor, *Metaphysics,* Foundations of Philosophy Series (Englewood Cliffs, N.J.: Prentice-Hall, 1963), p. 43.

24. See Davis, *Theory of Action,* pp. 109–123.

25. Dray, *Laws and Explanation.*

26. Ibid., p. 122.

27. Richard Taylor, *Metaphysics,* p. 51.

28. Ibid., p. 52.

29. Charles Taylor, *The Explanation of Behavior,* ch. 1.

30. Davis, *Theory of Action,* p. 103.

31. Joseph F. Rychlak, *The Psychology of Rigorous Humanism* (New York: Wiley, 1977).

32. Ibid., p. 508.

33. Arturo Rosenblueth, Norbert Wiener, and Julian Bigelow, "Behavior, Purpose, and Teleology," *Philosophy of Science* 10 (1943): 18–24, reprinted in Walter Buckley, ed., *Modern Systems Research for the Behavioral Scientist: A Sourcebook* (Chicago: Aldine, 1968), pp. 221–225.

34. Richard B. Braithwaite, *Scientific Explanation: A Study of the Function of Theory, Probability and Law in Science* (Cambridge: Cambridge University Press, 1955), chapter 9; Ernest Nagel, *The Structure of Science: Problems in the Logic of Scientific Explanation* (New York: Harcourt, Brace & World, 1961), pp. 401–428. Von Wright says: "Braithwaite expressly takes the view that teleological explanation, both of intentional goal-directed activities and purposeful behavior generally, is reducible to (forms of) causal explanation. Nagel's attitude to the question of reduction of teleology to causal (nonteleological) explanatory patterns is more guarded. It seems a fair rendering of Nagel's position to say that he considers teleological explanations in *Biology* 'reducible' to causal explanations" (*Explanation and Understanding,* p. 177).

35. Von Wright, *Explanation and Understanding,* pp. 22–23.

36. See Braithwaite, *Scientific Explanation.*

37. George Sommerhoff, *Analytical Biology* (London: Oxford University Press, 1950); also sharing this view are Braithwaite, Nagel, and Morton Beckner.

38. Example is from *Encyclopedia of Philosophy*, 1967 ed., s.v. "Teleology," by Morton Beckner.

39. See Arthur Koestler, *The Ghost in the Machine* (New York: Macmillan, 1967), for a summary of this position and of his notion of "holon," a neologism taken from *Holos* or whole and *On*, which, as in pro*ton* or neut*ron*, suggests a particle or part (p. 48).

40. See Edna Heidbreder, "Functionalism," in David L. Krantz, ed., *Schools of Psychology: A Symposium* (New York: Appleton-Century-Crofts, 1969), reprinted in Mary Henle, Julian Jaynes, and John J. Sullivan, eds., *Historical Conceptions of Psychology* (New York: Springer, 1973), pp. 276–285.

41. Melden, *Free Action*; Anthony Kenny, *Action, Emotion, and Will* (London: Routledge & Kegan Paul, 1963); G. Elizabeth M. Anscombe, *Intention* (Oxford: Basil Blackwell, 1957; 2nd ed., 1963).

42. Ryle, *Concept of Mind*, p. 109.

43. J. L. Austin, "Performative Utterances," in J. O. Urmson and G. J. Warnock, eds., *J. L. Austin: Philosophical Papers* (Oxford: Oxford University Press, 1961), pp. 220–239; and J. L. Austin, *How to Do Things with Words*, ed. J. O. Urmson and Marian Sbisa, 2nd ed. (Cambridge: Harvard University Press, 1975).

44. P. F. Strawson, "Truth," *Analysis* 9 (1949), reprinted in Margaret MacDonald, ed., *Philosophy and Analysis* (New York: Philosophical Library, 1955).

45. See Paul Ricoeur, "Philosophy," in UNESCO, *Main Trends in the Social and Human Sciences*, vol. 2 (The Hague: UNESCO, 1978), pp. 1073–1567.

46. Georg Henrik von Wright, "The Logic of Practical Discourse," in Raymond Klibansky, ed., *Contemporary Philosophy: A Survey*, vol. 1 (Florence: La Nuova, 1968).

47. Ricoeur, *Main Trends*, p. 1388.

48. See Ernest R. Hilgard, Richard C. Atkinson, and Rita L. Atkinson, *Introduction to Psychology*, 6th ed. (New York: Harcourt, Brace, Jovanovich, 1975), pp. 330–331.

49. A. N. Prior, *Time and Modality* (Oxford: Oxford University Press, 1957); see Ricoeur, *Main Trends*, p. 1390.

50. See Ricoeur, *Main Trends*, p. 1388.

51. Ibid., pp. 1390–1391. See also Hans-Georg Gadamer, *Reason in the Age of Science*, trans. Frederick G. Lawrence (Cambridge, Mass.: MIT Press, 1981), for a thorough discussion of practical reason (*phronesis*) and its grounding in Aristotle's ethics. Gadamer relates the use of practical reasoning to hermeneutics.

52. Jürgen Habermas, "Postscript to *Knowledge and Human Interests*," *Philosophy of Social Sciences* 3 (1973): 157–189, pp. 171–172.

Chapter Six: Existential-Phenomenological and Hermeneutic Systems (*Pages 201–240*)

1. Gerard Radnitzky, *Contemporary Schools of Metascience* (Chicago: Henry Regnery, 1973).

2. Joseph J. Kockelmans, "Theoretical Problems in Phenomenological Psychology," in Maurice Natanson, ed., *Phenomenology and the Social Sciences*, vol. 1 (Evanston, Ill.: Northwestern University Press, 1973), p. 246.

3. Ibid., p. 252.

4. Kockelmans uses the term *functional* in its mathematical rather than sociological sense. In sociology, "function" refers to the usefulness of a role or institution in accomplishing the "purpose" of the whole social system. In mathematics, "function" refers to a relationship in which a variable is so related to another variable that for each value assumed by one there is a value determined for the other. For example, in $y = 3x + 7$, if y is 10, x is 1; if y is 13, x is 2; etc.

5. Kockelmans, "Theoretical Problems," p. 257.

6. See Thomas Luckmann, ed., *Phenomenology and Sociology: Selected Readings* (New York: Penguin Books, 1978).

7. Harold Garfinkel, *Studies in Ethnomethodology* (Englewood Cliffs, N.J.: Prentice-Hall, 1967).

8. Amedeo Giorgi, W. F. Fisher, and Rolf Von Eckartsberg, eds., *Duquesne Studies in Phenomenological Psychology*, vol. 1 (Pittsburgh: Duquesne University Press, 1971); Paul F. Colaizzi, *Reflection and Research in Psychology* (Dubuque, Ia.: Kendall Hunt, 1973).

9. Ronald S. Valle and Mark King, eds., *Existential-Phenomenological Alternatives for Psychology* (New York: Oxford University Press, 1978).

10. Alfred Schutz, *Collected Papers*, ed. Maurice Natanson, 3 vols. (The Hague: Martinus Nijhoff, 1973); Maurice Merleau-Ponty, *Phenomenology of Perception*, trans. Colin Smith (New York: Humanities Press, 1962).

11. See Don Ihde, *Experimental Phenomenology: An Introduction* (New York: Putnam's, 1977) for the use of visual examples as a means for grasping the essential notions of phenomenology.

12. Erazim V. Kohák, *Idea and Experience: Edmund Husserl's Project of Phenomenology in "Ideas I"* (Chicago: University of Chicago Press, 1978), pp. 13–19, 216 n. 14.

13. Merleau-Ponty, *Perception*.

14. Merleau-Ponty, *Perception*, pp. 67–72; Richard M. Zaner, *The Problem of Embodiment: Some Contributions to a Phenomenology of the Body* (The Hague: Martinus Nijhoff, 1964), pp. 129–197; Elizabeth A. Behnke, "The Philosopher's Body," *Somatics*, Spring/Summer, 1982, pp. 44–46.

15. Franz Brentano, *Psychology from an Empirical Standpoint*, 1874, ed. Linda L. McAlister, trans. Antos C. Rancurello, D. B. Terrell, and Linda L. McAlister (New York: Humanities Press, 1973), pp. 155–270; Antos C. Rancurello, *A Study of Franz Brentano* (New York: Academic Press, 1968), pp. 41–66. See also Eugene T. Gendlin, "Experiential Phenomenology," in

Maurice Natanson, ed., *Phenomenology and the Social Sciences*, vol. 1, pp. 281–319.

16. Richard M. Zaner, *The Context of Self: A Phenomenological Inquiry Using Medicine as a Clue* (Athens: Ohio University Press, 1981), p. 245. See Merleau-Ponty, *Perception*, p. 228, for perception under the influence of mescaline, and p. 244 for Stratton's experiments with inversion glasses.

17. Eugène Minkowski, *Lived Time: Phenomenological and Psychopathological Studies*, 1933, trans. Nancy Metzel (Evanston, Ill.: Northwestern University Press, 1970).

18. Erwin W. Straus, "Aesthesiology and Hallucinations," 1948, trans. Erwin W. Straus and Bayard Morgan, in Rollo May, Ernest Angel, and Henri F. Ellenberger, eds., *Existence: A New Dimension in Psychiatry and Psychology* (New York: Basic Books, 1958), pp. 139–169.

19. V. E. von Gebsattel, "The World of the Compulsive," 1938, trans. Sylvia Koppel and Ernest Angel, in May, Angel, and Ellenberger, *Existence*, pp. 170–187.

20. Ernest Keen, "Psychopathology," in Valle and King, *Existential-Phenomenological Alternatives*, pp. 234–264.

21. Alfred Schutz and Thomas Luckmann, *The Structures of the Life-World*, trans. Richard M. Zaner and H. Tristram Engelhardt, Jr. (Evanston, Ill.: Northwestern University Press, 1973). See Luckmann, *Phenomenology and Sociology*: "It is, however, undoubtedly the lawyer-economist Alfred Schutz, the student of Max Weber and Edmund Husserl and the friend of Aron Gurwitsch, who is the central figure in the phenomenological reorientation of social theory. The direct influence of his work on sociology in the United States, the European continent and, recently, Great Britain is considerable. Furthermore, the thought of Schutz influenced Harold Garfinkel and Aron Cicourel and is thus one of the sources of what came to be known as ethnomethodology. His teaching at the New School for Social Research in New York City decisively influenced a whole generation of students of philosophy and sociology which included among others Maurice Natanson in the former and Peter Berger in the latter field" (p. 12).

22. Quoted in George Walsh, "Introduction," in Alfred Schutz, *The Phenomenology of the Social World*, trans. George Walsh and Frederick Lehnert (Evanston, Ill.: Northwestern University Press, 1967), p. xxiv.

23. Ibid., p. xxviii.

24. Examples of research using the methods developed by Giorgi are contained in the three volumes of the *Duquesne Studies in Phenomenological Psychology* (1971, 1975, 1979; see note 8).

25. Amedeo Giorgi, *Psychology as a Human Science: A Phenomenologically Based Approach* (New York: Harper & Row, 1970), p. 181.

26. Maurice Merleau-Ponty, *The Structure of Behavior*, 1942, trans. Alden L. Fisher (Boston: Beacon Press, 1967), p. 184.

27. Amedeo Giorgi, "The Relations among Level, Type, and Structure and Their Importance for Social Science Theorizing: A Dialogue with Schutz," in Giorgi et al., *Duquesne Studies.*, vol. 3., p. 83.

28. Ibid., p. 87.

29. Ibid., p. 91.

30. Emily Stevick, "An Empirical Investigation of Anger," in Giorgi et al., *Duquesne Studies*, vol. 1., pp. 132–148.

31. Stevick, "Anger," p. 144.

32. Giorgi et al., *Duquesne Studies*, vol. 3., p. 179.

33. Ibid., p. 179.

34. Ibid., p. 180.

35. Aron Gurwitsch, *The Field of Consciousness* (Pittsburgh: Duquesne University Press, 1964); see Richard M. Zaner, *The Context of Self: A Phenomenological Inquiry Using Medicine as a Clue* (Athens: Ohio University Press, 1981).

36. H. P. Rickman, *Understanding and the Human Studies* (London: Heinemann, 1967), p. 30.

37. See Richard E. Palmer, *Hermeneutics: Interpretation Theory in Schleiermacher, Dilthey, Heidegger, and Gadamer* (Evanston, Ill.: Northwestern University Press, 1969), p. 35.

38. Wilhelm Dilthey, "The Rise of Hermeneutics," 1900, trans. Thomas Hall, in Paul Connerton, ed., *Critical Sociology* (New York: Penguin Books, 1976), pp. 104–116.

39. Quoted in Palmer, *Hermeneutics*, p. 84.

40. Quoted in Josef Bleicher, *Contemporary Hermeneutics: Hermeneutics as Method, Philosophy and Critique* (London: Routledge & Kegan Paul, 1980), p. 14.

41. Ibid., p. 19.

42. Quoted in Michael Ermarth, *Wilhelm Dilthey: The Critique of Historical Reason* (Chicago: University of Chicago Press, 1978), p. 303.

43. Quoted in Bleicher, *Contemporary Hermeneutics*, p. 23.

44. Quoted in Nicholas F. Gier, *Wittgenstein and Phenomenology: A Comparative Study of the Later Wittgenstein, Husserl, Heidegger, and Merleau-Ponty* (Albany: State University of New York Press, 1981), p. 33.

45. Philip Wheelwright, *The Burning Fountain: A Study in the Language of Symbolism* (Bloomington: Indiana University Press, 1954), pp. 24–29.

46. Bleicher, *Contemporary Hermeneutics*, p. 23.

47. See Theodore Plantinga, *Historical Understanding in the Thought of Wilhelm Dilthey* (Toronto: University of Toronto Press, 1980) for an extensive discussion of the importance of this change in Dilthey's position. Plantinga holds that Dilthey was side-tracked into considering psychology and the study of "inner experience" as the ground for the human sciences. It was in the post-1900 period that Dilthey gave up on basing the human sciences on the introspective study of one's own consciousness and turned to the creations and expressions of "life," that is the "objective spirit" as the data base for human science. It was this turn from psychology that brought forth the emphasis on hermeneutics as the approach to understanding these expressions. Thus introspection was the method for exploring the data of "life" while Dilthey held that the source of the data was the inner experience

of a person's consciousness; when Dilthey changed to holding that the expressions of life should be taken as the data of the human sciences, then the method for understanding these expressions was to be hermeneutics.

48. Quoted in Ermarth, *Wilhelm Dilthey*, p. 210.

49. Ibid., p. 210.

50. Ibid., p. 211.

51. Ibid., p. 289.

52. See Richard Rorty, *Philosophy and the Mirror of Nature* (Princeton: Princeton University Press, 1979).

53. Ibid., p. 6.

54. See Keith Hoeller, "Phenomenology, Psychology, and Science," *Review of Existential Psychology and Psychiatry* 16 (1–3) (1978–1979): 147–175.

54a. E. D. Hirsch, Jr., *Validity in Interpretation* (New Haven, Conn.: Yale University Press, 1967), p. 259.

55. Martin Heidegger, *What Is a Thing?*, trans. W. B. Barton and Vera Deutsch (Chicago: Henry Regnery, 1967), p. 10.

56. See Paul Ricoeur, *Interpretation Theory: Discourse and the Surplus of Meaning* (Fort Worth: Texas Christian University Press, 1976), p. 78.

57. Palmer, *Hermeneutics*, p. 48.

58. Emilio Betti, *Hermeneutics as the General Methodology of the Geisteswissenschaften*, 1962, reprinted and trans. in Bleicher, *Contemporary Hermeneutics*, pp. 51–94.

59. Betti, *Hermeneutics*, p. 79.

60. Hirsch, *Validity*, p. viii.

61. Ibid., p. 164.

62. Ibid., pp. 173–176.

63. Ricoeur, *Interpretation Theory*, p. 79; see Karl Popper, *The Logic of Scientific Discovery*, 1934 (New York: Basic Books, 1959), pp. 251–281.

64. Ricoeur, *Interpretation Theory*, p. 78.

65. E. D. Hirsch, Jr., "Gadamer's Theory of Interpretation," *Review of Metaphysics*, March 1965, reprinted as Appendix II in Hirsch, *Validity*, p. 245.

66. Ibid., pp. 244–245.

67. Ibid., p. 245.

68. Paul Ricoeur, *Freedom and Nature: The Voluntary and the Involuntary*, 1950, trans. Erazim V. Kohák (Evanston, Ill.: Northwestern University Press, 1966).

69. Paul Ricoeur, *Freud and Philosophy: An Essay on Interpretation*, trans. Denis Savage (New Haven, Conn.: Yale University Press, 1970).

70. Paul Ricoeur, "The Model of the Text: Meaningful Action Considered as a Text," 1971, reprinted in John B. Thompson, ed. and trans., *Hermeneutics and the Human Sciences* (Cambridge: Cambridge University Press, 1981), pp. 197–221.

71. Ibid., p. 206.

72. Ibid., p. 218; see also "Structure and Hermeneutics," 1963, trans. Kathleen McLaughlin and reprinted in Paul Ricoeur, *The Conflict of Inter-*

pretations: Essays in Hermeneutics, ed. Don Ihde (Evanston, Ill.: Northwestern University Press, 1974), pp. 27–61.

73. Clifford Geertz, "Thick Description: Toward an Interpretive Theory of Culture," in *The Interpretation of Cultures* (New York: Basic Books, 1973), pp. 3–30.

74. Paul Rabinow and William M. Sullivan, eds., *Interpretive Social Science: A Reader* (Berkeley: University of California Press, 1979), p. 1.

75. Joseph J. Kockelmans, "Toward an Interpretative or Hermeneutic Social Science," *Graduate Faculty Philosophy Journal: New School for Social Research* 5(1) (1975): 78.

76. Charles Taylor, "Interpretation and the Sciences of Man," *Review of Metaphysics* 25 (1971): 3–34, 45–51, reprinted in Fred R. Dallmayr and Thomas A. McCarthy, eds., *Understanding and Social Inquiry* (Notre Dame, Ind.: University of Notre Dame Press, 1977), p. 105.

77. Ibid., p. 128.

78. Ibid., p. 129.

79. Ibid., p. 130.

80. Ibid., p. 127.

Chapter Seven: Human Science Research (*Pages 241–281*)

1. E. D. Hirsch, Jr., *Validity in Interpretation* (New Haven, Conn.: Yale University Press, 1967), p. 175.

2. Ibid., p. 180.

3. Ricoeur, *Interpretation Theory*, p. 78.

4. Ibid., p. 100.

5. Jürgen Habermas, *Theory and Practice*, 1971, trans. John Viertel (Boston: Beacon Press, 1973), pp. 16–32.

6. See Thomas McCarthy, *The Critical Theory of Jürgen Habermas* (Cambridge, Mass.: MIT Press, 1978), pp. 303–304; Thomas McCarthy, "A Theory of Communicative Competence," *Philosophy of the Social Sciences* 3 (1973): 135–156, reprinted in Paul Connerton, ed., *Critical Sociology* (New York: Penguin Books, 1976), pp. 470–497.

7. Stephen Toulmin, *The Uses of Argument* (Cambridge: Cambridge University Press, 1958).

8. McCarthy, *Critical Theory*, p. 305.

9. Ibid., p. 305.

10. Gadamer disagrees with Habermas on the grounds that we do not operate in such ideal speech situations but in real, finite situations. Although the notion of such an ideal speech situation may serve as a regulative ideal, it may also serve as a regulative illusion that we have the possibility of some kind of transparent communication going on when we argue for one knowledge claim or another.

11. See "Evolutionary Epistemology" in chapter 4.

12. See "Charles S. Peirce" in chapter 4.

13. James Ogilvy, *Many Dimensional Man: Decentralizing Self, Society, and the Sacred* (New York: Oxford University Press, 1977).

14. Ibid., p. 348.

15. Ibid., p. 191.

16. Noam Chomsky, *Aspects of the Theory of Syntax* (Cambridge, Mass.: MIT Press, 1965), pp. 18–21.

17. Norman K. Denzin, *Sociological Methods: A Source Book*, 2nd ed. (New York: McGraw-Hill, 1978), pp. 339–380.

18. Gregory Bateson, *Mind and Nature: A Necessary Unity* (New York: E. P. Dutton, 1979), pp. 68–88.

19. Kenneth J. Shapiro and Irving E. Alexander, *The Experience of Introversion: An Integration of Phenomenological, Empirical, and Jungian Approaches* (Durham, N.C.: Duke University Press, 1975).

20. Eugene T. Gendlin, *Focusing*, 1978 (New York, Bantam Books, 1981).

21. See Radnitzky, *Contemporary Schools of Metascience*, pp. 226–227.

22. Jürgen Habermas, *Knowledge and Human Interests*, trans. Jeremy J. Shapiro (Boston: Beacon Press, 1970), pp. 214–245.

23. Donald Polkinghorne, "The Reductions and Existence: Bases for Epistemology," in Anna-Teresa Tymieniecka, ed., *Analecta Husserliana: The Yearbook of Phenomenological Research* (Dordreckt, Holland: D. Reidel, forthcoming).

24. Aron Gurwitsch, *The Field of Consciousness* (Pittsburgh: Duquesne University Press, 1964).

25. Richard M. Zaner, *The Context of Self: A Phenomenological Inquiry Using Medicine as a Clue* (Athens: Ohio University Press, 1981), p. 68.

26. Paul Ricoeur, *The Rule of Metaphor: Multi-Disciplinary Studies of the Creation of Meaning in Language*, 1975, trans. Robert Czerny (Toronto: University of Toronto Press, 1977).

27. Jason Brown, *Mind, Brain, and Consciousness: The Neuropsychology of Cognition* (New York: Academic Press, 1977).

28. Stephan Strasser, *Phenomenology of Feeling: An Essay on the Phenomena of Heart*, trans. Robert E. Wood (Pittsburgh: Duquesne University Press, 1977), pp. 159–164.

29. Alfred Schutz, "Common-Sense and Scientific Interpretation of Human Action," in *Collected Papers*, ed. Maurice Natanson, vol. 1 (The Hague: Martinus Nijhoff, 1973), pp. 5–6.

30. Ulric Neisser, *Cognitive Psychology* (New York: Appleton-Century-Crofts, 1967), quoted in Arnold L. Glass, Keith J. Holyoak, and John L. Santa, *Cognition* (Reading, Mass.: Addison-Wesley, 1979), p. 343.

31. A. Attneave, "Transfer of Experience with a Class Schema to Identification Learning of Patterns and Shapes," *Journal of Experimental Psychology* 54 (1957): 81–88, cited in Glass , Holyoak, and Santa, *Cognition*, p. 344.

32. Glass, Holyoke, and Santa, *Cognition*, p. 341.

33. See Milič Čapek, *Philosophical Impact of Contemporary Physics* (Princeton, N.J.: D. Van Nostrand, 1961); Hans Jonas, *The Phenomenon of Life: Toward a Philosophical Biology* (Westport, Conn.: Greenwood Press, 1966).

34. See J. H. van den Berg, *The Changing Nature of Man: Introduction to a Historical Psychology*, 1961, trans. H. F. Cross (New York: Dell Books, 1964).

35. Stephan Strasser, *Phenomenology and the Human Sciences* (Pittsburgh: Duquesne University Press, 1963), p. 7.

36. See chapter 2 for a discussion of the "introspectionist" controversy.

37. Paul Ricoeur, *Interpretation Theory: Discourse and the Surplus of Meaning* (Fort Worth: Texas Christian University Press, 1976), pp. 20–21.

38. Jacques Derrida, *Of Grammatology*, trans. Gayatri C. Spivak (Baltimore: Johns Hopkins University Press, 1974).

39. See chapter 6; John R. Searle, *Speech Acts: An Essay in the Philosophy of Language* (Cambridge: Cambridge University Press, 1969).

40. However, even in a face-to-face speech situation, we can fail to say what we mean. We can be so influenced by the situation that we do not say directly what we mean. If we fear the other's response we may say something other than what we mean.

41. Sidney M. Jourard, "Experimenter-Subject Dialogue: Paradigm for a Human Science of Psychology," in Sidney M. Jourard, ed., *Disclosing Man to Himself* (Princeton, N.J.: Van Nostrand, 1968), pp. 18–34.

42. Michael Scriven, *Reasoning* (New York: McGraw-Hill, 1976), pp. 104–108.

43. Researchers are not always able to gather random samples from a population. When they do, the research can be called a "true-experiment." When samples are not random, such as comparing performances of members of two classrooms, the research is called a "quasi-experiment." Research which is not able to manipulate the independent variable, such as research correlating cancer and smoking, is *ex post facto* or nonexperimental research.

44. Gary R. Gruber and Edward C. Gruber, *Preparation for the Miller Analogies Test* (New York: Monarch Press, 1972).

45. See Amedeo Giorgi, "The Relations among Level, Type, and Structure and Their Importance for Social Science Theorizing: A Dialogue with Schutz," in Amedeo Giorgi, R. Knowles, and D. L. Smith, eds., *Duquesne Studies in Phenomenological Psychology*, vol. 3 (Pittsburgh: Duquesne University Press, 1979), pp. 81–96.

46. Edward S. Casey, *Imagining: A Phenomenological Study* (Bloomington: Indiana University Press, 1976).

47. Casey, "Comparative Phenomenology of Mental Activity."

48. Casey, *Imagining*, p. 25.

49. Ibid., p. 92.

50. Ibid., p. 95.

51. Ibid., p. 102.

52. Ibid., p. 103.

53. Ibid., p. 110.

54. Ibid., p. 118.

55. Ibid., p. 116.

56. Ibid., pp. 200–201.

57. Ibid., p. 178.

58. Ibid., pp. 203–233.

59. Paul Richer, "A Phenomenological Analysis of the Perception of Geometric Illusions," *Journal of Phenomenological Psychology* 8 (1978): 133.

60. Ibid., p. 134.

61. Ibid., p. 123.

62. Ibid., pp. 124–125.

63. Ibid., p. 126.

64. Ibid., p. 131.

65. Ibid., p. 125.

66. Ibid., p. 131.

67. Ibid., p. 131.

68. These two examples can be supplemented by many more. The various questions addressed to the human realm and some examples of studies concerned to answer these questions are listed below.

(1) What is the overall—the deep—organizational structure of the life-world? See Franz Brentano, *Psychology from an Empirical Standpoint*, 1874, ed. Linda L. McAlister, trans. Antos C. Rancurello, D. B. Terrell, and Linda L. McAlister (New York: Humanities Press, 1973), pp. 177–200, for a definition of descriptive psychology; Jean Piaget, *Psychology and Epistemology: Towards a Theory of Knowledge*, 1970, trans. Arnold Rosin (New York: Viking Press, 1971), for a description of cognitive structures; Henri Ey, *Consciousness: A Phenomenological Study of Being Conscious and Becoming Conscious*, 1963, trans. John H. Flodstrom (Bloomington: Indiana University Press, 1978), for a study of the architectonics of consciousness; Schutz, *Collected Papers*, for a description of the structures of the lifeworld; and Strasser, *Phenomenology of Feeling*, for a inquiry into the nature of the stratification of consciousness.

(2) What are the relationships among the "parts" or substructures of the lifeworld? See Gurwitsch, *Field of Consciousness*, for a study of the figure and ground relationship in perceptual experience, and Zaner, *Context of Self*, for an investigation of the contextural character of consciousness.

(3) What are the different characteristics of the various substructures? See Edward Casey, "Comparative Phenomenology of Mental Activity: Memory, Hallucination, and Fantasy Contrasted with Imagination," *Research in Phenomenology* 6 (1976): 1–25, for a description of the various modes of presentation within consciousness; Max Wertheimer, "Gestalt Theory," in W. Ellis, ed., *A Source Book of Gestalt Psychology* (London: Routledge & Kegan Paul, 1938), pp. 1–11, for the study of the Gestalt principles of perception; and N. C. Waugh and D. A. Norman, "Primary Memory," *Psychological Review* 72 (1965): 89–104, for a study of long–term and short–memory.

(4) What is the relationship between individual patterns of experience and the social milieu? See Benjamin L. Whorf, *Language, Thought, and Reality: Selected Writings of Benjamin Lee Whorf*, ed. J. B. Carroll (Cambridge, Mass.: MIT Press, 1956), for an investigation of the relationship between language and experience, and Max Weber, *The Protestant Ethic and the Spirit of Capitalism*

(London: Allen & Unwin, 1930; reprint, New York: Scribner's, 1958), for a study of the relationship between economic system and religious tradition.

(5) What is the relationship between experiential patterns and action? See Arthur W. Combs, Anne C. Richards, and Fred Richards, *Perceptual Psychology: A Humanistic Approach to the Study of Persons*, 1949, rev. ed. (New York: Harper & Row, 1976), for a description of the relationship between perceptual experience and action; Erving Goffman, *The Presentation of Self in Everyday Life* (Garden City, N.Y.: Doubleday, 1959), for a description of dramaturgical theory; and Harold Garfinkel, *Studies in Ethnomethodology* (Englewood Cliffs, N.J.: Prentice-Hall, 1967), for a presentation of ethnomethodological theory.

(6) How do structural patterns organize experience? See Edmund Husserl, *Ideas Towards a Pure Phenomenology and Phenomenological Philosophy*, 1913, trans. W. R. Boyce Gibson (New York: Macmillan, 1931; reprint, New York: Collier, 1962), for an investigation of essential structures such as judgment and classification; and Maurice Merleau-Ponty, *Phenomenology of Perception*, trans. Colin Smith (New York: Humanities Press, 1962), for an investigation of the relationship of embodiment to perception.

(7) How are structural patterns developed? Piaget's studies of genetic epistemology and Strasser's analysis of the process of strata formation are examples of investigations in this area.

(8) What is the relationship between the organic and neurological structures and the organization of experience? This question has been addressed by Brown's study of isomorphism between neurological formation and the development of consciousness and by Ey's and Merleau-Ponty's analyses of destructuration of consciousness and neurological lesions.

There are, of course, many other kinds of questions addressed by human science. Historians have been concerned with the change of social patterns and the effect of actions on subsequent developments. Anthropologists have examined the effect of infrastructure on social and personal patterns of experience. Psychologists have studied individual differences and universally shared structures. Linguists have focused on the effect of organizational patterns on the creation of language. And sociologists have been concerned with the connection between social structures and the formation of personal experience.

69. See Sigmund Koch, Stephen Toulmin, and Donald Campbell, "Psychology in a Postpositivist World: Three Perspectives," symposium given at the American Psychological Association 88th Annual Convention, Montreal, September 1980.

70. Karl Popper, *The Logic of Scientific Discovery*, 1934 (New York: Basic Books, 1959); Larry Laudan, *Progress and Its Problems: Toward a Theory of Scientific Growth* (Berkeley: University of California Press, 1977); Dudley Shapere, "Scientific Theories and Their Domains," in Frederick Suppe, ed., *The Structure of Scientific Theories*, 2nd ed. (Urbana: University of Illinois Press, 1977), pp. 518–599; Gerard Radnitzky, *Contemporary Schools of Metascience* (Chicago: Henry Regnery, 1973); Stephen Toulmin, *Human Under-*

standing: The Collective Use and Evolution of Concepts (Princeton, N.J.: Princeton University Press, 1972).
See Harold I. Brown, *Perception, Theory and Commitment: The New Philosophy of Science* (Chicago: University of Chicago Press, 1977), for appreciation of a postpositivist physical science.

Appendix: The Term "Human Science" (*Pages 283–289*)

1. John Stuart Mill, *A System of Logic*, Book V, "On the Logic of the Moral Sciences," in Philip P. Wiener, ed., *Readings in Philosophy of Science* (New York: Scribner's, 1953), p. 256.
2. Ibid., p. 255.
3. See Rudolf A. Makkreel, *Wilhelm Dilthey: Philosopher of the Human Studies* (Princeton, N.J.: Princeton University Press, 1975), pp. 35–37.
4. See Michael Ermath, *Wilhelm Dilthey: The Critique of Historical Reason* (Chicago: University of Chicago Press, 1978), which incorporates the extensive Nachlass materials in its analysis of Dilthey's work.
5. Herbert A. Hodges, *W. Dilthey: An Introduction* (London: Routledge & Kegan Paul, 1944), and *The Philosophy of Wilhelm Dilthey* (London: Routledge & Kegan Paul, 1952); H. P. Rickman, *Understanding and the Human Studies* (London: Heinemann, 1967), and *Wilhelm Dilthey: Pioneer of the Human Studies* (Berkeley: University of California Press, 1979); Makkreel, *Wilhelm Dilthey*.
6. Ermarth, *Wilhelm Dilthey*, p. 359.
7. Giorgi, *Psychology as a Human Science*; Stephan Strasser, *Phenomenology and the Human Sciences* (Pittsburgh: Duquesne University Press, 1963); Paul Ricoeur, *Hermeneutics and the Human Sciences*, ed. and trans. John B. Thompson (Cambridge: Cambridge University Press, 1981).
8. Richard E. Palmer, *Hermeneutics: Interpretation Theory in Schleiermacher, Dilthey, Heidegger, and Gadamer* (Evanston, Ill.: Northwestern University Press, 1969); Josef Bleicher, *Contemporary Hermeneutics: Hermeneutics as Method, Philosophy and Critique* (London: Routledge & Kegan Paul, 1980); John B. Thompson, *Critical Hermeneutics: A Study in the Thought of Paul Ricoeur and Jürgen Habermas* (Cambridge: Cambridge University Press, 1981).
9. Michel Foucault, *The Order of Things: An Archaeology of the Human Sciences* (New York: Pantheon Books, 1971).
10. Rickman, *Wilhelm Dilthey*, p. 62.
11. See Giddens, *New Rules of Sociological Method*, pp. 11–13.
12. Fred N. Kerlinger, *Behavioral Research: A Conceptual Approach* (New York: Holt, Rinehart & Winston, 1979), p. 2.
13. UNESCO, *Main Trends of Research in the Social and Human Sciences*, 2 vols. (Paris: UNESCO, 1970, 1978).
14. Réne Maheu, "Preface," in UNESCO, *Main Trends*, vol. 1, p. xiv.
15. Ibid., p. xiv.
16. Jean Piaget, "The Place of the Sciences of Man in the System of Science," in UNESCO, *Main Trends*, vol. 1, p. 2.

Bibliography

Achinstein, Peter. *Concepts of Science*. Baltimore: Johns Hopkins University Press, 1968.

Angyal, A. *Foundations for a Science of Personality*. Cambridge: Harvard University Press, 1941. Excerpts from chapter 8 reprinted in *Systems Thinking*, edited by F. E. Emery, pp. 17–29. New York: Penguin Books, 1969.

Anscombe, G. Elizabeth M. *Intention*. Oxford: Basil Blackwell, 1957; 2nd ed., 1963.

Apel, Karl-Otto. *Towards a Transformation of Philosophy*, translated by Glyn Adey and David Frisby. London: Routledge & Kegan Paul, 1980.

Argyris, Chris. *Inner Contradictions of Rigorous Research*. New York: Academic Press, 1980.

Atkinson, R. F. *Knowledge and Explanation in History: An Introduction to the Philosophy of History*. Ithaca, N.Y.: Cornell University Press, 1978.

Austin, J. L. "Performative Utterances." In *J. L. Austin: Philosophical Papers*, edited by J. O. Urmson and G. J. Warnock. Oxford: Oxford University Press, 1961.

————. *How to Do Things with Words*, edited by J. O. Urmson and Marian Sbisa, 2nd ed. Cambridge: Harvard University Press, 1975.

Ayer, Alfred Jules. *Language, Truth and Logic*. 1936. 2nd ed. New York: Dover, 1952.

Baron, Robert A.; Byrne, Donn; and Kantowitz, Barry H. *Psychology: Understanding Behavior*. Philadelphia: W. B. Saunders, 1977.

Bateson, Gregory. *Mind and Nature: A Necessary Unity*. New York: E. P. Dutton, 1979.

Bell, Philip Brian, and Staines, Phillip James. *Reasoning and Argument in Psychology*. London: Routledge & Kegan Paul, 1981.

Behnke, Elizabeth A. "The Philosopher's Body." *Somatics*, Spring/Summer, 1982, 44–46.

Berger, Peter L., and Kellner, Hansfried. *Sociology Reinterpreted: An Essay on Method and Vocation*. Garden City, N.Y.: Anchor Books, 1981.

325

Bergson, Henri. *Creative Evolution*. 1907. Translated by Arthur Mitchell. New York: Random House, 1944.

Bertalanffy, Ludwig von. *Modern Theories of Development*. 1928. Reprint. New York: Harper & Row, 1962.

————. "General System Theory: A Critical Review." In *Modern Systems Research for the Behavioral Scientist*, edited by Walter Buckley. Chicago: Aldine, 1968.

————. *General System Theory: Foundations, Development, Applications*. New York: George Braziller, 1968.

Betti, Emilio. *Hermeneutics as the General Methodology of the Geisteswissenschaften*. 1962. Reprinted in translation in *Contemporary Hermeneutics: Hermeneutics as Method, Philosophy and Critique*, edited by Josef Bleicher, pp. 51–94. London: Routledge & Kegan Paul, 1980.

Bleicher, Josef. *Contemporary Hermeneutics: Hermeneutics as Method, Philosophy and Critique*. London: Routledge & Kegan Paul, 1980.

Bosanquet, Bernard. *Knowledge and Reality*. 1885. Reprint. St. Clair Shores, Mich.: Scholarly Press, 1976.

Bradley, Francis H. *Appearance and Reality*. 1893. Reprint. Oxford: Oxford University Press, 1962.

Braithwaite, Richard B. *Scientific Explanation: A Study of the Function of Theory, Probability and Law in Science*. Cambridge: Cambridge University Press, 1955.

Brentano, Franz. *Psychology from an Empirical Standpoint*. 1874. Edited by Linda L. McAlister and translated by Antos C. Rancurello, D. B. Terrell, and Linda L. McAlister. New York: Humanities Press, 1973.

Brodbeck, May. "Explanation, Prediction, and 'Imperfect' Knowledge." In *Minnesota Studies in the Philosophy of Science*, vol. 3, edited by Herbert Feigl and Grover Maxwell. Minneapolis: University of Minnesota Press, 1962. Reprinted in *Readings in the Philosophy of the Social Sciences*, edited by May Brodbeck, pp. 363–398. New York: Macmillan, 1968.

————, ed. *Readings in the Philosophy of the Social Sciences*. New York: Macmillan, 1968.

Brody, Baruch A., ed. *Readings in the Philosophy of Science*. Englewood Cliffs, N.J.: Prentice-Hall, 1970.

Brown, Harold I. *Perception, Theory and Commitment: The New Philosophy of Science*. Chicago: University of Chicago Press, 1977.

Brown, Jason. *Mind, Brain, and Consciousness: The Neuropsychology of Cognition*. New York: Academic Press, 1977.

Brown, Richard H. *A Poetic for Sociology: Toward a Logic of Discovery for the Human Sciences*. Cambridge: Cambridge University Press, 1977.

Bubner, Rüdiger. *Modern German Philosophy*. Translated by Eric Matthews. Cambridge: Cambridge University Press, 1981.

Buckley, Walter. "Foreword." In *Systems Research for the Behavioral Scientist: A Sourcebook*, edited by Walter Buckley, pp. xiii–xxii. Chicago: Aldine, 1968.

Bunge, Mario. *Causality and Modern Science*, 3rd rev. ed. Cleveland: World, 1963. Reprint. New York: Dover, 1979.

Burtt, Edwin A. *The Metaphysical Foundations of Modern Physical Science*. Garden City, N.Y.: Anchor Books, 1954.

Campbell, Donald T. "Evolutionary Epistemology." In *The Philosophy of Karl R. Popper*, edited by P. Schilpp, 2 vols. La Salle, Ill.: Open Court, 1974.

Campbell, Donald T., and Stanley, Julian C. *Experimental and Quasi-Experimental Designs for Research*. Chicago: Rand McNally, 1963.

Campbell, Norman R. *What Is Science?* 1921. Reprint. New York: Dover, 1953.

Čapek, Milič. *Philosophical Impact of Contemporary Physics*. Princeton, N.J.: D. Van Nostrand, 1961.

Carnap, Rudolf. "Testability and Meaning." 1937. Reprinted in *Readings in the Philosophy of Science*, edited by Herbert Feigl and May Brodbeck, pp. 47–92. New York: Appleton-Century-Crofts, 1953.

————. *An Introduction to the Philosophy of Science*, edited by Martin Gardner. New York: Basic Books, 1966.

Casey, Edward S. "Comparative Phenomenology of Mental Activity: Memory, Hallucination, and Fantasy Contrasted with Imagination." *Research in Phenomenology* 6 (1976): 1–25.

————. *Imagining: A Phenomenological Study*. Bloomington: Indiana University Press, 1976.

Chapman, Harmon M. *Sensations and Phenomenology*. Bloomington: Indiana University Press, 1966.

Child, Irvin L. *Humanistic Psychology and the Research Tradition: Their Several Virtues*. New York: Wiley, 1973.

Chomsky, Noam. *Aspects of the Theory of Syntax*. Cambridge, Mass.: MIT Press, 1965.

————. *Cartesian Linguistics*. New York: Harper & Row, 1966.

Colaizzi, Paul F. *Reflection and Research in Psychology*. Dubuque, Ia.: Kendall Hunt, 1973.

Combs, Arthur W.; Richards, Anne C.; and Richards, Fred. *Perceptual Psychology: A Humanistic Approach to the Study of Persons*. 1949. Rev. ed. New York: Harper & Row, 1976.

Cook, Thomas D., and Campbell, Donald T. *Quasi-Experimentation: Design and Analysis Issues for Field Settings*. Chicago: Rand McNally, 1979.

Cunningham, Frank. *Objectivity in Social Sciences*. Toronto: University of Toronto Press, 1973.

Cutler, Jonathan. *Ferdinand De Saussure*. New York: Penguin Books, 1977.

Danziger, Kurt. "The Positivist Repudiation of Wundt." *Journal of the History of the Behavioral Sciences* 15 (July 1979): 205–230.

————. "The Social Origins of Modern Psychology." In *Psychology in Social Context*, edited by Allan R. Buss, pp. 27–45. New York: Irvington, 1979.

Davidson, Donald. *Essays on Actions and Events*. Oxford: Clarendon Press, 1980.

Davis, Lawrence H. *Theory of Action.* Englewood Cliffs, N.J.: Prentice-Hall, 1979.

Denzin, Norman K. "The Research Act." In *Symbolic Interaction: A Reader in Social Psychology,* 3rd ed., edited by Jerome G. Manis and Bernard N. Meltzer. Boston: Allyn & Bacon, 1978.

————. *Sociological Methods: A Source Book,* 2nd ed. New York: McGraw-Hill, 1978.

Derrida, Jacques. *Of Grammatology.* Translated by Gayatri Chakravorty Spivak. Baltimore: Johns Hopkins University Press, 1974.

Dilthey, Wilhelm, "The Rise of Hermeneutics." 1900. Translated by Thomas Hall. In *Critical Sociology,* edited by Paul Connerton, pp. 104–116. New York: Penguin Books, 1976.

Dray, William. *Laws and Explanation in History.* Oxford: Oxford University Press, 1957.

Driesch, Hans. *The Science and Philosophy of the Organism.* 1908. 2nd ed. London: A. & C. Black, 1929.

Ducker, Dalia. "Survey of Dissertations in Clinical and Professional Psychology Programs." Paper read at the American Psychological Association 88th Annual Convention, Montreal, September 1980.

Duhem, Pierre. *Aim and Structure of Physical Theory.* 1906. Reprint. New York: Atheneum, 1962.

Durkheim, Emile. *The Rules of Sociological Method.* 1895. Translated by Sarah A. Solovay and John H. Mueller, introduction by George E. G. Catlin. Chicago: University of Chicago Press, 1938: New York: Macmillan,1964.

————. *Suicide: A Study in Sociology.* 1897. Translated by John A. Spaulding and George Simpson. Glencoe, Ill.: Free Press, 1951.

Encyclopedia of Philosophy, 1967 ed. S.v. "Butler, Samuel," by T. A. Goudge; "Epistemology, History of," by D. W. Hamlin; "Explanation in Science," by Jaegwon Kim; "Functionalism in Sociology," by Dorothy M. Emmet; "Rickert, Heinrich," by Robert Anchor; "Teleology," by Morton Beckner; and "Windelband, Wilhelm," by Hayden V. White.

Ermarth, Michael. *Wilhelm Dilthey: The Critique of Historical Reason.* Chicago: University of Chicago Press, 1978.

Ey, Henri. *Consciousness: A Phenomenological Study of Being Conscious and Becoming Conscious.* 1963; enlarged ed., 1968. Translated by John H. Flodstrom. Bloomington: Indiana University Press, 1978.

Feigl, Herbert, and Brodbeck, May, eds. *Readings in the Philosophy of Science.* New York: Appleton-Century-Crofts, 1953.

Feyerabend, Paul. *Against Method: Outline of an Anarchistic Theory of Knowledge.* London: Redwood Barn, 1975; Verso Edition, 1978.

Filmer, Paul; Phillipson, M.; Silverman D.; and Walsh, David. *New Directions in Sociological Theory.* London: Collier-Macmillan, 1972.

Fisher, Constance T., and Wertz, Frederick J. "Empirical Phenomenological Analysis of Being Criminally Victimized." In *Duquesne Studies in Phenomenological Psychology,* vol. 3, edited by Amedeo Giorgi, R. Knowles, and D. L. Smith, pp. 135–158. Pittsburgh: Duquesne University Press, 1979.

Foucault, Michel. *The Order of Things: An Archaeology of the Human Sciences*. New York: Pantheon Books, 1971.

Freedman, Jonathan L.; Sears, David O.; and Carlsmith, J. Merrill. *Social Psychology*, 3rd ed. Englewood Cliffs, N.J.: Prentice-Hall, 1978.

Gadamer, Hans-Georg. *Wahrheit und Methode*. Tubingen: J. C. B. Mohr, 1960. *Truth and Method*, translated by Garren Burden and John Cumming. New York: Seabury Press, 1975.

————. *Philosophical Hermeneutics*, edited and translated by David E. Linge. Berkeley: University of California Press, 1976.

————. *Reason in the Age of Science*, translated by Frederick G. Lawrence. Cambridge, Mass.: MIT Press, 1981.

Garfinkel, Harold. *Studies in Ethnomethodology*. Englewood Cliffs, N.J.: Prentice-Hall, 1967.

Gebsattel, V. E. von. "The World of the Compulsive." 1938. Translated by Sylvia Koppel and Ernest Angel. In *Existence: A New Dimension in Psychiatry and Psychology*, edited by Rollo May, Ernest Angel, and Henri F. Ellenberger, pp. 170–187. New York: Basic Books, 1958.

Geertz, Clifford. *The Interpretation of Cultures*. New York: Basic Books, 1973.

Gendlin, Eugene T. "Experiential Phenomenology." In *Phenomenology and the Social Sciences*, edited by Maurice Natanson, pp. 281–319. Evanston: Northwestern University Press, 1973.

————. *Focusing*. 1978. Reprint. New York: Bantam Books, 1981.

Ghiselli, Edwin E.; Campbell, John P.; and Zedeck, Sheldon. *Measurement Theory for the Behavioral Sciences*. San Francisco: W. H. Freeman, 1981.

Giddens, Anthony. *New Rules of Sociological Method: A Positive Critique of Interpretative Sociologies*. New York: Basic Books, 1976.

————. *Studies in Social and Political Theory*. New York: Basic Books, 1977.

————. *Emile Durkheim*. New York: Penguin Books, 1978.

————. *Central Problems in Social Theory: Action, Structure and Contradiction in Social Analysis*. Berkeley: University of California Press, 1979.

Gier, Nicholas F. *Wittgenstein and Phenomenology: A Comparative Study of the Later Wittgenstein, Husserl, Heidegger, and Merleau-Ponty*. Albany: State University of New York Press, 1981.

Giorgi, Amedeo. *Psychology as a Human Science: A Phenomenologically Based Approach*. New York: Harper & Row, 1970.

————. "The Relations among Level, Type, and Structure and Their Importance for Social Science Theorizing: A Dialogue with Schutz." In *Duquesne Studies in Phenomenological Psychology*, vol. 3, edited by Amedeo Giorgi, R. Knowles, and D. L. Smith, pp. 81–96. Pittsburgh: Duquesne University Press, 1979.

Giorgi, Amedeo; Fisher, W. F.; and Von Eckartsberg, Rolf, eds. *Duquesne Studies in Phenomenological Psychology*, vol. 1. Pittsburgh: Duquesne University Press, 1971.

Giorgi, Amedeo; Fisher, Constance T.; and Murray, Edward L., eds. *Duquesne Studies in Phenomenological Psychology*, vol. 2. Pittsburgh: Duquesne University Press, 1975.

Giorgi, Amedeo; Knowles, R.; and Smith, D. L., eds. *Duquesne Studies in Phenomenological Psychology*, vol. 3, Pittsburgh: Duquesne University Press, 1979.

Glass, Arnold L.; Holyoak, Keith J.; and Santa, John L. *Cognition*. Reading, Mass.: Addison-Wesley, 1979.

Glucksmann, Miriam. *Structuralist Analysis in Contemporary Social Thought: A Comparison of the Theories of Claude Lévi-Strauss and Louis Althusser*. London: Routledge & Kegan Paul, 1974.

Glymour, Clark. *Theory and Evidence*. Princeton, N.J.: Princeton University Press, 1980.

Goffman, Erving. *The Presentation of Self in Everyday Life*. Garden City, N.Y.: Doubleday, 1959.

Goldman, Alvin I. *A Theory of Human Action*. Princeton, N.J.: Princeton University Press, 1970.

Gruber, Gary R., and Gruber, Edward C. *Preparation for the Miller Analogies Test*. New York: Monarch Press, 1972.

Gurwitsch, Aron. *The Field of Consciousness*. Pittsburgh: Duquesne University Press, 1964.

Habermas, Jürgen. *Knowledge and Human Interests*, translated by Jeremy J. Shapiro. Boston: Beacon Press, 1971.

————. "Postscript to *Knowledge and Human Interests*." *Philosophy of Social Sciences* 3 (1973): 157–189.

————. *Theory and Practice*. 1971. Translated by John Viertel. Boston: Beacon Press, 1973.

Hacking, Ian. *Why Does Language Matter to Philosophy?* Cambridge: Cambridge University Press, 1975.

Hampden-Turner, Charles. *Radical Man*. Cambridge, Mass.: Schenkman, 1970.

Hanfling, Oswald. *Logical Positivism*. New York: Columbia University Press, 1981.

Hanson, Norwood R. *Patterns of Discovery: An Inquiry into the Conceptual Foundations of Science*. Cambridge: Cambridge University Press, 1958. Reprint, 1969.

————. "Is There a Logic of Scientific Discovery?" In *Current Issues in the Philosophy of Science*, edited by Baruch A. Brody, pp. 620–633. Englewood Cliffs, N.J.: Prentice-Hall, 1970.

Harré, Rom. *The Philosophies of Science: An Introductory Survey*. Oxford: Oxford University Press, 1972.

Hart, H. L. A., and Honoré, A. M. *Causation in the Law*. Oxford: Oxford University Press, 1959.

Hegel, G. W. F. *Science of Logic*. 1812. Translated by W. H. Johnston and L. G. Struthers, 2 vols. New York: Macmillan, 1929.

Heidbreder, Edna. "Functionalism." In *Schools of Psychology: A Symposium*, edited by David L. Krantz. New York: Appleton-Century-Crofts, 1969. Reprinted in *Historical Conceptions of Psychology*, edited by Mary Henle,

Julian Jaynes, and John J. Sullivan, pp. 276–285. New York: Springer, 1973.

Heidegger, Martin. *Being and Time.* 1927. Translated by John Macquarrie and Edward Robinson. New York: Harper & Row, 1962.

———. *What Is a Thing?*, translated by W. B. Barton and Vera Deutsch. Chicago: Henry Regnery, 1967.

Hempel, Carl G. "The Function of General Laws in History." 1942. Reprinted in *Theories of History*, edited by P. Gardiner. Urbana: University of Illinois Press, 1959.

———. "Studies in the Logic of Confirmation." In *Mind.* 1945. Reprinted in *Readings in the Philosophy of Science*, edited by Baruch A. Brody, pp. 384–409. Englewood Cliffs, N.J.: Prentice-Hall, 1970.

———. *Fundamentals of Concept Formation in Empirical Science.* International Encyclopedia of Unified Science, vol. 2, no. 7. Chicago: University of Chicago Press, 1952.

———. "The Logic of Functional Analysis." In *Symposium on Sociological Theory*, edited by Llewellyn Gross, pp. 271–307. Harper & Row, 1959. Reprinted in *Readings in the Philosophy of the Social Sciences*, edited by May Brodbeck, pp. 179–210. New York: Macmillan, 1968.

———. "Explanation in Science and History." In *Frontiers of Science and Philosophy*, edited by R. G. Coloday. Pittsburgh: University of Pittsburgh Press, 1962. Reprinted in *The Philosophy of Science*, edited by P. H. Nidditch, pp. 54–79. Oxford: Oxford University Press, 1968.

———. *Aspects of Scientific Explanation and Other Essays in the Philosophy of Science.* New York: Free Press, 1965a.

———. "Explanatory Incompleteness." In *Aspects of Scientific Explanation and Other Essays in the Philosophy of Science.* New York: Free Press, 1965b. Reprinted in *Readings in the Philosophy of the Social Sciences*, edited by May Brodbeck, pp. 398–415. New York: Macmillan, 1968.

———. *Philosophy of Natural Science.* Princeton, N.J.: Prentice-Hall, 1966.

Hempel, Carl G., and Oppenheim, Paul. "Studies in the Logic of Explanation." In *Philosophy of Science* 15 (1948): 135–175. Reprinted in *Readings in the Philosophy of Science*, edited by Baruch A. Brody, pp. 8–27. Englewood Cliffs, N.J.: Prentice-Hall, 1970.

Hesse, Mary. "Is There an Independent Observation Language?" 1970. Reprinted as "Theory and Observation," in Mary Hesse, *Revolutions and Reconstructions in the Philosophy of Science.* Bloomington: Indiana University Press, 1980.

———. *The Structure of Scientific Inference.* Berkeley: University of California Press, 1974.

———. *Revolutions and Reconstructions in the Philosophy of Science.* Bloomington: Indiana University Press, 1980.

Hilgard, Ernest R.; Atkinson, Richard C.; and Atkinson, Rita L. *Introduction to Psychology*, 6th ed. New York: Harcourt, Brace, Jovanovich, 1975.

Hirsch, E. D., Jr. *Validity in Interpretation.* New Haven, Conn.: Yale University Press, 1967.

Hodges, Herbert A. *W. Dilthey: An Introduction*. London: Routledge & Kegan Paul, 1944.

————. *The Philosophy of Wilhelm Dilthey*. London: Routledge & Kegan Paul, 1952.

Hoeller, Keith. "Phenomenology, Psychology, and Science." *Review of Existential Psychology and Psychiatry* 16 (1–3) (1978–1979): 147–175.

Homas, George C. *The Nature of Social Science*. New York: Harcourt, Brace, & World, 1967.

Howarth, C. I., & Gillham, W. E. C., eds. *The Structure of Psychology: An Introductory Text*. London: George Allen & Unwin, 1981.

Husserl, Edmund. *Ideas Towards a Pure Phenomenology and Phenomenological Philosophy*. 1913. Translated by W. R. Boyce Gibson. New York: Macmillan, 1931; reprint, New York: Collier, 1962.

Ihde, Don. *Experimental Phenomenology: An Introduction*. New York: Putnam's, 1977.

Jakobson, Roman O.; Fant, C. G. M.; and Halle, M. *Preliminaries to Speech Analysis*. 1952. Cambridge, Mass.: MIT Press, 1965.

James, William. *Essays in Radical Empiricism*. New York: Longmans, Green, 1940.

Jarvie, I. C. "Understanding and Explanation in Sociology and Social Anthropology." In *Explanation in the Behavioral Sciences*, edited by Robert Borger and Frank Cioffi. Cambridge: Cambridge University Press, 1970. Reprinted in *Understanding and Social Inquiry*, edited by Fred R. Dallmayr and Thomas A. McCarthy, pp. 189–206. Notre Dame, Ind.: University of Notre Dame Press, 1977.

Jonas, Hans. *The Phenomenon of Life: Toward a Philosophical Biology*. Westport, Conn.: Greenwood Press, 1966.

Jourard, Sidney M. "Experimenter-Subject Dialogue: Paradigm for a Human Science of Psychology." In *Disclosing Man to Himself*, edited by Sidney M. Jourard, pp. 18–34. Princeton, N.J.: Van Nostrand, 1968.

Kaplan, Abraham. *The Conduct of Inquiry: Methodology for Behavioral Science*. Scranton, Pa.: Chandler, 1964.

Keen, Ernest. "Doing Psychology Phenomenologically: Methodological Considerations." Mimeograph. Lewisberg, Penn., 1975.

————. "Psychopathology." In *Existential-Phenomenological Alternatives for Psychology*, edited by Ronald S. Valle and Mark King, pp. 234–264. New York: Oxford University Press, 1978.

Keiter, Kenneth. *A Primer on Ethnomethodology*. Oxford: Oxford University Press, 1980.

Kenny, Anthony. *Action, Emotion, and Will*. London: Routledge & Kegan Paul, 1963.

Kerlinger, Fred N. *Foundations of Behavioral Research*, 2nd ed. New York: Holt, Rinehart & Winston, 1973.

————. *Behavioral Research: A Conceptual Approach*. New York: Holt, Rinehart & Winston, 1979.

Kinneavy, James L. *A Theory of Discourse: The Aims of Discourse.* New York: W. W. Norton, 1971.

Koch, Sigmund. "Epilogue." in *Psychology: A Study of a Science*, vol. 3, edited by Sigmund Koch. New York: McGraw-Hill, 1959.

———. "Psychology and Emerging Conceptions of Knowledge as Unitary." In *Behaviorism and Phenomenology*, edited by T. W. Wann. Chicago: University of Chicago Press, 1964.

———. "A Possible Psychology for a Possible Postpositivist World." Paper read at the symposium on "Psychology in a Postpositivist World: Three Perspectives" at the American Psychological Association 88th Annual Convention, Montreal, September 1980.

Kockelmans, Joseph J. "Theoretical Problems in Phenomenological Psychology." In *Phenomenology and the Social Sciences*, edited by Maurice Natanson, vol. 2., pp. 225–280. Evanston, Ill.: Northwestern University Press, 1973.

———. "Toward an Interpretative or Hermeneutic Social Science." *Graduate Faculty Philosophy Journal: New School for Social Research* 5(1) (1975): 73–96.

Koestler, Arthur. *The Ghost in the Machine.* New York: Macmillan, 1967.

Koffka, Kurt. *Principles of Gestalt Psychology.* New York: Harcourt, Brace, 1935.

Kohák, Erazim V. *Idea and Experience: Edmund Husserl's Project of Phenomenology in "Ideas I."* Chicago: University of Chicago Press, 1978.

Kolakowski, Leszek. *Husserl and the Search for Certitude.* New Haven, Conn.: Yale University Press, 1975.

Kremyanskiy, V. I. "Certain Peculiarities of Organisms as a 'System' from the Point of View of Physics, Cybernetics, and Biology." *General Systems* 5 (1960): 221–230. Reprinted in F. E. Emery, ed., *Systems Thinking: Selected Readings*, pp. 125–146. New York: Penguin Books, 1969.

Kretch, D.; Crutchfield, R. S.; and Ballachey, E. L. *Individual in Society.* New York: McGraw-Hill, 1962.

Kruger, Dreyer. *An Introduction to Phenomenological Psychology.* Pittsburgh: Duquesne University Press, 1979.

Kuhn, Thomas S. "History of Science." 1968. Reprinted in Thomas S. Kuhn, *The Essential Tension: Selected Studies in Scientific Tradition and Change.* Chicago: University of Chicago Press, 1977.

———. *The Structure of Scientific Revolutions*, 2nd ed. Chicago: University of Chicago Press, 1970.

———. "Mathematical versus Experimental Traditions in the Development of Physical Science." *Journal of Interdisciplinary History* 7 (1976): 1–31. Reprinted in Thomas S. Kuhn, *The Essential Tension: Selected Studies in Scientific Tradition and Change.* Chicago: University of Chicago Press, 1977.

———. *The Essential Tension: Selected Studies in Scientific Tradition and Change.* Chicago: University of Chicago Press, 1977.

Lakatos, Imre. "Falsification and the Methodology of Scientific Research Programmes." In *Criticism and the Growth of Knowledge: Proceedings of the*

International Colloquium in the Philosophy of Science, London, 1965, vol. 4, edited by Imre Lakatos and Alan Musgrave. Cambridge: Cambridge University Press, 1970.

Laszlo, Ervin. *Introduction to Systems Philosophy: Toward a New Paradigm of Contemporary Thought.* New York: Gordon & Breach, 1972. Reprint, New York: Harper & Row, 1973.

Laudan, Larry. *Progress and Its Problems: Toward a Theory of Scientific Growth.* Berkeley: University of California Press, 1977.

Leahey, Thomas H. *A History of Psychology: Main Currents in Psychological Thought.* Englewood Cliffs, N.J.: Prentice-Hall, 1980.

Leary, David E. "Wundt and After: Psychology's Shifting Relations with the Natural Sciences, Social Sciences, and Philosophy." *Journal of the History of the Behavioral Sciences* 15 (July 1979): 231–241.

Leichtman, Martin. "Gestalt Theory and the Revolt against Positivism." In *Psychology in Social Context*, edited by Allan R. Buss, pp. 47–75. New York: Irvington, 1979.

Lévi-Strauss, Claude. *Structural Anthropology.* 1958. Translated by Claire Jacobson and Brooke G. Schoepf. New York: Basic Books, 1963.

Lewin, Miriam. *Understanding Psychological Research.* New York: Wiley, 1979.

Losee, John. *A Historical Introduction to the Philosophy of Science*, 2nd ed. Oxford: Oxford University Press, 1980.

Luckmann, Thomas, ed. *Phenomenology and Sociology: Selected Readings.* New York: Penguin Books, 1978.

McCarthy, Thomas A. "A Theory of Communicative Competence." *Philosophy of the Social Sciences* 3 (1973): 135–156. Reprinted in *Critical Sociology*, edited by Paul Connecton, pp. 470–497. New York: Penguin Books, 1976.

————.*The Critical Theory of Jürgen Habermas.* Cambridge, Mass.: MIT Press, 1978.

McCawley, James D. *Everything that Linguists Have Always Wanted to Know about Logic.* Chicago: University of Chicago Press, 1981.

McGuigan, F. T. *Experimental Psychology: A Methodological Approach*, 3rd ed. Englewood Cliffs, N.J.: Prentice-Hall, 1978.

Macksey, Richard, and Donato, Eugenio, eds. *The Structuralist Controversy: The Languages of Criticism and the Sciences of Man.* Baltimore: Johns Hopkins University Press, 1970.

Maheu, René. "Preface." In UNESCO, *Main Trends of Research in the Social and Human Sciences*, vol. 1. Paris: UNESCO, 1970.

Makkreel, Rudolf A. *Wilhelm Dilthey: Philosopher of the Human Studies.* Princeton, N.J.: Princeton University Press, 1975.

Malinowski, Bronislaw. "Anthropology." In *Encyclopedia Britannica*, 13th ed. Supplement I. Chicago, 1926.

Mandelbaum, Maurice. *History, Man, and Reason: A Study in Nineteenth-Century Thought.* Baltimore: Johns Hopkins University Press, 1971.

Marcel, Gabriel. *Being and Having.* 1935. Translated by K. Farrer. London: Collins, 1965.

Melden, A. I. *Free Action.* London: Routledge & Kegan Paul, 1961.

Merleau-Ponty, Maurice. *The Structure of Behavior*. 1942. Translated by Alden L. Fisher. Boston: Beacon Press, 1967.

————. *Phenomenology of Perception*. Translated by Colin Smith. New York: Humanities Press, 1962.

Merton, Robert K. *Social Theory and Social Structure*, rev. ed. Glencoe, Ill.: Free Press, 1957.

Mill, John Stuart. *A System of Logic*, Book V, "On the Logic of the Moral Sciences." In *Readings in Philosophy of Science*, edited by Philip P. Wiener. New York: Scribner's, 1953.

Minkowski, Eugène. *Lived Time: Phenomenological and Psychopathological Studies*. 1933. Translated by Nancy Metzel. Evanston, Ill.: Northwestern University Press, 1970.

Moore, G. E. "External and Internal Relations." 1919. In G. E. Moore, *Philosophic Studies*. 1922. Reprint. London: Routledge & Kegan Paul, 1960.

————. "A Defence of Common Sense." 1923. In *Philosophy in the Twentieth Century*, edited by William Barrett and Henry D. Aiken, 3 vols., vol. 2, pp. 145–167. New York: Harper & Row, 1962.

Nagel, Ernest. *The Structure of Science: Problems in the Logic of Scientific Explanation*. New York: Harcourt, Brace & World, 1961.

Nidditch, P. H., ed. *The Philosophy of Science*. Oxford: Oxford University Press, 1968.

Ogilvy, James. *Many Dimensional Man: Decentralizing Self, Society, and the Sacred*. New York: Oxford University Press, 1977.

O'Hear, Anthony. *Karl Popper*. London: Routledge & Kegan Paul, 1980.

Olafson, Frederick A. *The Dialectic of Action: A Philosophical Interpretation of History and the Humanities*. Chicago: University of Chicago Press, 1979.

Palmer, Richard E. *Hermeneutics: Interpretation Theory in Schleiermacher, Dilthey, Heidegger, and Gadamer*. Evanston, Ill.: Northwestern University Press, 1969.

Peirce, Charles S. "The Fixation of Belief." 1877. Reprinted in *Philosophical Writing of Peirce*, edited by Justus Buchler. New York: Dover, 1955.

Phillips, D. C. *Holistic Thought in Social Science*. Stanford, Calif.: Stanford University Press, 1976.

Piaget, Jean. *The Origins of Intelligence in Children*. New York: International Universities Press, 1952.

————. *Structuralism*. 1968. Edited and translated by Chaninah Maschler. New York: Basic Books, 1970.

————. "The Place of the Sciences of Man in the System of Science." In UNESCO, *Main Trends of Research in the Social and Human Sciences*, vol. 1. Paris: UNESCO, 1970.

————. *Psychology and Epistemology: Towards a Theory of Knowledge*. 1970. Translated by Arnold Rosin. New York: Viking Press, 1971.

Plantinga, Theodore. *Historical Understanding in the Thought of Wilhelm Dilthey*. Toronto: University of Toronto Press, 1980.

Polanyi, Michael. *Personal Knowledge: Toward a Post-Critical Philosophy*. Chicago: University of Chicago Press, 1958. Reprint. New York: Harper & Row, 1964.

Polkinghorne, Donald. "The Reductions and Existence: Bases for Epistemology." In *Analecta Husserliana: The Yearbook of Phenomenological Research*, edited by Anna-Teresa Tymieniecka. Dordrecht, Holland: D. Reidel, forthcoming.

Popper, Karl. *The Logic of Scientific Discovery*. 1934. New York: Basic Books, 1959.

————. "The Myth of the Framework." In *The Abdication of Philosophy: Philosophy and the Public Good. Essays in Honor of Paul Arthur Schilpp*, edited by E. Freeman. LaSalle, Ill.: Open Court, 1976.

————. *Objective Knowledge: An Evolutionary Approach*, 5th rev. ed. Oxford: Clarendon Press, 1979.

Prior, A. N. *Time and Modality*. Oxford: Oxford University Press, 1957.

Putnam, Hilary. "What Theories Are Not." In *Logic, Methodology, and Philosophy of Science: Proceedings of the 1960 International Congress*, edited by E. P. Nagel, P. Suppe, and A. Tarski, pp. 240–251. Stanford, Calif.: Stanford University Press, 1962.

————. *Meaning and the Moral Sciences*. London: Routledge & Kegan Paul, 1978.

Quine, Willard van Orman. "Two Dogmas of Empiricism." In *From a Logical Point of View*. Cambridge, Mass.: Harvard University Press, 1953.

Rabinow, Paul, and Sullivan, William M., eds. *Interpretive Social Science: A Reader*. Berkeley: University of California Press, 1979.

Radcliffe-Brown, A. R. *Structure and Function in Primitive Society*. Glencoe, Ill.: Free Press, 1952.

Radnitzky, Gerard. *Contemporary Schools of Metascience*. Chicago: Henry Regnery, 1973.

————. "Disappointment and Changes in the Conception of Rationality: Wittgenstein and Popper." Paper read at the 10th International Conference on the Unity of the Sciences, Seoul, Korea, November 1981.

Rancurello, Antos C. *A Study of Franz Brentano*. New York: Academic Press, 1968.

Reichenbach, Hans. *Experience and Prediction*. Chicago: University of Chicago Press, 1938.

————. *The Rise of Scientific Philosophy*. Berkeley: University of California Press, 1951.

Reilly, Francis E. *Charles Peirce's Theory of Scientific Method*. New York: Fordham University Press, 1970.

Richer, Paul. "A Phenomenological Analysis of the Perception of Geometric Illusions." *Journal of Phenomenological Psychology* 8 (1978): 123–135.

Rickman, H. P. *Understanding and the Human Studies*. London: Heinemann, 1967.

————. *Wilhelm Dilthey: Pioneer of the Human Studies*. Berkeley: University of California Press, 1979.

Ricoeur, Paul. *Freedom and Nature: The Voluntary and the Involuntary.* 1950. Translated by Erazim V. Kohák. Evanston, Ill.: Northwestern University Press, 1966.

————. "Structure and Hermeneutics." 1963. Reprinted in *The Conflict of Interpretations: Essays in Hermeneutics*, edited by Don Ihde, pp. 27–61. Evanston, Ill.: Northwestern University Press, 1974.

————. "What Is a Text? Explanation and Understanding." 1970. Reprinted in *Hermeneutics and the Human Sciences*, edited and translated by John B. Thompson. Cambridge: Cambridge University Press, 1981.

————. *Freud and Philosophy: An Essay on Interpretation.* Translated by Denis Savage. New Haven, Conn.: Yale University Press, 1970.

————. "The Model of the Text: Meaningful Action Considered as a Text." 1971. Reprinted in *Hermeneutics and the Human Sciences*, edited and translated by John B. Thompson. Cambridge: Cambridge University Press, 1981.

————. *The Rule of Metaphor: Multi-Disciplinary Studies of the Creation of Meaning in Language.* 1975. Translated by Robert Czerny. Toronto: University of Toronto Press, 1977.

————. *Interpretation Theory: Discourse and the Surplus of Meaning.* Fort Worth: Texas Christian University Press, 1976.

————. "Philosophy." In UNESCO, *Main Trends in the Social and Human Sciences*, vol. 2, pp. 1073–1567. The Hague: UNESCO, 1978.

Robinson, James M. "Hermeneutic since Barth." In *The New Hermeneutic*, edited by James M. Robinson and John B. Cobb, Jr. New York: Harper & Row, 1964.

Roche, Maurice. *Phenomenology, Language and the Social Sciences.* London: Routledge & Kegan Paul, 1973.

Rorty, Richard. *Philosophy and the Mirror of Nature.* Princeton, N.J.: Princteon University Press, 1979.

Rosenblueth, Arturo; Wiener, Norbert; and Bigelow, Julian. "Behavior, Purpose, and Teleology." *Philosophy of Science* 10 (1943): 18–24. Reprinted in *Modern Systems Research for the Behavioral Scientist: A Sourcebook*, edited by Walter Buckley, pp. 221–225. Chicago: Aldine, 1968.

Rudner, Richard S. *Philosophy of Social Science.* Englewood Cliffs, N.J.: Prentice-Hall, 1966.

Russell, Bertrand. "Descriptions." 1919. Reprinted in *Readings in the Philosophy of Language*, edited by Jay F. Rosenberg and Charles Travis, p. 161. Englewood Cliffs, N.J.: Prentice-Hall, 1971.

————. *Our Knowledge of the External World.* Chicago: Open Court, 1929.

Rychlak, Joseph F. *The Psychology of Rigorous Humanism.* New York: Wiley, 1977.

Ryle, Gilbert. *The Concept of Mind.* New York: Barnes & Noble, 1949.

Sampson, Geoffrey. *Schools of Linguistics: Competition and Evolution.* London: Hutchinson, 1980.

Sanford, R. Nevitt. *Self and Society.* New York: Atherton, 1966.

Sarason, Seymour B. *Psychology Misdirected.* New York: Free Press, 1981.

Saussure, Ferdinand de. *Course in General Linguistics.* 1907–1911. Edited by Charles Bally and Albert Sechehaye, translated by Wade Baskin. New York: McGraw-Hill, 1966.

Schrag, Calvin O. *Radical Reflection and the Origin of the Human Sciences.* West Lafayette, Ind.: Purdue University Press, 1980.

Schultz, Duane. *A History of Modern Psychology,* 2nd ed. New York: Academic Press, 1975.

Schutz, Alfred. *Collected Papers,* edited by Maurice Natanson, 3 vols. The Hague: Martinus Nijhoff, 1973.

————. "Common-Sense and Scientific Interpretation of Human Action." In *Collected Papers,* edited by Maurice Natanson, 3 vols., I, pp. 3–47. The Hague: Martinus Nijhoff, 1973.

Schutz, Alfred, and Luckmann, Thomas. *The Structures of the Life-World.* Translated by Richard M. Zaner and H. Tristram Engelhardt, Jr. Evanston, Ill.: Northwestern University Press, 1973.

Schwartz, Howard, and Jacobs, Jerry. *Qualitative Sociology: A Method to the Madness.* New York: Free Press, 1979.

Scriven, Michael. "A Possible Distinction between Traditional Scientific Disciplines and the Study of Human Behavior." In *Minnesota Studies in the Philosophy of Science,* vol. 1, edited by Herbert Feigl and Michael Scriven. Minneapolis: University of Minnesota Press, 1956.

————. "Explanations, Predictions, and Laws." In *Minnesota Studies in the Philosophy of Science,* vol. 3, edited by Herbert Feigl and Maxwell Grover. Minneapolis: University of Minnesota Press, 1962. Reprinted in *Readings in the Philosophy of Science,* edited by Baruch A. Brody, pp. 88–104. Englewood Cliffs, N.J.: Prentice-Hall, 1970.

————. "Views of Human Nature." In *Behaviorism and Phenomenology,* edited by T. W. Wann. Chicago: University of Chicago Press, 1964.

————. *Reasoning.* New York: McGraw-Hill, 1976.

Searle, John R. *Speech Acts: An Essay in the Philosophy of Language.* Cambridge: Cambridge University Press, 1969.

Seung, T. K. *Structualism and Hermeneutics.* New York: Columbia University Press, 1982.

Shaffer, Jerome A. *Philosophy of Mind.* Englewood Cliffs, N.J.: Prentice-Hall, 1968.

Shaffer, John B. P. *Humanistic Psychology.* Englewood Cliffs, N.J.: Prentice-Hall, 1978.

Shapere, Dudley. "Discovery, Rationality, and Progress in Science: A Perspective in the Philosophy of Science." In *PSA 1972: Proceedings of the 1972 Biennial Meetings of the Philosophy of Science Association. Boston Studies in the Philosophy of Science,* vol. 2, edited by K. F. Schaffner and R. Cohen. Dordrecht, Holland: D. Reidel, 1974.

————. "On the Introduction of New Hypotheses in Science, and on the Notion of Rationality in Science." Unpublished manuscript. Quoted in *The Structure of Scientific Theories,* 2nd ed., edited by Frederick Suppe. Urbana: University of Illinois Press, 1977.

————. "Scientific Theories and Their Domains." In *The Structure of Scientific Theories*, 2nd ed., edited by Frederick Suppe, pp. 518–599. Urbana: University of Illinois Press, 1977.

Shapiro, Kenneth J., and Alexander, Irving E. *The Experience of Introversion: An Integration of Phenomenological, Empirical, and Jungian Approaches*. Durham, N.C.: Duke University Press, 1975.

Skinner, B. F. *The Behavior of Organisms*. Englewood Cliffs, N.J.: Prentice-Hall, 1938.

————. *Science and Human Behavior*. New York: Macmillan, 1953.

Sommerhoff, George. *Analytical Biology*. London: Oxford University Press, 1950.

Spiegelberg, Herbert. *The Phenomenological Movement: A Historical Introduction*, 2 vols. 2nd ed. The Hague: Martinus Nijhoff, 1976.

Stamps, Jeffrey S. *Holonomy: A Human Systems Theory*. Seaside, Calif.: Intersystem, 1980.

Stevick, Emily. "An Empirical Investigation of Anger." In *Duquesne Studies in Phenomenological Psychology*, vol. 1, edited by Amedeo Giorgi, W. F. Fisher, and Rolf Von Eckartsberg, pp. 132–148. Pittsburgh: Duquesne University Press, 1971.

Strasser, Stephan. *Phenomenology and the Human Sciences*. Pittsburgh: Duquesne University Press, 1963.

————. *Phenomonology of Feeling: An Essay on the Phenomena of Heart*, translated by Robert E. Wood. Pittsburgh: Duquesne University Press, 1977.

Straus, Erwin W. "Aesthesiology and Hallucinations." 1948. Translated by Erwin W. Straus and Bayard Morgan. In *Existence: A New Dimension in Psychiatry and Psychology*, edited by Rollo May, Ernest Angel, and Henri F. Ellenberger, pp. 139–169. New York: Basic Books, 1958.

Strawson, P. F. "Truth." *Analysis* 9 (1949). Reprinted in *Philosophy and Analysis*, edited by Margaret MacDonald. New York: Philosophical Library, 1955.

Suppe, Frederick. "Afterword—1977." In *The Structure of Scientific Theories*, 2nd ed., edited by Frederick Suppe, pp. 617–730. Urbana: University of Illinois Press, 1977.

————. "The Search for Philosophic Understanding of Scientific Theories." In *The Structure of Scientific Theories*, 2nd ed., edited by Frederick Suppe, pp. 3–232. Urbana: University of Illinois Press, 1977.

Sutherland, John W. *A General Systems Philosophy for the Social and Behavioral Sciences*. New York: George Braziller, 1973.

Tarski, A. "The Semantic Conception of Truth and the Foundations of Semantics." 1944. Reprinted in *Readings in Philosophical Analysis*, edited by Herbert Feigl and W. Sellars, pp. 52–84. New York: Appleton-Century-Crofts, 1949.

Taylor, Alfred E. *Elements of Metaphysics*. London: Methuen, 1903.

Taylor, Charles. *The Explanation of Behavior*. London: Routledge & Kegan Paul, 1964.

————. "Interpretation and the Sciences of Man." *Review of Metaphysics* 25 (1971): 3–34, 45–51. Reprinted in *Understanding and Social Inquiry*, edited by Fred R. Dallmayr and Thomas A. McCarthy, pp. 101–131. Norte Dame, Ind.: University of Notre Dame Press, 1977.

Taylor, Richard. "Comments on a Mechanistic Conception of Purposefulness." *Philosophy of Science* 17 (1950): 310–317. Reprinted in *Modern Systems Research for the Behavioral Scientist: A Sourcebook*, edited by Walter Buckley, pp. 226–231. Chicago: Aldine, 1968.

————. "Purposeful and Non-Purposeful Behavior: A Rejoinder." *Philosophy of Science* 17 (1950): 327–332. Reprinted in *Modern Systems Research for the Behavioral Scientist: A Sourcebook*, edited by Walter Buckley, pp. 238–242. Chicago: Aldine, 1968.

————. *Metaphysics*, Foundations of Philosophy Series. Englewood Cliffs, N.J.: Prentice-Hall, 1963.

Thomas, David. *Naturalism and Social Science: A Post-Empiricist Philosophy of Social Science*. Cambridge: Cambridge University Press, 1979.

Thompson, John B. *Critical Hermeneutics: A Study in the Thought of Paul Ricoeur and Jürgen Habermas*. Cambridge: Cambridge University Press, 1981.

Toulmin, Stephen. *The Philosophy of Science: An Introduction*. London: Hutchinson, 1953. Reprint. New York: Harper & Row, 1960.

————. *The Uses of Argument*. Cambridge: Cambridge University Press, 1958.

————. *Foresight and Understanding: An Enquiry into the Aims of Science*. Bloomington: Indiana University Press, 1961. Reprint. New York: Harper & Row, 1963.

————. *Human Understanding: The Collective Use and Evolution of Concepts*. Princeton, N.J.: Princeton University Press, 1972.

UNESCO. *Main Trends of Research in the Social and Human Sciences*. 2 vols. Paris: UNESCO, 1970: 1978.

Valle, Ronald S., and King, Mark. *Existential-Phenomenological Alternatives for Psychology*. New York: Oxford University Press, 1978.

van den Berg, J. H. *The Changing Nature of Man: Introduction to a Historical Psychology*. 1961. Reprint. Translated by H. F. Cross. New York: Dell Books, 1964.

van Peursen, Cornelis A. *Phenomenology and Analytical Philosophy*. Pittsburgh: Duquesne University Press, 1972.

Wallace, Walter L. *The Logic of Science in Sociology*. Chicago: Aldine, 1971.

Walsh, David. "Varieties of Positivism." In *New Directions in Sociological Theory*, edited by Paul Filmer et al., pp. 37–55. London: Collier-Macmillan, 1972.

Walsh, George. "Introduction." In Alfred Schutz, *The Phenomenology of the Social World*, translated by George Walsh and Frederick Lehnert, pp. xv–xxix. Evanston, Ill.: Northwestern University Press, 1967.

Wann, T. W., ed. *Behaviorism and Phenomenology: Contrasting Bases for Modern Psychology*. Chicago: University of Chicago Press, 1964.

Waugh, N. C., and Norman, D. A. "Primary Memory." *Psychological Review* 72 (1965): 89–104.

Weber, Max. *The Theory of Social and Economic Organization*, edited by Talcott Parsons. New York: Free Press, 1964.

————. *The Protestant Ethic and the Spirit of Capitalism*. London: George Allen & Unwin, 1930. Reprint. New York: Scribner's, 1958.

————. *Economy and Society*, Edited by Guenther Roth and Claus Wittich. New York: Bedminister Press, 1968.

Weingartner, Rudolph H. *Experience and Culture: The Philosophy of Georg Simmel*. Middletown, Conn.: Wesleyan University Press, 1962.

Wertheimer, Max. "Gestalt Theory." In *A Source Book of Gestalt Psychology*, edited by W. Ellis, pp. 1–11. London: Routledge & Kegan Paul, 1938.

Wheelwright, Philip. *The Burning Fountain: A Study in the Language of Symbolism*. Bloomington: Indiana University Press, 1954.

Whorf, Benjamin L. *Language, Thought, and Reality: Selected Writings of Benjamin Lee Whorf*, edited by J. B. Carroll. Cambridge, Mass.: MIT Press, 1956.

Winch, Peter. *The Idea of a Social Science and Its Relation to Philosophy*. London: Routledge & Kegan Paul, 1958.

————. "Understanding a Primitive Society." *American Philosophical Quarterly* 1 (1964): 307–324. Reprinted in *Understanding and Social Inquiry*, edited by Fred R. Dallmayr and Thomas A. McCarthy. Notre Dame, Ind.: University of Notre Dame Press, 1977.

Wittgenstein, Ludwig. *Philosophical Investigations*, 3rd ed., translated by G. E. M. Anscombe. New York: Macmillan, 1968.

————. *On Certainty*. edited by G. E. M. Anscombe and G. H. von Wright, translated by Denis Paul and G. E. M. Anscombe. London: Basil Blackwell, 1969. Reprint. New York: Harper & Row, 1972.

Wright, Georg Henrik von. "The Logic of Practical Discourse." In *Contemporary Philosophy: A Survey*, vol. 1, edited by Raymond Klibansky. Florence: La Nuova, 1968.

————. *Explanation and Understanding*. Ithaca, N.Y.: Cornell University Press, 1971.

Zaner, Richard M. *The Problem of Embodiment: Some Contributions to a Phenomenology of the Body*. The Hague: Martinus Nijhoff, 1964.

————. *The Context of Self: A Phenomenological Inquiry Using Medicine as a Clue*. Athens: Ohio University Press, 1981.

Index

343

Mind-body relationship, 177, 233–34
Minkowski, Eugène, 206
Modus ponens/modus tollens
distinction, 69–70, 73
Moore, G. E., 107
Moral sciences (Mill), 283
Motivation, theories of, 196–97

Nagel, Ernest, 74, 99
Naturalism 19, 28, 89
Nature, consistency of, 16, 78
Necker cube, 114, 204
Neo-Hegelian school, 138
Neo-Kantian school, 22–24, 47, 109,
138
Neo-positivism. *See* Logical positivism
Neurath, Otto, 60
Newton, Isaac, 16
Nomothetical-deductive system. *See*
Deductive-nomological model
Nomothetic/idiographic distinction, 23,
55, 288
Nondeterminism, 182–83
Noumena (Kant), 64, 127

Observation: and instruments, 66, 96,
175–76; and theory, 71–72, 95–97,
107, 114–15, 121, 122
Ogilvy, James, 250
Operationalism, 99, 304
Oppenheim, Paul, 73
Organicism, 138–40, 143, 187

Paradigmatic/syntagmatic distinction,
158–59, 163
Paradigms: revolutions of (Kuhn), 113,
132
Parallelism (mind-body), 177
Parole/langue distinction, 157–58, 164,
214, 265
Peirce, Charles S., 119–28, 131,
248–49
Perception: and abduction, 123–24; and
apperception, 34; of bivocal objects,
276–78; inner (Brentano), 39;
internal (Wundt), 35
Perelman, Chaim, 198
Performative theory, 194–95
Phenomena (Kant), 63
Phenomenalism, 63–64, 244, 296
Phenomenology, 296; of emotions,
212–13; existential, 46–47, 203,
205–206, 210; Husserlian, 41–45,
203–205, 206; of imagination,
273–75; of perception, 276–78
Phi phenomenon research, 53–54
Physicalism, 64–66, 216

Piaget, Jean, 165, 166, 245
Plato, 10
Pluralism: in Wittgenstein, 107–109. *See
also* Epistemology, pluralistic;
Syncretism
Polanyi, Michael, 94, 113
Popper, Karl, 74, 84, 85–86, 117,
129–30, 131
Positivism: history of, 16–18; and
language, 63, 71; primary themes of,
18–19; as single-method tradition,
18–19; triumph of, 19, 20, 51–52.
See also Logical positivism
Postpositivism: conception of science,
2–3, 12–13, 241–44, 279–81
Pragmatism: and Peirce, 119, 126,
248–29
Prague school (linguistics), 160–62
"Precision fallacy," 262, 269
Predicates: attributive vs. relational,
68–69
Prediction: and explanation, 73–75;
failure of, 93, 137, 142, 179, 238–39
Prior, A. N., 198
Probability, 100, 101–102, 130, 147,
195, 270; and Keynes, 230, 245
Prototype, 262
Psychognosie (Brentano), 38
Psychology: behavioristic, 55, 89, 98,
174–76, 183; descriptive (Brentano),
37–38, 40; folk (Wundt), 33, 35–36;
functional, 192, 308; genetic
(Brentano), 37; Gestalt, 52–54, 114,
152, 210, 215–16; humanistic, 54–56;
phenomenological, 55, 203, 210–13,
273–78; physiological (Wundt), 33,
35–36; and structuralism, 165–66
Purpose: vs. function, 150–51, 189–91
Purposiveness, 171

Qualities, emergent, 55, 56, 137, 138,
141, 142, 165, 187, 216
Quine, Willard van Orman, 96

Radcliffe-Brown, A. R., 148–49
Radnitzky, Gerard, 116, 119, 128–31
Rationalism, 41
Rationality: and language games, 111;
universal (Jarvie), 112. *See also*
Reasonableness
Realism, 126–27, 129; historical
(defined), 116
Reason: in Hegel, 136; historical
(Dilthey), 27, 220; practical (Kant),
22; pure (Kant), 27, 220; theoretical
(Kant), 22. *See also* Reasoning